YOUR SEARCH IS OVER

At last! Here you'll find thousands of non-traditional names suitable for yourself, your children, or just about anything else. This entertaining and infinitely useful reference provides a magical, Wiccan perspective on the origins, folklore, meanings, and symbolism of names past and present—from names of ancient Rome to those used in contemporary science fiction.

If you're a Wiccan, you're aware that a magical name holds an inherent power. However, you may not know how to choose the magical name that reflects your inner essence and your capacity to grow into the person you want to be. This book will allow you to use your magical name as the transformational tool that it can be. In addition to a lexicon of almost 5,000 names, you'll find naming rituals, spells, exercises, and meditations that will help you activate the magical power in any name.

In order to select the magical name that perfectly mirrors your individuality, potential, and spirit, you must first recognize your strengths, weaknesses, hopes, and fears. That process—and this book—will help you along your path to self-discovery.

ABOUT THE AUTHOR

Phoenix McFarland is an irreverent Wiccan priestess who lives in British Columbia. She and her husband, Kerr Cuhulain, founded the O.O.D.C. (Our Own Damn Coven), a small but earnest group of extraordinary human beings. Phoenix has had many articles published in Pagan publications, including the column "Rainforest Echoes" in *Hole in the Stone* Wiccan journal.

Phoenix holds a college degree in earth science (geology). She worked briefly as a coal mine geologist; she also worked with satellites to map the Earth from space, as an Old West history researcher, as an environmental hazardous waste clean-up technician, and as a newsroom secretary and reporter. Writing, however, is in her blood. Her mother was an English teacher, her father was a writer, a grandfather and uncle were poets, and a great-grandfather was a publisher. With the great playwright Tennessee Williams as a distant relative, becoming a writer was inevitable, like a family curse (or a blessing; she's not sure which).

TO WRITE TO THE AUTHOR

If you wish to contact the author or would like more information about this book, please write to the author in care of Llewellyn Worldwide, and we will forward your request. Both the author and publisher appreciate hearing from you and learning of your enjoyment of this book. Llewellyn Worldwide cannot guarantee that every letter written to the author will be answered, but all will be forwarded. Please write to:

Phoenix McFarland
℅ Llewellyn Worldwide
P.O. Box 64383, Dept. K251-8, St. Paul, MN 55164-0383, U.S.A.
Please enclose a self-addressed stamped envelope for reply, or $1.00 to cover costs.
If outside U.S.A., enclose international postal reply coupon.

FREE CATALOG FROM LLEWELLYN WORLDWIDE

For more than 90 years, Llewellyn has brought its readers knowledge in the fields of metaphysics and human potential. Learn about the newest books in spiritual guidance, natural healing, astrology, occult philosophy, and more. Enjoy book reviews, new age articles, a calendar of events, plus current advertised products and services. To get your free copy of *Llewellyn's New Worlds of Mind and Spirit,* send your name and address to:

Llewellyn's New Worlds of Mind and Spirit
P.O. Box 64383, Dept. K251-8, St. Paul, MN 55164-0383, U.S.A.

LLEWELLYN'S MODERN WITCHCRAFT SERIES

The Complete Book of MAGICAL NAMES

Phoenix McFarland

1996
Llewellyn Publications
St. Paul, Minnesota 55164-0383 U.S.A.

FIRST EDITION
Second Printing, 1996

Cover design and interior illustrations: Anne Marie Garrison
Book design, layout, and editing: Jessica Thoreson

An effort has been made to acquire proper permission for the use of copyrighted material used in this book. We apologize for any errors or omissions. Upon notification, we will make appropriate acknowledgements in subsequent editions.

Material from *The Kalevala: An Epic Poem after Oral Tradition* by Elias Lonrot (Keith Bosley, trans.), © 1986, used by permission of Oxford University Press.
Material from *The Long, Dark Tea-Time of the Soul* by Douglas Adams reprinted with the permission of Simon & Schuster. Canadian rights granted by Reed Books, London. Copyright © 1988 by Serious Productions, Ltd.
Material from *The Morrigan* by Teara Jo Staples, used by permission. From the album *The Seeker,* Earth Tone Studios, 49 Alafaya Woods Blvd., Oviedo, FL 32165.
Excerpt from *God was a Woman,* © 1990, used by permission. From the album *Hand of Desire.* Written by Sparky T. Rabbit and Greg Johnson. Performed by Lunacy. Refrain adapted from "The Goddess Chant" by Deena Metzger and Caitlin Mullin.
Material from *The Homeric Hymns* (Apostolos N. Athanassakis, ed.), © 1976, reprinted by permission of the Johns Hopkins University Press.
Material from *The Mists of Avalon* by Marion Zimmer Bradley, © 1982, reprinted by permission of the author and the author's agents, Scovil Chichak Galen Literary Agency, Inc., New York.
Material from *Thendara House* by Marion Zimmer Bradley, © 1983, reprinted by permission of the author and the author's agents, Scovil Chichak Galen Literary Agency, Inc., New York.
Material from *Firelord* by Parke Godwin, © 1980 by Parke Godwin, reprinted May 1994 by AvoNova Books. Used by permission.
Material from Dinesen, Isak. *Out of Africa.* © 1985, Vintage Books, an imprint of Random House. Used by permission.

Cataloging-in-Publication Data
McFarland, Phoenix, 1955—
    The complete book of magical names / Phoenix McFarland. -- 1st ed.
      p.   cm.
    Includes bibliographical references and index.
    ISBN 1-56718-251-8 (pbk.)
    1. Magic. 2. Names, Personal--Miscellanea. I. Title.
    BF1623.N3M37 1996
    133.4'3--dc20
                                     95-49695
                                         CIP

Llewellyn Publications
A Division of Llewellyn Worldwide, Ltd.
P.O. Box 64383, Dept. K251-8, St. Paul, MN 55164-0383

ABOUT LLEWELLYN'S MODERN WITCHCRAFT SERIES

Witchcraft is a word derived from an older word, *Wicca* or *Wicce*. The older word means "to bend" or "wise." Thus, those who practiced Wicca were those who followed the path of the Wise. Those who practiced the craft of Wicca were able to bend reality to their desires: they could do magic.

Today, Witchcraft is different from what is was eons ago. Witchcraft is no longer robes and secret rites. During the Aquarian Age—the New Age—the mystical secrets of the past are being made public. The result is a set of spiritual and magical systems with which anyone can feel comfortable. Modern Witchcraft—Wicca—may be the path for you!

Llewellyn's Modern Witchcraft Series of books will not only present the secrets of the Craft of the Wise so that anyone can use them, but will also share successful techniques that are working for Witches throughout the word. This will include philosophies and techniques that at one time were considered foreign to "the Craft," but are now being incorporated by modern Wiccans into their beliefs and procedures.

However, the core of Wicca will stay the same—that is the nature of Witchcraft. All of the books in this series will be practical and easy to use. They will all show a love of nature and a love of the Goddess as well as respect for the Masculine Force. You will find that this series of books is deeply rooted in spirituality, peacefulness and love.

These books will focus on Wicca and Wiccans today, not what was done a hundred, a thousand, or ten thousand years ago. They will help you to expand your horizons and achieve your goals. We invite you to follow this series and look toward the future of what some have called the fastest growing religion in the world, a religion that is personal, non-judgmental and non-institutional, natural and magical—that brings forth the experience of the sacredness of ALL life. Witchcraft is called "the Old Religion" and it is found present in the oldest myths and artifacts of humanity. This series will help you see what it will develop into tomorrow.

DEDICATION

I dedicate this book first, to my love, my husband, Kerr Cuhulain, a man who honors a hero's name. He brings magic, joy, laughter, and contentment into my life. My inspiration to write this book came from Amber K, who has borne many magical names and who inspired me with her gentle wisdom. Finally, I dedicate this book to all the people in the Denver Pagan community who made me feel my possibilities were limitless. You accepted me, empowered me, and believed in me. I couldn't have done it without you. You are all named "friend."

Of what use are we singers
what good we cuckoo-callers
if no fire spurts from our mouths
no brand from beneath our tongues
and no smoke after our words!

—Elias Lonnrot
The Kalevala

TABLE OF CONTENTS

Preface ix

Introduction xi

1

"Wigfrith! Aethelweard! Safe-on-High! ... Dinner!" 1

2

Some Curiosities in the Folklore of Nomenclature 21

3

The Naming of Our Offspring 29

4

The Power of the Magical Name 33

5

Naming Rituals, Spells, Exercises, and Meditations 39

6

Pagans and Christian Names 69

7

Names From the Planet Earth and Beyond 73
*Elemental Names • Rocks • Wheel of the Year Names • Birds • Names
From Plants and Trees • Celtic Tree Alphabet • Spices • Celestial Objects*

8

Ancient Names 133
*British • Egyptian • Finnish • Greek • Indian • Irish/Celtic • Norse •
Phoenician • Roman • Welsh • Names From English History*

9

Magical Names From Distant Circles 171
Afghanistan • Arabia • Armenia • Basque • Burma • Cambodia • Denmark
• Ethiopia • Finland • France • Greece • Hawaii • India • Italy • Ireland •
Kenya • North American Indian • Norway • Scotland • Names of Mythical
Places • Geographic Place Names

10

Names for Covensteads and the Things Which Lurk Inside Them 183
Covenstead Names • Animal Names • Tool Names

11

Which Witch Goes by Which Name? 197
Discordian and/or Unusual Magical Names • Coven Names • Festival
Monikers

12

Names From Whence We Came 201
Greek Names • Latin Names • Celtic/Gaelic Names • Teutonic Names •
English, Welsh, and Anglo-Saxon Names

13

Names From Literature 217

Appendix 1

Index of Names by Characteristic 257

Appendix 2

Pronounciation Guide for Difficult Names 281

Bibliography 283

Index 289

Preface

In this book I have strived to use inclusive language. I have also assumed the reader has some understanding of Wiccan rites and philosophy. For those who aren't Wiccan, there are a few terms that need to be clarified. I have never met any three Pagans who agree about the definitions of these words. So, I will use my own definitions. Under these definitions, I am a Wiccan, a Witch, and a Pagan.

I use the term "Pagan" to refer to the religions and their followers who do not have a scripture upon which they base their beliefs. Many major religions are "revealed" faiths, where deity speaks to a chosen few, who then translate what was said. These are religions which work with intermediaries between deity and the masses (Christianity, Judaism, Islam). Pagan religions are "imminent," meaning there is nothing standing between deity and the people. "Witch" refers to a person who practices any Goddess-centered religion. "Wiccan" describes one who follows the religion of Wicca, specifically a modern revival of Celtic tribal religion. Many Neo-Pagans who worship the Goddess in a non-Celtic pantheon call themselves "Wiccan," even though the term "Witch" would be more accurate. Many do so because of the negative connotation of the word "Witch." In general terms, the word "Pagan" refers to a non-Christian. The word "Witch" refers to a Goddess worshiper and "Wiccan" refers to one who specifically honors the Celtic deities.

The term "magic" refers to the reality-altering work that Witches do. It involves non-mysterious techniques such as visualization, psychology, self-control, imagination, and practice in accordance with will. The pulling-rabbits-out-of-the-hat brand of magicians are people presenting the illusion of someone doing magic. In fact, they are doing sleight-of-hand tricks and are little better than tricksters who have come to be socially acceptable entertainers. The term "covenstead" refers to the dwelling in which Pagans practice their magic; it can also be their home.

I have endeavored to use, whenever possible, pronounciation guides next to hard to pronounce names. In addition, I have included a brief explanation of pronounciation rules for Welsh and Finnish names in Appendix Two. Most pronounciations are written phonetically, based on American English.

Introduction

The Christian church has long had a hand in what we named our children. The emphasis shifted over the years as to which Christian names were most popular, but Christian names steadfastly remained the norm. It is indicative of this trend that it is customary to refer to one's first name as a "Christian" or "given" name.

In light of the death of the Piscean Age and the birth of the Aquarian Age, the names by which we call our children and even ourselves take on new meanings. When one explores the philosophy and power behind names, the idea of voluntarily choosing a Christian name for a non-Christian person of the coming age seems ludicrous. The idea of choosing a name for a woman which is a feminized version of a man's name is insulting in this day of feminist enlightenment. Yet we still do it. What the church once had to force us to accept, we now accept without a second thought. Biblical names are simply considered to be "normal" names, and we help support this notion by condemning unique names and clinging to the standard ones. We often don't even realize that the cute name we like actually harkens back to the Bible. We are generally unaware of what our names mean. We have all thumbed through the little grocery store check-out books of baby names and were fleetingly amused to find our name means honor, beauty, or intestinal fortitude, but our knowledge of the names by which we are known usually stops there. This apathetic attitude has robbed us of the ability to use one of the most powerful tools we have at our disposal.

Many Pagans, especially Wiccans, choose a special name called a magical name which, in essence, is a name for the magical part of themselves. As Pagans, many of us have come to learn the power of the magical name. It is more than a "cool" name, it is a very powerful magical tool. As with any power, knowledge is the beginning of mastery of that power. When you understand where our names came from, what they mean, how they evolved, and how different cultures look at them, you will have a deeper appreciation of names as tools of magical transformation. When the church captured our naming practices they stole something akin to our very souls, which was their intent. Now it's time to take the practice back.

1 ☆

"Wigfrith! Aethelweard! Safe-on-High! Dinner!"

A CHRONICLE OF NAMES THROUGH HISTORY

From the dawn of humanity, from the time we began to speak, there were names. The custom of naming offspring is one every society shares. The mystique and importance of our names grew over many thousands of years. Nomenclature (the system of naming) is a fascinating study because it clearly reflects the mores, customs, and history of society. Because we put our names on public documents and record the births and deaths of our loved ones, we have access to the history of nomenclature.

Our names have changed as we as a culture have changed. Throughout Europe, traditions of naming changed after an invasion to reflect the customs of the new ruling influence. The dark spectre of the medieval church dictated generations of baby names (these names were often ugly, ridiculous, and oozing piety). Conformity was the order of the day and any variation from it put one at risk. In those dark times, choosing an unusual name could lead to death by burning, hanging, or being crushed under a great weight of stones.

As the Puritan influence waned, other sources became the inspiration for new generations of names. The poets waxed romantic and our babies had new names. A

1

queen was popular and much loved by her subjects, and her name echoed on in future generations.

In the modern era, actors play beloved characters on television or in the movies and new names become popular. We are now in a time which allows great freedom. We are free to choose names for our children and even for ourselves which are not dictated to us by conquest, an oppressive ruler, the church, or any social convention. We can now leave "Joseph" and "Mary" behind and venture into the new age of nomenclature.

We are entering an age of seeking understanding and perspective which we achieve, in part, by looking to the past. We look to history. We look beyond the frightened fundamentalists of today, beyond the misogynistic murderers* of the Middle Ages, and back to an era before Christianity. We begin in the golden days of classical Paganism and the early, peaceful days of tolerant co-existence with the early Christians. We are looking back to a time when wisdom was valued, nature was revered, and the feminine was venerated; a time before humans believed they held "dominion" over nature. The ancient rites and rituals may have been lost in the mists of antiquity, but we can look back at what we do know and bring some things from that era forward. The ancient names we chose for ourselves, before we were named after saints, are links to the past.

When our primitive ancestors held a new baby wrapped warmly in the skins of animals and gave the child a name, they probably used methods of naming which would seem odd to us today. Of course, we don't know what the ancients named themselves; their languages have faded from memory many thousands of years ago. The oldest names we know tell us that tribes might choose names for children based on birth order, a desired trait, deities held sacred by the tribe, totem animals, rocks, plants, or weapons. Each little village would build up stocks of name words and as villages intermingled through trade or war, these names would be spread to new villages and the name pools expanded. Indo-European cultures combined two elements from their name stocks without caring if the name had a coherent meaning. (For example, Wigfrith means "war-peace.")

English names spring from an intermingling of several different cultures and languages brought to Britain by her various conquerors. Celtic tribes from Europe invaded Britain in 1000 BCE (Before Common Era). The mighty Roman legions of Julius Caesar conquered Britain in 55 BCE. In CE 410 (Common Era), a group of Angles, Saxons, and Picts began looting along her shores; 300 years later, Anglo-Saxon was the tongue of "Angle-land." Viking sea raiders also sought the tempting treasures Britain held and ravaged her shores in CE 750. In 1017, the Danish King Canute sat upon the English throne. The Norman-French invaders came in 1066, and for 200 years tried to impose the French language upon the peoples of Britain, without much success. Geoffrey Chaucer's *Canterbury Tales* was published in 1400 and is evidence of a lingering

---

* This refers to the perpetrators of the Inquisition (part of which is also called "The Burning Times") in which a number ranging from a few hundred thousand (Catholic church figure) to millions of women and men were murdered for their beliefs. I say misogynistic because this was a battle primarily against the women who were the practitioners of the Old Religion, and against the Goddess herself, as the church fought for the eradication of the Old Religion. I intend no disregard for the men who died. Although it was a "war" against the women, the male victims suffered as well.

French influence. By the time of Shakespeare's death (1616), Britain was undergoing a surge of English nationalism and rejected the French influence. Societal, political, and religious pressures also contributed to the creation of the English language we use today. This rich history is reflected in the names our ancestors chose for their offspring and in the names we bear today.

Each culture had its own ways of choosing names for its children. Some of the ancient Germanic names include words that mean war, strife, battle, protection, rule, counsel, raven, wolf, and bear—all of these were important to the prehistoric Germanic tribes. The literary classic *Nibelungenlied* (a Germanic epic written in CE 1203) is full of wonderful Germanic "warrior" names (see Chapter 13). Many of the methods of name-making which our ancestors used are still used today by native tribes in Africa.

1000 BCE: THE CELTIC INFLUENCE

The Celts (pronounced "kelts"), a group of warrior tribes spread across Europe, emerged as one of the continent's most powerful people in the first millennium BCE. They invaded England in 1000 BCE and settled there, lending the Celtic tongue to the inhabitants of England. The Celtic language has two modern variants: Q-Celtic or Goedelic (Gaelic) languages, including Erse, Scottish, and Irish; and P-Celtic or Brythonic languages, including Manx, Breton, Cornish, and Welsh. The main difference between the two is that the "c" or "q" sounds in Q-Celtic are replaced with "b" or "p" sounds in P-Celtic. For example, the prefix "Mac" found in many Scottish names is the Q-Celtic word for "son." "Mac Donald" means "son of Donald." In Welsh (P-Celtic), the word becomes "map" or "mab." The influence of the Celts is strongly felt in nomenclature. A number of names in current usage are from Irish or Scottish Gaelic, or Welsh. It is from this name stock that many Pagans choose their magical names.

55 BCE: THE ROMAN INFLUENCE

The Roman invasion of Britain in 55 BCE had a profound effect upon life in the British Isles, from changes in nomenclature to adaptations in the ways in which the people worshipped their Gods. The Romans brought with them the fashion of creating images of their deities, which the Celts hadn't developed (this is why there are so few images of Celtic deities). The influence of the Roman Empire had a binding and homogenizing effect on most of the civilized world, and language pools melded into one general vocabulary as Roman rule expanded across Europe and Britain. After the downfall of Rome, the medieval church took over as a unifying power and became a dominant force in molding nomenclature for the next 2000 years.

In Rome, the system of names was very complicated, involving an individual having several names which indicated paternity and tribal association, as well as the name of the individual. Slaves in the Roman Empire had no individual names and were given the names of their masters, followed by the suffix *-por* (meaning "boy").

*Marcus Tullius Marcifilius
Cornelia Tribu Cicero*

—A Roman name

*Afterwards a son was born
to him, a young boy in his
house, whom God sent to
comfort the people: he had
seen the sore need they had
suffered during the long
time they lacked a King.
Therefore the Lord of Life,
the Ruler of Heaven, gave
him honor in the world:
Beowulf was famous, the
glory of the son of Scyld
spread...in the Northlands.*

—Beowulf

Later in history, Roman slaves were given sexless Greek names followed by the name of their owners as a token of dishonor. This reminds me of the custom, which offends most feminists, of naming women with versions of men's names (Joan or Jane for John, Danielle for Daniel, Roberta for Robert, Patricia for Patrick).

CE 400: ANGLO-SAXON OR OLD ENGLISH

"Anglo-Saxon," in the general sense, describes the Teutonic tribes (Angles, Saxons, and Picts) who invaded England around CE 400-500. Anglo-Saxon or Old English also describes the language of those peoples. By CE 700, the language spoken in "Angle-land" was Anglo-Saxon. The epic poem *Beowulf* was written in CE 700 and is considered a classic in Anglo-Saxon literature. The influence of the Germanic (Teutonic) languages emerged in Old English nomenclature. In Old English it was common to use name words consisting of two parts, as in Aelfraed (aelf, "elf" and raed, "counsel"). This system of naming can be traced back as far as 3000 BCE to the prehistoric Indo-Europeans. In modern times, this is a popular method of choosing a name for some Pagans, resulting in names like "Moon Drummer" or "Foxsong." Most Old English names did not survive past the thirteenth century and were forgotten, thanks to the strong arm of the church. The only names which were allowed to emerge out of the distant antiquity of classical Paganism were those attached to Christians.

Elements Found in Old English Names

Aelf/Alf/Elf: Elf.
Beald/Bald: Bold.
Aethel/Ethel: Noble.
Beorht/Bert: Bright.
Beorn/Born: Bear; warrior.
Ead/Ed: Happiness, prosperity.
Frith/Fred: Peace.
Helm: Helmet, protection.

Herd/Heard/Hurd: Strong, hard.
Her/Here: Army, soldier.
Mund/Mond: Protection.
Os: Deity.
Raed/Rede/Red: Counsel, wisdom.

Ric/Rick: Rich; rule.
Vin/Win/Wine: Friend.
Weald/Wald: Power; rule.
Weard/Ward: Guard, protection.
Wil/Will: Resolve.

Old English or Anglo-Saxon Names

Aethelweard
Aethelwine
Aethelwulf
Alfeah
Aelfric
Aylwyn
Cada
Cuthwulf
Dene
Edmund
Edward
Ethelbert

Hereward
Hereweard
Hilda
Kragg
Mildburh
Mildgyth
Mildred
Mildthryth
Regenbeald (later Reynebaud,
    then Rainbow)
Regenweald
Thurbeorht

In Old English, although they did not use last names, family ties were created by choosing names which all began with the same letter, or all used the same prefix or suffix. Thus daughters of the same family might be called Mildthryth, Mildburh, and Mildgyth.

CE 750: THE VIKING INVASION

Powerful Viking sea raiders from Denmark, Sweden, and Norway ravaged the coastal settlements of Scotland and England around CE 750. The raids often involved the abduction of local women, who then became the property of the victors. The Danes finally conquered England in CE 1017, when King Canute of Denmark and Norway ruled England and made serfs of the Anglo-Saxons. The Scandanavians who settled in Britain made their mark on the culture and their history speaks to us through the fossils of current names. Names like Osborne, Booth, Svegn, Thorkill, Woolf, Seagram, and Osmond may come from ancient Viking raider ancestors.

Current Names and Their Ancient Viking Roots

Osborne (Asbiorn, God-Bear)
Booth (Bothe, Herdsman)
Secker (Sekkr, Sackmaker)
Woolf (Uhlfr, Wolf-Cunning)

Seagram (Saegrmr, Sea-Guardian)
Knowles (Knol, Turnip-Head)
Knott (Knutr, Square-Body)
Osmond (Asmindr, Protector)

CE 1066: THE NORMAN INVASION

William the Conqueror and his army of Norman warriors were of Scandanavian descent, which is to say that they were of Indo-European origin. The Normans came to England after having conquered parts of France. Although the Normans and Anglo-Saxons both originally used a dithemic system (a stock of name words), Norman customs changed slightly after their invasion of France. In France, the language was of Latin descent and people did not use the dithemic system. When the Normans stormed England they brought a very limited stock of name words with them, fewer name words than there had been for 400 years previously. This accounts for the overuse of a few men's names, such as Richard and Robert. Using the few names they had, they dramatically altered the face of English nomenclature. The Normans brought with them Biblical names, saint's names, and Old German names. Almost all the Old English names disappeared within three generations. By 1313, a list of 800 jurors in the Eyre of Kent showed only five Old English names; the rest were Norman.

The Normans instituted the first survey of England. Twenty-one years after their arrival in Britain, an army of clerks armed with quills and thin sheets of vellum invaded every home and interviewed the lord of every manorhouse. Production of crops, numbers of workers, sizes of homes, and heads of livestock were noted. From this information the Norman rulers were able to assess and charge taxes. The information, now only barely readable, was assembled into a two-volume set of books known as the *Domesday Book* (1087). In terms of nomenclature, it is an invaluable resource for historians. The *Domesday Book* indicated that, a mere twenty-one years after the Normans came to England (a very short period of time in terms of nomenclature), Norman names were most prevalent. In fact, virtually every name in the Domesday survey book was Norman.

Norman Names

Emma	Ralph
Helewis (Heloise)	Richard
Henry	Robert
Hugh	Roger
Matilda	Walter
Maud	William

What eclecticism there was decreased by the middle of the thirteenth century. Unless an ancient name was associated with an early Christian saint, it probably dropped out of use. This was because the early church made repeated attempts to obliterate all memory of Pagan classical history, the source of such names. Old Germanic and English names were almost entirely replaced by the names of saints, although some Old English, Norman, Breton, and Latin names were occasionally used.

CE 1300: THE NICKNAMES ERA

By the 1300s, Old English (Anglish) was replaced by a new form of English which was a mixture of Anglo-Saxon and French words, with a Norman influence. In 1380, this "new" English became the official language for Oxford and Cambridge Universities in England. Twenty years later, Geoffrey Chaucer wrote *Canterbury Tales*. The "English" he used in this work is known as Middle English.

Original Middle English

Whan that Aprille with his shoures soote
The droghte of Marche hath perced to the
roote,
And bathed every veyne in swich licour
Of which vertu engendred is the flour ...

Modern Translation

When April with his sweet showers has
Pierced the drought of March to the root,
And bathed every vein in such moisture
As has power to bring forth the flower ...

—Geoffrey Chaucer
The Prologue of the *Canterbury Tales*

By 1300, one-third of the males in England were called either William or John. It was therefore necessary, to avoid confusion, to be called by a nickname. For example, Roger was known as Hodge, and Robert as Hob. In fact, the late Middle Ages became the great era of nicknames. A man born Richard might never be called Richard, but Dick, Rich, Hitch, Hick, Dickon, or Ricket. Robin Hood, Will Scarlet, and Little John are good examples of nicknames in the Middle Ages. The name John today is frequently altered to Johnny or Jack. In the age of nicknames, however, shortened forms were used much more often and more creatively than they are today. In the Middle Ages, John was transformed into Jack, Johnny, Jenning, Jenkin, Jackcock, Jacox, Brown John, Mickle John, Little John, or Proper John. In addition to distinguishing a specific person from others of the same

In the olde dayes of the
Kyng Arthour,
Of which that Britons
speken greet honour,
Al was this land fulfild of
fayerye.
The elf-queene, with hir joly
compaignye,
Daunced ful ofte in many a
grene mede.
This was the olde opinion,
as I rede;
I speke of manye hundred
yeres ago.
But now kan no man se
none elves mo ...

—Geoffrey Chaucer

My father's family name
being Pirrip, and my Christ-
ian name Philip, my infant
tongue could make of both
names nothing longer or
more explicit than Pip. So, I
called myself Pip, and came
to be called Pip.

—Charles Dickens
Great Expectations

name, nicknames were also often a way to advertise one's trade or profession, such as Arthur the Smithy. The advent of the Puritan movement saw the end of the age of nicknames, as the pious Puritans saw diminutive forms of Biblical names as irreverent. The Puritan era was when manners became very important and titles of "Miss," "Sir," and "Ma'am" came into common usage.

Some Nickname Forms in the Fourteenth and Fifteenth Centuries

Adecock (cock is a reference to one who
     is "cocky," or masculine)
Adkin
Alison
Annot/Annora/Alianora
Batcock
Colin
Dawkin
Diccon
Dickin
Diot
Dobbin
Drewet
Eliot
Emmott
Gib and Tib (what many people named
     their cats)
Gibbon
Gillot
Gilpin
Hallet
Hancock

Hankin
Hitchcock
Hopkin
Huggin
Hutchin
Ibbett
Jeffcock
Jeffkin
Lampkin
Larkin
Lesot
Marion
Maycock
Peacock
Perrin
Pipkin
Robin
Simcock
Tibot
Tillot
Tonkin
Warinot (later Warren)

At the beginning of the Middle Ages (CE 1050), the people of England, Scotland, and Wales had no surnames. As time went on, the name pools these cultures drew upon became too limited; as the population grew, it became confusing because so many people bore the same name. Surnames were once called "sir names," because the nobility were the first to adopt this second name. The method by which the gentry chose a surname was usually by association with their property. Thus, Robert, Lord of Blackstone Castle or Edward, Earl of Thornfield Hall were titles which the gentry passed down to successive generations. By the year 1250, these titles were passed on whether the child was residing in the manor or not. Many of the people in England had adopted a second name by the thirteenth or fourteenth centuries, but even by 1465 the use of last names was not yet universal.

Before hereditary surnames evolved, the first surnames were patronymic (named for the father by adding "son" to a father's name: "Fitz" in Teutonic or "Mac" (Mc) in Gaelic); more were place names (indicating residence or origin); others were names of trade or nicknames which described a characteristic of the person. Thus William Jackson, Robin of Loxley, Alywin the Smythe, or Bodrick the Forgetful were representative thirteenth-century names.

Many societies clung to the patronymic system, even though naming through the mother's line is much more accurate, as maternity, unlike paternity, is never questionable. There is evidence that some cultures were matriarchal, but with the advent of the patriarchal warrior tribes, customs changed. With patriarchy came the notion of female virginity at marriage and strict monogamy as means of assuring paternity. It was under this patronymic system that a woman first began to take the name of her husband. This was one of the profound changes in cultural history which is well illustrated by the history of nomenclature. Within these subtle changes of nomenclature, history can bear witness to the subjugation of women in Western culture.

Patronymic Names

Fitzgerald
Jackson
Johnson
MacGregor
Wilson

Place Name Elements

Ay/Ey: Island, marshy meadow.
By: Farm, hamlet, town.
Cott: Cottage.
Croft: Fenced-in field.
Den/Dene: Valley, pasture.
Don/Dun: Hill, slope.
Garth: Homestead, enclosure.
Gea: Castle.
Hale/Hall: Corner; house.
Ham: Farm, homestead.
Holt: Wood.
Holm: Island.

Law/Low: Small hill.
Lay/Lee/Ley: Clearing, meadow.
Mor/More/Moor: Marshy or barren land.
Shaw: Small wood.
Stan/Staun: Stone.
Stow: Place.
Thorpe: Settlement.
Ton: Village, town.
Wal: Foreigner; wall.
Wald/Weald: Forestland.
Wick/Wich/Wyck: Farm (esp. dairy farm).
Worth: Enclosure, homestead.

Names From Locations

Atwood: Forest dwellers.
Bradford: The broad ford.
Cheney: From the oak-wood.
Dean: Valley dweller.
Endicott: From the end cottage.

Ford: Place to cross a stream.
Shaw: Shady glen.
Standish: A stony place.
Winthorp: From a friendly village.

Names From Trades

Baxter (Baker)
Brewster (Brewer)

Butler
Carpenter

Carter
Clark (Scholar)
Cook
Currier (Tanner)
Fowler
Gardener
Harper
Mason
Taylor
Tyler
Wainright (Wagon builder)
Ward
Webster (Weaver)

They shall take unto them a surname either of some towne, or some colour as blacke or brown, or some art or science, as smythe or carpenter, or some office, as cooke or butler.

—The law passed by King Edward IV

In the days of Edward IV (1465), a law was passed to compel Irish outlaws to take a surname (conceivably, it was easier to identify and keep track of such people with a surname). It wasn't until King Henry VIII (early 1500s) that people in England began keeping a single hereditary surname. Henry VIII drafted edicts to the people of Wales trying to force them to adopt the custom of surnames, which had been popular in England for some time. King Henry VIII's full hereditary name was "Henry VIII, By the Grace of God, King of England, France, and Ireland; Defender of the Faith, the Supreme Head and Sovereign of the Most Noble Order of the Garter." In Wales and remote Ireland, however, the people rejected surnames so strongly that there are people in the recent past who still bore a single name.

CE 1500: THE INCREASED INFLUENCE OF THE CHURCH

On Halloween night in 1517, beneath the light of the full moon, a German monk named Martin Luther nailed a proclamation to the door of a church and changed history. Luther, a Dominican monk in a small backwater village in Germany, did not like what he saw of Catholicism. His views presented a gentler, more forgiving God than the punitive one of the Catholics. He might have become one of hundreds of disgruntled monks the Vatican frowned upon and muzzled into silence but for the availability of technology. While the Ecclesiastical hierarchy in Rome was deciding the best way to silence this troublemaker, Luther had his ideas printed and distributed all over Germany. The social and religious rebellion which Luther inspired led to division and uproar. As the pendulum swung toward a gentler religion with Luther, it swung back with another leader. This time it was a Frenchman named Calvin, whose tenets were grim and filled with sin, describing the basic depravity of humanity and its inevitable end in fire and brimstone. This added to the reformation already in progress, and change swept across Europe. The Protestant Reformation shaped the lives of people at a deep level by making them submit to an intense scrutiny of their private lives and personal conscience, paving the way for the atrocities which were to come later in the Burning Times.

The Protestant Reformation also caused an upheaval in the customs of naming babies in England and the New World. Until then, people used only a few Biblical names, but mostly non-Biblical saint's names. These were not mentioned in the Bible but were names of supposed local saints, some of whom doubtless were whitewashed versions of local Goddesses and Gods. The church preached the virtues of naming children after Biblical saints, but the advice was not taken enthusiastically until after the Council of Trent (1545–63), when the Roman Catholic Church required a baby to bear the name of a canonized saint or angel in order for the child to be baptised. The variety of saint's and Biblical names was much greater than the old stock of name words and thus increased the number of names available for name making. Even so, there was still not a very wide assortment of names from which to choose. Only 3,037 male names and 181 female names are given in the Bible. This new, albeit limited, supply of names, combined with the very strong pressure from the church, contributed to a complete switch in nomenclature customs. All the names of non-scriptural saints fell into disgrace and were no longer used. Austin, Bride, Blase, Hilary, Quenton, and Valentine all but disappeared in the sixteenth century. These changes did not happen overnight, however. Most of the name changes didn't happen until the Reformation took stronger hold and as the attitudes of a movement known as Puritanism developed.

CE 1580: THE PURITAN ERA

The Puritan era was my favorite period of time only in terms of its curiosities of nomenclature. It is good to find something of interest and amusement in these times; the Puritan era lies within those horrible years we have come to call "The Burning Times," and there was little to laugh about during this reign of terror.

Reformation abolished the old system of nomenclature, while Puritanism supplied a new one. The Puritans turned the Reformation into a crusade against all Catholic dogma and ceremonies. With obsessive zeal overpowering their good taste and common sense, the Puritans changed the customs of nomenclature in Britain and in the recently settled (1620) Massachusetts. Puritans were fundamentalists in the extreme. The custom of picking names from the Bible was taken beyond any other custom to date. Some very unlikely names were pressed into service. Old Testament names, incidental Biblical references, Biblical place names, and ordinary words and phrases were used as first names. Names were sometimes assigned without regard to the sex of the bearer. An example is a custom of using Maria as a man's name, while Dennis and Matthew were used as women's names. The extent of the Puritan influence on nomenclature decreased to the north in the British Isles, with Scotland scarcely having any Puritan names at all. The Puritans were in the minority in England, but in America they flourished. In the New World, this religious fundamentalism launched a revolution in nomenclature that saw the almost complete abandonment of all Norman names in the New World.

'Tis good to impose such names as expresse our baptismal promise. A good name is as a thread tyed about the finger, to make us mindful of the errand we came into this world to do for our master.

—William Jenkin
Presbyterian minister
Christ Church, London
(1652)

Some Actual Puritan Names (CE 1500–1640) Found in English Birth Records

Abstinence
Abuse Not
Acceptance
Accepted, Thankful (Sons of a rector)
Acts-Apostles
Adulterina
Aholiab
Anger
Arise
Asa
Ashes
Assurance
Barnabus
Be Steadfast
Be Thankful
Be Strong Philpott
Be Courteous Cole
Beloved
Bezaleel
Caleb
Changed
Charity
Chastity
Clemency
Consider
Continent
Deliverence

Delivery
Depend
Desiderius
Desire
Discipline
Do Good
Dust
Earth
Ebenezer
Elihu
Elilama
Eliphalet
Erastus
Experience
Ezekiel
Faint Not
Faith
Farewell
Fear God
Fear-Not
Fight the Good Fight of Faith (a first
     name)
Flea-Fornication (or Flee-Fornication)*
Fly Fornication Richardson
Forsaken
Free-Gift
From-Above
Gamaliel ("camel of God")
Give Thanks
God Reward
Godly
Habakkuk ("the wrestler")
Hariph ("the flower of life")
Hate Evil
Help on High
Helpless
Hephzibah ("my pleasure or delight
     in her")
Hezekiah ("strong in the Lord")

Honor
Hope
Hopestill
Humble
Humiliation
Ichabod ("the glory has departed")
Increased
Isaiah ("salvation of the Lord")
Jaell ("ibex")
Jedidiah ("praise of the Lord")
Jehostiaphat Star ("the Lord judges")
Joab ("the Lord")
Joy
Joy In Sorrow
Joy-Again
Judas-Not Iscariot
Justice
Kerenhappuch ("splendor of color")
Kill Sin Pimple
Lament
Lamentation
Learn Wisdom
Live Well
Lively
Love
Love God
Magnify
Mahershalalhashbaz Christmas
(Mahershalalhashbaz means "haste to
     the spoil, quick to the prey")
Make Peace
Malachi ("angel of the Lord")
Merciful
Mercy
Meshach ("agile or expeditious")
Misericordia-Adulterina**
More Fruit
More-Triall
Muche-Merceye

---

* This was a popular name for foundlings who were conceivably born outside the bonds of matrimony. The Puritan rationale was that the abandoned child was actually fleeing the sinful ways of its fornicating parents. It was also used as a cruel reminder to the foundling of its "sinful" origins. Such a name would constantly bring to mind the parent's moral weakness, and the child would therefore be warned against any inherited tendencies to sin.

** Misericordia ("mercy") and Adulterina are like the name Flee-Fornication: names often given to babes born to unwed parents to shame, stigmatize, and warn them from the "wrong" path.

No-Merit
Obedience
Obey
Onesiphorus ("profit bearing")
Patience
Persist
Phineas ("mouth of brass")
Pleasant
Pontius Pilot Pegden
Postumus
Preserved
Prudence
Reformation
Refrain
Rejoyce Lord
Remember
Renewed
Repent
Repentance
Revolt Morecock
Riches
Sabbath Clark
Safe-on-High
Savage
Search the Scriptures
Shadrach ("rejoicing in the way")
Shelah ("prayer or sent shooting forth")

Silence
Sin Deny
Sin-No-More
Sirs ("Sirs, what must I do...")
Solomon
Sorry for Sin
Stand Fast on High
Steadfast
Supply
Temperance
Thank
Thankful
The Peace of God
The-Lord-is-Near
Tremble
Tribulation Wholesome
Truth
Unfeigned
Virtue
Weakly
Wealthy
Welcome
Zachariah ("remembrance of the Lord")
Zaphnathpaaneah ("sorrow of the age;" mentioned in Genesis)
Zeal of the Land

Of particular interest is the seventeenth-century Barebone family. One or two members of this family may be referred to by the name of "Barebones," but that is not accurate. The Barebone family consisted of at least four brothers who were named:

Praise-God
Fear-God
Jesus Christ Came Into the World to Save
If Christ Had not Died for Thee Thou Hads't Been Damned

Due to his bad reputation, the Puritan taboo against shortening given names was waived by the public when referring to Dr. "Damned" Barebone.* Praise-God Barebone was imprisoned after the Reformation, was released shortly afterward, and died an old man in obscurity in London.

Strange as it may sound, we can learn from these seemingly silly Puritan names and use them to become more powerful people. While the Puritans had rebellion and fundamentalism as the motivation in choosing their names, they stumbled onto a

---

* The editor of *Notes and Queries* (March 15, 1862).

magical principle. Many of the names they stumbled upon, such as Prudence, Silence, Wealthy, or Pious, are a way of using the name as a magical tool to bring the qualities of the name to the wearer. If we shift the perception from a Christian perspective to a Pagan perspective, we can use this idea to our advantage. If one wished to have more money, being called Wealthy would help. On the other hand, if one wished to save money, the name Frugality would be appropriate. If we were to rewrite the quotation from a few pages earlier and see it from a slightly different perspective, it might have more meaning to Pagans and might cause us to see the Puritans in a slightly different light. (See sidebar.)

It's good to take magical names that express our relationship with the Goddess. It will act as a string around the finger, to remind us of our place in the Universe, our roles as priest or priestess, our personal goals, and our responsibility to the earth.

My own family were farmers, and (ack!) one married the sister of the sinister clergyman Nicholas Noyse of Salem. The names I found in my genealogical research were representative of the Puritan influence of the day. These names were names my family bore during the persecution era. At the 300th commemoration of the Salem Witch trials at Dragonfest Pagan gathering in Colorado, I met another Pagan whose ancestor married another one of Noyse's sisters. At the same festival was a descendant of one of the victims of the Salem Witch hunt. Now we're all on the same side, Witches all. It added an eerie and uplifting element to the ritual to know this information and see how far we had all come.

Puritan Influence in my own Family

Abel
Abiel
Asa
Asahel
Azariah
Calvin Ely
Cyrus
Ebenezer
Elias
Eldad
Eliakim
Eliphalet
Elisha
Enoch

Ephraim
Hannah
Hezakiah
Hiram
Huldah
Isaac
Israel Ela
Jemima
Luther
Moses
Nathan

○

*Maria Ann Isabella
Margaretta Beatrix
(died 1762)*

*Charles Caractacus
Ostorius Maximilian
Gustavius Adolphus
(born 1781)*

*Dancell Dallphebo Mark
Anthony Dallery Gallery
Caesar Williamson II*

—Examples of persons
with multiple names

○

CE 1600: POST-REFORMATION

Following the piety of the Reformation came a period in which change crept quietly over society, especially in terms of nomenclature. One of the ways in which our naming practices changed was by using surnames as first names, even for girls. Names such as Gilford, Ashford, Rutherford, Ashley, Hill, Dudley, Stanley, Keith, Douglas, and Graham began to appear as early as the early 1600s during the reign of Elizabeth I. The church and pious community leaders condemned the use of these names, but to no avail. Usually the names were maternal family names used as first names to keep the names from dying out. The fashion is still popular today. Despite the desire of the church to retain control over nomenclature, the pendulum had begun to swing in the opposite direction and there was nothing that could be done to stop it.

The seventeenth century saw few other changes in naming practices, except for the adoption of multiple names. The giving of at least one additional name remains popular to the present time. As with most trends in nomenclature in England, new names were adopted by royalty, then became popular among the gentry, then the lower classes. It was the aristocracy who initially embraced this trend so enthusiastically that it appeared to be a contest to see how many ostentatious names could be hung on a child. The double names Mary Anne and Anna Maria appeared after the revolution of 1688, named for Queens Mary and Anne. Double names lasted to the nineteenth century, and gradually became confined to the lower classes and eventually relegated to the Southern United States.

THE EIGHTEENTH CENTURY

The eighteenth century saw classical or Latinized names for women take hold in fashionable society. Names such as Anna from Anne and Maria from Mary came into vogue.

Latinized Women's Names

Anna   Cecilia
Sophia   Juliana
Olivia   Maria
Evelina

In addition to this Latin influence in the eighteenth century, there was also a revival of the medieval names of Old English. Names which had been put aside for hundreds of years suddenly enjoyed a burst of popular appeal. Names such as Edgar, Edwin, Alfred, Galfrid, Emma, and Matilda flourished.

THE NINETEENTH CENTURY: THE ROMANTIC MOVEMENT

Many old names were taken out of the history books and dusted off for use in the nineteenth century, thanks to a social and a religious movement. First, the Romantic Movement (1798-1832) introduced escapism, mysticism, and a new surge of imagination in literature. Poetry of the time revived old legends of ancient Gods and Goddesses, fairies, elves, and the tales of Robin Hood and King Arthur. Gothicism, a return to Celtic and Scandinavian mythology and a sentimental interest in the relics of an idealized past, was also characteristic of Romanticism. As an enthusiastic response to this "new age," thought-provoking authors such as Scott brought us names like Wilfrid, Guy, Roland, Nigel, Quentin, and Amy. The romantic, idealized medievalism of Tennyson and the pre-Raphaelites popularized names such as Lancelot, Walter, Hugh, Aylmer, Roger, Ralph, Ella, Alice, Mabel, and Edith.

Religiously, the Tractarian Movement was responsible for the acceptance of several antiquated saint's names, such as Aidan, Augustine, Alban, Theodore, Benedict, and Bernard.

Romantic Era Names

Aidan   Benedict
Alban   Bernard
Augustine   Clarissa

Cristabel	Lancelot
Guinevere	Marmaduke
Gwendolyn	Theodore

The Victorian Era (1837-1901) saw the addition of names taken from vocabulary words, including names for gemstones, flowers, plants, and birds.

Names From Vocabulary Words

Cherry	Orchid
Daisy	Robin
Fern	Rose
Ivy	Ruby
Lilly	Violet
Opal	

THE TWENTIETH CENTURY:
NAMES FROM POPULAR CULTURE

The twentieth century has seen the fashions of nomenclature grow increasingly eclectic in the United States as well as England. There is a practice of using names from all over the world and from a variety of new sources. Novels, television, and the cinema have influenced our names and methods of name-making. It became popular in the early twentieth century to simply "make up" a name, or to combine two existing names to form a new one. It seems that about every ten years a new group of names becomes popular and the names which reigned the decade before are ousted. The names Doris, Peggy-Sue, Sunshine, Tiffany, and Morgan can be associated with the 1940s, 1950s, 1960s, 1980s, and 1990s respectively.

Frank Zappa, a rock musician, has also etched a place in popular nomenclature by virtue of his choice of names for his children. They are named Moon Unit, Dweezil, Diva, and Ahmet. Moon Unit (a girl) was first-born; if she had been born male, her name was to be Motorhead. When the Zappas went to the hospital to have their son Dweezil, the admitting nurse became annoyed when Frank answered "Musician" to the question "What is your religion?" When she found out the parents intended to name the baby Dweezil, she pleaded with them to name him something else. Despite the fact that Ms. Zappa was in labor, the nurse was determined to let her stand at the admitting desk until they thought of a "proper" name for the baby. The angry parents rattled off an assortment of names of people they knew, and as a result the baby was legally called "Ian Donald Calvin Euclid Zappa." Of this name, the nurse approved. The child, nevertheless, was called Dweezil. He was five years old before he discovered his legal names on his birth certificate. Dweezil was upset and pleaded with his parents to legally change his name to Dweezil, which they did. Diva (a girl) and Ahmet (a boy) came along later, and presumably no one tried to enforce traditional names on these members of the Zappa family. Traditional, especially religious, input is not worthless to Frank Zappa, however. He found it useful in disciplining his children. When his children misbehaved, he would make them watch a televangelist. Eleven-year-olds do not find this to be fun and it was successful as a form of discipline.

Musical history played an important part of the naming process for actress Valerie Bertinelli and her rock-star husband Eddie Van Halen when they chose a name for their son. In honor of the 200th anniversary of Wolfgang Amadeus Mozart's death and out of respect for his genius, the couple named their son Wolfgang Van Halen. I applaud their creativity and individuality in choosing Wolfgang. A grand old name!

Celebrities seem drawn to unusual names, perhaps because as members of the "special" rather than the "ordinary," they may see an advantage in helping their children to be special, too. Billy Ray Cyrus, the country music star, has broken out of the Southern tradition of double nickname forms (Billy Ray, Bobby Jack, Billy Joe) and has named his two children Blaison Chance (a boy) and Destiny Hope (a girl). Actors Demi Moore and Bruce Willis named their daughters Rumer, Scout, and Tallulah. Writer Tom Robbins named his child Fleetwood Starr. The Phoenix family includes Rainbow, Liberty, Summer Joy, Leaf, and River. Jefferson Starship singer Grace Slick named her daughter China.

The ever-increasing popularity of science fiction, fantasy, and the swords and sorcery genres of literature and cinema has contributed to popularizing creative new names and opening our imaginations to accepting new and interesting names. I have listed a number of unusual names from many books of this genre in the latter half of this book (Chapter 13).

Creating names by flights of imagination is a long-standing American tradition. This method began in the Southern United States, but soon grew in popularity in the north as well. This method involves new ways of spelling old names, such as Kathryn or Madalynne, or combining syllables from existing names in new combinations, such as Lauretta and Luvenia. Another American fashion, especially in the South, is to use pet name forms as formal names. Former President "Jimmy" Carter, for example, is legally named James, but insists on being called by his pet name.

People make a lot of fuss about my kids having such supposedly "strange names," but the fact is that no matter what first names I might have given them, it's the last name that is going to get them in trouble.

—Frank Zappa

Undine Celeste Mandala Palantine Thompson

Myrddin Emrys Arthur Gunter Pinder Thompson

—Children of Michael Thompson, bookseller, collector of rare science fiction books

Historical nomenclature is useful to us to examine the culture and influences of the day and learn something of the people who bear the names. At first glance, one would assume that this modern practice of making up new names is obscuring the clarity of historical nomenclature and confusing its social significance. Some Western countries have agreed with this notion and have created legislation to combat these trends. In France, for example, the Revolutionary Law of Germinal XI (1803) decreed names were to be chosen only from persons known in ancient history, or in use in the various calendars. Germany's laws state that a name must be one that can be proved to have been used before. While such laws keep the waves of modern popular names at a minimum, they simultaneously restrict the natural evolution of nomenclature. On one hand we are creating generations of meaningless, artificial names (which does say something about the culture in which we live); on the other hand, others are simply spinning out new generations of older name clones (which also says something about that culture). So by the very nature of our superficiality and resistance to change, historical nomenclature is as socially significant as ever.

2

Some Curiosities in the Folklore of Nomenclature

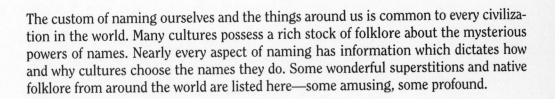

The custom of naming ourselves and the things around us is common to every civilization in the world. Many cultures possess a rich stock of folklore about the mysterious powers of names. Nearly every aspect of naming has information which dictates how and why cultures choose the names they do. Some wonderful superstitions and native folklore from around the world are listed here—some amusing, some profound.

NAMES TO BRING LUCK

Theater people are, by nature, creative, sensitive, emotional, and superstitious. There are many superstitions having to do with luck and the theater. One play in particular seems to attract a lot of "bad luck." It is considered unlucky to speak the name of the play *Macbeth* aloud, the only known exception being when a religious leader (more recently, Witch) has blessed the theater first. It is believed by many actors that if an actor unwittingly says "Macbeth," s/he must immediately step outside the theater and recite anything else written by Shakespeare to remove the "curse."

    Some bizarre customs exist even though there is ample evidence to show that the superstition isn't true. For example, in England it is believed that any boy named George will never be hanged, despite the fact that several Georges have been hanged.

It is considered lucky to have initials that spell a word. My late mother-in-law was born Beatrice Agnes Brownie Young (B.A.B.Y.). (Her father, the artist Charles Warburton Young, couldn't think of anything else starting with "b," so he chose "Brownie.") Many of the quaint practices found in folklore harken back to legitimate ideas and habits which have passed out of memory. The curiosities of letters and words perhaps were once the domain of a few learned people, and so to the ignorant peasantry this might seem like magic, and thus lucky.

NAMES TO AVOID ILLNESS

There are many names given to children in hopes of avoiding illness or misfortune. In the Midlands of England, there is a curious belief that any person named Agnes will invariably go mad. Sometimes a sickly English child was given many names of saints and dead relatives in an attempt to elicit supernatural aid on the child's behalf. Yet there is also a widely held superstition that if a child is named for another child who died in infancy, the same fate awaits the child who bears its name.

The name is seen as the link, in many cases, between illness and good health. Thus, by changing the name you could also change the physical condition of the name bearer. In several groups of North American Indians, when a person became ill, it was thought that his name was disagreeing with him and the name was "washed off" and a new one chosen. This is a primal, symbolic ritual which is shared by many cultures.

NAMES TO HONOR OTHERS

We all are aware of the practice of naming a child after someone to honor that person. This is a common occurrence today. When Alexander the Great entered Palestine in 333 BCE, legend has it that all Jewish boys born that year were named Alexander. Whether this was done out of respect or by force is not known.

On a deeper level, the giving of a name of a great warrior, healer, or thinker has the resonance of sympathetic magic to it. (Sympathetic magic is the invocation or evocation of a desired trait by mimicry.) Ancient Norsemen honored their dead in hopes that the good characteristics would be reborn in their children.

HOW NAMES ARE CHOSEN

This area of folklore yields the greatest diversity in naming customs. The naming of a child is an important event. We have always named our children and always will, but the ways in which these names are chosen is evolving. The ancient Jews had a custom of naming the baby after the first thing the mother saw after the birth of her child, so a woman in labor was surrounded by pleasant things. Priests interpret dreams for the natives of Brazil before choosing a name for a child. In Derbyshire, England, it was common to select a baby's name from the first name the eye fell upon when opening the Bible, regardless of the sexual orientation of the name. In Burma, a child is named according to the day of the week on which s/he is born. Each day has letters associated with it, and the child's name begins with one of those letters. Native Hawaiian children are usually named with words describing nature. Some examples of Hawaiian name words are Lani (sky), Lei (child), Kapu (sacred), Kala (sun), and Nana (beautiful). Many people choose a name based upon the number of letters in the name.

Many tribal peoples recognize a link between people, especially people of a common tribe. Tribal kinship is described as a "seamless web of humanity" by villagers in Ghana in western Africa. Kinship ties are strong and extend to the whole tribe. In Ghana, a child is given two names: one a soul's name (from a deity associated with its birthday), and the second given by the father. In New Guinea and western Africa, a name is chosen by divination. The behavior of the child is observed in response to certain objects belonging to dead ancestors, or its reaction while a list of ancestors is recited. The baby is used as a divining tool to find its own name.

A people's relationship with deity may have a hand in the naming process. Hindus believe God is manifested in everything. They may name a child after common household objects, because every time they say the name they are pronouncing the name of God and reminding themselves that deity is all around them. Other sources of Hindu names are nature, made-up names, rivers, and Hindu Gods.

Names in Uganda indicate birth order, describe family circumstances, or express hopes for the future. A child's name may be amended up to ten years later. A child's name often reflects the tribe's totem (a plant, animal, or object that serves as an identifying emblem for the clan).

NAMES AND SECRECY

Having a secret name is a powerful idea that children like to use in their play, along with secret passwords and secret codes. Every wizard had secret names, as did secret agents, cowboys, and most superheroes. When a Wiccan is asked to choose a "secret" name, it touches on the inner child excitement. Although it was expedient during the Inquisition, the need to keep names (especially inner-self and magical names) secret went further back than the dangers of the Burning Times. In many North American Indian cultures, it was believed that everyone and everything had a name that may remain hidden, perfectly describing one's innermost nature. The name might be revealed confidentially at some point, but the word had such sacredness to it that it was considered an extreme discourtesy to utter it aloud.

Secret names known only to the owner have to do with a belief in name-soul connection. In myths and folklore, the discovery of the secret name gives the discoverer power over the owner of the name. In many religions, the names of the Gods are the secret property of the priests, and thus the power of the Gods was held by the clergy. Many cultures thought it was unlucky to reveal the name of a newborn to anyone outside the family before the child was christened.

When it is necessary that a person's name be kept secret to protect that person from ill will from his/her enemies, many cultures name people after their children, reasoning that children have no enemies. So people are named "Mother of so-and-so," or "Father of that child." As any parent can tell you, when one is a parent s/he is often called "Cheryl's father" or "Trey's mother," by other parents who you think of as "Little Erica's mom."

NAMES AND DEITY

Along with the idea of secrecy goes the notion of compromised security if the name is revealed. As the Romans approached a city, they would have their priests lure the city's guardian deity to their side, promising many sacrifices and better offerings. Thus the name of the protective deity of Rome was kept a secret lest some foe lure their own Gods away.

In many Pagan traditions, it is common to choose a secret "inner court" name to be known only by one's covenmates and never revealed to outsiders. This is done not so much for security anymore but for the name's magical properties and the transformative idea of taking a name. In the past, however, the taking of a secret name was a great defense against discovery.

In some Pagan traditions, it is considered inappropriate to name yourself after a Goddess or God. Similarly, in the ancient Egyptian, Babylonian, and Hindu religions, just naming the Gods compelled them to answer, so these names were not used for fear of their Gods. Today, most Pagans are encouraged to have at least one Goddess or God name to instill the idea that we are all deity, that we are Goddess and God. This way, names act as a transformational tool to help us accentuate our God/dess-like traits.

This idea is also used in reverse to try to convince the powers of death that a child is unattractive. Often a child in India is given an unpleasant name to trick the Gods into not taking the child away. The Nigerian Ibo tribe treasures children, and often gives them an unpleasant name such as Chotsani (take-it-away) in an affectionate attempt to hide their joy so ancestors or deity won't take back the infant.

CHANGING NAMES

There are endless opportunities for new names. I have heard of Pagans who take a new magical name each year to reflect personal growth. Names can be used to mark the seasons or the turning of the years. The Kwakiutl Indians of British Columbia had both winter and summer names.

Among some African cultures, a child is given a name at birth (a childhood name) which describes the birth or the baby's appearance. Seven to forty days later, the child is given an adult name by the parents or paternal grandparents. Adults often change their names when the person has reached some sort of crossroads in life, or has achieved a personal milestone. A name is descriptive of the person who bears it and since we are always evolving and changing, it seems logical that our names evolve with us.

NAMES TO INVOKE CHARACTERISTICS

To shout at a baseball game calling the batter a less than flattering name is a form of magic. You are labelling the batter in a derogatory fashion in hopes that the person will take on the traits of the name and perform badly. This common kind of curse is not very powerful against the batter, but it is an old sort of curse. Some societies call their enemies by names suggesting clumsiness, because they believe that such attributes will attach themselves to their enemies, rendering them harmless. They are careful not to use the real names of these enemies lest their foes regain power and attack and slay the careless name-droppers. Similarly, some cultures will call a dangerous foe by a mild-mannered name to encourage it to become less of a threat. Tribes in India and Africa will call a snake by names meaning a stick or a strap to convince the snake to lie still and act like a harmless stick.

He who is called a bear is apt to act like a bear.

—Finnish proverb

NAME TABOOS

The fear of and reverence for totem animals lends us many interesting naming customs and taboos. North American Kiowa Indians say that unless you are named for the bear, you must not say "bear." They believed that a bear could render one insane just by saying its name.

The ancient Finns believed that if you knew the secret name for something, then you could control the thing. The ancient Finns used the phrase "words of power" frequently. Finns believed in a pantheon of spirits and deities which could be controlled by magic; the magic was in knowing its name. The Finns also believed in the taboo against uttering the name of a totem animal aloud for fear of needlessly invoking it. So, speaking of a bear, a Finn says "The little brother in the warm coat," Baltic peoples say "Beautiful honey-paw," "Broadfoot," or "Grandfather." Ural-Altaic peoples of Siberia call him "Little old man," "Grandfather," "Dear uncle," or "Wise one." The Tete de Boule Indians in Quebec also call the bear "Grandfather." In Sumatra, the tiger is called "He with the striped coat." In Java, the crocodile is called "Old One." To the Bechuanas, the lion is called "Boy with a beard." To the Kols, the elephant is known as "You, with the teeth."

To the ancient Greeks, the names of priests who performed the Eleusian mysteries might never be uttered during their lifetimes. After a rite of consecration into the mysteries, the names of these priests were written down and thrown into the sea to hide them from the eyes of humans. They then were given new and sacred titles. They did not wish the powerful priests to be lessened by someone calling them by their old mundane name.

The misogynistic attitude of the Christian church and the societies it has influenced has lead to many naming customs which were used to subjugate and belittle women. The taking of the husband's last name while the woman loses her own is a good example of this. The Christian idea of women being the root of all sin and menstruation being a "curse" is shamefully used in some naming customs. Most restrictive customs are especially confining when a woman is menstruating. In several cultures there is a taboo against women speaking the name of their husbands, their husband's male relatives, or their own son's name. To do so results in death to the person whose name the woman uttered. Many tribes also will not allow women to speak the name of valued livestock, but refer to animals with descriptive terms, such as "the woolly ones" for sheep.

NAMING RITUALS

The naming ritual is a profound one. Most religions have a ritual for the giving of a name. Christians have christening and Wiccans have Wiccaning. Choosing the time when children are to be named is a source of many interesting customs. The Yoruba tribe in Nigeria names their boys on their ninth day, girls on their seventh day, and twins on their eighth day. Until the naming day, a child is called Ikoko Omon (newborn child). In the naming ritual, the baby's mouth is touched with substances to signify hopes for the future: water for purity of body and spirit, red pepper for resolute character, salt for power, honey and oil for happiness and prosperity, and kola nut for good fortune. After the child's name is pronounced, the feasting and dancing continues until the next day. The naming of a child and the first cutting of his hair was cause for an important ritual and celebration among the Incas. The custom became so popular that it spread to several forest tribes of the upper Amazon.

A name ritual can help transform negative traits of the person to whom the name belongs. In Finland, it is believed that if you shout the name of a young thief over a cauldron of medicated boiling water, then clap the lip on tight, leaving the name to steep in the medicated water for several days, then the thief will be reformed.

NAMES AND MISFORTUNE

The connection between the name and the soul was recognized by the early Egyptians. They believed that cursing a man by name may destroy his soul and when the name of a dead man was ritually placed on his statue, that statue became the residence of his soul. In Ireland, it is believed to strike a line through a person's name would end that person's life.

We learn from folklore how names were once considered to be powerful, magical tools which helped shape the destiny of those who wore them. Let's look now at how we can shape the destiny of our children by the names we give them today.

Sticks and stones may break my bones but names can never hurt me.

—English proverb

3

The Naming of
Our Offspring

In naming a child, you must first decide just how conventional or unconventional you want to be. There are arguments on either side of this issue. The drawbacks of giving a child a unique name are that people do have a tendency to strive toward commonality and conformity and may pressure the child or discriminate against her/him. Unusual names interfere with social interaction and makes the child a bit of an outcast. You may not want to name your son something as unorthodox as Ichabod, Dweezil, or Sherlock, or your daughter Cinderella, Tallulah, or Tinkerbell. Those who bear odd names may also suffer from less attention given in classrooms and the prejudice of potential employers. Bear in mind that you do not know what sort of person this baby will grow up to be. As unlikely as you think it to be now, s/he might well want to be a corporate lawyer or stock broker. It would be very difficult as Cinderella Leilani or Kennocha Pagan.

Despite the trouble the mundane world may give to a child with an unusual name, I feel that there are compelling arguments in favor of, at least, a moderately unique name. On the plus side to giving the child an unusual name, by setting it apart from the "norm" of society, he or she may see life differently than the average "Joe." This may be a good thing. In my view, most of the truly brilliant, sensitive, creative, and ethical people are outcasts. Most Pagans are outcasts, and they are better people for the experience. You might want to look at the society from which your child may be outcast. Did you really want your child to fit in with those people? Being from a family of Neo-Pagans, Wiccans, or New Agers will set the child apart in the first place, so sticking it with a

MAUDE: No beautiful names, okay? Not Nicholas or Christopher or Adam or Jonathan.
ROB: Or Jennifer or Gwyneth or Cherish or Innocence.
MAUDE: And no politics, right? Not America or Peace and Freedom...just short and to the point...Joe, Gus, Eddie. Not Edward, Eddie.
ROB: Sue, Pat—American Bandstand names, right? So, it's settled. If it's a girl, it's Tallulah No-Nukes Salinger.
MAUDE: And if it's a boy, it's Bartholomew Zachary Save-the-Whales Chastity-Belt Salinger.

—*Mickie and Maude*
1984

name like "Mary" or "Joseph" won't make the child fit in any better. If you look at the members of any metaphysical or spiritual community, you will see that we are all different from the "norm." We are set apart and we have come to see a great advantage in this. Why would we want less for our children? In addition, the traditional name stocks from which we choose names are primarily Christian in origin, and now is a good time to stop using them for non-Christian people.

If enough people begin naming their children unconventional names, soon it will become the accepted practice. In fact, this trend is on the rise; fewer people want to name their children conventional names. If you choose to take the road less travelled in picking a name for your child, tread thoughtfully. If little Kennocha Pagan does grow up to be a lawyer who longs to be called Lloyd, he can always change his name.

When choosing a name, the question of the sexual orientation of the parents (they are not always hetrosexual or monogamous) and the idea of gender identification comes up. As time goes by, names which had traditionally belonged to one sex were sometimes claimed by the other. For example, at one time, it was common to find boys named Maria, Marion, Leslie, Clare, Lucy, Ann, Patsy, Caroline, Vivian (Vyvyan), Carol, Dorris, Evelyn, Jean, and Shirley. As interesting as that fact might be, to choose a name which is sexually confusing takes its toll on the child. The unhappy truth is that most North Americans are homophobic and frightened by anything which rocks the boat in terms of sexual identity. This fear usually takes the form of aggression against the dissident. Androgynous names can also become an object of ridicule and result in battery in the schoolyard.

There is also the question of extremes in sexuality in choosing a name. If you are all frilly and perfumed and love ultra-feminine names, please be aware that your daughter may end up a rough-and-tumble tomboy or athlete. Picking a very masculine or feminine name could be embarrassing or overwhelming to your child.

As unfair as it is, names for boys have a more devastating impact on the youngster than girl's names. It's not easy being a young boy growing up in the school yard, especially if your name is Rocky or Rambo. Other boys will expect a certain level of testosterone to accompany a name like that. If you don't want your son to be a punching bag, a determined pugilist, or a red-necked homophobe, stay away from the very "guy" names. In the same way, however, you can take it too far the other way. A boy named "Mortimer" or "Francis" will not have it any easier. It might be said that boys are under more pressure to conform than girls, and so the degree to which a boy's name may be unusual is more confining than it is for a girl. You might venture further out for a daughter's name, but come in closer to the norm for a son's. Researchers have found that boys who had peculiar first names had a higher incidence of mental problems than boys with common ones; no similar correlation was found for girls. Keep in mind that your "clever" choice of a name could end up causing your baby black eyes and split lips. My parents told me that if I had been born a boy, I would have been named Bruce Gustoff. This may explain why I was born a female this time around; I heard the name they had chosen and did some fast reorganizing. The threat of being a potential "Goosey-Brucy" is enough to change the DNA molecules of any sensitive fetus.

I was named Laurel at birth. It was an unusual name which, as I was often told, meant "honor." It set me apart from the many girls named more conventional names. So, from the time I was little, I learned to see beyond the norm of society. People frequently commented on the beauty of my name, which made me feel somehow special and magically empowered. I took the meaning of my name very seriously and strove toward honor. I think that my name helped me to develop magically. Try to imagine what effect the name you are considering might have on the child. Some of the impact of the name comes from what you tell the child about the name you chose. My parents often told me that my name was about beauty, honor, and triumph (resting upon one's laurels). Remember that your child is his/her own person, a separate soul who may have other plans than adopting your religion. Perhaps the kindest thing to do would be to give the child a name that would reflect your Pagan beliefs but work equally well in other worlds. Laurel was such a name for me. The only difficulty in being a Pagan who bore the name Laurel was when it came time to pick a magical name—I already had a beautiful one.

Often, even after the most thoughtful and well-intentioned parents choose what they consider to be the "perfect" name for their baby, the baby may grow up loathing his or her "perfect" name. A beautiful name to one person may be hideous to someone else. You do the best you can with what you have, and little Kennocha Pagan—I mean young Lloyd—will just have to deal with it as he sees fit. Names are not forever, even legal ones. Many people have legally changed their names for the sake of their careers, or just for their own pleasure. My cousin and her fianceé didn't like either of their last names, so when they married they chose a new last name and both had their names legally changed. If your parents did not discover your true name, take up the quest and discover it for yourself. Take control of the name by which the world knows you; own it or disown it.

4

The Power of the
Magical Name

As we set foot on a spiritual path, we begin to change. Life, well lived, is change. To walk the spiritual ways, especially the path of the newly resurgent feminist, Goddess-based religions, involves an enormous amount of personal transformation. We change. We grow. We evolve into new people many times over as we progress through life. We are no longer static and unchanging; we no longer "fit" the names given to us by someone else, which we have carried all our lives. After having met the challenges the Goddess gives us, after having studied and developed our power and wisdom; having learned to work magic, the healing of the sick, the divination of the future; after having been the vessel of the Gods themselves, we just simply are no longer a Kathie or a Dan.

We all wear many names through life's changes. We wear baby names, little child names, adolescent names, nicknames our friends give us, adult nicknames our colleagues give us, pet names our lovers give us. Women often take different names each time they marry or divorce. We take initiation names and often rename ourselves at each degree along the magical path. We name our tools, our homes, our pets, our children, and our covens. The reason we have so many names is that we are constantly evolving, and for each new stage in our development we choose a new name. If chosen thoughtfully, each name can be used as a tool to hasten our spiritual evolution and our understanding of ourselves.

Of all the times in our lives when we take on a new name, one of the most meaningful is the initiation rite. The ritual of initiation is one of the most significant religious

First, the initiate is given a Witch name, which she or he has chosen beforehand. The choice is entirely personal. It may be a God-name or Goddess-name expressing a quality to which the initiate aspires, such as Vulcan, Thetis, Thoth, Poseidon or Ma'at....Or it may be the name of a legendary or even historical figure, again implying a particular aspect, such as Amergin the Bard, Morgana the Sorceress, Orpheus the Musician, or Pythia the Oracle. It may even be a synthetic name made up of the initial letters of aspects which create a balance desirable to the initiate (a process drawn from a certain kind of ritual magic). But whatever the choice, it should not be a casual or hurried one; thoughtful consideration before the choice is in itself a magical act.

—Janet and
Stewart Farrar
The Witches' Bible

experiences in the history of human spirituality. This is an act which invokes great change, not only in the religious arena of a person's life but over his or her entire life. The ceremonial renaming of initiates is an archaic and powerful tradition still practiced today by Neo-Pagans, Wiccans, and even Christians. Catholic nuns may, and often do, choose a new name upon becoming nuns. Catholic popes traditionally choose a new name upon election by the College of Cardinals. This custom began in CE 844 when a priest named Boca de Porco was elected pope. (Boca de Porco means "Pig's Mouth.") Pope Pig Mouth was perhaps not in keeping with the image the church wished to have.

Baptismal names are customarily chosen for the Christian version of the initiation ritual. The rebirthing experience which occurs in many initiations includes the taking up of a new appellation to represent the newly "born" initiate. The new name is also used to introduce the new person to the Gods and the powers of the elements, as well as to the companions witnessing the ritual. Most of all, however, the new name is intended for the benefit of the initiate. If the name is the initiate's true name, the act of discovering it will have been a meaningful exercise in self-discovery. A person's true name is believed to resonate to the sound of his or her soul.

Another powerful renaming rite is the manhood/womanhood ritual. There is a trend in North America to reinstate rituals of adolescent initiation. The coming of age rituals are transformative ceremonies which span nearly every society, past and present. As with religious initiations, a coming of age initiation may involve a renaming of the initiate to reflect the mature personality as contrasted with the youthful personality. The rituals involve a clear understanding of the qualities of that which is sought (manhood or womanhood). It involves the initiate's understanding of his or her strengths and weaknesses. Having undergone a trial of some kind to prove his or her worth to the coven, community, and most of all, to him or herself, the individual is given his or her first adult name. (See Chapter 5.) This concept appears in many novels of the science fiction/fantasy genre.

There are many tools and traditions available to us as we walk the path of the Goddess. People involved in the New Age disciplines use many of these. Many tools are offered to help us understand our power, and some tools work better for us than others. Some use Tarot cards, some candle magic; both are effective and both have merit. One of the tools often overlooked by Pagans is the power in the name we bear.

The source of our power is in our own minds. To understand ourselves is to gain control over that which creates our reality. Most of us haven't a clue as to who we are. Perhaps such understanding begins with the name by which we call ourselves. This may be a key to spiritual transmutation.

The names we choose for ourselves can serve as magical tools as we travel on our individual paths. A name can be an inspiration (Venus, Athena, Phoenix); it can label us by our attributes (Quicksilver, Elder, Oak, Golden) or our failures (Iccarus, Chocolate, Crabapple, Machupa), and can inspire us to change. Our names can associate us with elemental powers and bring that energy into our lives (Ariel, Sundance, Cascade, Terra). A name can help to improve how we feel about ourselves (Willendorf, Gaia, Balder, Plato). It can emphasize where we are now or where we hope to go. It can make us feel more powerful, wiser, more beautiful, more commanding, gentler, stronger, more female/male, more exotic, more innocent, more sexual, more enthusiastic, more fertile, etc. There is no limit to what a name can bring into our lives, except for those limits we put on it ourselves.

For example, if you are skinny, shy, and awkward and long to be confident, powerful, commanding, and assured, a name change may be a positive and helpful tool for transformation. Take some time and think about yourself the way you are and the way you'd like to be. Let your inner voice guide you in choosing a new name. To become empowered, fire names (Wildfire, Spark, Glow, Ember) or powerful God or Goddess names (Diana, Eros, Zeus, Thor) or simply a name of someone you see as having these attributes is an appropriate choice. Conversely, if you are learning to control an angry temper, then a change to a cooler water name might help put out the excess fire

On the day the boy was thirteen years old, a day in the early splendour of autumn while still the bright leaves are on the trees, Ogion returned to the village from his rovings over Gont Mountain, and the ceremony of passage was held. The Witch took from the boy his name Duny, the name his mother had given him as a baby. Nameless and naked he walked into the cold springs where it rises among rocks under the high cliffs. As he entered the water, clouds crossed the sun's face and great shadows slid and mingled over the water of the pool about him. He crossed to the far bank, shuddering with cold but walking slow and erect as he should through that icy, living water. As he came to the bank, Ogion, waiting, reached out his hand and clasping the boy's arm, whispered to him his true name.

—Ursula LeGuin
A Wizard of Earthsea

(Spring, Rain, Lagoon, Twilight). There are endless images which can help to change your life.

There is no reason for limiting yourself by having only one name. A name is a tool. You don't own just one tool and refuse to get others because of the one at home. "I can't get a wrench; my parents gave me a perfectly good screwdriver already! It's a family screwdriver, we all share the same one, generations of us. I plan to give it to my son." You have as many tools as you need and sometimes you use a tool for only a brief period of time. If it does the job, what difference does it make how long you used that tool? It is the same with magical names. Use as many as you need. The Witches I've known who used the power of names have been known within their own coven by scores of names, but to reduce confusion, they were publicly known by only one name.

I find that everyone has a season in which he or she feels best and seasons which are harder to bear. For example, some people are summer people. I am not. While others bask in the sun, I sit in the basement, swatting at mosquitoes, covered with calamine lotion for prickly heat, waiting impatiently for autumn. An ancient custom of British Columbian Indian tribes is to take a seasonal name. (I could choose Sunstroke or Calamine to describe myself in the summer, or Summerwind or Phoenix to help me deal better with the fire energy.) Taking seasonal names is another way in which we can become more connected to the changing seasons and the turning of the wheel of the year. Again, the most important connection made by taking up a name is the connection to yourself and who you are; in this case, who you are during each season. Some examples of seasonal names are Mabon, Brisk, Autumn, Solstice, Litha, Jack Frost, Blizzard, Robin, Tulip, Sunny, and Summer.

Children grow rapidly and seem to be different people each time you look. They go through so many changes in their personalities that you, as well as they, can lose track of who they are. Magical names are wonderful tools children can use to illustrate the characteristics they see growing in themselves. These can be public names by which everyone in the metaphysical community calls the child, nicknames just the child's friends use, or they can be names which

The beginning of wisdom is to call things by their right names.

—Chinese proverb

are used in the family setting only. Making an effort to call the child by his or her new name (even if he or she is going through dozens of them) tells the child that you accept and respect those changes and that you approve of who he or she is and who the child is becoming. It also shows the child, in a clear way, how he or she has changed over a period of time.

Magical names for children, as well as for adults, can help our minds manifest the magic. Our minds are the only real tool needed to work magic, and intuition is the only tradition which is necessary. All the rest is helpful props or someone else's ego trip.

5

Naming Rituals, Spells, Exercises, and Meditations

Ritual has the ability to solidify ideas, to amplify intentions, to legitimize fantasies, and to influence the subconscious in a profound way. Some psychologists think that the loss of ritual has led to many of the ills of today's society. Ritual is more than pomp and circumstance and outmoded tradition. Effective ritual speaks to the subconscious and can bring about powerful change in the individual.

Using rituals for naming is a necessary step toward effectively using names as the powerful tools they are. Whether the name involved is a new magical name for an initiate, a baby's name, or a name chosen for a transition into another phase of life (such as adolescence or cronehood), the use of ritual is an integral part of the naming process.

THE NAME CHANT

To empower yourself, try chanting your name (mundane, magical, or private or "inner circle" name, whichever aspect of you that requires empowerment). If you are a member of a coven or other spirtual group, you might try empowering one member of the group by surrounding that person and chanting his or her name. Adding the person's positive traits to the mantra not only helps create a positive self-image for the person, but also helps to share the group's impressions of him or her. This technique would also work in achieving a desired result which is not yet manifested. For example, if a covenmate is ill, the group could chant his or her name and add short comments like "Healthy body!", "Clean lungs!" (or whatever is affected), "Radiant health!", etc. Be sure to include only comments from a positive perspective, because the subconscious doesn't readily process negatives. To prove this point, try telling yourself *not* to think of elephants. The mind must think of an elephant in order to know what not to think of. Comments, then, that communicate "Healthy body" are a better choice than "No more illness."

This technique is useful for groups or individuals and can be used to bring any number of attributes or changes into one's life. Chant the name in association with health, prosperity, happiness, a new home, a job, more fire, water, earth or air energy (see Elemental names in Chapter 7 for some words to intone), or anything which you desire for yourself. Always remember to think about the ramifications of all magic! Ask yourself if this will harm anyone (including yourself) before you do any magic. Be careful about the wording of your spells; this exercise *is* a spell. Remember that words are magic, so choose them with due consideration.

TOOL NAMES

Each tool has its own individual feel. Many Pagans name their swords, athames, drums, wands, staffs, and chalices. Incorporating a naming ceremony into the consecration ritual for your tools is a wonderful idea. Try meditating on the tool in question to seek its name. Remember the ancient notion that to know the name of something is to be able to control it. You can name your athame, for example, and ritually link the blade to you by linking the name of your athame to your inner circle magical name. By writing both your magical names on the blade (in

By ancient custom, for the next seven days, there was but a single task with which [the father] would seriously occupy himself: the selection of a name for his first-born son. It would have to be a name rich with history and with promise, for the people of his tribe—the Mandinkas—believed that a child would develop seven of the characteristics of whomever or whatever he was named for... Out under the moon and the stars, alone with his son that eighth night, [the father] completed the naming ritual. Carrying little Kunta in his strong arms, he walked to the edge of the village, lifted his baby up with his face to the heavens, and said softly, "Ffend kiling dorong leh warrata ka itea tee." (behold—the only thing greater than yourself.)

—Alex Haley
Roots

water, if you want to keep them secret), you further emphasize the bond. You may also use the name of your blade in a dedication ritual by pledging your heart and your blade to the Goddess.

QUICKIE NAME EXERCISE

We all have different aspects to our personalities. To find a name for some of these parts requires much thought. Other aspects come to mind immediately. One exercise with a group is to give the group members ten seconds to think of new names for themselves, then take turns telling their new names and why they appealed to them. This off-the-top-of-your-head method is effective for naming certain aspects of oneself. It is also a good way in which to grow closer to coven mates by seeing, naming, and discussing their various "selves."

NAME QUEST

A meditation for finding your magical name, a name for your baby, a pet's name, a covenstead's name, or the name of anything you care to name is what I call a Name Quest. In a Name Quest, go into a safe, meditative space (whether this means lighting candles and incense, putting up a circle, creating sacred space, closing the bathroom door, or merely closing your eyes), and mentally state your purpose before you begin by thinking "I am seeking the name for my athame" (or baby, cat, myself, etc.). Go into a meditative state in your favorite way. Visualize going deep within the thing in question (to the heart of the child, the core of the blade, etc.). Feel the essence of the thing, notice any visual characteristics, be open to any other incarnation (or former owner's) experiences imprinted on the thing, sense the strengths and weaknesses, note how it makes you feel—do you sense a smell associated with the object, do you hear anything? When you feel you have a handle on the essence of the object, tell it your most secret name and ask to know the name of the object. If a name does not make itself immediately known to you, do not despair. It may occur to you over the next few days spontaneously or appear in a dream one night.

NAMES FROM DESCRIPTIVE WORDS

As people did in ancient times, one can use name elements to create a new name. The ancient Anglo-Saxons put elements like "Aelf" and "Weard" together to make the name Aelfweard, which means "Elf-Guard" or "protected by the elves." We can create new and totally unique names for ourselves from descriptive word elements. This exercise is also a good way to get to know oneself. Make a list of several positive traits of the person to be named (like brave, strong, noble, wise), and a list of objects which appeal to that person (such as elf, silver, singer, moon, music, woman). If it is a name for a baby, list the traits you hope the child will have. Make these lists as long and as descriptive as you can. This is also a good exercise for building self-esteem or awareness of what we feel about the person being named. Simply combine as many elements as you like from the two lists until you find a combination which suits you, such as Elfsinger Moonman, Silver Musicwoman, or Wise Elf.

SEARCH THE WORLD OVER FOR YOUR NAME

Reference books are good places to look for magical names. The technique of bibliomancy, or using books as one might use a crystal ball or tarot deck to scry the needed information, is a wonderfully fun way of looking for your name. If, for example, your magical totem animal is a cat and you wish your magical name to reflect this energy, you could turn to these books for help. Under the listing of "cat" in *Webster's New World Thesaurus,* for example, you find: "House cats include the following: Maltese, Persian, Siamese, Manx, Burmese, Angora, Tortoise-shell, Alley, Tiger, Calico....[Other cats are:] Lion, Tiger, Leopard, Puma, Wildcat, Cheetah, Lynx, Bobcat, Mountain Lion, Ocelot, Cougar, Jaguar." Any of these would make a wonderful feline-oriented name. A search through the foreign language section of the library gives us the names Paka (Swahili, "cat"), Sanura (Swahili, "kitten"), and Nyan Nyan (Japanese, "kitten"). So just from this short excursion into the reference section of the local library we can come up with names like Sanura Manx, Alley Paka, or Angora.

SEXUAL ORIENTATION SWITCH

Many people have expressed a desire to become more comfortable with the opposite sex, especially when it comes to the little boy/girl who lives inside all of us. It is a valid technique for a man who seeks to be at ease with his feminine self to take a woman's name as part of this process. It needn't be a public name, if he is shy about it. Women would also do well to name the little boy within. I have been to an inner child party given by some Pagan friends. We all came in our inner personas, played with crayons and toys, ate peanut butter, and drank Kool-Aid. We all also were called by our inner child names. It was a fun and powerful experience. Naming our opposite sex selves helps to accept these parts of ourselves and also draws us closer to the Goddess and God aspects which we all reflect. This is a healthy exercise for all of us who have clawed our way out of a misogynistic/homophobic society. We all have some aspects of that attitude lurking within our psyches. To openly name and covet the opposite aspect of ourselves will help us understand our motivations and may lead us to discover and abolish some of our hidden prejudices.

NAME, NAME, GO AWAY!

That addiction to cigarettes! That uncontrollable eating problem! That nasty temper! We all have traits we wish we didn't. They line our dark side like trees along a country road. To help rid yourself of these unwanted tendencies, try giving them a name. Remember the wisdom of the ancients—to know a thing's name is to control that thing. For example, give your temper a name. When you are choosing its name, think about it and what motivates it to explode. You will come to have a better understanding of it, and even an acceptance of it as part of yourself. It becomes more personal when you know it well enough to name it. Then when your temper erupts you won't add guilt on top of it by feeling bad about it, you'll simply acknowledge it as "Old Hothead" or "Firebreather." You can work on overcoming its negative aspects by giving them watery names to reduce their fire power. You can do spells and meditations to break it into its parts (a temper is anger, insecurity, frustration, fear, desire to be noticed, and many other things specific to the individual). Keep and rename the valuable aspects, such as deeply felt emotion and your need for attention. Banish the unwanted parts, like unwarranted anger and fear. Your temper serves a purpose or you wouldn't have developed one. Find a way for you to express what needs expressing and toss out the rest. Name the parts you want to banish and do a ritual in which you burn the unwanted aspect's name or erase it, transform it into something useful, or flush it down the toilet. Use your imagination.

The same idea works for ridding yourself of addictive habits, such as an eating disorder or a drug or alcohol addiction. Try naming that from which you wish to be free, and then ritually destroy that name. You could write the name for your problem on a piece of paper and tear it into many pieces, saying encouraging and forceful commands with each tear. Or you may choose to name the part of you which desires to be sober, clean, or in control of your addictions and empower that aspect. Give that aspect a power name filled with strength and wisdom and do exercises such as the Name Chant (discussed earlier) to help yourself become stronger and fight against the addiction. But, as with all magic, remember the old saying, "As above, so below." In addition to the magical working, you also need to work on a mundane level to fix the problem. Find a support group or go see a counselor.

A NAME FOR ANY SEASON

You can incorporate the idea of name magic in any seasonal ritual (Sabbat) to create seasonal growth. For example, if at Beltane you felt ready for a spiritual growth period, you could choose a growth-oriented name like Sapling and ritually rename yourself. Pagans of my acquaintance commonly set seasonal goals for themselves at Beltane to be achieved by Samhain, and again at Samhain to be accomplished by Beltane. These goals would be more easily achieved by adding name magic to the ritual already taking place. Be sure to reward yourself if you meet your goals and give yourself a new name. Try using your name as a signpost along the path, marking your progress as each goal is achieved. Go from Acorn to Sapling to Oak to Mighty Oak to Oak Forest.

BLESS THIS HOUSE

When Pagans move into a new home, one of the first things they do is a House Blessing ritual. This ritual is basically blessing the house with the four elements of Air, Fire, Water, and Earth; the easiest method is by using incense (Air and Fire) and salt water (Earth and Water). If there is some lingering negativity from the previous owners, a banishing is done before the blessing. A good way to ritually banish an area is to use a ritual broom to symbolically "sweep" away all that isn't welcome. When you are blessing the house, begin by formally naming the house and use the new name in your ritual. In essence, you are consecrating the house as you would a magical tool. You can add desired aspects (such as protection, safety, sanctuary, love, coziness, happiness, and comfort) to the ritual to further enhance the home magically. As a symbol of the protection I seek, I paint tiny pentagrams in clear nail polish on all the windows in my house as part of the ritual. This is symbolic of the invisible barrier to any unwanted negativity or trouble. The nail polish becomes mostly invisible, unless you see it from a certain angle when the light is right, then suddenly what looks like a crystal pentagram seems to appear in the window. You might want to carve or paint a sign with the house's name to hang by the front door. Working on the house's name sign while in circle will add to its effectiveness and magical potency. (For house name ideas, see Chapter 10.)

HANDFASTINGS AND NAMES

Handfastings (Pagan wedding ceremonies) are highly personal rituals which cannot be generically produced for use by the masses. They are written from the heart and tailored to reflect the tastes and feelings of the happy couple (or threesome, etc.). It is for this reason that I did not put a Handfasting ritual in this chapter. I can, however, make some general comments which can be incorporated into one's ceremony.

In Pagan traditions, Handfastings do not require the woman to give up her name. Some women take their new husbands' names, some do not, and some couples change both their last names to new ones of their own invention. Some choose new magical names to reflect the union. One advantage to changing magical names rather than mundane names is that you reflect the changes that come from being "married" without having to change your driver's license.

Handfastings are more than just a way to acknowledge the love and/or commitment people feel for each other. The Handfasting ritual can help deepen the bond between people. Many feel that Handfasting will help those so bound to recognize the other in the next lifetime.

Many people exchange some kind of vow or promise during the ritual; this section inevitably includes using your names. ("I, Phoenix, do promise...") Some people choose to use their mundane names in the ceremony and some use their magical names. Because we name different aspects of ourselves when we take a name, it might be a good idea to use all our names in this ritual. The mundane names, circle names, magical names, inner court names, outer court names, and pet names should be included in the Handfasting ritual. This way it is a bonding of two (or more) complete people. All aspects are merged and shared equally with the other. This deepens the effects of the ritual on many levels. I was at such a Handfasting not long ago when two people spoke the words with six different names.

OTHER MAGICAL USES FOR MAGICAL NAMES

Using magic to empower a name before taking it on will help to boost the power of the name. Try making a name amulet filled with your new name, appropriate spices, stones, oils, and imagery representative of the changes you are seeking. Every time you smell the oils and spices, every time you feel it around your neck, the magic will be helped along. If you are working with elemental energy, it is also helpful to bring the energy of the direction into your environment. For example, if you are seeking to have calm water energy in your life, burn blue candles, hang photos of ocean scenes on your walls, put sea shells in blue bowls on tables, and make an effort to wear sea colors. All these things will work with your new magical name to trigger your subconscious and help manifest change. (Remember: As above, so below!) Magical names react with the inner child, the younger self within all of us. This is the part of you that likes dramatic robes, magical jewelry, elaborate rituals, candlelight and incense. The more magical trappings you attach to your new name, the greater the effect on the subconscious. The subconscious mind will then work the magic and the growth will occur.

A NAMING RITUAL FOR ANY NEW NAME

Set up an altar and quarter altars (if desired). If the name you have chosen has a visual symbol, use it in decorating your altar (with the name Old Owl, for example, use an owl feather to accent the altar). Include a piece of paper, a pen, and a mirror on the altar. Make sure candles, incense, water, and salt are available, as well as any musical instruments you have. Call the quarters, cast the circle, and invite the deities.

> *I,* [old name], *stand before you for the last time as* [old name]. *I have grown. I have changed.* [Feel free to illustrate ways in which you have changed into this new person.] *I have evolved to be the person here today. I am no longer described by* [old name]; *I no longer can be contained within that name.*

Go to the altar and write your new name on the piece of paper. Wave the paper through the smoke of incense, saying:

> [New name] *be consecrated and empowered by the powers of air to lend me strength of intellect, clarity of vision, and purity in the dawn of the life of this new name.*

Hold the paper between you and the candle, seeing the light illuminate the name (but do not let it catch on fire), saying:

[New name] *be consecrated and empowered by the powers of fire to give me determination, strength, drive, and energy, the fiery spark of enthusiasm during the noontime of the life of this new name.*

Sprinkle the paper with water from the altar, saying:

[New name] *be consecrated and empowered by the powers of water to lend me gentle intuition, deep understanding, and a deeper awareness of the mysteries of myself during the twilight of the life of this name.*

Bury the name in the salt dish on the altar, saying,

[New name] *be consecrated and empowered by the powers of earth to give me strength and solidity, deeper connection to my own earthiness, and a fearless awareness of the dark sides within myself during the nighttime of the life of this name.*

Take the name from the salt. Light it on fire and drop it into the censer, saying:

I am now [new name]. *By air, fire, water, and earth I bear this name proudly. I am* [new name]! *I am* [new name]! *I am* [new name]!

Go to the four quarters and say the following at each direction:

Hail, East [South, West, North]! *It is I,* [new name]. *Know me when I call to you by this name. Help me by sharing with me your* [intellect, strength, intuition, groundedness, etc.].

Go to the altar and call the deities.

Hail [deity names and specific greetings to them]! *I am your child. I am your priest/ess. My names change to reflect my movement upon your path, but my heart remains true and steadfast. Know me, Mother/Father, I am* [new name], *your child. Bless me, Mother/Father, for I am your child. Know me by my heart which is true, my mind which strives for knowledge, my hands which shape your images, my eyes which behold your magnificence, my lips which speak your holy name which is all names, for you are ALL. Bless me, Mother/Father, for I now am* [new name].

Spend some time in contemplation, if desired. You might drum and chant your new name, weave it into your favorite chants, or drone it out in a meditative way. You can illustrate how your new name makes you feel in dance or song. You might want to look into a mirror and chant "I am (new name), I am God/dess." The Name Chant (above) is good to do here to help reinforce the name in your mind and in the minds of your coveners. When you are finished revelling, dismiss the quarters using your new name, bid farewell to the deities, and take down the circle. Stay aware of the impact of the new name upon your life. (It will have an impact!)

Like all rituals, this is to be adapted to your personal needs. Change the traits the elements lend to the new name; change what you seek to become. Put in your deities and their qualities. Add, subtract, and tailor it to fit your life. Breathe *your* life into this ritual!

WICCANING RITUAL

For this celebration of birth, set up the altar, call the quarters, cast the circle, and invite the deities.

We have come together to celebrate the birth of this soul. We all began so. We all were once so small. We grow and learn as we walk on the path of the Goddess. This person has begun again and will learn again. There WILL be growth, for that is life. Change is the only constant. From infant to parent to elder. From elder to death to rebirth. Such is the path of the circle of life. In our excitement in the beginning of life, we do not forget the turning of the wheel. We honor the maiden, mother, and crone. We are here to celebrate a new beginning, to welcome a new person into our midst, and to name that person.

Ask the parents to bring the baby forward to the altar.

Who is this person?

Parents answer with the child's name.

Welcome, [new name]!

Take the censer and trace a pentacle before the child saying:

[New name], *by fire and air I honor you.*

Draw a pentacle on the baby's third eye in salt water, saying:

[New name], *by water and earth I honor you.*

Hold the child and turn to the east, saying:

Hail, East! Know [new name], *a child walking once more upon the path. Help* [new name]. *Protect* [new name]. *Bless* [new name]. *Let* [new name] *fly into the unlimited skies of imagination and thought. Send* [new name] *gentle breezes and freshening winds to gently guide him/her along his/her path. Favor* [new name] *with all the airborne powers of the East!*

Stepping to the South, hold the child and say:

Hail, South! Know [new name], *a child walking once more upon the path. Help* [new name]. *Protect* [new name]. *Bless* [new name]. *Let* [new name] *warmly pursue his/her life's desire. Let* [new name] *bask in the glory of the golden light of passion. Let* [new name] *run with the lions of courage, never shrinking from the light of day. Send* [new name] *purifying candles to light his/her way and gently guide him/her along his/her path. Favor* [new name] *with all the fiery, sunlit powers of the South!*

In the West, hold the child and say:

Hail, West! Know [new name], *a child walking once more upon the path. Help* [new name]. *Protect* [new name]. *Bless* [new name]. *Let* [new name] *swim uninhibited in the waters of the Mother. Let* [new name] *dive freely into the depths of his/her own feelings. Allow* [new name] *to swim with the blue dolphins and sing with the mermaids. Send* [new name] *the soothing sounds of the waves to calm his/her ruffled emotions. Favor* [new name] *with all the blue-roaring waterfall powers of the West!*

To the North, hold the child and say:

Hail, North! Know [new name], *a child walking once more upon the path. Help* [new name]. *Protect* [new name]. *Bless* [new name]. *Let* [new name] *walk safely within the darkest places. Lead* [new name] *to safety in the night. Let* [new name] *climb the apple trees, stroke the animals, and learn the wisdom in the sounds of an untouched forest. Send* [new name] *the cool, damp smell of a pine forest in the moonlight to ground and balance him/her. Favor* [new name] *with all the earthly solidity of the North!*

Give the child back to the parents.

Hail, [new name], *and welcome! May the Goddess bless you as you grow. May the God protect you your whole life long. Remember, parents of* [new name], *that this is a distinct and separate soul, not an extension of your own. Allow* [new name] *to flourish in his/her own way.*

Since we do not introduce babies or children into our religion before they are old enough and wise enough to understand the meaning of what they are doing, we do not come here today to make you a Wiccan. We simply welcome you and wish you great blessings.

The existence of this new little body for this very old soul makes us more aware of the wheel of life as it ends and begins again. Merry meet. Merry part and merry meet again!

Have cakes and wine (or in some circles, it's more accurate to say cookies and juice). Give Wiccaning gifts to the parents. Close the circle, dismiss the quarters, and say farewell to the deities.

FIRST MOON RITUAL FOR GIRLS

Part One: The Challenge of the Path

When a girl moves into adolescence and begins her menstrual cycle, she has passed into a new phase of her life in a physical sense. As many of us have come to realize, that does not mean that she is automatically a woman. The fact that many of us who are middle-aged wives and mothers still think of ourselves as girls caused a desire to create a ritual to help bring us and our daughters into womanhood. By ritually expressing this transformation, a change takes place which allows ourselves and others to see us as women, not as aging girls. A ritual of this type should play an important part in society. The fact that we have lost our rituals to make men out of boys and women out of girls leaves us feeling incomplete, unfinished, and sometimes unsure of what is expected of us as adults. Once upon a time we had these rituals in place; many cultures still do, and those rituals can help define who we are as a people and mold honorable men and women from uncertain youths.

This ritual is for women only. It takes place as soon as possible after the girl's first period. It can be robed or skyclad as your preferences dictate. I have written it as robed; skyclad needs no additional description.

I have included Goddesses from a few different pantheons for those of you who follow a particular one. The ritual calls for a Goddess in each quarter. Take your pick.

GREEK

East: Artemis   West: Demeter
South: Aphrodite   North: Hecate

FINNISH

East: Kyllikki   West: Ilmatar
South: South Daughter   North: Kalma

IRISH

East: Eire   West: Fodhla
South: Morrigan   North: Banbha

ROMAN

East: Diana   West: Juno
South: Venus   North: Nox

The idea is that in the East is a maiden or young woman, in the South is a lover or warrior, in the West is a mother, and in the North is a crone. Use whatever characters exhibit these traits. You can even use modern "pantheons," such as:

East: Deanna Troi   West: Beverly Crusher
South: Tasha Yar   North: L'waxana Troi

You may laugh at the idea of using characters from *Star Trek: The Next Generation,* but they are valid archetypal images which may speak more meaningfully to the young girl in this ritual. Don't forget that filmmaker George Lucas worked with Joseph Campbell, the great student and teacher of mythology, in creating the Star Wars trilogy, which was based on Campbell's exploration of the hero in myth.* Whatever pantheon you choose is fine, but realize that they are but symbols for the deeper energies; the symbols are not what is important in Wicca. The mistake that many Christians made was in worshipping the messenger while ignoring the message.

The girl is brought into the circle by a tyler (a person who remains outside the circle, traditionally to keep a look-out for intruders). All the quarters are faced outward in the

---

* From Mickey Hart's *Drumming at the Edge of Magic: A Journey into the Spirit of Percussion,* p. 46.

circle with their backs toward the center of the circle. There is at least one tyler who stays outside the circle. The altar can be decorated with photos of women the girl admires, heroines, or family photos of women the girl loves. There can be photos of her which mark her growth. A crystal chalice is central to the altar, along with a Goddess statue and green candles.

Priestess: Congratulations! You have chosen to walk the path of woman-hood. You have attained your first moon. This does not mean that you are now a woman. All females menstruate. That is nature, not maturity. You have come into this circle to set your feet upon the path toward woman-hood. This is the first of two rituals to see you to that end. In another twelve moons [or whatever time frame seems likely], *if you have had the courage to change, the maturity to temper your faults, and the wisdom to allow transformation to occur, then you will have earned the second ritual, the door to womanhood. Not all who set their feet upon this path make it to that door. There are many aging girls in the world who never achieve womanhood. They achieve all the outward signs of womanhood—they get married, they bear children, they have successes in parts of their lives— but they never feel complete. They often feel as if they are playing at being a grown-up. They feel as if their lives are a charade. We hope that you will not be one of them. It is our hope that you will be powerful enough to be considered a woman.*

In life there are balances. There are tears along with the laughter; there are gifts and there are challenges. A woman does not let the gifts make her lazy and does not allow the challenges to overpower her determination. A woman accepts the gifts of life gratefully and graciously, as her due. She deserves it. A woman also accepts her challenges gratefully as a blade is grateful for the grinding stone. It is our challenges which mold us and make us strong, wise, powerful, and happy. Are you ready to receive the gifts of the Goddess?

Girl: Yes.

Priestess: Are you ready to receive the challenges of the Goddess? Before you answer, know that you must be prepared to change your habits, behav-ior, or even your way of thinking if you seek to meet these challenges. Are you willing to do that to become a woman? Do you seek to be a woman we can respect?

Girl: Yes.

Priestess: Very well. That took courage. I will take you to the Goddess where everything begins and where everything ends.

The girl is lead to the East Goddess.

Priestess: It is here that I leave you. You are in the hands of the Goddess now and I can do nothing more to help or guide you.

Priestess goes to the center of the circle where she sits and meditates, not looking at or directing the girl in any way.

The maiden aspect of the Goddess is dressed in flowery, flowing robes, or perhaps in the modern dress of a young girl wearing popular clothes. This might have more impact than the robes of an ancient and alien culture. The whole idea behind this ritual is to reach the girl and communicate important information. The more you do to tailor the ritual to her level of understanding and relating, the more effective the ritual will be. The girl must "grok"* the magic.

> *East: I am the laughing Goddess of youth and girlhood and I bless you and wish you well on the path toward womanhood. Youth! Exuberance! Laughter! Excitement! Growth! School! Friends! This is a time of your life which will never come again in this lifetime. You are only young once, they say. This is true, but it is not the end. Those who revere only me desire to be forever young. They worship and adore me, but they make me sad. They are stuck in childhood. Those who never want to grow up are spiritually retarded and never satisfied. This time is fleeting; savor it fully, enjoy your youth, but have the wisdom to move on when the time is ripe. Your time has come.*
>
> *You said that you were ready to receive the gifts and challenges of the Goddess. Here, then, is your gift. I give to you the gift of laughter which will heal your hurts, make you strong, and reduce the impact of the pain in your life. She who can laugh in the face of adversity has great power over her world. [She may give the girl a humorous book or a video of a favorite comedian's routine.] Take the laughter of youth with you into womanhood. You will have need of it. Let the gift of laughter extend to yourself. Learn to laugh at yourself, and you will achieve much in the way of a balanced personality.*
>
> *I have a challenge for you as well, for a gift is not enough to make you whole. I give you this challenge with as much love as I gave the gift. I challenge you to _____.*

The challenges applicable for the East are those to do with intellect and, of course, will need to be specific to the girl's situation. Every one has her own challenges to meet.

They might include:
> thinking before speaking
> doing her homework
> improving her grades
> getting through a particularly difficult class which stretches her abilities
> reading particular books which will help her in some way
> reducing the number of hours she watches television and replacing that time
>   with intellectual activities
> becoming a tutor for other students
> teaching a workshop at a Pagan festival on her own.

* "Grok" is to fully understand. From *Stranger in a Strange Land* by Robert Heinlein.

This challenge must be given your best effort and continuously met for the period of time before you will be considered to be ready for womanhood. Do you understand? There will be no excuses for failure, but one, and that is that you are not ready for womanhood. Do you have any questions? Do you accept this challenge? Give me your word, and remember that a woman's word is her bond; no honorable woman would give her promise falsely. [Wait for girl to reply.] Very well, you have given your word to the Goddess and woe be it onto anyone who breaks a vow to me.

The East then turns her back on the girl. She is left standing there, unsure as to where to proceed. She gets no direction from anyone. After a bit the Goddess in the South turns to face the girl and waits for the girl to come to her. If the girl just stands there, the Goddess can look stern and command the girl to pay attention to what she is doing and use her head. Women do not need to be told what to do at every moment. Women think and reason for themselves. The Goddess will speak in such tones until the girl moves to the South. The South Goddess is the lover. She can be robed in revealing Grecian robes like Aphrodite, or she could wear a sexy black sheer nightgown or a garter belt, if you prefer. The idea to get across is sexuality. This will be a part of the young girl's life soon and she needs to see it in a positive light.

South: I am the Goddess of sexuality. I am she who plays the temptress, the lover, the passionate, orgasmic, wet and ready lover of the God. I am also the lover of women. I am that which drives women to love's door. I am passion. I am love. I am the fire in your loins, that which catches your breath and burns in your brain. I am dark and wet and wonderful. My sounds are that of nature, my smells are that of my ocean, my face shines on the faces of all while in the act of love. I am the pure, fiery essence of sexuality. Do not be ashamed of me. I may come to couples, groups, or to an individual alone. The acts of sexual pleasuring that occur are all beautiful. I am feared by some, but I cannot be denied, only masked in shame. Do not fear me, or put the ugly faces of shame and guilt on me. Explore with me the music of life which is ecstasy. My passions are not blind or aimless. You can be aware of what you are doing and capable of picking the proper place and season for your love. Allow yourself the freedom to worship the Goddess of sex, but keep in mind that there are diseases which will end or mar your life. There are also babies which can be conceived before their time. Take precautions against these dangers. Shield yourself. To protect your body is the first act of sexuality. Love yourself first.

The gift I have for you is the freedom to love yourself. By exploring first your own sexuality, you prepare yourself for sharing that sexuality with another. [A practical gift here is a vibrator and a book about sexuality.] *Sexuality is linked with womanhood but does not define it. You cannot prove your womanhood by simply losing your virginity or bearing a child. A true woman values her sexuality as a treasure, not a mask to be worn. A woman does not use her sexuality in hurtful ways, and she does not need to use it to prove anything to herself or others.*

Part of sexuality is passion. This is where I find your challenge. I, the bright, burning Goddess of sexuality, challenge you to _____.

This challenge should be about passion and will-power. Again, it is tailored to the girl's situation.

Some ideas for the challenge are:
> to control her temper
> to be more assertive
> to get through an assertiveness training course
> to develop and prove her determination or will-power in some significant way
> to become committed to something outside herself, a passionate cause
> to get through an Outward Bound course (will-power).

This is an important challenge, for you cannot be a woman without these skills. Will you accept this challenge? Do I have your word that this challenge will be met with your best effort? [Awaits answer.] Very well. You have spoken your bond with the Goddess. So mote it be, or woe onto she who breaks her bond with me.

The Goddess turns her back on the girl. The Goddess in the West turns to face the girl. The Goddess of the West is a mother figure, ripe with fertility. A pregnant woman is best, or you can simulate her appearance. She wears leaves in a garland about her head and carries a cornucopia filled with guavas, pomegranates, eggs, nuts, money, shells, etc., or she can hold a baby.

West: In the West the waves sweep the shore and the smell of woman is in the air. To the West is water. Here are moods, inspiration, and intuition. Here pulse the rhythms and cycles of motherhood. I am the mother Goddess, Gaia [Juno, Ilmatar, Fodhla, Demeter, etc.]. I am the symbol of fertility. I was once revered as the magical being I am. I create life where there was no life. This is the deepest magic. They saw my cycles in the moon, the tides, and in the monthly bleeding of women. Each month women experience a cycle of the Goddess. Menstruation is the time of the crone, the time at which we are most magical and powerful. After the crone comes the maiden who is lighthearted and joyous. The ripe and thrusting passion of the lover comes with ovulation and the natural desire to mate. The mother comes before the moon time with its hormonal upsets, like those of a pregnant woman. And around again goes the moon.

The mother aspect is the most fertile, allowing much growth and power. It is also a place of great responsibility. Motherhood is a great teacher. The mother aspect also brings the fulfilment of motherhood. One day, perhaps, you will experience this. For now, I give you a gift of surrogate motherhood, for the time is not yet ripe for you to bear a child.

If it is something the girl desires and the girl's parents allow, a gift of a kitten or puppy is appropriate. For concentration's sake the animal is kept out of the ritual room, to be seen afterward. It can be brought to the outside of the circle and shown to the girl at this time, then taken away.

This is your gift and your challenge. Your challenge will come in caring for the animal. You will come to see that being a mother is not always the easiest thing and sometimes it hurts. You must shoulder the entire responsibility for the care and happiness, training and love of this animal entirely on your own. Will you accept this challenge? Give me your word that you will do your best to be a good mother to the animal. So mote it be! You have spoken your vow before the mother of all things; do not forget this, for woe be it onto she who breaks her word with the mother!

The North Goddess turns and faces the circle as the West turns away. The North is dressed as a crone in black, or as a Grandmother would.

North [in an almost whispery voice]: *In the North, it is dark. The hour is late and the forests of the night are hushed and silent. The tread of hooves is heard in the snow and the quiet is such that you can hear the fall of the snowflakes upon the earth. This is my realm. I am Hecate* [Halma, Banbha, Nox, Rhiannon, etc.], *dark Goddess and ruler of the crossroads* [death, night, or underworld]. *You reached a crossroads in life and you set your feet on the path which leads to womanhood. This is a noble ambition. To help you reach the end of your path, I give you the gift of secrecy.* [A good gift here would be a beautiful moon journal or diary with a special pen.] *Use these to record your inner thoughts and feelings. Write in it on a regular basis. You will come to learn from this the secrets of your self. My challenge for you is _____.*

The challenges here are to do with groundedness; some examples are:
    learn to keep silent
    do not gossip
    get and keep a job
    save a certain amount of money
    perform some added task on an ongoing basis
    raise a herb or vegetable garden by herself.

The attainment of this challenge will bring you the grounding you require to become a woman. Will you swear to meet this challenge to the best of your ability? [Wait for a reply.] *Very well, I have your word and woe be it onto anyone who swears a falsehood to the Goddess of darkness.*

She turns away. After a moment, the Priestess begins to speak from where she is sitting as she rises to face the girl.

Priestess: The Goddesses have spoken. Have you heard them? [Wait for a response.] *Good. Much is expected of you. Womanhood is not easily attained, which is why we respect and revere women. To be a woman is to possess the traits of the laughing girl who teaches* [her eastern challenge], *the passionate lover who teaches* [southern challenge], *the responsible mother who teaches* [western challenge], *and the silent crone who teaches* [northern challenge]. *To be a woman is to be all of these things and more.*

What is your name, child? [Her name is given.] *That is the name of a child. That is the name of a girl who has not walked this noble path. Although you have not achieved womanhood, you have had the courage and wisdom to set your foot upon this path, and that in itself is a worthy accomplishment. To show that you have accomplished this and to help you on the path, we have a new name for you. This girl on the path to woman-hood is now called* _____ [this name should be a growth-oriented name or a maiden's name—see index by characteristic for ideas]. *This name is ripe with promise and potential. This name will help you meet your challenges. The Goddess gives all women challenges to overcome. The difference between a girl and a woman is how she deals with the challenges in her life. If you face your challenges squarely and attempt to overcome them, then you will have earned the right to a woman's name. As you work on your lessons, ponder what that name will be. For a child is given a name, but a woman chooses her own.*

You have been given the gifts of laughter, pleasure, motherhood, and secrecy. You have been challenged to [list chosen challenges] *and you have agreed to meet these challenges. In the next twelve moons* [or however long] *we will be watching you, to see how you meet your challenges. The person who meets her challenges head on and masters them will be called woman. The person who shrugs away her challenges, ignores them, for-gets them, or attacks them halfheartedly is still a child. No one will urge you to get after them. No one will remind you or caution you that time is running out. If you seek womanhood, you seek it on your own. Your suc-cess or failure is in your own hands and no one else's. Women shoulder many burdens and challenges and must be able to handle them, for only children have others meet their obligations for them. If you fail, it will be up to you to come to us and ask for another chance. We won't ever ask you. Good luck.*

Cakes and wine are shared. A cake decorated with a scene of a girl walking along a path toward a door marked "WOMEN" is appropriate, and champagne is drunk to celebrate the moment. The tylers can be cut into the circle now and the puppy/kitten can be brought in to share in the excitement. The circle is closed.

The Priestess will keep track of the girl to see that she properly addresses herself to her challenge. If she doesn't, she should under no circumstances get the second rit-ual. Womanhood is not of value if it is given away without being earned. It will have no meaning. If she does not make the time limit, another can be set, but she must ask for it herself.

Part Two: The Rite of Passage

This ritual is to take place only when all the conditions of the previous ritual are accomplished, to the best of the girl's abilities. No excuses should be made to "go easy" on the girl. This ritual should be earned to have value.

There are five "characters" in this ritual, all women:

The student: Represents intellectual achievement and the continued pursuit of understanding. She wears a graduate's cap and gown. She holds books on self-discovery and Wicca. She stands in the East.

The warrior priestess: Represents courage, determination, honor, and spirituality. She can be dressed as a High Priestess who carries a sword (which represents will). She stands in the South.

The mother: Represents the nurturer, protector, and the life-giver. She should be played by the girl's mother, if possible. She stands in the West. She carries a locket shaped like a heart.

The achiever: Represents career, success, and achievement. She should be dressed in a business suit. Her attire should symbolize success in the business world. She carries a briefcase. She stands in the North.

The lady: Represents honesty, integrity, and self-esteem. She can be dressed in any costume which conveys pride. Some suggestions are a medieval costume of a fabled lady, a Greek-style gown, or a conservative suit (like something Queen Elizabeth II might wear) worn by a woman the girl respects and admires. She carries a mirror. She stands in the Center.

Purify the space, cast the circle, and call the applicant, who was given time to take a ritual bath and meditate. She is nude.* Bring her to the circle. The Priestess has the option to be skyclad or robed. There are two chairs by the altar. The girl is stopped at the circle.

> *Priestess: Stop! This is a circle of women; why do you approach?* [Applicant says she wishes to be a woman.] *What have you accomplished to gain access to this circle?* [Girl recounts all her challenges from the previous ritual and how she met them.] *Very well, you have exhibited great* [name the traits she needed to accomplish her tasks]. *You may enter this circle of women.*

They step to the altar where the priestess anoints the girl's third eye with salt water and smudges her with incense.

> *Give me your name, child.* [Applicant answers with the name given to her at the last ritual.] *I take this name from you. This is a girl's name, a child's name. You will be given a woman's name later. Sit with me, nameless one.*

They sit near the altar. From the East comes the student and stands before the two women.

> *Student: I am what makes a girl a woman. I am she who seeks knowledge. I explore what I do not know until I understand it. I am curious, intelligent,*

---

* Performing ritual skyclad can emphasize the importance of the working. In my coven we use skyclad only on special occasions. I found that being skyclad only for serious workings has much more effect than if you were skyclad every Thursday night.

wise, and on a neverending voyage of discovery. I seek to know all I can about the world around me, the people in it, the wisdom of the past, and the events of today. Most of all, I wish to know and understand myself. I study things about Wicca and the Goddess to better understand my beliefs. I am open to new ideas and I see through to the truth in everything. I am what makes a girl a woman!

Priestess: Is it so? Then perhaps you will open this chest for me. [She places a chest, trunk, or jewelry box which locks in front of her.] *This is the box that can only be opened by that which makes a girl into a woman.*

The student tries and fails to open the box. She looks within her books but cannot find the way in to the box. She says so.

Warrior: What you need is a warrior priestess to open your box! She joins the student to stand in front of the girl.

Priestess: What makes you think you can open this which only she who makes a girl into a woman can open?

Warrior: Because I am she who makes a girl a woman! I am the warrior priestess who gives her strength to endure hardship, determination to see things through, courage to overcome fear, and the will to be victorious in whatever challenge is set before her. No girl can be a woman without me at her side. I shall open your box.

Warrior tries and fails. She even tries hitting the box with her sword, to no avail. She admits her defeat.

Mother: It takes neither head nor spirit to open such a box. It takes the understanding of the mother to make a woman! [Mother steps forward to stand near the box.] *I am she without whom girls cannot become women. A woman is compassionate, she cares about others, she nurtures those around her, she tends the sick and feeds the soul of those she loves, she loves little children and looks after the elderly. She is understanding, sympathetic, loving, and supportive. Without these things, how can a girl become a woman? I will be the one to open the box, surely.*

Mother tries and fails to open the box. She waves the pendant near the box to entice it to open with the power of love, but fails. The achiever comes forward.

Achiever: I am a symbol of womanhood; perhaps I can accomplish this task. I am she who sees a girl promoted to womanhood! I am success. I strive to achieve things in life. I stand for independence, self-reliance, self-confidence, achievement, and the rewards which go with success. I am she who inspires women to stretch their limitations and achieve more. I inspire them to be more than what they are. No girl can achieve what I allow women to do! I, then, shall succeed where the others failed.

She tries to open the box, but fails. The lady approaches the group.

Lady: You've all tried so hard to do this task. I'm sorry you were disappointed; if it were up to me, you would all deserve to open the box on your own. I'm sorry to disappoint you, though, because it is I who make a woman from a girl. I am the lady. I bring the traits which allow the woman to hold her head high. I give pride, self-respect, honesty, trustworthiness, and honor to women. Under my guidance, a woman's word is golden. She speaks well of others and always keeps secrets which are trusted to her. She never is malicious or cruel toward others. This soft gentility will open your box.

She tries and fails. The priestess stands and picks up the box.

Priestess: What makes a girl a woman, then? [She gestures to each person she speaks about and draws them near.] *Indeed, that which quests for understanding is an important part of being a woman.* [East approaches and helps support the box.] *The brave warrior priestess makes a woman brave and bold.* [South comes forward and helps support the box.] *The loving heart of the mother is part of every woman, whether she bears children or not.* [West comes forward and kisses the girl, handing her the heart locket, then moves to help support the box with the others.] *The spirit which strives to succeed at life is an important part of womanhood* [North approaches], *and the gentle ways of the lady are part of womanhood as well* [Center comes forward].

None could open the box because none of these things make a girl into a woman. [Characters are surprised and protest briefly.] *Come here, girl.* [Candidate comes forward.] *You have a locket. It represents love: love of the self, love of others, and love of the Goddess. Without love you are no woman. Open it.* [Inside the locket she finds a key.] *What none of you can do, not student or warrior or mother or the achiever or the lady or love alone can do. You can all do together, for a woman is all of you.*

Priestess moves aside and lets the girl put the key in the lock. All the characters help her open the box. Inside is a gift, a token of her womanhood. The nature of the gift is entirely up to the planners of this ritual. It should be personalized to the girl's situation. When they have finished, the priestess calls the girl to the altar.

Priestess: Come here, nameless one. It is time to make you a woman.

The girl is made to kneel near the altar. The East comes before her. She anoints her third eye with oil:

Student: Let me live here in your mind.

Warrior anoints her breasts with oil:

Warrior: Let me live here in your heart.

Mother anoints her abdomen with oil:

Mother: Let me live here in your womb.

Achiever anoints her hands with oil:

Achiever: Let me live here in your deeds.

Lady anoints the area around her lips:

Lady: Let me live here in your words.

Priestess: if you are wise enough to listen to the words spoken here today, you will be a truly remarkable woman of whom we can all be proud. We are proud of you now, young woman.

Student: You learned quickly.

Warrior: You have met your challenges with spirit and determination

Achiever: And have succeeded!

Mother: You have made me proud, and always will.

Lady [holds up mirror to the applicant]: *When you look here, you will see me within you.*

Priestess: What is your chosen name, young woman? [Applicant responds.] *Today you are a woman! Rise,* [new name].

Each character approaches to hug and kiss and say the new name of the woman. Cakes and wine are shared. The circle is closed.

CRONING RITUAL

This ritual is a bit different from the others. It is ritual drama. To be successful, the participants should have at least a feel for acting. Lines should be memorized and rehearsed until the ritual flows smoothly. When performing the drama, the participants should get into a ritual "head space" prior to the ritual and should maintain this throughout the drama. Remember to look the candidate in the eyes; it is more effective to do so. Attention to props and costumes always pays off in a moving and effective ritual. To avoid the complex differences between a croning for a man and a croning for a woman, I have elected to write one from the woman's point of view. The ideas will be similar and you should be getting a pretty good idea of what's involved for a male sage ritual. It makes sense for me to write the woman's rituals (as I am a woman) and leave the men's for a man to write.

This ritual is preferably held outdoors in a temperate time of year. The woman candidate is dressed in her ritual robes. She is lead along a path by a tyler. A young maiden in a garland of spring flowers and pastel Grecian robes stops them. If a spinning wheel or a hand spinner can be attained, it would be even better to have the girl spinning thread when the candidate approaches.

Maiden: Hello, sister. I see you have come through my land. You have tread the paths lined with springtime's flowers and green grasses. You have worn the heart of a young girl who dreamed and laughed and hoped. You were a child, then a girl radiant in her virginity. You set your maidenhood aside and knew love and lust. You spun your thread at the wheel of life and danced underneath the springtime moons. I give you a token that you have passed me by. [She places a wreath of spring flowers upon the head of the candidate.] *Go now, along the path, but do not forget what you have experienced in my realm.*

The candidate is then led down the path. Pictures of her life as a mother are seen along the way in little shrines set up by each of her children (or covens if the woman had no children and mothered only her students. In the event that the woman had no covens, then mementos of her life during those years can be used). The pictures should be in chronological order so she sees the children in order of birth from babies to adults as she walks along. A woman dressed in earth-colored robes who is made to appear pregnant is seen carefully weaving thread. (It is often difficult to find a loom upon which to weave, but even a loop weaving set used by children is acceptable. One can have the mother surrounded by woven goods and skeins of yarn to illustrate the point.)

Mother: Hello, sister. You have walked the path called motherhood. You have known the birth of babies and held the hands of tiny children as they walked. You have gone through the worries of parenthood. You have seen your children grow up and go on to lives of their own. You were once swollen with the giving of life and ripe with fertility. You felt the changes life imprints upon the bodies of mothers. You wove the thread of life into your own tapestries and sang hymns to the harvest moons. I shall give you a token that you have passed me by. [She places a sheaf of wheat in her arms.]

The candidate is lead further along the path. She comes upon an old woman dressed in black, surrounded by black yarn which is woven from branch to branch in the bushes behind her. The old woman is snipping the threads very carefully and retying the ends to other strands.

Crone: Hello, sister. You have travelled long to get here. I see by your tokens that you have come through the realm of the heart and that of the body. You have spun and woven the threads of life. You approach the realm of the cutter of the threads of life. You have learned many lessons. Are you wise enough to enter the realm of the mind? [Candidate answers.] *What, then, was the most important lesson life has taught you?* [Any answer is acceptable.] *You are indeed wise. You have not yet reached the pinnacle of your wisdom, however. You are just entering the land of the crone, the grandmother, the wise woman, the teacher. You have much learning ahead of you and much work. You who are about to enter the area of wisdom and teaching, of she who ponders beneath the winter moons. Are you prepared to take on these lessons? Very well, then; I admit you to my realm and give you a token that you have set foot on my path.* [She places a beautiful scarf shot with silver threads across the shoulders of the candidate.]

The candidate is brought to a place where there is a large cauldron suspended by three poles. Inside the cauldron is a grate, a few inches down from the top; below the grate is some dry ice; above the grate is a bowl containing an exotic fruit juice. A woman is standing there, holding a dipper. She is dressed to look like the Goddess Cerridwen.

> *Cerridwen: I am she you have yet to meet in this lifetime. It is to me you will come upon death and into my vast cauldron you will go. It is also from my cauldron you will emerge reborn. I am Cerridwen, giver of life as the sow is a giver of life. Like the sow, I am prolific. I am also the dark Goddess, the taker of life. I will devour my children that they may live again. I am the ultimate initiator. I dispense the ultimate knowledge and inspiration from my cauldron. Taste now my draught so you will not fear me when you come, at last, to me. Savor its sweetness tinged with the essence of all life itself. This is the drink of life; savor it.* [Cerridwen dips into the bowl and offers a dipper of the juice.]

The candidate is taken back to the beginning. (Preferably the ritual is staged to be in a circle.) There cakes and wine and croning gifts await. The other participants can go to this place following their parts to await celebrating with the newly croned woman.

WARRIOR INITIATION

This is a ritual for men as well as women, for warriors are of both sexes. Do not mistake this archetypal warrior for a mere soldier or hero. The difference is in the spirit of the being. Soldiers march, warriors dance. A warrior may be a peaceful being. It has nothing to do with war and battle as such. A warrior has to do with fighting the inner battles, overcoming one's own hardships, limitations, mistakes, and addictions. A warrior is one who is noble, honorable, trustworthy, and responsible. S/he is one who understands the phases of life and seeks wisdom in living them to the fullest. A Pagan who truly lives the craft is a warrior.

This ritual requires five main participants (plus several hecklers) to take the following parts:

Boudicca ("BOO dick ah"): A warrior queen of the Celtic tribe called the Iceni. She is famous for having nearly defeated the Roman armies in an uprising to fight against the injustices done to her by the Romans occupying Britain in her time. Her name means "victory."

Cuchulainn ("coo HUH lin"): Legendary warrior of Irish myth. His name means "Hound of Culann."

Scathach ("SCAH hah"): The demi-Goddess who taught Cuchulainn his warrior skills. Her name means "The Shadowy One" or "She Who Strikes Fear."

Fionn Mac Cumhail ("FINN Mac COOL"): Another legendary warrior. Captain of the Irish Fianna. Possessor of all knowledge after catching and consuming the mythical "salmon of knowledge." For this ritual, he will bear a chalice or cup.

The Morrigan ("MORE ee gan"): Irish Goddess of war and sex. Her name means "the great queen."

The candidate will have selected a suitable warrior name by which he/she wishes to be known. As part of the Warrior initiation, he/she will take this new name. The candidate should dress in clothing which does not limit movement or entangle his or her limbs. Track pants, a sweatshirt, and running shoes are more suitable to this ritual than robes.

The persons having roles in the initiation ceremony will take their places along the path. Boudicca will stand at the entrance to the path. She will be armed with a spear or a sword. Cuchulainn stands next along the path, his sword sheathed. Scathach is encountered after him. She holds a spear. Fionn Mac Cumhail comes next, with a cauldron set beside him, containing some sort of fruit beverage. Then comes the Morrigan.

The candidate will retire to a secluded place before the initiation ceremony in order to ground, center, and reflect on the approaching initiation. The candidate will know that it is time to approach the path to receive initiation when he or she hears a prearranged signal, such as a blast on a horn or the sound of drums. The sound of the drums will indicate to the candidate where the entrance to the path is located. It might be a good idea, to prevent the candidate from stumbling onto places he or she should not see until later, to place emergency glow lights (available at surplus stores) leading toward the entrance to the path. As the candidate approaches the path, he or she will be challenged by Boudicca, who brandishes her weapon:

> *Boudicca: Hold!* [The drumming ceases.] *This is the path of the Circle of the Fianna* [pronounced "fee AH nah"], *an army of warriors in Ireland who swore their allegiance to the Ard Ri* [pronounced "ard ree"], *the High King. They walked this earthly path many centuries ago, but the spirit of the warrior lives on. This is also the path of the lucht tighe* [pronounced "luck tie"]. *These were the king's personal guard, whose honor and dependability are renowned. None but warriors may tread this hallowed place. I am Boudicca, the aire echta* [pronounced "air eckta"]. *I represent the king's personal champion. I am a champion of the oppressed, guardian of the gate. We are the embodiment of the warrior's spirit and we have gathered together in this magical place upon this magical night. We are warriors all. Who approaches this hallowed place?*

The candidate gives his/her mundane name (not his/her warrior name; this comes later).

Boudicca steps up to the candidate and places the point of her weapon on the candidate's chest, saying:

> *Boudicca: What is your purpose here?*

The candidate will state his/her desire to walk the path and be initiated as a warrior in his/her own words.

Boudicca: All on this path have faced a challenge or trial to make them worthy of the title "warrior." What trials have you endured to earn your place here?

The candidate briefly describes what challenges or trials he or she has overcome to improve him or herself.

Boudicca: This is good. But all who enter this path are dedicated to something beyond themselves. Mere heroes are loyal to themselves. They seek to impress themselves and others. But the warrior is loyal to a greater cause, and places this cause before his or her own interests. This is the first lesson of the warrior, the lesson of transpersonal commitment. Have you learned this lesson? If so, to whom or to what do you pledge your fealty?

The candidate states what he or she is loyal to.

Boudicca: This is good.

Boudicca withdraws the point of her weapon from the candidate's chest. She says:

Leave your blade outside this path, for on this path only warriors may carry a blade. [Candidate turns his or her athame over to Boudicca.] If you are truly determined to walk our path then, [mundane name of candidate], start upon this path and learn the further mysteries of the warrior's path in the company of the circle of the Fianna.

Boudicca brings the candidate onto the path and takes the candidate to the next point along the path, where he/she is presented to Cuchulainn, who carries his sword Cruaiden Cadatchenn (pronounced "CRAY don cah DATCH in," meaning "little hard one") in a sheath on his belt.

Cuchulainn: I am Cuchulainn, the Hound of Ulster. [Cuchulainn draws his sword and brandishes it, walking around the candidate as he continues.] I am the personification of action. I am the embodiment of energy. I am motivation made manifest. I am persistence and relentlessness in pursuit of goals. I leap into battle with my full energy, and seize the day. [Cuchulainn stops in front of the candidate.] Is it your intention to follow the warrior's path?

The candidate answers appropriately.

Cuchulainn: Then I give you your first challenge: Before us on the path is a net staked tight to the Earth. Using diligence, energy, persistence, and relentlessness, find a way to crawl under the net to achieve that which is waiting for you at the other end [he shines a flashlight on a package at the other end of the net]. A false, limited, and superficial person would wait until no one is looking and walk around to claim the prize falsely. A warrior, however, would face the trial and crawl beneath the net to earn the prize at the other end. What say you, are you a warrior or a cheat?

The candidate answers appropriately.

Cuchulainn: Then proceed with my blessing.

The candidate must crawl beneath cargo netting (available at most surplus stores for very little money) pinned down with stakes until very tight against the ground. After accomplishing the challenge, the candidate is urged to open the package. Within should be a nice token of this achievement, such as a token of a hawk symbolizing persistence and relentlessness.

Boudicca (who walks around the net and waits at the other side) next takes the candidate to Scathach, who is armed with a spear.

Scathach: I am Scathach, the tutor of Cuchulainn. I am the disciplinarian. I am the personification of control over mind and attitudes. Is it your intention to continue on the warrior's path?

The candidate answers appropriately.

Scathach: Then I give you your second challenge: You are to remain still. You will not move, or speak, look in any direction except straight ahead, or in any way abandon your concentration. You will remain immobile until I and only I come back for you. A lesser person might be distracted along the path, but a warrior remains focused. Are you ready to begin your challenge?

The candidate answers appropriately.

Scathach: Very good. Then eyes forward, arms at your sides, your feet shoulder-width apart. Excellent. Don't move! Now gather your self-discipline and await my return.

After a minute or two, a number of people come along, one by one trying to distract the candidate from his/her stance.

One might run up to the candidate, shouting at him/her, "Hey! Scathach said follow me! Didn't you hear her? Let's go, candidate! MOVE! What are you waiting for? She said it was all right; now, MOVE! Go forward on the path. She said it was okay."

Someone comes along carrying a bag full of foam balls and throws the balls at the candidate while shouting "Look out! Catch!"

An assortment of cheap, flashy dimestore toys can be waved in the candidate's face or put in the candidate's hands, while the distractor yells things like: "Here! Take this! You'll need it ahead. Really!"

Streamers can be waved in the candidate's face and swirled around his/her body.

Feathers can be used to gently brush the candidate's skin and body to elicit a response.

People can sneak up to the candidate and try to startle him/her into movement by leaping out and shouting "Boo!"

A person of the opposite sex can make sexual overtures to the person.

A person can heckle the candidate, trying to lead him/her into an argument by saying things designed to make the candidate upset and emotional.

The spouse or parent (if possible) comes along and tries to get the candidate to leave. "What are you doing here? Get home this instant!"

An older person can come along and dismiss all the other distracters, saying "Very good! You did it. You can relax now. You've done very well. Let us proceed along the path."

If the candidate responds to any but Scathach, he/she will be encouraged to move along the path as if he/she passed. But Scathach will leap out at the candidate, shrieking her ire and menacing with her spear until the candidate backs up to where he/she was challenged. Directions are given again, and the challenge repeats with the helpers improvising their distractions. After a period of five minutes, if the candidate does not waver, then Scathach may return.

> *Scathach: Candidate! You have exerted great self-discipline and control over yourself and your emotions. You have acted as a warrior might. You have earned this token.*

A gift is given pertaining to immovability. A stone carved into a shape or set in a ring symbolizing solidity and immovability would be appropriate.

Boudicca next takes the candidate to Fionn Mac Cumhail, who stands by a cauldron.

> *Fionn Mac Cumhail: I am Fionn Mac Cumhail, Captain of the Fianna. I am the personification of courage. To achieve courage, one must attain knowledge, judgement, and clarity of thinking. The warrior knows what action is appropriate through clarity of thinking and discernment.* [Fionn takes the cup and fills it from the cauldron. He hands it to the candidate and bids the candidate to drink.] *Drink then from the cauldron of courage. Learn about your strengths and weaknesses.* [He takes the cup back.] *The braggart does not know his/her limitations and romanticizes his/her invulnerability. The warrior realistically assesses his/her capacities and limitations in every situation. Warriors know what they want and they know how to get it. The secret that enables a warrior to reach clarity of thought is living with the awareness of his or her own imminent death. Every act counts. This is the true meaning of courage. Is it your intention to continue on the warrior's path?*

The candidate answers appropriately.

> *Fionn Mac Cumhail: Then I give you your third challenge.* [He points with a flashlight to a package placed on a branch high in a tree, near which is a rope ladder or a simple rope for the more youthful and hearty of candidates.] *There is your goal. It is up to you to achieve it. A coward would shake the tree and cause the package to fall into his/her hands without effort. A manipulative person would get another person to go get the package, claiming illness, age, fear, or a dysfunctional childhood as the reason he or she cannot do it. A warrior would climb the rope and attain the goal. Can you summon the courage to scale these dangerous heights and achieve your goal?*

The candidate answers appropriately.

Fionn Mac Cumhail: Then proceed with my blessings.

The candidate climbs the tree, claims the package, and climbs down with it. The gift of a statue or pin of a lion represents courage.

Boudicca next takes the candidate to the Morrigan, who stands by a large stone.

Morrigan: I am the Morrigan, the Goddess of battle and destruction. I am a destroyer only of that which needs to be destroyed in order for something new and fresh, more alive and virtuous to appear. I obliterate corruption, tyranny, oppression, injustice, obsolete and despotic hierarchies, unfulfilling life-styles and job situations, and bad relationships so that better civilizations, better ventures, and better relationships may take their place. A warrior must have the ability to destroy his/her negative traits, to destroy obsolescence, tyranny, corruption, or oppression as needed. Destruction is a part of your life, or nothing better would ever spring up, new and fresh. As the darkness of night is necessary to understand the brilliance of day, so destruction is to creation. Are you willing to destroy that which traps you? Are you willing to pull down your limitations and destroy your ignorance? Is it your intention to continue on the warrior's path?

The candidate answers appropriately.

Morrigan: Then I give you your final challenge: Get through this barrier symbolizing that which keeps you from the circle of the Fianna. Get past your limitations. A fool would deny the existence of any barrier. A conceited person would claim he or she didn't need to attain the circle of the Fianna and would ridicule those warriors who attained it. But a warrior would fight his or her way through all barriers to the attainment of self-respect. The choice is yours.

By any means the candidate must make his or her way through a wall built of flimsy wood which will come down with repeated kicking. Words can be painted on the wall, such as "self-doubt," "ignorance," "foolishness," or any words meaningful for the candidate to overcome.

Boudicca meets the candidate and hands him or her a final gift. (A necklace with a Thor's hammer symbol would be appropriate.) The candidate will find him or herself standing close to the circle of the Fianna. All the characters in the ritual are standing within the circle. For an added theatrical effect, cardboard Grecian-style pillars can be bought from a theatrical supply company. (They look startlingly realistic in the moonlight.)

Boudicca walks up and hands the candidate his/her own blade, which had been left behind at the entrance to the path. Boudicca leads the person into the circle from a doorway cut in the northeast. They walk to the altar. The candidate's gifts are placed on the altar.

Boudicca: Prepare yourself to take the oath of the warrior. You have been taught persistence, control of your mind, courage, and the necessity of destruction. You have been given tokens representing the persistence of the hawk, the solidity of a rock, the courage of a lion, and the destructive attributes of Thor's hammer. These are all tools of the warrior. These are tools to help the warrior live his/her life. The warrior's oath binds you to this path. Are you ready to take the ancient and traditional warrior's oath to join the circle of the Fianna?

The candidate expresses his/her desire to take an oath.

Boudicca: Have you chosen a warrior's name for yourself? If so, what is it?

The candidate announces his/her chosen warrior name.

Boudicca: [Warrior name], *repeat after me. I have performed the challenges given to me today by the Gods on this sacred path. I will strive to nobility of cause, honesty of word, faithfulness of heart and, in short, to live by the motto of the Fianna: Truth in my heart, strength in my hands, and consistency in my tongue. I swear by all that I hold sacred, that until the heavens with all its stars falls upon me, and the earth gives way beneath me, and the sea bursts its bounds to drown the land, I will strive to live my life as a warrior. If I prove false to my oath, then may my weapons turn against me and leave me at the mercy of the Goddess. From this day forth, I will seek to live up to the mighty name of* [warrior name[.

The candidate repeats.

Boudicca [after embracing the candidate]: *Welcome to this warrior's circle. You have learned what it is to be a warrior, but be ever mindful that there is more to you than this. Know that warriors combine their skills with the skills of the king* [or queen, depending on the sex of the candidate], *and practice sound leadership. Know that warriors combine their skills with those of the Witch, to give them mastery and control over themselves and their powers. Finally, know that warriors combine their skills with those of the lover. This gives the warrior compassion and a sense of connectedness with all things. A warrior knows that there is no greater power in all the world than that of love. To be a balanced and effective human, you must be part warrior, king* [or queen], *Witch, and lover.*

Cakes and wine are served. Participants come forward to congratulate the new warrior. The circle is closed when the feasting ends.

6

Pagans and Christian Names

Since the Norman Conquest of England, the church has influenced or dictated to the English-speaking world the names by which our children would be known. Of course, many people did not choose Biblical names simply because the church encouraged it, but because they were motivated by sincere religious reverence or in loving memory of someone who once bore that name. Later, after the Protestant Reformation, names were chosen out of the Bible in a new manner to illustrate the tenets of the religious reorganization of the day. The church was still dictating, even more loudly than ever, by what names our children were to be called, and more people complied out of fear. In these dark days, deviating from the Christian norm was severely punished and very soon no one walked alone. People may have been marching to a different drummer internally, but to the world they marched as Christian soldiers, all named the same. From 1750 to the present, the most commonly given names are drawn from a store of only 179 names. A dreary sea of Johns, Pauls, Josephs, and Marys washed over history for hundreds of years.

Today, many of us are not even aware of which names are Biblical, or to what they refer in the Bible. We simply have a stock of "normal" names from which we choose. We have chosen the same names for centuries. What the church once had to force upon us, we now accept as rote. We have blurred the boundaries between church and state in so many areas that we have come to find that certain ideas are frowned upon by the culture, but actually stem from the disapproval of the church.

I think it is time for a change, for many reasons. Names, as many ancient cultures used to know, have power. To choose a child's name from a religious tradition to which you do not subscribe is a meaningless, hollow concession to societal (and implied religious) pressure. How can this name ever have power and meaning to the child to whom it is so thoughtlessly given? How can a name so commonplace vibrate in harmony to the essence of so many people who carry that name? A name, ideally, is a reflection of the person who bears it. We have lost a sense of our own individuality and we perpetuate this trend by choosing names which do not represent the individual.

Another good reason to vary the program with regard to choosing traditional Christian names is boredom! We have used Joseph, Peter, Mary, John and the derivations of these names for 800 years. Aren't we bored yet? When someone tells you they have just named their new baby John, do you ever comment "Zonkers! What a rollickingly fascinating name! Wherever did you get a name like that? How on Earth did you come up with it? How original! How creative! Good name! How do you pronounce it again? By Jove, there's a keeper!"? Probably not.

Most of us were given our "given" names, and many of them are Christian names. Our parents may have been Christians, and had no inkling they were naming someone who would grow up to be a Pagan. The Christian name may have been given in a sentimental gesture, out of religious zeal, or just because the parents thought it was pretty and hadn't a clue that it was a Christian name. The names in the Bible were around a long time before Christianity came to be, so it may be argued that they are merely pre-Christian Hebrew names which happened to be used in the Bible. As such, don't they have as much power as any other non-Christian name? To a Pagan, I don't think so. For thousands of years, millions of people have put lifetimes worth of energy into the Bible. They prayed to many of the names in the Bible; they read it aloud as they set fire to innocent people—it is the basis of many wars and much bloodshed; many preached it on Sunday and ignored it on Monday. Much negativity and hypocrisy has been associated with the Bible and the names in it. In terms of the collective unconscious, Biblical names have "copped an attitude." If you disagree with me, try thinking about naming your son Judas, a popular name once upon a time, and see if the name isn't tainted by all that has gone before. There was certainly good and sincere energy attached to Biblical names, but to our subconscious, which is the level in which names hold power, the names still say "Christian." It could be argued that Peter, for example, means "rock," so why not use it for stability and grounding work? Because to our subconscious, Peter carries the Biblical images, not those of rocks. Why try to reshape and redefine all that energy when by choosing a name free from Christian imagery, you can also make a statement about nonconformity and help to free society from the clutches of the church?

So, here we are, all fired up with an anarchistic, innovative, revolutionary fire in our collective belly. We are ready to chuck all the Johns, Marys, Josephs, Pauls, and Matthews right out the window and begin fresh with different, non-Biblical names. We can now choose ancient Pagan names or make up our own. The trouble is, in regard to ancient Pagan names, what are they? Second, how do you go about making up a name? It would be helpful to review how the pre-Christians chose their names. Below is a listing of methods of picking names used prior to the Christian influence, as well as some modern techniques. All these techniques lend themselves well to selecting a mundane name as well as a magical name.

METHODS OF NAME MAKING

Ancient

Metronymic: Named for the mother. This makes great sense, because maternity is irrefutable. Merlin Stone speculated in *When God Was a Woman* that cultures as far back as the Upper Palaeolithic Period were matrilineal (based upon mother kinship). The metronymic method of name-making has been recently revived and used by feminists and in fiction work, such as the Darkover novels by Marion Zimmer Bradley. This method was the way in which the Free Amazons were named. In Denmark, it is law that a person can choose to adopt the name of his or her father or mother.

Patronymic: Named for the father. This system superseded the metronymic system. In this system, David Paulson is David, son of Paul; David's child would be Eric Davidson or Eric Davidsdaughter.

Habitational: Where you live. Robin Oceanside, Laurel of White Rock, and Kerr of Gull Cottage are examples of habitation names.

Occupational: Baker, Weaver, Wainright, and Smyth are such names.

Nicknames: David the Forgetful, Atilla the Hun, and Becka the Buxom are names derived from affectionate or descriptive nicknames.

Anecdotal: Based upon a significant experience in the person's life. This method is one used by the Blackfoot Indian tribe. Some anecdotal Blackfoot surnames are "Old Sorrell Horse," "Over the Mountain," and "Shot in Both Sides." Another example of an anecdotal name is the name "Dances With Wolves" from the motion picture by the same name.

Seasonal: Based upon a time of year particularly important to its bearer (May, June, Mabon).

Interests: Based on what the person does, perhaps as a hobby (Mason, Gardener, Healer, Harper).

Physical attributes: Based upon the person's physical characteristics, such as "Aelfrick the Red."

From this day forth I swear I will never again be known by the name of any man, be he father, guardian, lover, or husband, but simply and solely as [the daughter of my mother].

—Marion Zimmer Bradley
The Oath of the
Free Amazons from
Free Amazons of Darkover

Ambitions: Hopes for what the bearer will achieve.

Mythological: Named after famous mythical Gods, Goddesses, or heroes.

Birth circumstances: Names chosen based upon birth order, birth process, or significant family feelings.

Totem animals: Named for the animal which makes itself known to be the person's totem animal.

Special objects: Names can come from many common sources (rocks, plants, flowers, herbs, spices, celestial objects, trees, animals, etc.).

Intellectual considerations: Based upon a person's special intellectual abilities or lack thereof, as "John Littlewit."

Geographic: Using the names of mountains, towns, or landforms as a source of names.

Modern

Media ideas: Using television, movies, poetry, or novels as a source of new names.

Foreign names: Picking names from other countries which mean something of significance to the bearer.

Elemental: Names from the four natural elements (air, fire, water, and earth). Examples of these are Sky, Firefly, Cascade, and Terra.

Historical: Looking to our past as a source of names for the future.

7

Names from the Planet Earth and Beyond

THE VOICE OF THE PLANET

The Earth is our mother. She is crucial to our existence and integral in our religious beliefs. Geology is the study of the Earth and her processes. The names used to describe these processes frequently are beautiful, mysterious, or at least interesting names. Geological names are for those who find the Earth a fascinating place and who dance to her rhythms and study her ways. There are many scientists in the Wiccan religion, especially geologists (for example, me). For those of us whose religious focus is the same as our career focus (the Earth), these would make interesting name choices. Even if one isn't a Geo-Pagan and doesn't know the first thing about geology, these names are still good choices because they are unique, beautiful, Earth-oriented, and interesting. They may also be good names for covens, covensteads, or familiars. These names are also Elemental names (relating to Air, Fire, Water, and Earth). The reason for grouping geological names according to elements is that the processes which form the Earth can be broken down into elemental forces.

Earth and Fire

The Earth is a result of the interaction of several major forces, and these forces can be interpreted as an interaction between elements. First, there is the force known as continental drift, which is the movement of the various continental plates of comparatively lighter rock which are, in effect, "floating" upon the more fluid liquid magma core of the Earth. These plates are pushed along by other plates and create certain tectonic phenomena along their leading edges. This process is also called plate tectonics. This force is the reason the continents are arranged the way they are. Originally, all the continents were one large landmass called Pangaea (pronounced "pan GAY ah"). It then broke into two continents called Gondawanaland ("gond WAWN ah land") and Laurasia ("LAUR asia"). Over millions of years, the continents moved slowly about until they reached the current configuration. The system is still at work moving the landmasses around. In North America, the plate is being pushed along by a rift in the Atlantic Ocean, where new earth is spewing forth in the form of erupting volcanos. This new land moves away from the rift, pushing the older rocks along. This process is slowly pushing North America westward at a rate of about one inch per year. On the West Coast, the older rocks are reabsorbed or subducted (literally pushed under California). In this way, the Earth recycles itself. Fiery volcanos erupt and spread new earth along the floor of the ocean, causing the very sea to boil and churn around it. Great clouds of steam escape from the roiling sea. The lava oozes into the sea, cools quickly, and, if the volcano is big enough, sometimes will create an island, the passionate offspring of Earth and Fire. Elementally speaking, continental drift is primarily an activity involving Earth and Fire.

Earth and Earth

The second part of the process of continental drift is where the reverse of a volcano happens. On the edge of the plate furthest away from the ridge where new land is being created, there is a place where the oldest land is being reabsorbed back into the molten core of the planet. The Earth is, in effect, swallowing its own tail. In North America, the Earth's crust beneath the ocean is colliding with our continent, and the ocean floor is being slowly pushed under us. Where two plates collide is a place of great tectonic disturbance. The reabsorption of the Earth's crust into itself creates enormous friction and heat. The collision causes tectonic activity in the topmost plate. It is manifested, specifically in California, in the San Andreas fault and its associated earthquakes. Along this front where Earth meets Earth, the top plate bends and ripples like a supple lover. Great coastal mountain ranges are pushed up, shearing and fracturing the rocks as they buckle and jump. The Earth trembles and shudders as the Pacific plate slides slowly beneath it. Volcanos erupt all along the coast and heat the water in geothermal springs. Like a lover, the land heaves and warms in the embrace. This is a process of Earth interacting with Earth.

Earth and Water

Additionally, the erosion process is at work. Let's look at the cycle from the point at which some soil is eroded from the bank of a stream. It is eventually deposited in larger and larger rivers until it is emptied into one of the oceans. Here it is mixed with the calcium from eroding shells of sea life and other chemicals which we pour into the ocean. This deposit will harden, under the pressure of millions of years worth of deposition, into a dense rock such as mudstone or sandstone. As the plates move around the globe, weather in any given place drastically changes. The seas rise and fall. The sea into which our soil was deposited may become land again. (This is why one can find marine sandstones in Iowa and tropical foliage fossilized in Antarctica.) As the rain falls upon our formerly marine sandstone, it erodes bits of the rock, breaking it into soil. The soil washes away into the stream and the cycle begins again. Like life, the cycle is neverending, but continually beginning again. Water is a very powerful force, capable of eroding through thousands of feet of solid rock. The Grand Canyon is the result of the relentless energy of one stream working away at the Earth. This cycle can take millions and millions of years. The erosional cycle is involved primarily with the forces of Earth and Water.

Earth and Air

As the radiation from the sun's energy warms the surface of the planet and the planet moves from day into night, temperature fluctuations create weather. Cloud development, storms, patterns of rainfall, and the location of various kinds of climate are all dictated by these processes. The spinning of the globe and the intense pull of the moon as it orbits the earth every twenty-eight days affect tides of the planet and those of its women. The interaction between the planet and weather patterns is important to maintaining the process of erosion. This interaction is primarily involved with Earth and Air.

Thus we have the planet interacting with the four elements of Fire, Earth, Water, and Air to create the major Earth-building forces. It is through this interaction that the Earth can provide the stunning vistas we love. It is also through these processes that we have an environment suited to support life at all. The "Gaia theory" proposed by some theoretical scientists proposes that we, as human beings, fit into the scheme of things as sort of walking nerve endings for the planet in the delicately balanced environment. As we interfere with the eco-balance, the planet adjusts with a counter-reaction. The scientists see the whole system as interdependent, and the Pagan in me tends to agree with them.

ELEMENTAL NAMES

Each of the four elemental Earth-shaping forces has a "voice" of its own, its own energetic feel. These four very different qualities of the Earth can be used for magical applications in the careful choosing of a magical name from any of these areas. The elements of Air, Earth, Fire, and Water are four powerful, natural forces for growth and change; as we have seen here, they shape the very face of nature. Why not use them to change the nature of yourself?

Air

The process of weather gives us many of the Air names. Air names bring airiness, lightness, and intellectual qualities. This is the quarter of dawn, when the clean and shining day begins. The power of Air can be the gentle, refreshing breezes reflected in a pretty name like Ariel, or a maelstrom of windborne power in a name like Thunder. Air names are for heightening intellectual prowess, clear and orderly thinking, for soaring high above the ground on the wings of thought. Air moves us. Choose a name to help move you where you want to go.

Wide open and unguarded are our gates,
Named of the four winds, North, South, East, and West;
Portals that lead to an enchanted land...
Here, it is written, Toil shall have its wage
And Honor honor; the humblest man
Stand level with the highest in the law.
Of such a land have men in dungeons dreamed
And with the vision brightening in their eyes
Gone smiling to the fagot and the sword...

—Thomas Bailey Aldrich
(1836-1907)

Aeolus: Greek God of wind.
Aleyn: Phoenician God of wind and clouds.
Aria
Ariel
Aurora
Boreas: Greek God of the North wind.
Breeze
Celestial
Cirrus
Cloudy
Cumulus
Cyclone
Doldrum
Dustdevil
Eos: The dawn.
Ethereal
Eurus: Greek God of the East wind.
Gale
Gusty
Hathor: Egyptian Goddess.
Hurricane
Jumala: Finnish sky God.
Maelstrom
Nimbus
Notus: Greek God of the South wind.
Puff
Skye
Storm
Stratus
Thor: Norse God of thunder.
Thunder

Tornado
Tradewind
Tsunami
Typhoon

Ukko: Finnish sky God.
Whirlwind
Wind
Zephyrus: Greek God of the West wind.

Fire

Fire names erupt like surging volcanos of change. Fire names are for bringing the passion and warmth of the south into your life. These names are for warmth, passion, determination, fiery conviction, increased sexuality, for becoming a "hot-blooded" person. As the volcanos erupt beneath the sea, so fire names ignite change and the reshaping energy fire can give. Fire names transform us. They bring determination, courage, unbending will-power, passion, enthusiasm, vivacity, sexual electricity, and drive. Read the following names and find one which reflects how high you want to turn up the heat.

Agni: Hindu fire God.
Aton: Egyptian sun God.
Arani: Hindu Goddess of sexual fire.
Ardor
Bask
Blaize or Blaze
Blast
Brighid: Irish "fiery arrow."
Crackle
Dazzle
Electric
Fever
Fire
Firecracker
Firefly
Flame
Flash
Glow
Grainne
Li: Chinese sun God.

Lightning
Lightning Bolt
Lightning Bug
MacGreine: Irish fire elemental.
Paiva: Finnish sun God.
Pyre
Ra: Egyptian sun God.
Salamander
Seb: Egyptian sun God.
Seker: Egyptian sun God.
Shamish: Babylonian sun God.
Solar
Spark
Sparkle
Sultry
Sundance
Sunny
Sunshine
Surya: Hindu sun Goddess.
Wildfire

Water

Water names are a good way for a person to tone down an overabundance of fire energy in one's life. Water names are cool, tranquil, and soothing, and even the most serene ones are able to quench a raging fire. Water names bring about a coolness of mind, a quenching of tempers, a watery, emotional, moon-driven, twilight merging with the Lady of the Lake. Water shapes us. Water names smooth over rough emotional terrains as water slowly smooths the craggy face of the planet.

Archelous: Greek river God.
Atlantic
Bay
Brook
Cascade
Cove
Creek
Deep
Drizzle
Dylan: Welsh sea God.
Ebb
Egeria: Roman water Goddess.
Flow
Geyser
Glacier
Hail
Harbor
Jet
Lagoon
Lake
MacCuill: Irish primordial water
    elemental.
Manannan Mac Lir: Irish sea God.
Marsh
Monsoon

Nu: Egyptian water elemental.
Ocean
Pacific
Pond
Rain
Rana: Norse sea Goddess.
Raindrop
Rainforest
Rapid
River
Sea
Sea Priestess
Shoney: Scottish sea God.
Snowflake
Splash
Spring
Stream
Tamesis: British river Goddess.
Tefnut: Egyptian moisture Goddess.
Vellamo: Finnish water Goddess.
Waterfall
Wave
Whirlpool
Whitewater

Earth

Earth names ground. These names help one become more rooted in reality, more stable, quieter and slower to speak, more thoughtful, fertile, and strong. Earth names heal us. One can use Earth names to heal old wounds and grow stronger as a result. Let your Earth name absorb your pain and ground it harmlessly. Earth energy is about endings and beginnings. As the Earth gives birth to itself, so it also destroys itself in an endless birth-death-rebirth cycle. The Earth is the final step through the elements back to where it all began and to where it all must finally end.

Acres
Aker: Egyptian earth God.
Chalk
Chestnut
Coast
Desert
Eartha
Faunus: Roman God of forests.
Flidais: Irish woodland Goddess.
Flora

Forest
Gaia: Greek earth Goddess.
Glade
Glen
Gondwanaland: An ancient landmass.
Grove
Inland
Island
Laurasia: Ancient continent.
Magma: Molten rock.

Meadow
Mesa: Plateau.
Mielikki: Finnish forest Goddess.
Moraine: Glacial debris.
Moss
Pangaea: Ancient continent.
Planet
Rhea: Greek "Earth."
Rock
Salt
Sandy
Savanna
Shore
Steppe
Stone
Talus: Debris at cliff bottom.
Tapio: Finnish forest God.
Terra: Roman earth Goddess.
Terrain
Terrestrial
Tundra
Tuulikki: Finnish forest Goddess.

*Ye who love the haunts of
  nature,
Love the sunshine of the
  meadow,
Love the shadow of the
  forest,
Love the wind among the
  branches,
And the rain-shower and
  the snow-storm,
And the rushing of great
  rivers
Through their palisades of
  pine-trees,
And the thunder in the
  mountains,
Whose innumerable echoes
Flap like eagles in the
  eyries;—
Listen to these wild
  traditions...*

—Henry Wadsworth
Longfellow
The Song of Hiawatha

The planet is controlled by the interaction of elemental forces with each other. Many of us have elemental energies which form parts of our personalities. Taking a name which reflects the merging of two or more elements may speak to the energies which are exhibited in your nature and help them flourish. For example, the names Sea Fire, Stream Pebble, Eagle Rock, and Whirlwind Cascade all combine elements and may suit those who are working toward an inner balance of elemental forces.

ROCKS

Rocks and minerals are the gems of the earth. As a gift of the planet to its children, rocks are an excellent choice for a source of names. The study of the power of crystals is well known, but all rocks give off a vibration and have unique qualities which can benefit the wearer. As with other magical names, rock names can be used to describe who you are, or can help you become what you want to be. In terms of the sympathetic magic aspect of names, rocks can lend one a wide variety of attributes, the most powerful of which is the groundedness that comes with these names.

Agate

Agates are magnificent stones with endless variations of brightly colored bands in swirling patterns. This is such a conspicuous and brightly-colored stone that it was probably one of the earliest stones to be noticed and used, especially in the carving of ancient religious symbols. Agates were at first thought to have supernatural powers which lend them such intriguing beauty. The name agate was given because the stone was first discovered by the ancient Greeks beside the river Achates. Agates were popular stones for carving magnificent works of art in ancient Egypt, and later in Greece and Rome. In fact, agate was used by nearly every ancient culture due to its workability, strength, and beauty. Agates have a very calming effect and are frequently used as worry-stones (polished versions kept in pockets and stroked when tension increases).

Agates are formed when lava from an erupting volcano flows and gasses escape from the lava to the air, leaving cavities which fill with concretions formed by the cooling rock solutions. Agates are hard and more durable than the rock around them. As the rock cools, the layers form in wild patterns which mimic the cavity in which they are formed. Sometimes the center of an agate is hollow space in which crystals form. Often crystals or fiery opals form some layers to create some of the most beautiful stones in the world.

As a magical name, Agate suggests a person of variety, unpredictability, fire, color, beauty, strength, durability, popularity, and age-old appeal. It is an especially fine name for a Pagan, as it is reflective of its birthplace in the Earth and because of its cultural history as a medium for some of the greatest works of Pagan religious art ever created.

Amber

Amber is a fossilized rock formed from prehistoric tree sap. It is a pale yellowish stone with a soft, waxy lustre, usually cloudy (but more transparent when heated). It is always a lightweight stone, sometimes containing fossils of Tertiary Period insects which had been caught in the tree sap as it flowed.

Amber was one of the most prized precious stones in primeval times. It was used for making simple ornaments and as a form of money during the Palaeolithic Period. Archaeologists have found ornaments made of amber dating from the second millennium BCE. Nearly every ancient society had its own name for amber, which reflects its popularity. To the Greeks amber was *elektron,* meaning lustrous metal; in Rome, *succinum;* to the ancient Germans, amber was called *bernstein,* derived from the word meaning "to burn" (amber does burn).

During the geologic period known as the Tertiary (fifty million years ago), dense forests grew and thick sap flowed from wounds on the trees. The drops of sap would fall from the trees to the earth below, and were buried by the process of sedimentation until they were exposed once more to the atmosphere. The sap from the trees in the

Tertiary Period was thicker and richer in resin and sometimes dripped over insects which rested on the trunk of the tree, resulting in a thick, sticky death. These creatures were sometimes preserved inside fossilized pieces of amber, as in one famous example of the specimen which held a complete prehistoric wasp.

In terms of its significance as a magical name, Amber brings to mind one who is pale, thin, durable (yet soft), natural, tempered by life experiences; an ancient soul, one with a connection to trees and their well-being; a slow-moving, thoughtful person; a well-grounded person; a solid, well-rooted individual; a forest lover or an environmentalist. Amber is an excellent choice for a magical name because of its connection to ancient life and its gentle, glowing, golden appearance. Amber brings a slowness to judge, gentleness, and a deep sense of patience and tolerance. Amber beads together with jet are traditionally worn by a high priestess. Amber beads are the tears of ancient trees.

Amethyst

Amethyst is a purple variety of the mineral crystal quartz. To the Greeks, amethyst was *amethystos,* which means "unintoxicating," and was thought to be a cure for inebriation. The Greek word from which the word crystal was derived means "ice." Ancient wealthy Roman patricians used quartz crystal balls to cool their hands and face in hot weather. Quartz stays cool; it is a very poor conductor of heat. Amethyst is also believed to be a cure for insomnia.

Amethysts have always been very popular stones. All quartz crystals were used early in history due to their beauty, abundance, strength, and their resistance to erosion by all external influences. Early tools were made of another form of quartz (flint) from the Palaeolithic Period to the Neolithic Period. The popularity of amethysts continues to the present day. In the Middle Ages, artists cut impressive goblets with magnificent carving out of amethysts and other varieties of quartz. Amethyst was used for jewelry and ornaments during the Renaissance. All manner of quartz crystals became popular during the Victorian era, decorating lamps and chandeliers. The awareness of crystals as amplifiers of energy was well-documented from the writings of Pliny the Elder all the way up to the present day. A great surge of popular interest in the magical properties of amethysts (and all other stones) surfaced with the advent of the New Age movement.

Amethyst is thought to be a gentle stone, yet a powerful protector by those who use crystals in healing. Keeping a large cluster of amethyst in your home is thought to protect the space from negativity. It is used in meditation to help channel away any negative feelings from the bearer. It is suggested that amethyst should accompany any ritual of protection and purification.

Amethyst is a good magical name for someone who is (or who wants to be) sharp, clear-thinking, regal, cool-headed, sober, resistant to societal pressure, naturally attractive; an honest person who is a transparent liar; a catalyst or a spokesperson for organizations; a sharp and battle-seasoned warrior; someone who needs protection from negativity; a trustworthy friend, but a poor enemy; and a person of strong psychic abilities.

Aquamarine

A clear, light bluish-green variety of beryl is called aquamarine. Aquamarines are formed in connection with coarse-grained granites, called pegmatite. Aquamarine (blue-green), heliodor (golden), morganite (pink), and emerald are all forms of the crystal beryl.

Aquamarine is a fine name for one who is ruled by a water sign, who is beautiful, colorful, emotional, intuitive, cool-headed, drawn to the ocean, tends toward depression and feelings of inadequacy yet comes to realize his or her true worth. This is a good name to take after an especially transformative experience.

Arkose

Arkose is a sandstone composed mostly of quartz and feldspars, the most common and important rock-forming minerals. Arkose quite easily decomposes and is a vital source of nutrients for plant life.

This simple rock is not flashy, colorful, unique, or adorning the necklace of Cleopatra, but without it there might not have ever been any Cleopatra. This mineral-rich rock which easily erodes feeds the planet with its own quiet "death" and transformation.

This is a good name for one who is plain, hard-working, modest, unadorned; one who does not hold a position of power in any organization, yet without whom the organization would collapse; a nurturer, parent, or teacher; a good cook; a purist; an animal and plant lover or gardener; an unemotional, basic, back to nature, natural food-eating, vegetarian, middle-of-the-road sort of person. It is also a good name for developing a more modest and helpful side to one's personality.

Basalt

During the Tertiary Period (fifty million years ago), volcanos erupted and spewed forth glowing magma from the bowels of the planet. As the liquid rock flowed over the surface of the earth, it slowly cooled, creating a variety of rocks. Basalt is one of those rocks. Basalt is a rich, black rock which can sometimes be formed into interesting landforms such as Fionn Mac Cumhail's Giant's Causeway in Ireland (and Scotland), and Devil's Tower in Wyoming.

A person bearing the name Basalt may be one who has a temper; one who accomplishes many things; a creator; a fiery, passionate person who comes from an overly emotional, even violent home; a fire sign; a successful person who is at his best when thinking cooly and rationally (but who doesn't always do so); a dark, brooding personality who will rise to great heights of accomplishment. Basalt is a good choice for bringing more fire energy into your life.

Beryl

Beryl is a rock which commonly occurs within a coarse-grained granite called pegmatite. Varieties of beryl range in color from the deep green of emerald to the delicate blush pink of morganite. Plain beryl is not of gemstone quality. The crystals are sometimes very large and quite heavy. The largest crystal yet found weighs eighteen tons. Beryl crystals are milk-colored and opaque. They are valued for the manufacture of beryllium, one of the lightest metals.

Beryl is a pretty name. It is well-suited to a salt-of-the-earth sort of person who is occupied in building and maintaining foundations of organizations, relationships, or families. This is a plain person who can be quite large in size; someone who is pale in appearance; a person who is often thrust into the role of outcast, yet who out-performs those around her; a private person whose inner thoughts are hard to read—you never quite know what this person really thinks; someone who often has very beautiful off-spring and siblings. Beryl is a name for someone who gets things done. Beryl brings with it a sense of solidity and modesty.

Clay

Clay is a firm, fine-grained earth composed of aluminum silicate which is created by the erosion of fine rock particles mixed with water. It is used to make pottery, bricks, sculpture, and ceramics.

This is a nice magical name for one who is a sculptor, potter, or who works with ceramics. It is also a good name for becoming well-grounded. This name evokes a feeling of earthiness, the fertile potential without which growth cannot occur; it is a creative and fertile person.

Copper

Copper was very likely the first metal used by humans because of its abundance and the fact that copper is easy to work. The Romans called copper *cuprum*. Copper is a reddish-brown metallic element which is most frequently found covered by blue azurite and green malachite. Copper is used for jewelry, ornaments, wall and building coverings, and more recently in electronics, as copper is an excellent conductor of electricity.

Copper is an excellent name for a person with auburn or red hair, for one who is easy to get along with, who enjoys being "one of the guys (or gaias)," and for adept trance mediums and psychics. Copper suggests a charming and bubbly, sometimes highly sexual person. This is a name for working on a temper, becoming clean and tidy, and staying healthy; a good name for a hard-working and passionate activist. If you wish to play with fire names, then a name like Copper will bring fire energy to your life.

Crystal

Crystals of all kinds have played a major part in the history of humanity. It is likely that one of the first rocks to become important to primitive people was rock salt. By watching the behavior of animals who came to lick the salty crystals for their important nutrients, early humans may have discovered this edible crystal. Later humans discovered and used many crystalline rocks, such as sharp-edged quartz, for tools and weapons, but ornamental crystals have always held an fascination for us. We fashioned jewelry out of them, sewed them onto our clothing, and imbedded them in the walls of our sacred temples.

The discovery of gold, copper, and bronze brought a way to fashion the beautiful crystals into ornaments to decorate the body. People have always liked the feel of crystals against the skin. Beautiful crystal jewelry has been found in tombs as ancient as the fourth century BCE. In the early days before we could explain the origins of these fascinating crystals, it was commonly believed that they were formed by (and in some cases possessed of) supernatural powers. Crystals were commonly worn as magical amulets.

The Greeks were adept at carving upon precious gems; the hard crystals of diamonds, rubies, emeralds, and others bore the work of accomplished artists. In Rome, the artisans acquired knowledge from a variety of sources and soon became superior to the Greeks. The Romans perfected the technique of carving the cameo.

In the Middle Ages, ownership of precious crystals was confined to rulers and the church. The natural joy of adorning the body with beautiful crystals and stones was frowned upon by the early Christian church. The emphasis then was on the life to come and the pleasure of gems was forbidden to the masses as a temptation to be avoided, although the high church officials and the churches were laden with magnificent jewels. The incredible developments in stone carving, especially the carving methods for the creation of the exquisite cameos, popular in the ancient world, withered into a faint memory until the art form finally faded into oblivion in Byzantine times.

In the eleventh century, Constantine Psellos wrote a book on the healing and magical powers of gemstones, which was based on the works of the ancient author Pliny the Elder, but with added ecclesiastical dogma. Even in this time the popularity of crystals could not be denied. Moonstones became exceedingly popular and were worn as amulets to enhance beauty and health, and attract money, glory, and happiness through their strange, supernatural powers.

The expansion of the arts in the thirteenth and fourteenth centuries triggered a rebirth in the carving of precious gems. As the degree of interest and craftsmanship rose, so did the demand for the crystalline raw material. Trade routes from the sources of the gems into much of Europe developed. The prices for the gems were once again very high.

Crystals became extremely popular during the Renaissance in the later part of the seventeenth century. The demand for precious stones was so great that the supply of diamonds and rubies became strained and artisans used quartz and amethyst instead.

Crystals have remained popular and enjoyed a recent upsurge of popularity with the advent of the New Age. As the knowledge of the powers of crystals resurfaced, it once again became popular to wear crystals against the skin. As the influence of the Christian church wanes, the natural joy we have always felt in the wearing of crystals against the body has returned, stronger than ever.

As a magical name, Crystal is a clear favorite. It is for becoming someone who sparkles and shines; a pretty, vivacious, clear-headed, well-spoken, honest, sincere person; one who communicates clearly and loudly when necessary; a concerned activist and boisterous opponent; one whose voice is clear and lilting, with a laugh as light as a bell. A truly likeable person. A great name for one who seeks to bring her light out from under the basket; this name will help shy people shine.

Diamond

Diamonds are an almost pure form of carbon. Coal, millions of years old, was exposed to massive forces of heat and pressure to create the diamond. It is a magical stone. To have come from such dark, earthy origins and be transformed into the clear brilliance and sparkling radiance of pure light has always been seen as extraordinary. These gems refract the light, splitting it into tiny sparkling rainbows of color, especially when cut to enhance this natural ability. Diamonds are also the hardest known natural substance.

The ancients used diamonds as jewelry. Pliny the Elder (23–79 BCE) wrote about diamonds. Issac Newton, the physicist, assumed that the diamond was combustible, based upon its exceptional ability to bend light rays. It was believed that a diamond would help maintain unity and love, and so it became traditional for use in wedding and engagement rings. It was thought that this power only worked when the diamond was freely given.

Diamond is a good name for one who is bright, clear-thinking, sharp, strong of will, stubborn, many-faceted, and who shines in intellectual pursuits. This is the name for a highly intelligent person. A tough-minded MENSA member would be well-suited to this appellation. Prepare to shine. This is a name to take to enhance your self-image in regards to your intelligence, to bring admiration of your speaking ability, and to appear confident and sharp.

Emerald

The deep green emerald is the most valuable variety of beryl. Emeralds have been mined and worn as far back as 1650 BCE in ancient Egypt. Cleopatra had her image carved on an emerald. The ancient Romans (and later, the Arabs and Turks) came to Egypt and searched for the elusive and valuable emerald. The mines which lured these cultures are now deserted. Trade routes known as the "Emerald Road" led to the emerald mines.

It is said that the natives of Peru worshipped an emerald the size of an ostrich's egg. Montezuma, the Aztec emperor from 1502–1520, is said to have owned at least one very large cluster of emerald crystals. Today, in a remote Buddhist temple in the jungles of Sri Lanka, is an ancient statue of Buddha carved from a huge single piece of emerald.

In terms of magical names, Emerald is a fine choice. It brings to mind a lucky individual, a beautiful person (perhaps with a green tint to his or her eyes), someone who seems to outshine those around him or her, a hard and enduring personality who overcomes all adversities and comes up shining, an attractive person to whom beauty is important, or one who may have come from humble beginnings but who is destined to attain a measure of greatness. This, then, would be a good name to attract employment or success of any kind.

Emery

Emery is a compact form of corundum, a variety of rock which includes rubies and sapphires. This crystal is found in deposits of metamorphic rocks (those rocks which have undergone metamorphosis by heat and pressure) and in alluvial deposits (deposits of the eroded debris of metamorphic rocks). It is mined for use as abrasives for polishing (emery boards).

This magical name is one suited to someone who has had a hard time, especially in the past. This difficult time has tempered the individual and also, perhaps, has interfered with the proper development of self-esteem, confidence, or trust. This is a wounded bird, but one who can soar. This may be a bitter and abrasive person on the surface, with a warm heart underneath. This is a name to take as a part of getting over a dysfunctional relationship or recovering from family disorders. Emery is a transitory name which may help lead one to a better place, for emery is abrasive, yet it helps to bring a glowing polish to dull, lifeless things.

Flint

During the Stone Age, flint was commonly used for tools and weapons. Flint is the brownish-black mixture of chalcedony and quartz which, because of how the stone broke when it was chipped, was easily formed into sharp-edged tools. This type of tools made by prehistoric peoples were common from the Palaeolithic to the end of the Neolithic Period. In addition to its exceptional ability to be shaped into useful tools, flint (and quartz in general) was widely available because it was sturdy and resistant to the forces of erosion. Most old arrowheads one still finds in the West were made of flint.

Flint is a strong magical name. It is suitable for one who is tough, useful, and helpful; one who is able to remain unswayed by pressure; a rugged survivor, there is little of softness in this person. A sleek, athletic person; one who uses and understands the use of tools; or perhaps a woodworker or a sculptor might choose the name Flint. Flint is a strong name; if you are dealing with fear in your life, take a strong name like this one to help see you through.

Galena

Galena is a shiny grey stone made of lead sulphide, which cleaves into perfect cubes when struck. It is a very common mineral of ore veins and occurs in tandem with many other substances.

Galena was mined and processed to remove the lead from it as early as the time of the ancient Roman and Babylonians. The Romans used lead from galena to make water pipes for their famous sewer systems. The Babylonians used the lead to form lead vases. The process of extracting the lead from the galena was fairly simple, and known and used in early times.

In terms of Galena as a magical name, it is for one who works well with others; whose hidden, inner core is strength; a glowing individual with a shining intellect; a well-grounded person; one who may be prone to weight problems; a predictable, organized person; one who is neat and tidy; a person with an excellent memory; and one who might have a number of good partners. This is a good magical name for a student who seeks to share the shining intellect of galena.

Garnet

Pliny the Elder used the term *carbunculus,* meaning "small, red-hot coal" to describe the garnet. The garnet group includes minerals of similar composition which mix with one another. They include a greater variety of colors that any other mineral. They often form granular to large clusters in rocks. They vary in color from ruby red to green, yellow, or violet. Pyrope, a deep red variety of garnet, is named from the Greek *pyropos,* "fiery-eyed." Another kind of garnet is almandine, named for its discovery in the ancient Turkish city of Alabanda. Almandine garnets have a violet hue. The demantoid garnet is the most valuable. It shines with its dispersive power, or its ability to break up white light into the colors of the spectrum. Garnets are among the most widespread minerals.

Garnets occur under a variety of conditions, but always under high temperatures. They are very resistant to weathering and so occur in alluvial deposits. Rocks which form on the boundary between igneous (volcanic) rocks and other rocks often consist of garnet rocks.

Garnet is an excellent name for a redhead or one with fire playing an important role in his or her life. Garnet is a fiery, in-the-fray kind of opponent; he or she is always on the edge of dissent. If there is a confrontation, you can bet this person will be close at hand. This is an opinionated, hard-headed, stubborn, smart, and vociferous individual. Someone who will not be swayed by public opinion, who will not shut up and hang back; this is a fiercely independent, feisty, likable person. This name brings great courage, determination, grit, staying power, and often a ruddy-cheeked beauty. These individuals are able to take a nasty thunderstorm of confrontation and turn it into rainbows of understanding. This is a person you need as a public spokesperson or organizer of events. The sparkle you always see in Garnet's eye will soon spread to those around him or her, like fairy dust.

Gold

Gold has played a major role in the history of humanity. Archaeologists tell us that gold was probably the first metal worked by the ancients. The oldest gold decorative objects date back to the early Stone Age, and gold coins were used as early as the seventh century BCE. In the Dark Ages, gold was used to adorn churches and the clothing of priests. The allure and power of gold has touched practically every culture, from the Aztecs to the California gold prospectors. Gold is the metal that is symbolic of the God, where silver is the metal of the Goddess.

Gold does not oxidize and normally does not combine with other elements, so it is found in nature in a relatively pure state. It occurs in the original rock through deposition from hot water or through decomposition of gold-bearing sulphides, such as pyrite. Gold is very soft and is usually cast with harder metals to lend it strength and durability. Only platinum surpasses the density of gold.

Gold or Golden as a magical name conjures up images of the sun. This is generally a man's name, as it is a symbol of the sun and the God energy. Gold is a rarity; it is soft and pliant, bright and beautiful. The man who chooses this name is sentimental, flexible, soft; tender, yet sometimes easily manipulated; one who must rely upon his partner for strength; one whose early years may have been spent in mental abuse or emotional turmoil. He is a handsome man who doesn't indulge in harmful habits, such as smoking or drinking, and who is concerned about his health. This is an individual who is like no one else. His attitudes and preferences set him aside from the mainstream of society and he has learned to accept this ostracism. This is a man who prefers the company of men to that of women.

Granite

Granites are intrusive rocks (volcanic rocks which solidified before they reached the surface of the earth). They are used primarily in sculpture and for architectural uses. Granites are a combination of feldspar, orthoclase, quartz, mica, and sometimes larger crystals. Granite is the most abundant rock in the world and is commonly found beneath the earth's crust. Mountains are landforms largely made of granite, which have been thrust up into the atmosphere from below the surface. Granites appear white to pinkish with sparkling bits of mica or crystal.

Granite is a strong name, one which leaves a lasting impression on people. This name is for one who is strong, with a mixture of spirituality, self-knowledge, and well-grounded energy. This is a name bringing earth energy, for having one's feet on the ground; practicality; reality; surviving a violent past, and yet crediting the violence of the past as a character-building experience.

Gypsum

Gypsum is formed from massive beds of decaying shells which were deposited on the ocean floor. Gypsum is easy to identify, as it can be scratched with the fingernail. Gypsum is quite soft and occurs in crystals. When these crystals are clear, white, or transparent, it is known as selenite; when granular, it is alabaster; and when it's fibrous, it's called satin spar. In the Sahara Desert, perfectly formed gypsum crystals are found lying loosely in the sands. (This variety contains a great deal of sand.) They appear as flat crystals, usually quite large, and grouped into clusters resembling rose petals or leaves. They are called "desert roses" and are formed by evaporation of water from salty lakes.

It was believed that gypsum was a lucky stone which would bring good fortune to its owner.

Gypsum is used to create plaster. When you heat gypsum it yields plaster of Paris, which sets hard after being mixed with water. Pliny the Elder, who wrote a great deal about rocks and minerals and how his culture used them, mentioned the use of gypsum by the sculptor Lysippus to make a mold of a human face. This was the first recorded time plaster was made from gypsum.

Gypsum is a name for water energy, especially ocean energy. It suggests sensitivity, being easily hurt, and showing this when injured. Gypsum is a carefree name of a plant lover, one who carries the whisper of the ocean in the eyes, an environmentalist, a highly emotional person, an intuitive being with great spiritual depth to their souls. For those who wish to be more water-oriented, more emotional and intuitive, then bearing Gypsum as your name would help accomplish this.

Jade

Jade is one of the toughest known minerals and is widely used as an ornamental stone for carving, due to its strength. The Chinese have carved ornaments from jade for thousands of years. The cool, smooth, waxy feel to jade is characteristic of the stone.

The very mention of the name "Jade" conjures images of oriental beauty and mystery. There are stories regarding the mystic and magical properties of jade stones. It is said that jade transmits wisdom, clarity, justice, courage, and modesty. Jade is a fertile and lush name. Jade suggests cool, quiet mystery. It brings to mind lush, tropical plants and plenty of running water. Jade is a wise name, a name for one who understands life's mysteries, who has many gifts and much luxury (or the appreciation for it). This is a name for understanding one's gentle strength. This is one who works on instinct and emotion before calculated thought. This is a growth-oriented name. Jade is a name for bringing tranquil, watery energy to one's life.

Jasper

Jaspers are brightly colored stones with wild patterns and designs similar to those of agates, but more beautiful. The colors vary greatly from piece to piece. The layers or bands create the wild designs, which may be cloud-shaped or rainbow patches where one color gradually blends into another. The designs are so intricate in jasper that it sometime appears to be a landscape scene drawn onto the stone rather than the natural, random layers of rock. The extreme beauty of a jasper may be why it is called "the mother of all stones." Crystals often form at the edges of jaspers. Jasper is formed by crystallization of hot solutions in cracks of igneous (volcanic) rocks. The minerals in this volcanic rock were decomposed by the hot solutions. This siliceous gel oozed into the cracks in the original rock, where it crystallized into an opaque quartz containing chalcedony. The various colors come from minerals dissolved in the solution.

The ancient Egyptians, Romans, and Greeks used jasper for making ornaments and magical amulets. Magic signs and religious carvings were engraved on the surface of jasper in ancient days. Pliny the Elder wrote about the colorful splendor of jasper. This popularity lasted through the Middle Ages. The chapel of one Bohemian castle has walls decorated with blood-red jaspers which date from 1347. A table made of jasper was once considered one of the wonders of the world. A large tabletop from Emperor Rudolf II's collection, made of a great many colored jaspers which depicted the countryside, was one of the most famous examples of the incredible beauty of jasper. The Winter Palace of the Russian Tsars holds many ornamental works in jasper, including huge pillars carved from single pieces of jasper.

Jasper is a beautiful name for a Pagan. This is a name for developing inner beauty, the beauty which comes from the subtle intricacy of the mind and the beauty of the soul. Jasper suggests the hard-won ease and luxury which adorns one like a mantle. This is a name for a delicate and shining person; someone who may have been hurt in the past, but who has come out a lovely person much improved by the trial. Jasper is a name for a survivor.

Lapis

In Latin, lapis means "stone." The stone lazurite or lapis lazuli was always popular as a precious stone due to its beautiful blue hues. Marco Polo (1254–1324) first describes lazurite mined in what is today Afghanistan. The ancient Egyptians used the stones from these mines for amulets, especially for those representing the sacred scarabs. When lapis was ground it was used as paint, perhaps to adorn the eyes of Cleopatra. Oriental artisans also carved ornamental objects from lapis and prized its rich blue to mauve tones. It was believed that lapis lazuli would bring tranquillity and happiness.

Lapis is another cool water name, evoking the cool blues of a tranquil stream or lagoon, soothing the fires of temper or confusion. A name bringing a happy smile and a light and cheery disposition is enjoyed by all.

Mica

Mica is a mineral which can be split into individual plates of transparent, elastic, thin material ideal for window panes prior to the use of glass. It is also prevalent in a large number of rocks, which fit into my very unscientific childhood category of "magic sparkle rocks." The sparkle you see when you look at some granites is mica.

Mica is a great magical name for a seeker, because it reflects the desire to see through the veils. Mica is not hard, tough, or resistant to change, quite the contrary; but Mica's very weaknesses make it special. This is a good name for a psychic or trance channeler.

Obsidian

Obsidians, together with flints, were among the first rocks used by primitive people because they took on a sharp cutting edge when chipped.

Obsidian is a glassy black extrusive rock (volcanic rock which solidified on the Earth's surface). Obsidian is often called volcanic glass, but its hardness is not comparable to glass.

Dark stones are thought to be good for grounding, for connection with the earth energies. Apache tears (obsidian) are also thought to be good for ridding yourself of negative thoughts; transfer the thoughts to the stone, then toss it away with a spell to keep anyone else from ever picking it up. In this way, Apache tears act as a kind of emotional handkerchief for throwing away bad moods.

Obsidian is a good name for a sharp, tough, clear-thinking, and well-spoken activist. Obsidian is also good for getting in touch with the Dark Goddess aspects. This name suggests being deeply motivated by issues and quick condemnation of those who aren't in complete agreement. It is a name which brings the ability to see beyond tomorrow in terms of possible changes and their repercussions, although these forecasts are almost always gloomy. This is a good name for an environmentalist.

Ochre

When the bodies of priests and priestesses were laid to rest during the Stone Age, many cultures laid them out in the ground in the fetal position and painted their bodies with red ochre to represent blood. Virgil mentioned the beauty of certain red crystals in *The Aeneid;* these were a type of hematite in the same family as ochre.

Ochre is a marvellous magical name for a mother, a midwife, a healer, or a painter. It is one rich in humanity, earthiness, robust fertility, fire, and life. This could be a name for a redhead or a ruddy-cheeked individual. People who wish to increase their fertility might do well to choose Ochre.

Onyx

An agate with black and white bands (see Agate). Onyx is a good name for someone with the qualities mentioned in Agate (above), but who tends to see things in simple terms, either black or white. This might also be a good choice for those who seek less confusion in their lives.

Opal

The mysterious opal wraps us all in its subtle spell. It is said that it is unlucky for any but one born under the sign of Libra to wear opals. Despite this unlucky folklore, people began to use them early on in history. The earliest example of objects made from opal dates from 500 BCE. The Greek poet Onomakritos in the sixth century BCE praised the inner fire of the opal. A Roman senator named Nonius owned a valuable engraved opal; rather than give up the stone to Marcus Antonius, he chose exile. Empress Josephine owned the famous "Trojan Fire" opal, which was part of the French crown jewels. It disappeared during the French Revolution.

The flat precious stone called opalus [opal] is the most valuable of all the stones, but it is difficult to define it and describe it. It has the gentler fire of the ruby, the brilliant purple of the amethyst, and the sea-green of the emerald, all shining together in an indescribable union.

—Pliny the Elder

Opals are as much as 34 percent water, and are often stored in water to keep the dryness of the air or changes in temperature from cracking the delicate stones. They form in cracks or in veins in rock and the amount of water in them determines the mix of colors present in the stone. The colors vary from the milky iridescence of delicate pastel hues of the precious opal, the brilliant fiery reds in a fire opal, to the dark reds, blues, greens, and purples emanating from a black opal. These stones captivate and fascinate like no other stone can do. They are indeed magical.

The name Opal brings a quixotic unpredictability. This is a name for bringing quicksilver intensity, sparkling beauty, milky softness, gentle but undeniable power, emotionality, intuition, and water energy.

Pyrite

The Greeks called this *par*, which means "fire," because when you break it, sparks fly. (I have a Manx cat by this name, and believe me, sparks do fly!) Throughout history it was thought to have magical healing powers and so was popular in amulets. Pyrite is believed to heal blood disorders. It was valued as a mirror to the Incas and they buried it with their dead. Pyrite occurs in coal seams. Its shiny gold appearance resembles gold, and its oxidized form is brightly colored with blue, red, and green. It decomposes and releases sulphuric acid. Since it oxidizes so easily, it is unsuitable for decorative purposes.

As a magical name, Pyrite is a name for a minx. This is a trickster name, one who is all stern fire and metal one moment then dissolving into rainbows of softness the next. This is a name for bringing unpredictability, mystery, changeable moods, twinkling fiery energy, humor, carefree abandon, and independence. The name also suggests the finer qualities of humanity, yet down deep isn't the gem it appears to be. Thus, it may be a good name for dealing with our social masks and true selves. This name is also for persons who get into trouble with addictive scenarios. Yet they are sparklers, unique and memorable tricksters. This is a good name for those who seek to loosen up and live less rigidly.

Quartz

(Also see Amethyst, a variety of quartz; and Crystal.) The Greek word from which crystal was derived means "ice." Quartz was a popular medium in ancient times. The crystal ball into which the stereotypical mystic gazes is made from solid quartz. It is an excellent conductor of psychic energy.

Quartz crystals were used early in history due to their abundance, strength, and resistance to erosion by all external influences. The first tools were made of this mineral (in the form of flint), dating from the Palaeolithic Period to the Neolithic Period. The popularity of the varieties of quartz continued to the present. In the Middle Ages, impressive goblets with magnificent carvings were made from quartz. It was used for jewelry and ornaments through the Renaissance; during the Victorian Era, it became popular on lamps and chandeliers. The awareness of crystals as amplifiers of energy was renewed during the New Age movement. Quartz crystals are good for promoting clarity of thought, amplification of one's personality, and a variety of healing qualities.

Quartz is a name for bringing insight, strengthening one's intuitive abilities, honesty, clear thinking, cool and thoughtful actions in crisis, and for motivation of yourself and others.

Quicksilver

Liquid mercury is formed from cinnabar decomposition. The ancient Greeks called it *hydragyrum,* from *hydor* (water) and *argyros* (silver). The word quicksilver is an Old English term. It is the only liquid mineral aside from water. Its name fits it, as you know, if you have ever handled it. It defies order and uniformity. You can't herd quicksilver where you want it to go; it will merely break up into a dozen smaller droplets and scatter.

As a magical name, Quicksilver is an interesting choice. It denotes someone who is quick to change; a shining, soft, liquid personality who easily melts from one attitude into another, leaving others breathless and intrigued. It is a name for a shimmering, glowing, energetic, effusive, enthusiastic, funny, and totally guileless human being. This is a name to choose for encouraging change in one's life or to become less rigidly controlling.

Ruby

The deep red ruby is of the corundum family, which also includes the sapphire. The ruby has long been a popular precious stone, especially in India. The ruby mines of India were known from as early as the sixth century BCE. The Bohemian crown of St. Wenceslas (1346) holds the largest ruby in history. The Indian Princes and the Shah of Iran possessed some of the largest rubies in the world. Rubies are believed to have the power to gather and enhance energy.

Ruby is a good name for a fiery, redheaded person; a clear and vociferous speaker; or a passionate, sexual, womanly female. This is a person who is sizzlingly sensual, tempestuous, fickle, sparkling, angry, vengeful, and (sometimes) heartless. This is a name to bring the fires of passion into your life.

Silver

There is nothing as beautiful as the lustre of pure silver taken directly from the Earth. Soon, however, oxidation occurs, creating a dark layer of silver sulphide. In the Earth, silver occurs as a tangle of winding silver wires intertwined in a lump. Silver is created during the decomposition of silver sulphide ores, like galena.

Silver has been used as far back as the jewelry of the Chaldean kings in the fourth century BCE, and has never lapsed in its popularity. Silver is very soft and is unable to be used for ornamental work, except in compounds with stronger metals.

The cool, silvery color is symbolic of the lunar influence and hence the feminine aspect of the universe, the Goddess. Silver is seen as the Goddess' metal, whereas gold represents the Sun or the God form.

Silver, because of the connection to the Goddess and the lunar influence, is an extremely popular and wonderful magical name. To differentiate yourself from the other Silvers out there, you might consider taking a second name in addition to Silver to more personalize the name. It is a name for a mysterious, cool, pale, intuitive, moon-driven, poetic, creative, Goddess-oriented night owl who burns the midnight oil, perhaps writing of magic and moonlight. Silver is a dancer in the night; a hunter; a shining, bright, illuminating individual. This is a psychic, rhythmic, cyclic, turner of the wheel of life. Silver is a good name to take for intuition, enlightenment, and for encouraging the lunar influence.

Slate

In the old days, slate was used to make school blackboards. Slate is a sedimentary, fine-grained, claylike stone which is made when deposits of sand, mud, calcium from seashells, and water are compressed under thousands of feet of earth deposited over millions of years. The heat and pressure compress the sandy, claylike mixture and harden it to form slate, and in some combinations of deposits, sandstones. Slate is dark, smooth, and tightly compressed.

As a name, Slate indicates a plain, dark individual upon whom impressions can be easily left. This is a quiet person, better at writing than at speaking, perhaps tending toward shyness; this is a sometimes a poetic and romantic person in a very quiet way. This is an earthy person, a night owl, and very often a good writer. A good student's name.

Topaz

Topaz may have been named from the island upon which it was found, yet some people think it was derived from the Sanscrit word *tapas,* meaning "fire." It is found in cavities in granite and in alluvial deposits associated with these granites. They are transparent crystals which are found in abundance all over the world. Topaz occurs in many colorful hues, including a honey-blonde, smoky, pink, pale blue, yellow, grey, violet, and clear. Many large topaz stones have adorned the crowns and jewelry of the rich for thousands of years.

Topaz as a name evokes an image of smoky uncertainty. This is a name to bring subtlety and mystery to one's personality.

Turquoise

Turquoise is usually thought of as being worn by North American Indians in the southwestern United States, and indeed it is so. They combined native turquoise and silver into beautiful and distinctive jewelry which is still popular today. Earlier than this, the Ottoman empire sought this precious stone and the ancient Egyptians used turquoise in their artwork and jewelry. The sky-blue stone, which is often veined with the brown stains of iron compounds, tends to symbolize the joining of the sky and the Earth.

Turquoise is a great magical name for an air sign person. This balance of blue and brown, of sky and earth is a great stabilizer. It can add lightness to an earth-bound person and stability to an overly airy personality. Its pure blue is refreshing and uplifting; the brown marks are intricate and can inspire the imagination.

Velvet

Velvet is another name for malachite. Because of its green color, it was called "rock green," then "the satin ore" and "the velvet ore." Velvet was believed to protect children from various misfortunes. The ancient Greeks and Romans used velvet in protective amulets. Its beautiful greenish layers form intricate patterns and lacy designs in the stone.

Velvet is a softly effective name. It suggests a soft, soothing, healing, protective, and maternal energy. This may be a good name for a teacher, nanny, nurse, mother, daycare worker, or social services worker. This is a name for learning the soft caress is better than the firm command. Velvet is a good name for softening one's style of human interaction, or for soothing that short temper.

ROCK MEDITATION

Visualize yourself in a tranquil state. Do whatever relaxation techniques you need to get yourself there. See yourself at the base of a lovely mountain. Ahead of you is a cave. Walk toward it, noticing what stones, if any, are underfoot outside the cave. As you move into the cavern, a light comes from within you and lights the area. As you move through the caverns, examine the walls and the floors of the cave and look to see of what rock the cave is formed. Is it a luminescent and fiery opal with rainbows of color darting from within its core? Is it a brilliant diamond, ruby, sapphire, or emerald? Is the floor a different stone than the walls? Move to the very back of the cave where there is evidence of ancient cave paintings on the walls; read what it says. As you turn to leave, look for a rock which catches your eye. If there is one that does so, pick it up and take it with you. Return from whence you came.

The thing to notice with this meditation is how what is on the surface differs from what is below, how the surface on the cave differs from the walls, and what message is found in the cave paintings. If a particular stone speaks to you, you might try to find it at a crystal or rock shop and carry it in an amulet, as well as wear it as a magical name.

WHEEL OF THE YEAR NAMES

Seasonal names are wonderful choices for magical names because they evoke a definite set of mental and emotional images in almost everyone who hears them. The names "April" or "Valentine" may remind most people of springtime and romance. To a Pagan,

April may also generate thoughts of the Maiden, a young girl approaching womanhood, innocence, sweetness, the budding Earth, the promise of fertility, warmth, or blustery emotions. Valentine conjures images of Eros or Cupid; the idea of romance, of course, but also passion, eroticism, flirtation, amorousness, and lust. Magical names, remember, are chosen to reflect who we are or who we *want* to be. From a Pagan perspective, each name holds a deeper and more profound and transformative meaning, which is why our magical names should be well thought out and treated with the respect we give our other magical tools.

April: A good name for a young girl or one born in April. A name of new beginnings; blustery, vivacious, enthusiastic beginnings.

August: A name which brings the wisdom of age and the fruitfulness of a well-tilled field.

Autumn: A nice choice for a fiery redhead, or for bringing abundance.

Beltane (BEL-tane): This name is for a passionate, sexual, generally "available" young person.

December: A wise, cool, older person. December brings to mind the end of the cycle of the year or of life. A good crone's name.

Eostar: A time of year (the Spring Equinox) when the light has become balanced with the dark. Its a good choice for a person who seeks balance.

Esbat: A full-bodied person representing the fullness of the moon, or a person with a strong lunar influence. A name which indicates fertility, as the full moon reflects the mother aspect.

Equinox: The times of the year (Eostar, Mabon) when the darkness and the light are equal. A balanced name for those who seek balance.

February: A cool person or one born in this month. A name which suggests enduring the last of the cold. A crone or sage's name.

Fall: A good name for either a fruitful redhead or a hopelessly clumsy person.

Imbolc: Meaning "the stirring of the light" or "in the belly." A good name for a newly pregnant mother or for someone coming out of a painful time who is beginning to see the light at the end of the tunnel. A growth name.

January: A cool, thoughtful, beautiful name for a new Witch. A beginning.

July: A hot-blooded, summertime name bringing passion and fire energy.

June: A summer name, but one filled with images of Beaver Cleaver's mom.

Lammas: A summer name for warmth and fertility.

Lughnasadh (Pronounced "loo NAH sah"): August celebration of the first harvest. A name for abundance and reaping rewards.

Mabon: A harvest name, indicative of the balance of light and dark of the Equinox and the fruitfulness of the harvest.

March: A blustery, springtime, warm, and youthful name.

May: Ah, May. Beltane time. Springtime, flowering buds, rising passion, love chases, sacred marriages, May Queens, mating, nesting birds, fertility and conception, freshness, youth, and sweetness are invoked with this name.

Midsummer: A warm, intense, sun-dominant time for people with warm personalities and/or an affinity for the summer season.

Moosemas: A discordian name for the offbeat personality.

November: An older, cooler, slower-paced person. A name that brings to mind the warmth and comfort of hearth and home on a cold November day. In some places it is also suggestive of a resplendent feast of Thanksgiving.

October: A name for an autumn person or a Libra.

Samhain (Traditional Gaelic pronunciation is "SOW in"): A darker personality with an appreciation for the shadow side would suit this name. It could also be a good choice for someone who has lost a loved one, as Samhain is the time for remembering the dead.

Season: A bright, earth-based personality. One who loves the turning of the wheel of the year and who rejoices with its changes.

September: The month which is traditionally used as a synonym for growing older (as in May/September weddings). A name for a time of reaping after a lifetime of sowing. An older, wiser person.

Solstice (as in Midsummer and Yule): A time when the sun is either at its longest exposure or its shortest. The name then indicates a person of extremes, an all-or-nothing individual. The sun at this point turns back toward the equilibrium it finds at the equinoxes; this might be a good choice for someone who is out of balance, yet who seeks to turn the tides toward balance.

Spring: A youthful, maiden, flowery name. A name for new beginnings.

Summer: A sultry, warm, fertile name.

Time: A name for either of the sexes which suggests the power of time, the changes time etches onto humans, and the pull of the wheel of the year.

Valentine: A name evoking the energy of Eros and Cupid; a romantic, amorous, flirtatious, sexual, charming name.

Winter: The cool, God-dominant portion of the year when Demeter hides her blessings from the earth. This is a name which suits an older, white-haired person who has the wisdom of experience; a cool, contemplative thinker; someone with a quiet, reserved demeanor; someone in darkness waiting for the light; or simply a lover of wintertime.

Yule: The time when the world is most in darkness; the celebration of the growing light. A dark person, one who loves hearth and candlelight and the quiet fruits of the wintertime.

BIRDS

Magical names taken from bird (or animal) names are usually chosen because the animal has special meaning to the individual. Perhaps a bluebird has a nest in the tree near where you do your magical work or a crow reminds you of how you act at times. Bird or animal names are highly individualized and they mean what you think they mean. I have listed some of the more interesting or beautiful-sounding bird names and briefly described what sort of bird they are. If any of the names interests you, watch that bird in nature (or on bird documentaries) to get a feel for the animal. Often it is helpful when contemplating a name to meditate on the names which you are considering. Your subconscious will guide you.

Sing a song of sixpence
A pocket full of rye
Four-and-twenty blackbirds
Baked in a pie
When the pie was opened
The birds began to sing
Wasn't that a dainty dish
To set before a king?

—Mother Goose rhyme

Blackbird

A species which is usually black with brightly colored splashes. This is a robin-sized marsh bird. One of the varieties makes a song like very rusty hinges. A good name for those who wish more movement and more water energy. There is a Mother Goose rhyme which features blackbirds.

Bluebird

The stunning bluebird is large-eyed, slender-billed, and usually a stout-legged songbird. They are among the finest songbirds. Most varieties are a brilliant turquoise blue or blue with other colors on the neck or chest. Some types appear dumpy and round-shouldered. The bluebird is sometimes referred to as "the bluebird of happiness," perhaps because its beauty and cheerful song brings happiness. A good name for a happy person, or for a sad person who wishes to be happy.

Brant

A small goose not much bigger than a mallard duck. These large waterfowl are generally larger, heavier-bodied, and longer-necked than ducks. They are quite noisy when flying. They are more terrestrial than ducks, and can be found in grassy marshes or stubble fields. A good, solid name for a male.

Condor

The huge condor is a vulture with a wingspan of up to nine and a half feet. They live in the mountains of California and nest in caves or holes in cliffs. Another soaring man's name, evoking power and freedom.

Crow

Crows are large, noisy, black birds with powerful bills. Crows tend to be chunky. This is a completely black bird with black bills and feet. Some are smaller beachcombing varieties. They often eat carrion. Crows are identified with the Crone aspect of the Goddess. Wrinkles around the eyes are called "crow's feet." Crows and ravens often warned of an impending death. Some forms of the Goddess which were seen as crows are Coronis, Badb Catha, and the Danish Goddess Krake. This is a good choice for a croning name or for those who seek wisdom with age.

Dove

Doves are plump, fast-flying birds that have low, cooing voices. Doves are related to pigeons. Both can be found in cities. Some varieties nod their heads as they walk. Doves are known as birds sacred to lovers, as lovers are known to "bill and coo" like doves. Doves are also symbols of peace; in Asia Minor, doves were symbols of the Goddess Aphrodite. Because doves were believed to bring immortalizing ambrosia to Zeus, they were raised in the temples of Aphrodite. In India, there is a Dove Goddess whose name means "Lust." The constellation the Seven Sisters, the Pleiades, means "the doves." A name which invokes peace, romance, and quiet.

Eagle

The mighty eagle is a diurnal bird of prey with a large hooked beak and strong hooked claws. They are larger than hawks, with longer wings. The bills are very powerful and almost as long as the head. They eat chiefly rabbits, rodents, fish, and snakes. Their wingspan is up to eight feet long. They have a majestic, flat-winged gliding and soaring flying pattern. Eagle comes from the Latin word *aquila,* from which the English word aquiline also springs. To the Roman emperors, the eagle was a symbol of power because it was sacred to the Gods Zeus and Jupiter. When a Roman emperor died, he was cremated and an eagle was released from above his pyre, because it was believed that the eagle carried the emperor's soul to heaven. A good name for a warrior (or one who seeks to be one); a soaring, passionate tribute to power and freedom.

Falcon

Falcons are streamlined birds of prey. Their wing strokes are rapid and their pointed wings allow for speed, not sustained soaring. For centuries, falcons have been trained and used by people as hunting birds. Falcons were, like eagles, released at funerals to symbolize the release of the soul. In Greek, the falcon is called *kirkos*. A good crone name or name for those who seek the wisdom of the dark God/dess aspects.

Flicker

The flicker is a wood-boring bird with a chisel-like bill. They have extraordinarily long tongues and stiff tails which help in climbing. Some varieties live in the saguaros, the giant desert cactus. A name for movement, determination, and swiftness.

Gannet

Gannets are large sea birds with pointed bills and tails shaped like rounded cigars. They fish by spectacular dives into the sea from the air. They eat fish and squid. Gannets are the sea birds of the cold oceans. Gannet is a good name for attracting water and air energy.

Gull

The word gull is from the Celtic, probably borrowed from the Welch word *gwylan*. The Cornish said *guilan,* the Bretons *gwelan,* and the Old Irish *foilenn*. The Old Celtic word was *voilenno*. These long-winged swimming birds are superb fliers. The are more robust, wider winged, and longer legged than terns. Gulls favor coasts, but also live inland. Coastal gulls usually frequent coastal waters, estuaries, beaches, piers, city waterfronts, and grassy parks. In storms, they fly inland and stay in farmer's fields by the thousands until the weather clears. Gull as a name suggests the seashore and the salt air, and determination, courage, and ingenuity.

Ibis

Ibises are long-legged marsh birds. They have long curved bills for eating their diet of crustaceans, insects, leeches, and fish. In Egyptian mythology, the ibis was associated with Thoth, the god of writing, spells, and magic. Thoth was the guardian of the moon gates in heaven. Ibis is a good name for a writer.

Jay

Related to the crow and the raven, a jay is a bold bird. Some are the size of robins; others get quite large. Jays are noisy, fearless, and often pesky birds which have been known to walk right up to a camper's plate and steal food. The word jay may, like robin, have come from a person's name.

The term jaywalker (one who crosses the road illegally) was based on the American use of the word jay to mean a fool or simpleton. A good name for a bold adventurer, a silly trickster, or the fool of the Tarot deck just about to go forth to seek his lessons. Don't forget; after his journey, the fool ends up with the world.

Lark

Larks are gregarious musical birds. They tend to be brown-streaked, terrestrial birds. The skylark's song while in hovering flight is a beautiful series of trills that is sustained for a very long time. Perhaps the long songs of the lark inspired the expression "happy as a lark." Lark is a joyful name for those who are sad or sing the blues (also Calandra, which is a Greek name meaning "lark").

Magpie

These are the only large black and white birds with long tails in North America. They are bold and noisily talkative birds. If kept in close association with humans, magpies can learn to imitate human speech. Magpies were associated with oracular abilities, probably because of their ability to "speak." It is believed that the term for an edible pie comes from the bird's name (which was originally pie) based on a comparison of the miscellaneous contents of pies with the hoard of assorted stolen treasures accumulated by the bird. A trickster name, full of magic and mirth.

Merlin

The merlin, or pigeon hawk, is a small, compact falcon about the size of a jay. Its wingspan is two feet. They are usually silent birds. When one takes the name of Merlin, one also gets all the wizardly connotations that go with it, but it is still a fine name for a doer of wizardly things.

Oriole

A small bird, smaller than a robin. Their songs are low-whistled notes of a human quality. They sing in disjointed fashion, much like a child learning to whistle. A good student's name.

Owl

The phrase "the wise old owl" may refer to the scholarly appearance of the owl. Owls are large, nocturnal birds of prey with large heads, flat faces with "facial disks" (which resemble large eyeglasses), and usually feathered feet. They eat rodents, birds, fish, insects, and snakes. The German word for owl is *uhu*. Owls are traditionally connected with Witches and wizards as well as many aspects of the Goddess. Athena is the Goddess most often associated with the owl, but Lilith, Minerva, Blodeuwedd, Anath, and Mari had close ties as well. A name for a wise one, a student, a seeker, or a judge.

Raven

The word raven is both the noun that refers to the bird and the verb "to raven," meaning "prey or plunder," only used today in the term "ravenous," which goes back to the Latin term meaning "seize by force." The German word for raven is *rabe,* the Dutch *raaf,* and the Danish *ravn.* The Old German word was *khrabnaz* or *khraben,* which may have been an imitation of the raven's harsh croaking. The raven is a large, black bird with a wedge-shaped tail. It is much larger than the crow. It flies like a hawk, alternating flapping with soaring. The raven is often gregarious. In England, there is a superstition which asserts that England will remain a power as long as there are ravens there. If the ravens were to leave, so the legend goes, England would fall. Ravens have otherworld ties by being sacred to the Goddesses Morrigan and Rhiannon. Ravens, like crows, were omens of death. Probably because of this otherworld association and the raven's ability to mimic human speech, they were seen as oracle birds. In Roman Mithraic temple initiations, the initiate took the title of Raven. In the Pacific Northwest, a native Indian culture had a Raven God who married the Goddess of the Earth. Raven is a trickster name; a wild, carefree, curious, irreverent, and mirthful being. (Also Brendan, which is Irish Gaelic for raven.)

Robin

The sight of robin "red breast" is said to be the sign of springtime. Robins are large-eyed, slender, yellow-billed birds which have a lovely song. Their eggs are a pale blue, referred to as "robin's egg blue." The original name for this bird was "Robin Redbreast," and the name robin was not used alone until the middle of the sixteenth century. It was, like the jay, a bird which bore a human name. In Britain, the myth of the robin who died by an arrow through the chest only to be reborn in the spring was typical of the resurrection myths. This scenario is repeated in the slaying of Cock Robin as well as Robin Hood. Robin is a great name for either a man or a woman; a solid, dependable person who is in balance with the wheel of the year and understands the cycles of death and rebirth.

Sandpiper

A long-legged, sea-combing bird of small or medium size. They frequent shores and marshes. Their long, slender bills are helpful for eating crustaceans and mollusks. They live in or near streamsides, wooded swamps, ponds, marshes, and beaches. Sandpiper is a name which is good for bringing water energy to one's life. It is also a good name for a bagpipe, flute, or tin whistle player.

Starling

The starling is a very gregarious, garrulous black bird. Starlings sometimes mimic other sounds. The starling was first called star in Old English *(staer).* A nice feisty, growth-oriented name.

Stork

They are large and long-legged, with long bills. Some varieties have wingspans of five and a half feet. Storks have come to be known in folk tales as the birds who deliver babies. This myth is very ancient. Because storks frequent marshes, it was further told that unborn babies waited in the murky water of such places for the proper mother. The stork is strongly connected to fertility magic. Because of the benefit to fertility that storks implied, nesting storks on a chimney of a house were taken to be a fortuitous event to hopeful parents. The name stork is derived from the Greek word for mother love. A good fertility or luck name.

Swan

The graceful swan is in the best known family of water birds. The swan is a huge, all-white aquatic bird with a very long neck. They are more aquatic than geese. In Greek myth, Zeus took the form of a swan to impregnate Leda, who then gave birth to twilight and dawn and Selene (the moon). Swans were sacred to Aphrodite and the Muses. In Saxon times, a Swan Knight named Lohengrin rescued women dispossessed by patriarchal laws. The Knight of the Swan was seen as a symbol for the servant of women. Swan is a graceful and beautiful name.

Wren

The wren is a small, brown, stumpy bird that eats spiders. They are often gifted songbirds. The Druids considered them supreme above all other birds. Wrens were the sacred bird of the Isle of Man in Britain. Nursery rhymes tell of "Jenny Wren," who is really the Fairy Queen in a different form, which is why there are Christian traditions to hunt and kill the wren as part of the Christmas festivities. Wren is an ancient and lovely name for history buffs, music lovers, or druidic types.

BIRD MEDITATION

Get yourself into a quiet, meditative space. Visualize walking through the forest. It is a fine, sunny, spring day. There is new growth on all the trees and flowers are blooming on the forest floor. You hear the song of a bird ahead. Follow it. Come to a grove of apple trees which grow around a clearing, in the center of which is a well. There are flowers decorating the well, so you know that it is a sacred well. Drop the bucket into the well and draw yourself a drink of cool, fresh water. In the grove, there appears a beautiful woman dressed in white. She wears white flowers in her hair and lovely songbirds fly about her, chirping greetings. She is Rhiannon, Goddess of the underworld. Notice what kind of birds you see. What color are they? "Speak to me of what you seek, my child," commands the Goddess in a soft voice. Do so. She will reply. After she has finished speaking to you, pick a bouquet of flowers from the forest to leave at the well in thanks.

Rhiannon reaches out her hand to you and hands you an apple. Taste it; enjoy its sweetness and juiciness and the comforts of the grove. Sit in the dappled sunlight with Rhiannon and let yourself be lulled by the sound of her birds' singing. Allow complete abandonment to the sensations. Return back from whence you came, when you are ready.

The thing to focus on in this meditation is relaxation, allowing yourself to rest in the company of the Lady and let her rejuvenate your tired spirit. Keep in mind the birds you saw; when you are under stress, recall the birds and the lovely flutelike song they sang and take with you some of that contentment to counterbalance the stress.

NAMES FROM PLANTS AND TREES

Trees and plants have often been revered and held in awe by humanity. The early Celts devised a tree alphabet with each letter having a magical tree associated with it. (See page 119 for the Celtic tree alphabet.) Most Gods and Goddesses are associated with their sacred plants, flowers, or trees. It is extremely popular to choose one of these for a magical name. I have included the Old Celtic words for some of these trees, as they might make a more interesting choice than the common name. Also see the names in the spices section, where I list names from herbs, spices, and flowers that are used in magical herbalism.

Acorn

Not a tree, but the seed from the oak tree, the small, nut-like acorn is symbolic of great potential. This is why it would make a good student's name or a name for someone who is young, inexperienced, or just beginning on a new path. Acorn is a name for achieving one's potential.

Alder

One of the Druids' seven peasant trees (known as Fernn or Fearn in the Celtic tongue) and the fourth letter of the Celtic tree alphabet. Alder has a very distinctive perfume in spring. This tree is sacred to the Celtic God Bran. The alder is related to the element of fire and is prized as a raw material for charcoal by the Celts. Felling a sacred alder was once thought to bring about the burning down of one's house. The alder tree was used by the Celts to make milk pails and pilings for bridges and docks. They obtained fine red dye from its bark, green dye from its flowers, and brown from its twigs, relating to fire, water, and earth.

Alder is an excellent magical name for one who is secretive, changeable, a fire sign; one who loves color; a seamstress (or tailor) or an artist; one who loves incense, aftershave lotion, or perfume; a down-to-earth person who is a forest lover and a wise, experienced Witch. This is the sort of person who loves the drama of ritual, who likes to dance skyclad in the shadows of the forest. Alder will bring out the hidden sensitivity and sentimentality lurking within you.

Apple

Apple is one of the Druids' seven sacred chieftain trees (known as Aball). The Celts used its bark for tanning. The secret inside the apple is a well known bit of Pagan trivia. If you cut an apple in twain across the apple rather than down, a pentacle can be seen in the core. The sharing of an apple with a lover is a very old theme and part of the Gypsy wedding ceremony. The apple was seen as "the fruit from the tree of knowledge," and to the Christians it was considered a "sin" for a woman to eat of the fruit of knowledge. This didn't stop the fruit from becoming as popular and as "American as apple pie."

The name Apple brings to mind a rounded person, a ruddy (apple-cheeked), fertile, sweet, loveable (apple of my eye), alert, intelligent person who is thoughtful (apple for the teacher), funny, plump (juicy), happy, and generous.

Ash

One of the Druids' seven sacred chieftain trees (known as Iundius) and the third letter in their tree alphabet (Nion). The Celtic kings had their thrones made of ash. It was also used for the shafts of spears and arrows. Ash was considered sacred in many mythologies. Ash was sacred to the Sea God Poseidon; the mythical Norse world tree Yggdrasil was an ash tree. Odin's own runic alphabet was said to have been formed from ash twigs. Ash is attuned to the power of water.

As a magical name, Ash is an excellent choice. It is generally thought to be a male's name, but it would work well for women, too. It is a name for a leader, one who is a true warrior (not a mere limited soldier, mind you); one who has proven him/herself; a person comfortable with emotions and intuition; a strong, confident, brave, loyal, honorable, and decisive person. Ash is a good name for bringing leadership and teaching ability, both valuable qualities in a priest/ess.

Aspen

Aspen bark is used to make a remedy for fever. Aspens have white bark and large, broad leaves. This tree is also known as "quaking aspen" because of the fluttering movement its leaves make in the wind. Aspens are beautiful in the autumn. It is a common outing in the Colorado mountains to pack a lunch, drive into the mountains (aspens are most common in mountain areas), and "see the aspens turn." There are entire mountainsides covered with aspen, and when the leaves all turn golden, the effect is spectacular.

Aspen is a name for someone who is trying to face up to his or her own fears. It is a transformative name leading from fear into a fiery burst of courage. People who are shy, naive, or inexperienced could wear Aspen well. It could also be a good name for a dancer, a drummer, or anyone working with movement and rhythm. This is a mountain person's name. Aspens have a lot of potential.

Banyan

It is also known as the Indian God Tree. This is a tree revered by the Hindus, Hawaiians, and the peoples of Polynesia. As a name it evokes mystery and an aura of the Orient. An exotic name for an unusual person.

Barberry

Known in the Pacific Northwest as Oregon grape. It has yellow flowers and dusty blue berries. Its leaves often show autumn colors year round.

This may be a name for an artist. Barberry is a name for relating to one's own sexuality in a healthy way, for increasing one's confidence, self-esteem, motivation, strength, and stability.

Beech

Writing tablets used to made of beech; in fact, the word beech might be considered a synonym for literature. The English word book is etymologically connected to the word beech.

Beech is a name for becoming more intellectual than physical, more cerebral than sexual. This is a name of introspection, philosophical contemplation, learning, seeking, and becoming less aggressive, more studious, and wise. Beech is a good name for a writer or a student.

Bilberry

This is part of the heather family, which includes huckleberries and blueberries. It is a very popular fruit among Native Indians in British Columbia.

Bilberry is an unusual name for a sweet, gentle person. This name brings to mind warmth, sweetness, generosity, caring, sharing, and love.

Birch

One of the Druids' seven peasant trees (Beithe or Beth) and the first letter in their tree alphabet. Birch is believed to drive off evil spirits. For this reason, the Celts used it to make cradles. It was used throughout Europe for flogging delinquents and lunatics. It was thought that birch would drive away the evil spirits which afflicted the victim.

Birch is a cleansing name, full of light and purity. It is a name for one who deals well with children, the sick, or the elderly. It is a name for a nurse, a teacher, a parent, a social worker, or one who seeks social or political change by gentle means. Birch invokes purification.

Blackthorn

This is one of the Druids' seven shrub trees (Draidean). Blackthorn is a good name for a strong, dark person. A person with mighty shields and defenses might feel comfortable wearing this name. It is a place name that invokes a lot of protection, and so would be good for a house or covenstead.

Blueberry

A type of bilberry, part of the heather family. Blueberry is a magical name which suggests sweetness, purity, wholesomeness, and a totally guileless human being. These are good traits to strive toward.

Bracken

A very common fern. The young shoots or "fiddleheads" are edible and were eaten by many Native Indian groups. The Indians made bread out of the starch obtained from bracken rhizomes.

Bracken is a good young man's name. It is a name for youth, inexperience, and great potential. This is a person who is very impressive, if a bit too brash and sometimes boastful. This is a lover, a drinker, and an energetic person. Bracken is the name for a passionate young drummer, or a shy fellow who wishes he were more outgoing.

Briar

Briar is one of the Druids' eight bramble trees (Dris). Briar is an excellent magical name. It is a protective and powerful name, not for the faint of heart or the untried youth. This is someone who has won the rewards of battle and is peacefully ensconced in his or her position. This is someone who does not like to move, and who usually does it very badly. Briar is a sharp, brilliant, quick-tongued, bright-eyed, prickly person who has a great deal of knowledge and expects you to appreciate that fact. This person is resourceful, cunning, smart, defensive, strong, confident, and harsh, but an extra-ordinary teacher. A good name for an older person.

Broom

Broom is one of the Druids' eight bramble trees (known to the Celts as Giloch). Broom belongs to the gorse family. Local variations on the name include basam, bisom, bizzom, breeam, browme, brum, and green broom. It is used in the construction of the Pagan besom or broom and also used to weave baskets, and to some extent, thatch. Its yellow flowers are in bloom from April to July. The broom was adopted as the badge of Brittany by Geoffrey of Anjou. Fulke of Anjou followed this tradition, and it was passed on to his grandson, Henry II of England. Henry used its medieval name of Planta Genista, which is how his family name came to be the Plantagenets. It first appeared in England on Richard I's Great Seal. Several other nobles used it as a symbol, including Richard II of England and Charles V and VI of France. It was considered a sign of plenty because of its long flowering season. Its flowering tops were used for house decoration at the Whitsuntide festival. It was considered unlucky to use the flowering tops for menial purposes when they were in full bloom. Before the introduction of hops, it was used to flavor beer. Its bark contains a large amount of tannin, which was used in tanning.

Broom is a wonderful Witch's name. Of course, we jokingly refer to secretive Witches as being "in the broom closet," and we have many old customs and uses for the magical broom in circle and out. Many a Witch's wall is decorated with brooms dressed up with ribbons and dried herbs and flowers. The broom is the most famous tool of the trade for Witches, and so would naturally make a great magical name. Broom is a good name for people of either sex, and is just as applicable to a youthful person as it is to a crone. Broom is a name which suggests fertility, cleansing, honor, protection, and freedom.

Bryony

A poisonous climbing and twining plant. Black bryony is in the same family of plants as yams. White bryony is in the cucumber family. The root of the black bryony is used to make rubefacients and diuretics, but an overdose can produce a very painful death. The roots of European white bryony are used to make one of the best diuretics in medicine. Both are used to treat gallstones. The roots of white bryony, also known as English mandrake, were used to make purgatives, but this is not common any longer because of the plant's powerful irritant properties.

Bryony is a great name, good for those who are (or want to be) balanced between their male/female or their light/shadow sides. This is a good name for one who is too sensitive, too emotional, and who wishes to become more balanced. This name can help you move from a water-dominated space into a more grounded place.

Candleberry

Candleberry is also known as bayberry. Its bark and wax are used to make astringents and stimulants, and is emetic in large doses. The greenish-white wax from its berries was in some places used as sealing wax. Bayberry candles are burned at New Year's to insure good fortune for the following year in some Scottish folk traditions.

Candleberry or Bayberry are cleansing names which inspire the bearer to be more organized, cleaner, tidier, have more energy, more luck, and encourage silence.

Checkerberry

One berry bearing this name is also known as the partridgeberry or squaw vine. It has bright scarlet berries. It is taken by Indian women for weeks before childbirth to ease their labor pains. Another berry bearing this name was the wintergreen.

Expectant mothers, midwives, healers, and people going through difficult times would benefit from checkerberry as a magical name. The healing and pain-reducing properties of Checkerberry work when you use the name as well as the plant itself. This is a nice-sounding name which seems friendly, well disposed to deal with life's situations, and possessing a fine sense of humor.

Chestnut

It is believed that chestnuts fed to a loved one insure he or she will love you back. Chestnut is a good name for a brunette. It suggests warmth, home and hearth, and autumnal energy.

Chicory

Chicory is also known as succory. It is in the same family as dandelions. Its roots are used as a coffee substitute and its is cultivated in many places as a salad vegetable. It has lovely blue flowers.

Chicory falls off the tongue in an easy way and is memorable, yet not an overused magical name.

Chocolate

The chocolate tree is also known as the cacao or cocoa tree. Its seeds are used to make the popular confection called chocolate. It is a handsome tree, 12 to 16 feet high with light-colored wood and reddish flowers.

Cocoa has long been a popular name for a dark-skinned or dark-haired person. Cocoa or Chocolate is a good name for anyone who is warm, sweet, soft, or who is one of the millions of people addicted to the joys of chocolate.

Clover

Also known as trefoil. A fluid extract is used as an alterative antispasmodic. Its roots were a popular food amongst Native Indians. A clover with four leaves is considered to be a lucky charm. Children make necklaces and wreaths from the long-stemmed clover flowers.

Clover is a wonderful magical name. It brings to mind warm, sunny, summer days spent lying in the clover, listening to the droning of bumblebees and lazily watching clouds overhead. It is a comfort name—soothing and peaceful, warm and reminiscent of a happy childhood.

Daisy

Its Latin name, *bellis perennis,* is said by some to be derived from the Latin *bellus* (pretty or charming), but others say it came from the name of the dryad (woodland nymph) Belidis. Daisy comes from its Old English name "day's eye," as can be seen in Chaucer's writings: "Well by reason men call it maie, the Daisie, or else the Eye of the Daie." In Scotland it is the bairnwort, due to its popularity among children in making flower chains. An old saying is "When you can put your foot on seven daisies, summer is come."

Daisy is a summertime name which suggests honesty, sincerity, and innocence.

Dandelion

The name comes from the Old French name *dent de lion* (teeth of a lion), which its flower petals were supposed to resemble. Its old Latin name is *dens leonis,* and in Greece it was *leontodon.* It is used in salads and its roots can be used as a coffee substitute. Dandelion wine is also still popular.

Dandelion is a good name for becoming "one of the guys" (or gaias). It suggests fitting in with the flow of society, being one of many.

Drake

A grass also known as bearded darnel. Its Old English name was *cokil*. Its seeds are used by herbalists to make a sedative. The name darnel comes from the French word *darne* (stupefied), and in France it was called *ivraie* (from *ivre;* drunkenness), because large doses cause all the symptoms of drunkenness. The Arabs called it *zirwan*. In some parts of England, it was called cheat because it was sometimes used to adulterate malt and distilled liquors.

Drake, Darnel, Cokil, Darne, Ivraie, or Zirwan all are good names for a person who is gregarious and loves his cups (and what's in them). It then would be a good name for someone who is trying to understand the motivations of a drinker. It might be a good choice for a drug and alcohol counsellor.

Elder

Elder is one of the Druids' seven shrub trees (Trom). The dwarf elder was the twelfth letter in the Druids' tree alphabet (Pethboc), and the elder was the thirteenth (Ruis). This tree is traditionally associated with Witches. It is a tree of doom in many Christian myths. It is often said that the tree on which Judas hanged himself and Jesus' cross were both made of elder wood. The word elder comes from the Anglo-Saxon word *aeld* (fire), as the hollow stems of the young branches were used to blow up a fire. Early names for it were eldrun, hyldor, and hyllantree. In Germany, it is called hollunder. In Low Saxon it is ellhorn. The pith is easily pushed out of the young branches and these hollow stems were used to make pipes, hence the elder was often called the pipe-tree, bore-tree, or bour-tree. This name survives in Scotland as burtree. Its Latin name, *sambucus,* is adapted from the Greek word *sambuca*. The ancient Greeks used elder to make pan-pipes. In Danish mythology, a dryad named Hylde-Moer (elder tree mother) was supposed to live in the branches of the elder. Should the tree be cut down and used to build a chair, she would haunt it. It was also believed in Denmark that if you stood under an elder on Midsummer Eve you would see the King of Fairyland ride by, attended by his retinue. An old spell is to take the pith and dip it in oil, light it, and float it in a glass of water on Christmas Eve. This was supposed to reveal the whereabouts of any sorcerers in the neighborhood. Up until recent times in England many people would not trim it lest they attract bad luck. In many parts of Europe, its wood is thought to drive off ill fortune. In England it was thought that elder trees were never struck by lightning. It was once cultivated near English houses as it was thought to drive off Witches. It was often used as decoration at funerals, and elder branches were placed in graves to ward off evil.

Any of the names for Elder (Trom, Pethboc, Ruis, Aeld, Eldrum, Hyldor, Hylantree, Hollunder, Ellhorn, or Burtree) are good magical names. Some of the older names indicate an association with elves and fairies. These are names which invoke versatility, sturdiness, mystery, musical ability, luck, and a serious attitude about magic.

Elm

Elm is one of the Druids' seven peasant trees (Leam). It is resistant to water and used for building ships. Its durability lead to its common use in lining carts and wheelbarrows.

Elm is a solid name which is versatile and easy to remember. It also works for either sex. Elm depicts a person who is dependable, secretive, solid, trustworthy, reliable, honest, sober, and believable. A Pagan elder.

Fabiana

Also known as pichi. Fabiana is originally from South America. It bears white or purple flowers. Its dried leaves and twigs are used to make medicines to treat urinary and kidney disorders.

Fabiana and Pichi are lovely names for women. They suggest a feminine person, well-versed in a captivating sexuality. These names are earth-oriented. This name may bring fertility, sexuality, femininity, a dancer's grace, and an appreciation of music.

Fern

One of the Druids' eight bramble trees (Raith). Ferns are thought to bring powerful protection to the home.

Fern and Raith are quiet, earthy names. They suggest protection and a love of hearth and home. They are good names for delicate but flourishing people who have their priorities straight.

Fir

The silver fir was the fourteenth letter in the Druids' tree alphabet (Ailm). It is sacred to Artemis and the moon.

As a magical name, Fir is a cool, winter name for an older, wiser person. Fir suggests Yule and winter's cold, and one who possesses the knowledge gained in the turning of many seasons.

Goldenrod

Also known as verge d'or, solidago, goldruthe, or woundwort. Goldenrod as a magical name is suggestive of a healer; a gentle, tender person who is better at healing the wounds than participating in the battle. It may be a name for a male or female, although the golden imagery that goes with the name is more suggestive of masculine energy.

Gooseberry

Gooseberry is one of the Druids' eight bramble trees (Spin). It was formerly believed to cure all inflammations.

Spin may be one of the most profound magical names I've ever heard. Spin is what we do. We spin among the webs of life when we weave our magic. It is a superb name for a weaver, a seamstress, or a teacher. Like the name Broom, Spin is appropriate for *any* Witch. It is a name of action, motivation, change, growth, magic, and transformation.

Gorse

Gorse is an evergreen shrub whose flowers have a strong scent and which blooms for a very long time (spring to late August). It is an old English custom to include a spray of gorse in the bridal bouquet because of this. Gorse is in the same family as broom and furze. Gorse grows well near the sea. Its ashes are very alkaline and were used to make soap and an excellent fertilizer. The leaf buds have been used as a substitute for tea, and the flowers to make a strong yellow dye.

When gorse is out of bloom, kissing's out of season.

—Traditional

This is a romantic's name, a lover of love. This is the kind of person who likes to dance when he or she hears a romantic song, even if he or she is in a grocery store at the time. It is a name which suggests affection, sensitivity, creativity, imagination, tenderness, and love.

Hawthorn

It is also known as whitethorn, quick, thorn, haw, hazel, gazel, halves, hagthorn, or May (from which the name of the month comes). Hawthorn is sacred to the Goddess Maia. It is one of the Druids' seven peasant trees (Sceith) and the sixth letter in their tree alphabet (Uath). In general, considered an unlucky tree. In ancient Britain, Greece, and Spain, May was the month in which people went about in old clothes, a custom referred to in the old saying "ne'er cast a clout ere May be out" (meaning do not put on new clothes until the unlucky month is over). This is the origin of the current custom of buying new spring clothes (Easter bonnets). In Greece, all the temples were swept out and images of gods washed during the month of May. It was considered an unlucky month for marriage. This is why more people get married in June than any other month. The hawthorn was the tree of enforced chastity. It was considered extremely bad luck to cut a sacred

The fair maid who, the First of May
Goes to the fields at break of day
And washes in dew from the hawthorn tree
Will ever after handsome be.

—Traditional

hawthorn down. This tree was used by the Turks as an erotic symbol because, to many men, the hawthorn blossom has a scent of female sexuality. There is an old poem that speaks of the hawthorn's ability to make one beautiful.

Hawthorn or any of its other names are wonderful names for a Witch. They are steeped in craft custom and lore.

Hazelnut

The Druids considered white hazel to be one of their seven shrub trees (Fincoll). Hazel was the ninth letter in the Druids' tree alphabet (Coll). In Celtic myth, the nut was a symbol of concentrated wisdom.

Fincoll or Coll may be the best choices for this magical name. It is a good name for a wise, thoughtful, experienced Witch.

Heath

Heath was one of the Druids' eight bramble trees (Fraech). Heath is a superb name, and one which many Pagans have named their sons. The feminine version is Heather. Both names are good for magical names as well as mundane names. Heath is a name for a clean, honest, natural person who loves home and hearth, wife and family.

Heather

Heather is the sixteenth letter in the Druids' tree alphabet (Ur). Sacred to the Roman and Sicilian love Goddess Venus Eryncina.

Heather is a lovely woman's name. This is the name for a delicate, feminine, womanly, graceful, intelligent, quietly powerful person.

Holly

Holly is one of the Druids' seven sacred chieftain trees (Cuileann) and the eighth letter in their tree alphabet (Tinne). Also known as holm, hulm, and holme chase. Holly is an evergreen with shiny green leaves and bright red berries. Its timber was used by the ancient Celts to make chariot shafts. It is a tree of the waning year and has been used by Pagans and Christians alike to decorate their homes at Yule.

Holly is a festive name for a sexy, attractive, sharp-witted person. This is also someone who has a temper and can be prickly when crossed. Holly brings an improved outward appearance and better defenses.

Iris

The iris was considered in ancient times to be a symbol of power and majesty. It was dedicated to the God Juno. It was the origin of the sceptre, as the Egyptians used it to decorate the sceptres of their kings. The three leaves of its blossoms symbolized faith, wisdom, and valor. Iris is also the name of the Goddess of the rainbow in Greek myth.

Iris is a good choice for a magical name. Iris brings to mind a woman who is partial to wearing brilliant colors and flamboyant styles. This is one who is unique, faithful, brave, wise, and beautiful. It is a good name for improving communications, especially with the Gods.

Ivy

One of the Druids' eight bramble trees (Eideand) and the eleventh letter in their tree alphabet (Gort). Ivy is sacred to the God Dionysus, and it was once believed that binding it around one's brow prevented intoxication. October was the season of the Bacchanal revels, during which people rushed wildly about with a roebuck tattooed on their right arms and waving fir branches wrapped with ivy. Plutarch said that the Bacchantes were intoxicated as much by ivy as by wine. Ivy is dedicated to resurrection because only it and vine grow in a spiral. English taverns used to have the sign of an ivy bush over their doors, to indicate the excellence of their liquor, giving rise to the saying "Good wine needs no bush." Also sacred to Artemis (or Ariadne). Its leaves formed the poet's crown. The Greeks presented a wreath of ivy to newlyweds as a symbol of fidelity.

Ivy is thought to be a symbol of a clinging person, but it is much more than that. Ivy is a sober name, a name to wear on the other side of the tunnel after having come through a battle with alcoholism. It is aligned with the passion of the Bacchanal revels, but not without restraint. It reflects the power and mystery of the spiral path in its twining growth.

Ivy is a name for a faithful, stalwart, honest, poetic, humorous person who has walked a rocky path and who has learned well from that experience. This is the magical name of a person worthy of respect.

Juniper

Also called genevrier, ginepro, or enebro. Juniper leaves and berries were used in one of the earliest incenses. Juniper is thought to be a protective plant, and a necklace of the berries is thought to attract a lover. Juniper berries are used in the production of gin.

Juniper, as a magical name, is perfect for someone who is lively, spritely, excitable, vivacious, and protective. This is someone who longs to find his or her perfect mate and settle down and begin nest-building in earnest. Until then, Juniper enjoys a good party and lively society.

Lavender

Lavender is made into sachets and used in love spells. The scent of lavender oil was an identifying scent for European prostitutes. It is thought to be a powerful plant which brings joy and long life.

Lavender is a good option for a magical name. It is an appellation for one who is sweet, affectionate, funny, sentimental, and romantic (by that I mean ROMANTIC). It is a name which brings sensitivity.

Linden

The flowers of the lime tree. In Lithuania, women once made sacrifices to linden trees.

Linden is a name which tends to be more for a male than a female. Its a name which signifies fertility, youth, male beauty, and the sweet flower of manhood.

Mahogany

Indians believed that mahogany protects against lightning.

A good name for a brunette or a person with dark skin or eyes. This is a name for strength, durability, steadfastness, honor, and dignity.

Mandrake

Mandrake is used by herbalists to make emetics and purgatives. It was used in ancient times as an anesthetic. It was also believed to have the power to prevent "demonic" possession. Its roots often resemble human forms. Mandrake used to be placed on mantle pieces to avert misfortune and bring happiness and prosperity to the house. Ancient terms used to describe mandrake are phallus of the field, Satan's apples, hand of glory, and devil's testicles. It is very firmly entrenched in the ground and many customs have built up around the dangers involved in removing the roots.

This is a name steeped in sexuality for the male, and as such is a good name for improving (or perhaps advertising) male virility. Mandrake indicates a quiet man who is good with his hands, who is perhaps a sculptor or a painter. Mandrake is also a seer with a keen talent for telekinesis.

Mistletoe

Mistletoe was venerated by the Druids and believed to protect the possessor from all evil. Youths were sent about with branches of mistletoe to announce the new year. It is from this custom that the modern one of including mistletoe in the Christmas decorations comes. In Norse mythology, Balder, the god of peace, was slain by a weapon made of mistletoe. He was brought back to life by the other gods and the mistletoe was placed in the keeping of the Goddess of Love. She ordered that everyone who passed under it should receive a kiss, to show that the mistletoe had now become a symbol of love rather than hate. To this day, lovers still kiss under the mistletoe. Druids considered the white berries to be drops of the Oak God's semen.

Mistletoe is a lover's name. This is someone who loves love, sex, and is a championship flirter. This name invokes the rites of courtship and love.

Myrrh

It is also known as mirra, morr, didin, didthin, karan, and bowl. Used for centuries as an ingredient of incense, perfumes, etc. In Ancient Egypt, it was burned at noon to honor the sun God Ra and in the temples of Isis.

Myrrh is a noble name for a person who is a fire sign. This is someone who likes summer, the outdoors, and natural, aromatic scents. This is a mysterious person with exotic tastes.

Myrtle

The Druids considered the bog myrtle to be one of their eight bramble trees (Rait).

Myrtle is a very old name and a powerful magical name. Myrtle or Rait are names for an older woman, one who has the wisdom of silence and the will to keep it.

Oak

Oak is one of the seven chieftain trees of the Druids (Dair or Duir) and the seventh letter in their tree alphabet. Oak is sacred to Zeus, Jupiter, Hercules, the Dagda, Thor, and all other thunder Gods. It is also sacred to Janus in Greece and Llyr in Celtic myth. Our word door comes from the Celtic word for oak, *duir,* a wood favored for door construction due to its durability and strength. The sacred mistletoe grows in the branches of this tree of the waxing year. There is an old expression "Fairy folks are in old oaks."

Oak is one of the best magical names for a male because of its qualities of strength, fertility, and majesty. An old oak is a thing which inspires great awe. As a name, Oak is good for one who would be a high priest.

Orchid

Witches were supposed to use the tubers of orchids to make love potions. Orchids were said to be under the influence of Venus. Once believed to be the food of the satyrs, this plant was said to have excited them to excess. Orchis was the son of a satyr and a nymph who was killed by Bacchanalians for his insult to a priestess of Bacchus. His father prayed to Zeus, who turned Orchis into the flower bearing his name. The orchid is still a customary gift between courting lovers, especially at Valentine's Day and for special occasions, such as fancy balls.

Orchid is an exotic, beautiful name for a Pagan woman. Orchid is soft, pastel, beautifully scented and hued, and its petals resemble the female vulva. This is a name for a person who is very involved with womanhood and sexuality.

Pine

Pine is one of the Druids' seven sacred chieftain trees (Ochtach).

The name Pine is one with clean, healthy connotations. It is a name for an athlete or a healer. It may be good in combination with a second name.

Poplar

White poplar (or aspen) was one of the Druids' seven shrub trees (Crithach) and the seventeenth letter in their tree alphabet (Eadha). It was thought to be a shieldmaker's tree. It is a tree of the autumnal equinox and old age.

This is a good name for an older person, a warrior (of either sex) who is teaching young people the ways of Wicca.

Rowan

It is one of the Druids' seven peasant trees (Caerthann) and the second letter in their tree alphabet (Luis). One of the Ents in *The Lord of the Rings* by J.R.R. Tolkien was a rowan. Rowan is used as a charm against lightning and ill fortune.

Everybody and their dog is named Rowan these days. Why not try using some of the interesting folk names for rowan instead? It is known as delight of the eye, mountain ash, quickbane, ran tree, roynetree, Thor's helper, whitty, wicken tree, wiggen, wild ash, witchbane, witchen, and witchwood.

Shamrock

The three-leaf clover known as shamrock was originally seen as representing the triple Goddess, and was sometimes called "Three Morgans" or "Three Brigits." This triple Goddess connection to the Shamrock was common in Arabia and ancient Indus. Because of the connection to the Goddess, Christian authorities in Ireland were not comfortable with Ireland's fondness for the symbol. From this environment sprang the notion of the four-leaf clover being the lucky one (four being symbolic of the points of the cross).

This would be a good name for one who reveres the triple aspects of the Goddess.

Sycamore

The sycamore was thought to be a tree of the dead in which spirits lived. It was a tree long associated with the Goddess. In Greek myth, the sycamore was the tree under which Zeus lay with Hera.

Sycamore is a good magical name, as it is a tree sacred to the Goddess. It is a good name for a male or a female, and hasn't a specific age associated with it. It is an interesting name for a vital and earthy person.

Tamarisk

Used for thousands of years in exorcisms. In Egyptian myth, the tamarisk tree was the one which enveloped Osiris' sarcophagus.

Tamarisk is a beautiful name. It embodies beauty, mystery, uniqueness, purity, and power.

Vine

The tenth letter in the Druids' tree alphabet (Muin). Sacred to Dionysus and Osiris.

Vine is a name which is indicative of a climber. This is someone of great potential, a hard worker, a networker, perhaps a Yuppie who seeks a spiritual path, or a "Puppie" (Pagan Yuppie).

Willow

Willow is also known as osier. It is sacred to Hecate, Circe, Hera, Europa, Persephone, and the Muses. This is definitely a lunar tree. The Witch's besom is traditionally made of an ash stake, birch twigs, and osier binding. It is one of the Druids' seven peasant trees (Sail or Saille) and the fifth letter in their tree alphabet.

Willow is a wonderful name for a man or woman. It has more of a female feel to it, so it shouldn't be chosen as a name which will inspire masculine traits. This is a tree name of emotion, a water sign name; a liquid, moving, loving, moon-driven name.

Yarrow

Also known as arrowroot, eerie, gearwe, knyghten, soldier's woundwart, and yarroway. Used for protection and courage.

Yarrow is an excellent magical name. It, or any of its other names, is for one who is a warrior. This is a good name for either sex.

Yew

Yew is one of the Druids' seven sacred chieftain trees (Ibur) and the eighteenth letter in their tree alphabet (Idho). The Celts used it to make household vessels and breast-plates. It is sacred to the Goddess Hecate. In Ireland, wine barrels were made of yew. Considered to be a tree of death in many European countries. Its seasoned and polished wood has an extraordinary power of resisting corruption.

Yew is unique. This is a name of honor, steadfastness, protection, lunar influence, and durability.

GREENWOOD MEDITATION

As with any meditation, begin by relaxation, deep breathing, and a well-grounded (or centered) mindset. Imagine that you are the mythical Norse tree Yggdrasil. You are ancient beyond reckoning. Your mighty branches reach up to form the sky and spread over the world. Humans live in your leaves and make their homes on your bark. Your trunk is as wide as the Earth and in your mighty roots snuffles the dragon Nidhug. Your breathing slows; your thinking slows. You are the solid, stable body of Earth itself. The mighty tree of life. Notice how slow and accepting of life you are as a tree. Notice how the comings and goings of the humans affect you. Observe the interaction of the elements and how they impact you. Draw in the strength and patience of Yggdrasil and let your human insecurities and fears drain unneeded into your roots. Become strength. Become one with all of nature. Listen to whatever comes to you. Return to being yourself when ready.

The thing to be aware of in this meditation is the slowness of trees. This is a good trait to have in today's crazy world. Learn to use it. It will help slow down the frenetic pace of life and put things into perspective. This is a great grounding meditation.

THE TREE ALPHABET

A relic of the ancient Druids, the tree alphabet was passed down orally through the centuries. It consists of five vowels and thirteen consonants, with each letter named after a tree or shrub thought to be sacred to the Druids. The months of the year, in the Celtic calendar, were named after these consonant trees. I have included the dates these months covered. They reckoned time according to the lunar cycles, thus having thirteen months in a year. The Celtic months were Beth, Luis, Nion, Fearn, Saille, Uath, Duir, Tinne, Coll, Muin, Gort, Peith, and Ruis. The five vowel trees were assigned days which came thirteen weeks apart, on the solstices and equinoxes. I have included many names within this chart, and the properties they describe. For tree lovers, this may be a place to look for your magical name.

Letter	Dates	Modern	Celtic	Welsh	Aspects
B	12/24–1/20	Birch	Beth	Bedwen	Purification
L	1/21–2/17	Rowan, Quickbeam	Luis	Cerdinen	Learning, Quickening
N	2/18–3/17	Ash	Nion	Onnen	Rebirth, Water energy
F	3/18–4/14	Alder	Fearn	Gwernen	Fire energy
S	4/15–5/12	Willow	Saille	Helygen	Dark Goddess enchantment
H	5/13–6/9	Hawthorn	Uath	Draeenen	Bad luck, Enforced chastity
D	6/10–7/7	Oak	Duir	Derwen	Endurance, Triumph
T	7/8–8/4	Holly	Tinne	Celynnen	Increase, Plenty
C	8/5–9/1	Hazel	Coll	Collen	Wisdom
M	9/2–9/29	Vine	Muin	Gwinin-Ydden	Joy, Exhilaration
G	9/30–10/27	Ivy	Gort	Eiddew	Resurrection
P	10/28–11/24	Dwarf	Peith	(none)	Established power
R	11/25–12/22	Elder	Ruis	Ysgawen	White Goddess
A	12/23	Silver fir	Ailm	Ffynidw-Ydden	Birth Mother Goddess
O	Spring Equinox	Furze	Onn	Eithin	Encouraging young growth
U	Midsummer	Heather	Ura	Grug	Passion, Lust
E	Autumn Equinox	White poplar	Eadha	(none)	Old age
I	Yule	Yew	Idho	Ywen	Death

Brehon law in Ireland forbade the unlawful felling of certain trees or sacred groves. The law divided the trees into chieftain, peasant, shrub, and bramble, with the severity of punishment decreasing according to the category. The destruction of chieftain trees brought the severest penalty, sometimes even death.

Seven Chieftain Trees*

Oak (Duir)
Hazel (Coll)
Holly (Cuileann)
Yew (Ibur)
Ash (Iundius)
Pine (Achtach)
Apple (Aball)

Seven Peasant Trees

Alder (Fernn)
Willow (Sail)
Hawthorn (Sceith)
Rowan (Caerthann)
Birch (Beithe)
Elm (Leam)
Unknown (Idha)

Seven Shrub Trees

Blackthorn (Draidean)
Elder (Trom)
White Hazel (Fincoll)
White Poplar (Crithach)
Arbutus (Caithne)
Unknown (Feorus)
Unknown (Crann-Fir)

Eight Bramble Trees

Fern (Raith)
Bog Myrtle (Rait)
Furze (Aiteand)
Briar (Dris)
Heath (Fraech)
Ivy (Eideand)
Broom (Giloch)
Gooseberry (Spin)

---

* The lists of trees are from Robert Graves' *The White Goddess;* the pronounciations are my addition.

SPICES

Spice names are splendid choices for magical names. There are gentle, sweet names and wild, lustful, and spicy names. If you find a spice name which brings out your natural "flavor," then by all means, cook with it. Spice names correspond to images of coziness, hearth fires, warm and fragrant kitchens, and fresh-baked goods; in short, they invoke a feeling of home, at least to those of us who cook with herbs and spices. They are marvellous plants which improve our lives and enhance the flavor of our food. In the early days of sailing ships, adventurers risked their lives to seek the treasures of the Spice Islands, bringing back the precious cargo of spice. Spices are used for healing and in magical spells, and have a vast amount of folklore about their uses. I have also included some herbs and flowers in this list as well because some of them are used in tandem with spices in magical herbalism.

Some spice names are better for certain physical attributes than others, such as for a redhead the names Allspice, Paprika, Cinnamon, and Cayenne. A blonde may prefer the name Vanilla or Lavender. A dark-eyed, black-haired person would do well with names like Star Anise, Licorice, or Pepper. Physical correspondences such as these are one way of connecting to a spice name, but there are many others. For example, the red spices are representative of fire energy and could be chosen based on elemental magic. Black spices are connected to Earth energies. Sometimes there are interesting folk names for these spices; one of these may work for you.

Allspice

Allspice is used for magical healing and is burned to attract prosperity. Oil of allspice is good for invigorating convalescing patients. This is a name which can be worn by any physical type of person, but one who is passionate and feisty, and comfortable with that. It is an invigorating and healing name.

Allum

When the Ancient Egyptians had been robbed, they would burn allum together with crocus to discover the identity of the thief. A good name for a quiet, mysterious, psychic person.

Angelica

Angelica is used for its protective properties. It is a good name for a parent, teacher, healer, or for those who desire protection.

Anise

The essence of anise is said to be an aphrodisiac. Anise is very aromatic. It is thought to eliminate nightmares when you sleep on it. Many Witches use it in their ritual baths together with bay laurel. It is supposed to promote clairvoyance. It is also known in

Britain as sweet cicely or British myrrh. In the past, herbalists described the plant as "so harmless, you cannot use it amiss." Anise is a good name for a dark person. It brings deep passions.

Basil

Basil promotes harmony and a sympathetic connection between two people. Perhaps this was why Spanish prostitutes used to wear the scent. It is also known as alabahaca and the Witches' herb. Basil is used for purification, protection, exorcism, and to attract love.

Basil is a name for one who is seeking a mate. It will emphasize their attractiveness to the right person.

Bay

Also called baie, bay laurel, Grecian laurel, Roman laurel, or sweet bay. Bay is used for protection, improving clairvoyance, exorcism, and healing, and is believed to protect against lightning.

Bay is a water sign name. Laurel is also a beautiful name which brings honor, truth, and intuition.

Bittersweet

Bittersweet is used for protection and healing. It is good for curing vertigo.

This is a good name for one who seeks to balance his or her light and dark sides, or for one getting over a relationship and going through the transition period.

Chamomile

Also called maythen. Used for healing eye troubles, to increase prosperity, and to induce restful sleep.

Chamomile is a woman's name. As a magical name, it is for bringing quietness to one's life. This is a peaceful, restful, healing sanctuary of a name.

Caraway

Used for protection, to attract a lover, to strengthen memory, to protect against theft, and to insure fidelity.

Caraway is a good name for either sex, although it has a slightly more masculine feel to it.

Cayenne

A spicy red pepper. As a name, Cayenne brings out one's hidden passions and brings determination, righteous anger, and strong will.

Cinnamon

Cinnamon is used for bringing success, spirituality, lust, increased psychic powers, protection, and love. In the past, cinnamon-leaf wreaths decorated Roman temples.

As with the other red spices, this would be a good redhead's name. It also represents passion, temper, hard-won loyalty, deep spirituality, fierce love, and the protective powers of a mother lion defending her young. Many of these fiery qualities are commonly associated with redheads.

Clove

Used for protection, exorcism, attracting love and money, removing hostility, purification, stopping gossip, and attracting the opposite sex.

As a magical name, Clove is a solid choice. This is a stable, respectable name for a person who has (or wants to have) a bounty of blessings, from a good job to a happy home life.

Comfrey

Also called miracle herb or yalluc. Used for insuring safe journeys and attracting money.

Comfrey is a wonderful name for healers, herbalists, parents, teachers, or other people who are involved with making others feel better. This is a name for one who eases pain, one with great compassion and empathy for others. This is also a name to choose if you seek to be healed.

Coriander

Amulets containing coriander are used to attract love, health, and lust. Coriander is also used to ease headaches.

As a magical name, Coriander is likely to bring romantic qualities into your life. This is for a person who desires desire.

Cumin

Used for protection, fidelity, and lust. Cumin is worn by brides to insure happy weddings. Germans put cumin in bread to prevent the bread from being stolen.

Cumin is a name good for either sex. It is a happy, rollicking, fun, friendly, protective, sexy name.

Curry

Curry is used for protection rituals.

This is a spicy, exotic sort of name. Curry is an open person, sexual, attractive, and interesting. This name suggests fire.

Fennel

Amulets made with fennel are used for protection and hung in doors and windows.

Fennel is another name which is good for men or women. This name is for bringing wisdom, becoming well-established in the mundane world, or becoming a powerful priest or priestess.

Ginger

Ginger is used for attracting love, money, success, and power.

As a magical name, Ginger is interesting. It's a good name for a lively blonde, and brings many good things with it.

Honeysuckle

Also known as goat's leaf. Used to attract money and good luck. A sweet, feminine, charming name that can be used to attract success.

Laurel

A variety of the laurel tree was taken by priestess of the Delphic oracle prior to their oracular frenzies. It is a narcotic poison that contains levels of cyanide which can produce such delirium. In the Vale of Tempe, the name Laurel (or Daphne) was given to the priestesses. (Also see Bay.) A good name for developing psychic talents. A good priestess' name.

Marjoram

Also called joy of the mountain, mountain mint, and wintersweet. It is used in love spells, and is thought to brings happiness.

Marjoram is a woman's magical name which hints at the great wealth of inner qualities that are hidden from casual view. This is a deep person, one who is romantic, steadfast, honorable, intelligent, and beautiful. The great strength of this person is not in what is obviously charming on the exterior, but what is inside. This name suggests becoming valued for your true gifts.

Mint

Mint is grown for its healing properties (it relieves headaches and stomachaches) and is used in cooking. Because of the rich green color of mint, it is used in incenses which attract prosperity. Spearmint is also called *mismin* in Irish Gaelic and Our Lady's mint. The mints are used for healing, attracting love, and increasing mental powers.

Mint or its variations (Spearmint, Peppermint) are comfortable, feisty, funny, likeable names for Witches.

Nutmeg

Nutmeg is used in luck charms, and strung in necklaces with star anise and tonka beans for a potent herbal necklace. It is used for prosperity spells.

A wonderful name for a brown-haired person or one who desires riches.

Paprika

This is another great redhead name. A spicy, tumultuous, spirited name which brings fire energy.

Parsley

Parsley is also called devil's oatmeal. It promotes lust. It is believed that parsley protects food from contamination, which is why it is traditional to place it on plates at restaurants.

As a magical name, Parsley is a good choice. Parsley is a unique person with a strange sense of humor.

Pepper

Pepper is used in protection spells.

It is a great name for someone with black hair. This is a tempestuous, vivacious, sometimes depressed person. This name brings spirit.

Rosemary

Also called dew of the sea, elf leaf, sea dew, and guardrobe. Used for protection, cleansing, and improving memory. Used in healing and as incense for thousands of years. It is used in the bath to insure youth, hung in sick rooms to promote healing, and grown in the garden to attract elves. It is believed that rosemary makes one happy; this is a name which brings happiness.

Sage

Sage is used in promoting wisdom and in purification.

Sage is a wonderful name for an older, wiser person. As the sage smudge purifies a temple, so can this name bring blessings to your life. A good crone's (or sage's) name to bring wisdom into your life.

Star Anise

For developing psychic powers and bringing luck. It can be worn as beads to increase these attributes. Star anise is used to decorate altars because it empowers altars.

Star Anise is a unique name for a powerful priest or priestess. This name brings power.

Thyme

Thyme is used for promoting health, sleep, psychic powers, love, courage, and purification. A woman who wears thyme makes herself irresistible and able to see fairies, or so it is believed.

Thyme is an interesting magical name for a person of either sex. It is for someone who is well-rounded and interested in physical, metaphysical, and romantic matters.

Vanilla

A type of fermented orchid that inspires love, lust, and increased mental powers.

Vanilla is a good name for a blonde. It is a name full of sweetness, warmth, coziness, home, and hearth. This is a bright person, a person to whom the home is important, a lover of people.

Basically
Life is unsatisfactory
Because:
1) It is not perfect
2) We only get two weeks
of vacation each year
3) Our joys are
impermanent
4) No one gets out alive
5) Our bodies have to be
washed over and over
again
6) The freeway is crowded
7) We must be taught by
pain as well as pleasure
8) Our name sounds
dumb...

—Sujata
Beginning to See

SPICE MEDITATION

Relax. See yourself walking along a road, moving away from a city and into the countryside. You begin to notice fields of herbs and flowers. Walk into the fields. Notice that the fields all have Goddess statues in them. The plants aren't poisoned with chemicals and fertilizers, yet they grow green and lush. As you walk through the fields, smell the tart mint smell of spearmint, the tang of dill; rosemary, thyme, basils by the score are growing in abundance. Move toward the center of this magic garden, toward the Goddess statue upon an altar. On the altar are cords, cloth, and scissors for snipping herbs. Make yourself an amulet for whatever reason you choose. You may create one to attract a lover, to find a job, to be stronger or more sensitive. Roam through the field and let your intuition tell you which herb to take. Ask permission before you cut, and give thanks afterward. Take the cut herbs and bind them in the cloth. Tie it closed with the cord and allow for a length so you can wear it around your neck. Feel it hanging against your skin; smell the fresh-cut herbs mingling with your body's scents. Feel that which you seek. Associate this desire with the smell of these herbs. Whenever you have the need for bolstering this trait, remember the smell of these herbs. Leave the garden now and stroll along the dirt road. Notice the plants and flowers growing in lush display on either side of the trail. This road will lead you home in a very short walk. Notice the kinds of herbs you were attracted to and which flowers you saw on the way back. These may have meaning for you. Look them up in this chapter and find ways of using them in your life, such as amulets, incense, bath oil, perfume, or cooking with them.

NAMES FROM CELESTIAL OBJECTS

I have included a section on celestial objects in a book intended for members of an Earth-based religion because many of us are confirmed science fiction fans. For those who gaze at the stars in the summer skies and long "to boldly go where no one has gone before,"* I include some names you may find on your journey. Even if you aren't a space travel or science fiction fan, these are lovely names which stand on their beauty alone.

Alcyone: In Greek mythology, a daughter of King Aeolus. She was changed into a kingfisher. One of the stars of the Pleiades. A seeker's name; one who seeks to soar despite the risks.

Aldebaran: A star of the first magnitude in the constellation Taurus, forming the eye of the bull. A good name for those who require a strong inner vision and true insights.

Algol: A fixed star in Medusa's head in the constellation Perseus. It is a binary star and loses most of its brightness when eclipsed by its dark companion. A fine name for someone who was (or is) overshadowed by others.

Alioth: A star in the tail of the Great Bear. A name for someone who requires the strength of the bear.

Altair: The bird; a star of the first magnitude in the constellation Aquila. Altair is a name for one who seeks a broader perspective in life (a bird's-eye view).

Andromeda: In Greek legend, Andromeda was the daughter of Cepheus. Perseus rescued her from a sea monster and married her. It is also a constellation in the northern hemisphere. A name for a person who needs to feel safe, rescued, and secure.

Antares: A star of the first magnitude in the constellation Scorpio. It is also called scorpion's heart. For those who require strength of heart.

Aquarius: Latin for "the water carrier." It is a large central constellation of a man pouring water from a pitcher. It is also the eleventh sign of the zodiac. A good water energy name.

Arcturus: From *arktos* (bear) and *ouros* (guard). It refers to a fixed star of the first magnitude in the constellation Bootes. A strong, courageous name.

---

* From *Star Trek: The Next Generation.*

Aries: A northern constellation between Pisces and Taurus which outlines a ram. It is the first sign of the zodiac. A name which, like people who are born under this sign, is strong, self-absorbed, and fearless.

Asteroid: Any of the small planets (planetoids) found between the orbits of Mars and Jupiter. A name about movement, balance, and finding one's niche in life.

Astral: A word meaning starry or starlike, or referring to the field of energy which envelops the human form. This is a name for dreamers, poets, and others whose hearts soar upon the astral.

Aurora: In Greek mythology, Aurora was the Goddess of the dawn. It also refers to the beginning or early period of anything. It is the name of the magnificent crackling, shimmering displays of light which occur in the far northern and far southern skies. Many native cultures have taboos about being outside when the lights are active. An air elemental name which invokes a bit of fire as well.

Blue Moon: Because there are twelve months and thirteen moons, one month each year will have two full moons. The second of these full moons is known as a blue moon. A name for a person who wishes to be unique.

Bootes: A ploughman; from *bous* (ox), a northern constellation which includes the bright star Arcturus. A name for one who tills the earth.

Canis: Refers to the constellations Canis Major and Canis Minor, the greater and lesser dog. A name for a dog lover or someone who has a hound as a totem animal.

Capricorn: A southern constellation of the goat. Also the tenth sign of the zodiac, which the sun enters at the Winter Solstice (December 22, Yule). This is a name that brings images of the goat climbing easily to high, rocky crags, leaving everyone else below. This is a good name for an achiever, a social climber, one who cares about succeeding.

Cassiopeia: In Greek legend, Cassiopeia is the mother of Andromeda and the wife of Cepheus. It is also a northern constellation between Andromeda and Cepheus. A proud mother's name, but beware the price of pride.

Centaurus: A southern constellation between Hydra and the Southern Cross. The brightest star is Alpha Centauri, which is the closest star to earth. From centaur, a cross between a horse and a human. For bringing fleetness, strength, and courage. A good name for a horse lover.

Cepheus: In Greek mythology, husband to Cassiopeia and father to Andromeda. He was placed among the stars after his death. Also a northern constellation surrounded by Cassiopeia, Ursa Major, Draco, and Cygnus. A proud father's name.

Chiron: A new planet discovered in 1977. It is located on an irregular orbit between Saturn and Uranus. In mythology, Chiron was a centaur who was unlike other centaurs. He was wise, kind, and skilled in music and medicine. He was a friend to Hercules, but was accidentally injured by him. Because centaurs are immortal, he would not die but suffer endless pain, so he asked Zeus to grant him death. Zeus placed him in the stars after allowing him to die. Chiron is a name to bring an end to suffering and provide wisdom, skill, and faithfulness. It is a name for one who walks to the beat of a different drummer, and does not live as others expect you to live.

Comet: From *kome* (hair), because the tail of a comet is like long hair. A celestial body having a starlike nucleus with a luminous mass around and trailing after it. Comets follow an orbit around the sun. A name which brings fleetness, alertness, and fire energy; a quick, sparkling energy rather than a slow, steady flame. For those who seek fire elementals but who wish also for spontaneity and passion.

Crescent: Referring to the shape of the new moon. A lunar energy name bringing calm, growth-oriented energy. A good name for a student.

Deneb: Short for Dhanab Aldajajah, "tail of the hen" in Arabic. A first magnitude star in the constellation Cygnus (the swan). A meticulous, detail-oriented name. Good for one who desires more order and control in life.

Draco: From the Latin *draco* and the Greek *drakon,* meaning dragon. A constellation lying between the Big and Little Dippers. A subtle fire name for dragon lovers.

Earth: The fifth largest planet in the solar system and the third planet from the sun. Also referring to the soil covering the surface. One of the best names for becoming well-grounded. A great name for promoting fertility. A good choice for gardeners or a would-be parent.

Ephemeris: A collection of tables which show the various positions of the planets for any day in a given period. Ephemeris is a name which speaks of organization, planning, attention to detail, and reliability.

Ethereal: Very light, airy, delicate, or referring to the upper regions of space. One of the more beautiful names for those who seek the power of air names.

Falling Star: A meteor or shooting star. A romantic name for an air person, one which connotes splendor, luck, and a crone energy.

Full Moon: When the moon appears in the sky in its greatest aspect. Equated with the pregnant mother aspect of the Goddess. A time of monthly celebrating for Pagans known as the Esbat. A marvellous name for bringing fertility, ripeness, fullness, and fulfilment.

Galaxy: A grouping of millions of stars which appears to be a luminous band across the sky. Referred to as the Milky Way. A remote air name; although there is no "air" in space, such things are seen to live in the sky and thus are associated (distantly) as air names. Because stars are distant fires, starry names are also fire names. Galaxy has a marvellous lilt to the name with associated images of encompassing many things within it.

Gemini: A northern constellation between Cancer and Pollux represented by twins sitting together. Also the third sign of the zodiac, entered by the sun about May 21. Gemini brings a duality to one's life, a recognition of one's other side.

Half Moon: The moon when half its disc is visible. A growth-oriented name.

Jupiter: In Roman mythology, the supreme God figure equated to the Greek Zeus. It is also the largest planet in the solar system and the fifth planet from the sun. A name for power, leadership, control, and omnipotence.

Leo: A constellation between Cancer and Virgo which outlines a lion. Its brightest star is Regulus. A cat name, one which brings feline power, sleekness, and strength.

Libra: A southern constellation between Virgo and Scorpio which resembles a pair of scales. Also the seventh sign of the zodiac, which the sun enters about September 23 (the Autumn Equinox). A name which lends its bearer balance and harmony.

Lumina: A measurement of the flow of light. A fire name which sheds light on the darkness. A name for personal enlightenment.

Luna: In Roman mythology, the Goddess presiding over the moon and the months. In alchemy, luna refers to silver. A cool, calm, moon-driven name for those who wish to be in harmony with her cycles.

Lunar: Moonlike. (See above.)

Lyra: A northern constellation containing the white star of the first magnitude called Alpha Lyra. A poetic name with a hint of music to it (lyre).

Mars: The God of war in Roman mythology, similar to the Greek God Ares. Also refers to the fourth planet from the sun, which appears red. In alchemy, Mars refers to iron. A name which brings strength, power, victory, and bravery.

Mercury: In Roman mythology, the messenger of the Gods, God of commerce, manual skill, eloquence, cleverness, travel, and thievery; equated to the Greek Hermes. Also the smallest planet in the solar system and the nearest to the sun. A name that speaks of commerce, success, and movement along the economic scale. An ambitious person in business would do well using this name.

Meteor: A shooting or falling star. A small, solid body travelling in space which enters the atmosphere at a very great speed, and is made white-hot and thus visible by friction with the air. A fiery crone name.

Milky Way: A name for the galaxy in which we live. It appears to be a broad, faintly luminous band in the night sky consisting of innumerable stars and nebulae so distant as to be indistinguishable without a telescope. A name of encompassing complexity with a maternal (milky) edge to it.

Mira: From Latin *mirus,* wonderful. A star, Omicron Ceti, in the constellation Cetus, which is remarkable for its varying brightness increasing from the twelfth to the fourth magnitude in a period of six weeks. A flexible, variable, quixotic name for one who seeks to extend beyond limits.

Moon: The heavenly body that revolves around the earth once every twenty-eight days. A cool, tidal, changeable name.

Nebula: Any of several misty, light, cloudlike patches which consist of interstellar clouds of dust or gas seen in the night sky. An airy, subtle, and sparkling name.

Neptune: In Roman mythology, the sea God equated with the Greek Poseidon. Also the third-largest planet in the solar system. A strong water name to induce the power to deal with the deepest emotions.

New Moon: The moon as it appears in conjunction with the sun. It is visible as a narrow crescent. A growing, promising name full of potential. A good name for a student.

Northern Lights: The shimmering lights or curtains of color which appear in the night skies of the northern latitudes. (See Aurora Borialis and Aurora Australius.) A distant, magical, shimmering, air name, bringing subtle changes.

Nova: A star which suddenly increases in brilliance then gradually grows fainter. Nova is a name of brilliance and achievement.

Orion: In Greek and Roman mythology, a hunter whom the Goddess loved but killed. Orion was also thought to have desired the Pleiades and so ran after them. Zeus saved them by turning them all into stars. Also an equatorial constellation near Taurus containing the first magnitude stars Rigel and Betelgeuse. A name which brings quick instincts and basic desires.

Perseus: In Greek mythology, the slayer of the gorgon Medusa. A northern constellation between Taurus and Cassiopeia. A youthful hero's name that brings bravery and accomplishment.

Pisces: A constellation south of Andromeda resembling two fish. Also the twelfth sign of the zodiac entered by the sun around February 21. A water name.

Planet: Any heavenly body which shines by reflected sunlight and revolves around the sun. The major planets are Mercury, Venus, Earth, Mars, Jupiter, Saturn, Chiron, Neptune, Uranus, and Pluto; the minor planets are the planetoids which move in orbits between Mars and Jupiter. A good earthy name.

Pleiades: In Greek mythology, the seven daughters of Atlas and Pleione who were placed by Zeus among the stars. A large group of stars in the constellation Taurus. Six of them are visible, the seventh being the "lost" Pleiad. A good name for an all-female coven.

Polaris: The north star. A star of the second magnitude forming the end of the tail of Ursa Minor, it marks the position of the north pole. A name which involves polarity and alignment with the earth.

Rigel: The brightest star in the constellation of Orion. Rigel is a blue star of the first magnitude.

Sagittarius: From the Latin, meaning archer. A southern constellation depicting a centaur shooting an arrow. Also the ninth sign of the zodiac, which the sun enters about November 23. A hunter's name, bringing attributes of a stealthy hunter.

Saturn: In Roman mythology, the God of agriculture and husband to Ops, the Goddess of the harvest. He is equated with the Greek Cronos. Also the second largest planet in the solar system. A powerful fertility name for those who seek to make things grow.

Scorpio: A southern constellation resembling a scorpion located between Libra and Sagittarius. Also the eighth sign of the zodiac, which the sun enters about October 24. A fiery, passionate name.

Shooting Star: A meteor or falling star. (See Falling Star.)

Sirius: The brightest star in the heavens, located in Canus Major. It is sometimes called the dog star. Sirius is a good dog's name.

Star: In Middle English *sterre,* Anglo-Saxon *steorra,* Icelandic *stjarna,* Gothic *stairno,* Dutch *ster,* Old Dutch *sterne,* German *stern,* Latin *stella,* Greek *aster,* Cornish *steren,* and Persian *satarah.* A star is a heavenly body seen to be fixed in the night sky. Each of these points of light are distant suns. A fire name, bringing sparkle and illumination.

Taurus: A northern constellation which includes the Pleiades. Taurus outlines the shape of a bull. Also the second sign of the zodiac, entered by the sun about April 20. A powerful earth name; the great bull who is strong, large, and prolific.

Terra: Earth. A good name for grounding. Terra brings fertility and sensibility.

Vega: A blue-white star of the first magnitude in the northern constellation Lyra.

Venus: In Roman mythology, the Goddess of love and beauty equated with the Greek Aphrodite. The most brilliant planet in the solar system. Ancients called it Lucifer as the morning star and Hesperus as the evening star. In alchemy, Venus is related to copper. A name which is a powerful expression of self-worth, appreciation of beauty and love, and strong sexuality.

Virgo: The sixth sign of the zodiac, which the sun enters about August 22. Its symbol is the virgin. An equatorial constellation between Leo and Libra outlining the shape of a woman or virgin. Virgo contains 39 visible stars, of which Spica is the brightest. A maiden's name bringing youth and innocence.

Waning Moon: The moon anytime after it has been full until it is a new moon again. A good crone name. A name useful for ridding yourself of something.

Waxing Moon: The moon anytime after it is new until it has reached full illumination. A growth-oriented name.

World: In Middle English *werld,* and in Anglo-Saxon *weoruld.* The earth. An earth-energy name.

Zodiac: An imaginary belt in the heavens extending for eight degrees on either side of the apparent path of the sun and including the paths of the moon and the other planets. It is divided into thirteen equal parts, or signs, each named for a different constellation. A name which brings an awareness of the stars and astrology.

8

Ancient Names

MYTHOLOGICAL NAMES

Many Pagan traditions require their members to choose at least one Goddess (or God) name. On the other hand, some think that bearing the name of the Goddess is presumptuous. I tend to agree strongly with the former idea. There are little hidden bastions of Christianity which lurk inside many of us Pagans. I call them time bombs. This reluctance to bear the name of a deity sounds like a time bomb to me. The idea of being a God-fearing, humble, self-degradating person who is insignificant compared to deity is not embraced by the Wiccan religion. In Wicca, we recognize that there is nothing between the individual and deity. In fact, we assert that we *are* deity. All of us. Given this, how can it be presumptuous to call yourself what you are? It is one of your true names, that of the Goddess.

There are a number of good reasons to take a Goddess name. They are very powerful names, which seem to cause transformation more quickly than other names. I have gone through a string of Goddess monikers, and with each one I could easily spot the pronounced influence of that particular Goddess in my life. One note of caution: be careful which Goddess (or God) name you choose. I do not recommend some of the Goddesses of disease in the Finnish pantheon, for example, unless you are willing to undergo some painful learning experiences. To name yourself after an ancient fertility Goddess, such as Willendorf or Gaia, may cause an unwanted weight gain or unexpected increased fertility. They are strong names, capable of manifesting the lessons of life in a dramatic and colorful way.

Deity names may also help one feel more connected to the Goddess in her many forms. It is a wonderful way of getting to know a particular aspect of the Goddess. As you carry her name you are more aware of that aspect of yourself, you see it manifesting in your life in many ways, and the feeling of connectedness arises. There are brief

First she had a great abundance of hair, flowing and curling, dispersed and scattered about her divine neck; on the crown of her head she bore many garlands interlaced with flowers, and in the middle of her forehead was a plain circlet in fashion of a mirror, or rather resembling the moon by the light that it gave forth; and this was borne up on either side by serpents that seemed to rise up from the furrows of the earth ... "I am she that is the natural mother of all things, mistress and governess of all the elements, the initial progeny of worlds, chief of the powers divine, queen of heaven, principal of the gods celestial, the light of the goddesses: at my will the planets of the sky, the wholesome winds of the seas, and the lamentable silences of hell be disposed; my name, my divinity is adored throughout all the world, in divers manners, in variable customs and by many names."

—Lucius Apuleius
The Golden Ass

glimpses in this life of how bound together everything is, and all to her. It is a joy to, even momentarily, be still and listen to the music of life, and witness the ties that bind us all together. Bearing the name of the Goddess will help you do that. Remember, thou art Goddess!

British Goddesses

Ancasta: Mentioned only in a single inscription. A Goddess who is almost forgotten. Whoever she was, don't let her be forgotten.

Belisma: Celtic lake and river Goddess. A water name.

Damara: Fertility Goddess associated with the month of May. A feisty, sexual, and prolific name.

Godiva: On May Day, there were processions beginning with the crone representing winter, followed by the lovely young Godiva, riding naked on a white horse. She was the May queen who brought spring, the feminine compliment to the phallic Maypole. She represented fertility and youth. An unencumbered name which brings freedom, youth, maidenhood, and fertility.

Latis: Goddess of beer who fell in love with a salmon. Out of pity for her, the other gods turned him into a young warrior. But in the winter he turns back into a fish and she mourns him. The winter rains are her tears. A name which brings a single-mindedness, determination, a way of dealing with loss, and the idea that love conquers all.

Morgause/Margawse: Sister of King Arthur; wife of Lot; mother of Modred (Arthur's son), Gawaine, Agravaine, Gaheris, and Gareth. Usually seen as the villain, a scheming, selfish woman. However, the legends were perpetuated by the Christians and this could have colored the original story. A powerful name.

Ratis: Protective Goddess of the fortress. A name which brings security, safety, confidence, trust, and protection.

Tamesis: River Goddess who gave her name to the Thames. A water element name bringing the power of an ancient body of water.

Egyptian Goddesses

Athtor: Mother night, the primordial element covering infinity. A night or dark Goddess name brings quiet power, respect for the darkness, a heightening of our other senses.

Bast: Cat Goddess. A kindly Goddess of joy, music, and orgiastic rituals. A favorite name among cat fanciers. It is a happy, playful, sexual name. We have named our kitty condo "Chateau Bast."

Hathor: Goddess of beauty, love, and marriage. Represented as the sky. An air name which brings love and the power of self-love.

Isis: Wife of Osiris, mother to Horus, known as mistress of charms or enchantments. A name of mystery, dedication, determination, and magic.

Maat: Goddess who personifies honor, justice, truth, and steadfastness. A powerful name to bear when making a difficult decision.

Mafdet: Cat Goddess predating Bast. A name which conveys sleekness, skill, guile, mystery, wildness, and beauty.

Mert: Lover of silence in Egyptian myth, another name of Isis. One of the most valuable lessons a Wiccan learns is when to be silent. This name brings the wisdom of silence and constraint.

Tefnut: Goddess who carries away the thirst of the deceased, represented as a form of moisture. A water name bringing relief and attainment of one's dreams.

Finnish Goddesses

Annikki (pronounced "AHN ikki"): Nighttime Goddess. Known as "she of good name." As a magical name, this would be appropriate for work involving the shadow side.

Fir Daughter: Goddess of the forest. A name for grounding.

Ilmatar (pronounced "ILL mah tar"): Mother of the waters. Creation Goddess impregnated by the wind to give birth to the earth and stars and the first person

I know thee, I know thy name, I know the name of the Goddess who guardeth thee: "Sword that smiteth at the utterance of its [own] name, the unknown Goddess with back-turned face, the overthrower of those who draw nigh unto her flame" is her name.

—The Egyptian Book of the Dead

Thy sister put forth her protecting power for thee, she scattered abroad those who were her enemies, she drove back evil Hap, she pronounced mighty words of power, she made cunning her tongue, and her words failed not. The glorious Isis was perfect in command and in speech, and she avenged her brother.

—The Egyptian Book of the Dead

And she jerked her knee
and she shook her limbs:
the eggs rolled in the water
sink into the sea's billow
the eggs smashed to bits
broke into pieces....
The bits changed into good
*   things*
the pieces into fair things:
an egg's lower half
became mother earth below
an egg's upper half
became heaven above;
the upper half that was yolk
became the sun for shining
the upper half that was
*   white*
became the moon for
*   gleaming;*
what in an egg was mottled
became the stars in the sky
what in an egg was blackish
became the clouds of the air.
The ages go on
the years beyond that
as the new sun shines
as the new moon gleams.
Still the water-mother
*   swims*
the water-mother, air-lass
on those mild waters
on the misty waves
before her the slack water
and behind her the clear sky.

—Elias Lonnrot
The Kalevala

(a bard). A good fertility name, or one for renewal and important beginnings.

Juniper Daughter: Goddess of beauty and nature. Useful for self esteem work.

Kalma (pronounced "KAHL ma"): Goddess of death. A croning name which brings the mystery of the dark Goddess.

Kipu-Tytto/Kivutar (pronounced "KIPPU tewt tur" or "KIV ooo tar"): Goddess of illness. A name for confronting and dealing with serious illness.

Kyllikki (pronounced "KEWL likki"): Means "beautiful island flower." Maiden Goddess, equivalent to Persephone. She was abducted by a wanton and unlucky mate. This name suggests youth, beauty, and new beginnings.

Luonnotar (pronounced "LWOAN oh tar"): Daughter of nature. A name to bond with the earth.

Mielikki (pronounced "MY ay likki"): Forest crone Goddess. Creator of the bear. A fertility name which brings abundance and power.

South Daughter: Nature Goddess. A name for bringing warmth and growth.

Summer Daughter: Goddess of summer. A name for growth.

Tuonetar (pronounced "TWOAN etar"): Goddess of the underworld. For delving into one's own depths seeking the shadow self.

Tuulikki (pronounced "TOO il eekey"): Forest Goddess. Called upon to insure abundance of game. A name which brings abundance; especially powerful when used for animal rights and protection work.

Vammatar (pronounced "VAHM mah tar"): Goddess of pain and disease. Helps to overcome and go through illness. Not a name to take unless the need is great.

Vellamo (pronounced "VAYL ah moe"): Water Goddess. For insight, true feeling, and clear meaning.

Water Mother: Creation Goddess associated with the merging of air and water. She gave birth to everything, including the first human, a bard. This is a powerful fertility name, one for new beginnings.

Greek Goddesses

Aphrodite: Goddess of sexual love. Born of sea foam. A powerful name of beauty, sexuality, love, and desire. Especially powerful for work with building self-esteem.

Ariadne: Using a thread, she helped Theseus find his way into the labyrinth to kill the Minotaur and get out again. She eloped with him but he abandoned her. She then became a lover of Dionysus. A name which brings recovery of a broken heart, healing after a failed romance.

Artemis: Virgin, huntress. Protector of young girls. A strong, protective name for someone who has been victimized.

Aspasia: "The welcome." Mistress of Pericles, famous for her charm and intelligence. A noble choice for those who seek improved self-esteem.

Astra: Goddess of justice and purity, seen in the constellation Virgo. A name bringing balance, fairness, and unswerving devotion to justice.

Ate: Goddess of rash infatuation who leads men to ruin. Infatuation is one of the lessons we learn in youth. This is a good name for a young person to take to learn the wisdom of true emotions versus the folly of infatuation.

Atalanta: Would only marry any man she couldn't outrun. A good name for a runner, surely, but also for anyone who seeks pride in her accomplishments.

Athena: Goddess of wisdom, justice. Athena is a powerful name and a powerful force for change in our lives. To name yourself after the Goddess of wisdom allows great transformation and learning to occur. It is a most worthy name.

Bendis: A moon Goddess worshipped in orgiastic rites. A name which brings enlightenment, mystery, and seductive sexuality.

I have much to tell:
there is a maid in the
*   Northland*
a lass in the cold village
who will not accept bride-
*   grooms*
take to good husbands.
Half the north was praising
*   her*
for being very handsome:
the moon shone from her
*   brow-bones*
and from her breasts the
*   sun beamed*
the Great Bear from her
*   shoulders*
the Seven Stars from her
*   back.*

—Elias Lonnrot
The Kalevala

I begin to sing of Pallas
Athena, defender of cities,
awesome Goddess; she and
Ares care for deeds of war,
cities being sacked and
cries of battle, and she
protects an army going
to war and returning.
Hail, O Goddess, and
grant me good fortune and
happiness.

—Homer
The Homeric Hymns

Sing, O Muse, of Artemis, sister of the Far-darter, arrow-pouring virgin, who was nurtured with Apollo, she waters her horses by Meles with its tall rushes and thence on her golden chariot courses to Klaros, rich in vineyards, where Apollo of the silver bow sits waiting for the far-shooting arrow-pourer....

—Homer
The Homeric Hymns

Brimo: Fertility Goddess. A good name for hopeful mothers.

Chloris: Goddess of flowers. A good maiden's name, a name of springtime and youth.

Cytherea: Title of Aphrodite; from the island Cythera, where she was born out of sea foam. (See Aphrodite.)

Calliope: Muse of epic poetry. A lyrical name of whimsy, inspiration, poetry, and reflection.

Cybele: Goddess of caverns, of the earth in its primitive state. Ruled over wild animals. A wild and basic name, bringing an appreciation of primal instincts and natural wonders. I believe it is her voice which whispers in caves, caverns, and coal mines. I once worked in a coal mine, and this was where I first heard the voice of the Goddess. As the miners cut a new face into the rock, they would free ground water and tiny pockets of gases in the rock. As the gas moved through the wet face of the rock, it made an eerie, whispering song. I would work between shifts so I would be practically alone a mile or so below the surface of the earth, deep in the heart of the planet, listening to the song Cybele sang as I blessed and healed her wounds as I worked in the moist, cool, darkness.

Delight: Daughter of Eros and Psyche. A happy and uplifting name.

Delia: Moon Goddess Artemis' name, from her birth place on the island of Delos. (See Artemis.)

Demeter: Goddess of vegetation and fruitfulness. A name which brings maternal longing, worry, and sorrow, but also fruitfulness, joy, and bonding with her children.

Dike (DEE-kay): Goddess of justice; reported to Zeus the wrong-doings of men. This is a good name for anyone who watches out for wrong-doers: a police officer, a reporter, an environmental watchdog, or someone in charge of security at a Pagan festival.

Elara: The mother of a giant by Zeus. A name which brings greatness.

Eris: Goddess of discord. An unusual name which may bring confusion, arguments, upset, and certainly a degree of humor.

Gaia: Earth Goddess. A name which suggests fertility and plenty.

Hecate (Greek pronunciation is "heck AH tay" and Latin pronunciation is "HECK ah tay"): Goddess of the crossroads. Mysterious and powerful Goddess of ghosts and Witchcraft. A crone's name, or one who seeks the wisdom of the dark Goddess, especially at a crossroad in one's life.

Hera: Goddess of women and childbirth. Wife of Zeus. This name suggests healing and support, but Hera was also the most jealous and vindictive Goddess in the Greek pantheon.

Hestia: Goddess of the hearth, peace, and family. Of all Olympians, she is the mildest. A good name for a home, or bringing the feeling of home, security, warmth, comfort, and peace.

Iris: Goddess of the rainbow, messenger of the gods. A name which brings color, enlightenment, beauty, treasures beyond expectation, and happy endings to stormy periods.

Irene: Goddess of peace. A sweet, peaceful, serene, contented name.

Melanie: Means "the dark one," one of Demeter's titles. A name to choose to delve into one's dark side.

Nike (NIGH-key): Goddess of victory. For winning a battle or overcoming defeat.

Psyche: The wife of Cupid (Eros), she was the personification of the human soul. Zeus made her immortal.

Pythia: Serpent Goddess. For sleekness, guile, mystery, and femininity.

Rhea: "Earth." For fertility and abundance.

Selene: Goddess of the full moon. Unlike Diana, not a huntress or virgin. One of the Pleiades. A fertility name.

*Of golden-throned Hera
I sing, born of Rhea, Queen
of all the Gods, unexcelled
in beauty, sister and glorious wife of loud-thundering Zeus. All the Gods on
lofty Olympus reverence
her and honor her together
with Zeus who delights in
thunder.*

—Homer
The Homeric Hymns

*... Mid hushed, cool-rooted
    flowers, fragrant-eyed,
Blue, silver-white, and
    budded Tyrian,
They lay calm-breathing on
    the bedded grass;
Their arms embraced, and
    their pinions too;
Their lips touched not, but
    had not bade adieu,
As if disjoined by soft-
    handed slumber,
And ready still past kisses
    to outnumber
At tender eye-dawn of
    aurorean love:
The winged boy I knew;
But who wast thou, O
    happy dove?
His Psyche true!*

—John Keats
Ode to Psyche

Muses, sweet-speaking daughters of Zeus Kronides and mistresses of song, sing next of long-winged Moon! From her immortal head a heaven-sent glow envelops the earth and beauty arises under its radiance. From her golden crown the dim air is made to glitter as her rays turn night to noon, whenever bright Selene, having bathed her beautiful skin in the Ocean, put on her shining raiment and harnessed her proud-necked and glistening steeds, drives them on as their manes play with the evening, dividing the months. Her great orbit is full and as she waxes a brilliant light appears in the sky. Thus to mortals she is a sign and a token. Once Kronides shared her bed and her love; and became pregnant and gave birth to Pandeia, a maiden outstanding for beauty among the immortal Gods. Hail, Queen and white-armed Goddess, splendid Selene, kindly and fair-tressed!

—Homer
The Homeric Hymns

Suadela: Goddess of persuasion, an attendant of the Goddess of love. A great name for a salesperson, a lawyer, or anyone who needs a handle on the art of persuasion.

Goddess of India

Anumati: Goddess of the waning moon. A name to use for ridding yourself of unwanted aspects of your personality. (See chapter on naming rituals.)

Arani: Goddess of female sexual fire. For accepting one's own sexuality.

Chanda: One of the names of Devi, the great Goddess. A unique and powerful name.

Kundalini: "Coiled." The feminine serpent force, the life-force. Perhaps the most primal and elemental feminine aspect name. A profound name for enlightenment, fertility, all aspects of femininity.

Raka: Goddess of the full moon. For attainment of fertility and success.

Samdhya: Goddess of twilight. A nature Goddess. A name which is for transition into darkness, a croning name, and a name rich in abundance and mystery.

Suratamangari: "Sexual joy and blossom cluster." Associated with fairies. A name for sexual experimentation and recovery from sexual trauma work.

Surya: Goddess of the sun. A fire name bringing passion, warmth, and home energy.

Tamra: "Copper-colored." Ancestress of birds. A name which brings freedom, flights of intellect, warmth, and merriment.

Tara: Hindu star Goddess. A cool name for distancing one from trouble; a gentle teacher.

Irish/Celtic Goddesses

Anu/Anann: Irish. Sex and war Goddess. Part of the triple Goddess Anu, Badhbh, and Macha, known collectively as the Morrigan. This is a powerful choice for a woman who must do battle on the battlefields of sexual discrimination or abuse. These are powerful names not to be chosen lightly. The empowerment potential from these names is impressive. One very frightened Pagan male of my acquaintance told me in a hushed voice that one never spoke these names aloud out of fear of this Goddess. He was a wife-beater and a misogynist. He had reason to be wary. I hope his wife chooses this as her magical name. There is no Goddess or God whose names we dare not utter. That is god-fearing hierarchical orthodox religion, not Wicca.

Badhbh (pronounced "Bave"): Irish. Sex and war Goddess. Part of the triple Goddess Anu, Badhbh, and Macha, known collectively as the Morrigan. (See Anu.) Badhbh was seen as the crone aspect.

Banbha (pronounced "BAN vah"): Irish. Daughter of the Dagda, who asked that Ireland be named after her (along with her two sisters Fodhla and Eire, who also wanted that). The three sisters, of course, form a triple Goddess with Banbha as the crone.

Banshee (pronounced "BAN shee"): Irish. "Woman fairy." Can be heard keening near a house in which someone is about to die. She is attached to certain families (she keens for members of my husband's family). A good crone name.

Boann: (pronounced "pboo ANN"): Irish. Goddess of the River Boyne. She mated with the Dagda on November 1 (a Samhain rite), and the Dagda also mated with the Morrigan on the same day. Boann gave birth to Aengus mac Og. A fertility and sexuality enhancing name.

Brighid (pronounced "breed"): Irish. "Fiery arrow." Also Brigid, Brigit, Brid, Bride, or Bried. Goddess of fertility and inspiration. Daughter of the Dagda. The word "bride" is derived from this name. These names bring a fire of change to its bearer. They are for fertility, good fortune, inspiration, and new beginnings.

Cliona of the Fair Hair: Irish. Goddess of great beauty. Daughter of the Druid of the Tuatha de Danann. A name for building self-esteem, pride, and acceptance of one's appearance; an especially appropriate name for a blonde.

Damona: Celtic. A cow or sheep Goddess. A name for fertility and abundance.

Dana/Danu: Irish. The major mother Goddess figure. Goddess of the Tuatha de Danann (which means "children of the Goddess Dana"). A powerful name for a woman seeking motherhood, coming into her own power, or becoming a teacher.

Epona (pronounced "ee PONAH"): Celtic. Horse Goddess of British and European Celts. A name symbolizing power, energy, and fertility.

Erin/Eire: One of the three queens of the Tuatha de Danann. A daughter of the Dagda. She wanted Ireland to be named after her, and so it was. A name which brings the ancient call of Ireland with it. This aspect was representative of the maiden.

Ernmas: Irish. "She-farmer." The mother of the Irish triple Goddess persona. A fertility name.

Etain: Irish. "Horse riding." Symbol of reincarnation. Very beautiful. A rejuvenating name to bring about shining renewal.

*Lady raven, fly. Black wings
shadow falls over battle
fields, sacred fields and bring
the breath of Avalon, the
peace of the west. We have
tried, warrior maid, we have
fought, we have died 'til the
dolmens and groves have
run red with our blood.
Battle crone, are we lost as
your standing stones fall?
Do our own Wicca ways go
for naught? Morrigan, Morrigan. Do not cry, Wicca
child, for your life or your
ways. Know the peace of the
grave is a rest, not an end.
To my ways be reborn, for
the craft never died and my
time comes again, I am the
Morrigan, Morrigan. Lady
raven, fly, black wing's
shadow falls over city lights,
jewelled nights and come to
us from Avalon, come forth
from the west. See my black
feathered cape in the night,
moonless night. Know my
wing's shadow falls not to
hide, but protect. For each
wise one who calls, never
more shall they fall. And
from Avalon come I again.
Morrigan, Morrigan.*

—Teara Jo Staples
The Morrigan

Flidais: Irish. Woodland Goddess. Rode in a chariot pulled by deer. Married to Adammair, who was so lusty that when she was away he needed seven women to satisfy him. A name for increasing one's sexual appetite.

Fodhla (pronounced "FOW lah"): Irish. Daughter of the Dagda, who asked that Ireland be named after her (along with her two sisters, Banbha and Eire, who also wanted that). The three sisters form a triple Goddess with Fodhla as the mother aspect.

Garbh Ogh (pronounced "garb ock"): Irish. A giantess who who ate deer milk, and eagle's breasts, hunted with seventy hounds, and rode in a chariot drawn by elk. A powerful, large, intimidating woman's name.

Macha: Irish. War and sex Goddess. Part of the triple Goddess Anu, Badhbh, and Macha, known collectively as the Morrigan. (See Anu.)

Medbh (pronounced "meve"): Celtic. Queen Medbh was a fearsome and mighty warrior who commanded great armies. She was so powerful that her presence deprived her opponents of most of their courage and strength. She used the men in her army, sometimes several at once, for sexual encounters, which might suggests the idea of the God being a secondary consort to the more important Goddess. The warrior and sexual aspects hint strongly of the Goddess Morrigan. This is a powerful name bringing with it the feeling of sexuality, power, might, strength, control, and leadership abilities.

Melusine: Irish/Scottish. Dark aspect of Lucina. One whose power lay in her secrecy and anonymity. A good name for a hidden child of the Goddess, one whose situation does not allow her to be public.

Morrigan (pronounced "MORE ee gan"): Irish. War and sex Goddess. Pre-Celtic moon Goddess whose symbol was the raven. (See Anu.)

Nemontana: Celtic. A British Celtic war Goddess. A warrior's name bringing strength, stamina, fortitude, tenacity, and courage.

Scathach (pronounced "SKAH hock"): Celtic. Warrior Goddess who instructed Cuchulainn in martial arts on the Isle of Skye. A name for a teacher, a warrior, a strong and powerful person, one who desires to become fearless and skilled at combat.

Sulla (pronounced "silla"): Celtic. Also Sulis. Goddess of hot springs. For relief of arthritic complaints, a water element name which connotes healing, comfort, and energy. It would be appropriate to erect a shrine to Sulla near a hot tub to make it a safe and healing place.

Norse/Teutonic Goddesses

Freya: Norse. Goddess of love, beauty, and fertility. Another powerful name for building self-esteem, encouraging fertility, and increasing one's sexual appetite.

Holle: Teutonic. Also Holda or Holde. Moon/forest Goddess. She bathed in streams in the forest in the summer, but in winter she showered herself in snow by shaking the trees. A name for cleansing and purifying.

Induna/Udun: Teutonic. The source of the magic apples that allowed the Gods to be immortal. A name for rejuvenation, wisdom, cleansing, and healing.

Jarnsaxa: Teutonic. Wife of Thor. She was a giantess who gave birth to courage and might. A strong name, bringing realization of one's own power and unlocking great potential.

Kara: Norse. A Valkyrie, lover of Helgi. She charmed his enemies in battle by enchanting them with song, but in the end Helgi accidentally killed her. A name which brings the magic of music.

Laufey: Teutonic. Her name means "wooded isle." She gave birth to Loki, the trickster God. A name which brings tolerance, patience, maternal support, and the ability to laugh at one's troubles.

Nanna: Teutonic. Unfaithful wife of Balder. She was seduced by her husband's rival. She committed suicide on her husband's funeral pyre. A serious name bringing wisdom through folly, atonement through self-sacrifice, and the value of being true to one's word.

Nerthus: Teutonic. An early earth Goddess. A fertility name bringing peace and plenty.

Nix: Teutonic. Sirens of great beauty who would sit and sing on the banks of rivers, combing their long hair and luring sailors to their doom. The sound of their singing drove people mad. A name of devastating beauty which has an alluring and sexual connotation. A name which also suggests the great power of music.

Rana/Rania: Norse. Goddess of the sea. She cast her nets upon the sea and set her alluring daughters to tempt sailors into her trap. Once drowned, however, the men were welcome at her feast. A name for bringing forth the inevitable, for working on capturing that which tries to elude you. It also suggests a reward for following the call of the Lady.

Saga: Teutonic. A giantess who is a seer. A name which brings insight and shows one the big picture. A good name for those who have trouble seeing the forest for the trees.

Sjofna: Teutonic. Love Goddess. For feeling love and approval.

Skadi: Teutonic. She loved the mountains, but her husband favored the seashore. She eventually returned to the mountains. A name for following your bliss, being true to yourself, and learning to pay attention to your needs.

Phoenician Goddesses

Astarte: Goddess of love. A name which brings us in touch with the most powerful human emotion.

Baalat: Means "the lady." A generic name for all Goddesses. A name which brings the coalition of many thoughts.

Ghe: Means "Earth." Mother Earth Goddess, a derivation of Gaia. A fertility name with earth element properties.

Omicle: Mother figure in Phoenician creation myth. She gave birth to everything. Her mate was "desire." A name for new beginnings, fertility, rejuvenation, and the fulfilment of desire.

Re: Moon Goddess. A name for gentle teaching and quiet enlightenment.

Sapas: Sun Goddess. Torch of the Gods. For fire energy, passion, powerful enlightenment, harsh lessons, and quick growth.

Tanit: Moon Goddess. A fertility name bringing abundance, attainment of goals, growth, and fulfilment of desire.

Roman Goddesses

Aestas: Goddess of summer. A good seasonal name. A name which brings warmth, growth, nurturing, prosperity, and learning.

Annona: Goddess of the harvest. A name bringing abundance, attainment of goals, prosperity, and success.

Aradia: Goddess of Witches. Daughter of Diana. In folklore she came to earth to teach Witches Diana's magic. A powerful name for a teacher.

Befona: Also Befana. Italian. Witch fairy woman who flies down the chimney on Twelfth Night to bring presents to children. A good name for a good parent or teacher.

Bellona: Goddess of war. A war Goddess' name brings strength, power, courage, an overcoming of fear, and a respect for death.

Bona Dea: Also Fauna or Maia. Goddess of chastity and fecundity. A good maiden's name.

Cardea: Protection Goddess for the home. She evolved into one who guards over children. A fierce name for defending children's rights and protecting the home.

Ceres: Corn Goddess. A name which brings abundance and fertility.

Cerelia: Goddess of the harvest. A name bringing fertility, abundance, and success.

Cloacina: Goddess of drains and sewers. This may seem amusing at first, but in any crowded, densely populated city it is important to keep this Goddess happy. This is a good magical name for helping with household plumbing problems but also for our own internal plumbing. This is a good name for those who suffer from colitis, ileitis, chronic diarrhea, constipation, or any other intestinal upset.

Cynthia: New moon version of Diana. A good name for new beginnings, for new projects, growth, and maturation. A name for a woman who has just come through her rite of passage.

Diana: Goddess of the moon. A virgin huntress. A powerful, independent, strong, beautiful, and empowering name.

Egeria: An oracular water Goddess who foretold the fates of newborn babies. A name for bringing foresight, enlightenment, and intuition to those who deal with children.

Fauna: Also Bona Dea or Maia. Goddess of fertility, animals, farming, and chastity. Wife of Faunus. So faithful a wife she was made a Goddess after death. A good name for fertility and earthiness. A good choice for working out marriage difficulties.

Fides: Goddess of fidelity and honor. A good name to take to bring out these characteristics in you.

Flora: Goddess of flowers and gardens. She enjoyed perpetual youth. A youthful name, appropriate for a maiden.

Jana: Wife to Janus; guardian of doors and the turn of the year. A good name for initiation (opening of doors), movement, and growth; for dealing with aging and death.

Juno: Supreme Roman Goddess of marriage and childbirth. The month of June is named for her. A name for fertility and working out marital troubles.

Luna: Goddess of the moon. Luna brings the power of the night, the illumination of insight, and the wisdom of the Goddess.

Lucina: Midwife Goddess of childbirth; her name means "light." A fertility name which brings the wisdom of the parent.

Maia: Also Bona Dea or Fauna. Goddess of spring. One of the Pleiades. A good name for a maiden. A name conveying youthful energy, springlike renewal, and hope.

Minerva: A war Goddess who originally protected business, education, and industry. Goddess of wisdom and justice. Also called Athena in Greece. A strong name for achieving success in business, good grades in school, or in defeating an enemy of any description. A powerful name.

Nox: Goddess of the night. A name for exploring one's shadow self, the dark Goddess, or inner mysteries.

Pax: Goddess of peace. A name which brings serenity, relief from stress, cool deliberation, and freedom from strife.

Salus: Goddess of health. A good name for overcoming illness.

Terra/Tellus: Earth Goddess. For fertility and abundance.

Volupia: Goddess of pleasure. A feel-better name. One to take for increasing one's pleasure in life.

Venus: Goddess of love (more sexual in nature than Aphrodite). A great name for self-esteem work, for increasing one's sexuality, for working with tantric energy.

Vesta: Goddess of the hearth. A name for a home, surely, but also for bringing about hominess, safety, warmth, friendship, and family. A good name for people who need to feel more secure.

Welsh Goddesses

In Wales, myths were very important. The Welsh word for mythologist or storyteller was *cyfarwydd,* which means a seer and teacher who guides the souls of those who listen through the world of mystery. The Welsh word for story or myth comes from the root word which means "to see," and the word story means guidance, direction, instruction, knowledge and skill. The wise ones of Wales knew how to use their myths and the names found within them.*

Arianrhod (pronounced "air ee EN road"): Means "silver wheel." Goddess of reincarnation. Mother of Llew by Gwydion. A transformational Goddess whose name brings rebirth and acceptance of the cycles of life.

Branwen (pronounced "BRAN oo win"): She was the wife of the king of Ireland, who mistreated her. Her brother, Bran the Blessed, came to avenge her but was mortally wounded. She took his head, which continued to talk for several years. It finally asked to be buried. A good name for one who seeks to overcome oppression, leave environments of mistreatment, and listen to words of wisdom.

Cerridwen (pronounced "caer EED uin"): Mother, moon, grain Goddess. Mother of Creirwy (the most beautiful girl in the world) and Avagdu (the ugliest boy). Also the mother of Taliesin, the greatest of the bards. She is the owner of a cauldron called Amen in which she made a magic drink that gave inspiration and knowledge. A beautiful name which brings the cycles of life into focus; a rejuvenating name, a good crone's name. A name for knowledge, wisdom, and magic.

Cyhiraeth (pronounced "keh HEAR aeth"): Water Goddess who evolved into being a warning of impending death. This is a good name for bringing out one's awareness of death, and improving one's intuition and psychic abilities.

Don (pronounced "dohn"): Equivalent to the Irish Danu. Mother Goddess figure. Wife of Beli and mother to Arianrhod. A fertility name.

---

* From Caitlin Matthews' *Mabon and the Mysteries of Britain,* Arkana Publishers, 1987.

Dwyvach (pronounced "DWEE vach"): Husband to Dwyvan, with whom she built an ark to rescue many animals and escape a great flood in a pre-Christian myth. A name for an animal lover, a sailor, or a person who takes care of others, such as a mother or a teacher.

Goleuddydd (pronounced "go LEUTH theeth"): A fertility Goddess who appeared in the form of a sow. A fertility name.

Gwendydd (pronounced "GWEND eth"): Also Gandieda, Vivienne, and Nimue. Merlin's sister, to whom he gave his gift of prophecy. A name for a powerful Witch, a strong woman who has considerable psychic talents.

Gwenhwyfar (pronounced "gwen HOOEY far"): Also Guinevere or Gurneva. Arthur's wife. The queen in the medieval romances is a revision of her true role in Arthur's court, according to the Farrars.* In ancient times she played the role of the goddess-queen at Arthur's court, a focus of sovereignty in triad form. This is a name which brings with it, however, the power of both these mythologies. Gwenhwyfar is a name which brings the sovereignty of a queen, with its associated justice, wisdom, temperance, and tolerance. It also carries with it the unfaithful wife aspects of the myth which is more widely known (and thus empowered by the collective unconscious). Thus it brings with it elements of resignation to one's fate or karma, a tendency to follow one's bliss regardless of the consequences, and the ability to play a key role in events around you.

Morgan (le Fay): Means "of the sea." Best known as Arthur's half sister/lover. Earlier was known as a sea Goddess of the Isle of Avalon. She was associated with Merlin and from him received magical secrets. She was a healer as well. This is a name which brings a talent for both the arts of healing and magic. A water name, bringing with it soothing qualities and increased psychic awareness.

Olwyn (pronounced "OLL win"): An important character in the old king versus the new king struggle which is seen in many myths, in which the winner

"I am Rhiannon, daughter of Hyfaidd Hen, and I am being given to a man against my will. I have never desired any man, and that because of loving you. And I still don't desire one, unless you reject me; it is to know your answer to that that I have come."

"I swear to God," said Pwyll, "my answer to you is this: if I could choose from all the women and maidens in the world, 'tis you I would choose."

—The Mabinogi

*From Janet and Stewart Farrar's *The Witches' Goddess,* Phoenix Publishing, 1987.

becomes the consort to the Goddess. Olwyn is the daughter of Ysbadadden and the intended bride of Culhwch. If Olwyn marries Culhwch, then Ysbadadden must die. A sovereign Goddess name which brings with it power, justice, wisdom, and fate.

Rhiannon (pronounced "hree ANN in"): Fertility and underworld Goddess. For the swiftness of a swift steed or fluttering bird. For overcoming punishment mistakenly laid upon one, or for recovering from abuse. A good name for one intent on self-healing, or a counsellor of others who are healing. The birds of Rhiannon are said to have made such beautiful music that could "wake the dead and lull the living to sleep." This suggests an appropriate name for a singer or musician. There are a few very talented singers of Pagan music who share this name.

Scathach ("SKATH ach"): The Goddess who taught Cuchulainn the arts of war. This is a powerful name for one who wishes to become self-sufficient, strong, or a teacher.

GODS

To call yourself "God" is an important and almost unparalleled act of self-acceptance and empowerment. To bear the name of one of the Gods makes a man stand taller, feel braver, more confident, more in tune with his maleness, and more aware of the Goddess. These names are names accentuating the hero, the magician, the lover, the bard, and the warrior. These are very strong archetypal images which manifest powerfully in people who bear these magnificent names.

If your experiences with any deity speaks to you of different things than what I have written here then, for you, those things are what should be used to describe the deity and the deity's name. The bottom line is what does this name mean to you? You make the magic.

I have approached this from the perspective of women taking Goddess names and men taking God names, but only because that is the most common connection. Deity names work well for us, regardless of our current sexual affiliation. God names bring many good things to both sexes. Goddess names work well for men as well as women. Taking a deity name of the other sex, in fact, is a great way to understand more about the other sex. If you want to learn about men, who better to teach you than the God? What better female to lead you into the realm of womanhood than the Goddess?

Thou art God!

British Gods

Arthur: British/Celtic. The most popular mythic hero in British culture. He represented a savior God who is said to rise from his sleep on the Isle of Avalon when he is needed. He was the son of King Uther Pendragon and Ygraine, Duchess of Cornwall. Arthur was reared by Merlin the magician, upon whom he depended for advice and counsel. Husband to Guinevere, who loved Arthur's closest friend and bravest knight Lancelot. A name of honor, enlightenment, civilized behavior, and betrayal. It is a good name for getting over betrayal.

Balin and Balin: Knights of King Arthur's round table. Ancient names.

Gareth: Valorous knight of King Arthur; husband to Lynet. A name which connotes bravery and valor.

Gawain: Son of Morgause and Lot; knight of Arthur's court. A noble name.

Herne: A hunter God. He bears a rack of deer antlers upon his head and races across the sky with his red-eared hunting dogs. He is associated with fecundity and usually portrayed with an enormous phallus. This is a particularly potent name for one who desires increased sexual fertility, virility, or ability.

Launfal: A knight of the round table. Tryamon, a fairy princess, loved him and gave him money, provided he did not reveal their love. He inadvertently did so, and instantly lost his wealth. He was put on trial and commanded to produce the object of his boasts. Trymon appeared, supported his boasts, and blinded Guinevere. A name which teaches the wisdom of silence.

Llud (pronounced "hleth"): British Celtic river God. Also Ludd, Nuda, or Nudd. Very similar to Nuada of the Irish pantheon. He also had a silver hand. This is a name for water energy and overcoming one's handicaps.

Myrddin (pronounced "MERTH in"): British/Welsh. Also Merlin or Emerys. The British Zeus. Early legendary wizard and bard. England first bore this name as "Clas Merdin" (Myrddin's enclosure). He is said to have erected Stonehenge. He is a guardian of Britain said to rise when the world has need of him. He was dazzled by young Nimue (Nineve, Ninianne), who stole his magic and buried him within an oak tree (or beneath Stonehenge, at sea, in a dense forest on Bardsey Island, or within a crystal cave, say other myths). Has sky God attributes and his resting place is referred to as his airy tomb. A wise, magical, powerful, vulnerable, and protective name. A good name for a sage.

Nick: Water God. Derived from the Nix, Teutonic water sprites. This is a good water energy name.

"Immortals are what you wanted," said Thor in a low, quiet voice. "Immortals are what you got. It is a little hard on us. You wanted us to be forever, so we are forever. Then you forget about us. But still we are forever. Now at last, many are dead, many dying," he then added in a quiet voice, "but it takes a special effort."

"I can't even begin to understand what you're talking about," said Kate, "you say that I, we—"

"You can begin to understand," said Thor angrily, "which is why I have come to you. Do you know that most people hardly see me?...It is not that we are hidden. We are here. We move among you....You gave birth to us. You made us be what you would not dare to be yourselves. Yet you will not acknowledge us. If I walk along one of your streets in this...world you have made for yourselves without us, then barely an eye will once flicker in my direction."

—Douglas Adams
*The Long, Dark,
Tea-Time of the Soul*

Tannus/Tinnus: British and French. Means "oak." He survived as a thunder God, but early Etruscan myth names him Tina. Gaelic words derived from his name mean fire, and the word tinder comes from his name. This is probably more likely to be a lightning God involved with fire energy. This is a fire energy name, suggesting building energy, feeding the system, passion, fortitude, and self-sufficiency.

Uther: King of southern Britain as Uther Pendragon. Father of King Arthur. Husband to Ygraine, Dutchess of Cornwall. This is a noble name bringing leadership, bravery, diplomacy, and the ability to follow one's bliss.

Wayland: British/Celtic. Also Weland or Weyland the smith. A smith God. He was originally the Nordic God Volund. Son of Wade (Wada), King of the Finns. Grandson to Wachilt, a sea Goddess. Wayland was abandoned by his wife, stolen from, abducted, lamed, imprisoned, and forced to work. He killed the two sons of his captor, made drinking cups from the dead son's skulls as a gift to his captor, raped the man's daughter, and escaped with wings he made during his captivity. This is a name of a victim who is sorely abused and who dreams of revenge. It is a name for one stuck in pain and unhappiness but who is thinking of ways to escape. This is also a name for a silversmith who seeks to create wonderful work.

Egyptian Gods

Aker: God of the earth. A God who had the bodies of two lions with human heads, facing opposite directions. He ruled the underworld, guarding its gate. Aker is a name for those who are dealing with death or are undergoing any important new beginning.

Akhnaton (pronounced "auck NAH ton"): Revolutionary king who worshipped Ra the sun God. He has apparently been reincarnated into the body of an ex-Las Vegas card dealer living in Denver, Colorado (or so he claims). The interior of this man's house is covered with beautiful hieroglyphics and decorated according to the tastes of an Egyptian king. He holds court there and tells his students the secrets of the universe, for a price. Akhnaton is a good name for one who desires to think for himself, to be a rebel, or to think about things in a new way.

Amun-Ra: Also Ra. Sun God. A creation God from whose tears humanity sprang. Interestingly enough from a perspective of names, Isis tricked Ra into revealing his secret name to her and thus she acquired his magic powers. This is primarily a fertility name bringing warmth, insight, knowledge, and an awareness of the frailty of aging. This would be a good name to take if you are working on learning to keep secrets.

Anubis: God of embalming. Weighed the heart of the deceased against that of a feather to judge if the deceased was pure of heart. Like many underworld Gods, this name is good for introspection and accepting the cycles of life and death. Also good for self-improvement.

Apis: A series of sacred bulls in which is believed to live the soul of Osiris. The name Apis brings strength, fecundity, masculine prowess, and nobility.

Babi: Baboon God. A fierce and phallic God who feeds on humans, yet could protect humans from snakes. This is a name for getting in touch with one's warlike aspects and for improving one's virility.

Bes: God who protects women during pregnancy and birth. A happy God who delights in music, merrymaking, families, children, married couples, and eroticism. Sort of Pan with family values. This is a great name to take when one decides to become a father and to keep through the birth of the baby.

Horus: God of light. Son of Isis and Osiris. A name for enlightenment and understanding.

Khepera: God of the rising sun. The rising sun is seen as Khepera moving into the body of the sky Goddess. He is a creation figure; in one myth, he was said to form the world. His symbology has to do with life and procreation. As a magical name, Khepera is a positive, hopeful, creative, and rejuvenating name for those beginning again.

Min: God of sexual potency. He was shaped like a phallus with a human or a lion's head. He protected desert travellers who offered him flowers to assure the fertility of the Nile Valley. This is a name for enhancing one's sexual drive, endurance, potency, and sexual capacity.

Nu: Also Nun or Nunu. God of the primordial watery mass from which sprang the Gods; known as the father of the Gods. He and his wife were the first couple. This is a name for going back to the beginning and looking at your life. This is a starting over name. It also is a good name for new beginnings and the creation of new couples or groups.

Osiris: God of fertility, growing things (with his cycle of life, death, and rebirth), and the afterlife (he was a judge and caretaker of the dead). His reformation of the lands he touched was done without force but with charm, music, and sound ideas. Husband of Isis. He was torn apart by Set and his body hidden all over Egypt. Isis had to find all the parts to restore him to life. The only part she couldn't find was his penis, which had been eaten by a fish. It was from this myth that the custom of eating fish on Fridays sprang. The

The company of the Gods rejoiceth and is glad at the coming of Osiris's son Horus, and firm of heart and triumphant is the son of Isis, the heir of Osiris.

—The Egyptian Book of the Dead

[Ra said] "I have made the heavens and the Earth... I have stretched out the two horizons like a curtain, and I have placed the soul of the Gods within them. I am he who, if he openeth his eyes, doth make the light, and, if he closeth them, darkness cometh into being. At his command the Nile riseth, and the Gods know not his name."

—The Egyptian Book of the Dead

Hail to thee, Osiris, lord of eternity, king of the Gods...to thee are obedient the stars in the heights...Thou art the Lord to whom hymns of praise are sung in the southern heaven, and unto thee are adorations paid in the northern heaven...Thy dominion is eternal, O thou beautiful Form of the company of the Gods... Many are the shouts of joy that rise to thee at the Uak festival, and cries of delight ascend to thee from the whole world with one voice.

—The Egyptian Book of the Dead

sacramental imbibing of the flesh of deity began in this way and has persisted for thousands of years, thanks to the Catholics. This is a powerful name for those who seek to be in sync with the cycles of life, to accept death as part of life, and for those who seek to change the world in a gentle and profound manner. It is also a name for fertility, growth, intellect, charm, and balance.

Ptah: The opener; called the father of fathers and the power of powers; a Solar God. This is a name for creativity, craftsmanship, and skill.

Ra: Sun God of ancient Egypt. (See Amun-Ra.)

Set: Originally a sun God; he ended up being a God of the powers of the deathly dryness in the Sahara. This is a name which brings an awareness of one's own dark side. It is a name for examining one's shadow self and dealing with it.

Thoth: God of divine intelligence and writing. A name to take as you write or study.

Finnish Gods

Hisi (pronounced "hissy"): Malicious spirit trinity together with Paha and Lempo. Seemingly evil, malicious, or trickster Gods serve a purpose and their names can help us. This energy is part of us all; we are not made of sugar and spice and lots of white light. We have a dark side, as does nature, and these archetypes personify these aspects of life. These Gods serve the cycles and act as balance for the Gods of more pleasant things. Evil has been described as a lack of balance, and I think that this is very true. These names then can be used (carefully) to work with one's dark side. Knowing oneself is the key to being successful at life and at magic. Using names like these can dredge up our own "evil," that within us which is out of balance, and help examine it, understand why it came to be there, accept it, and, finally, work to bring it back into balance.

Ilma (pronounced "ILL mah"): Air God. Father of "Daughter of Nature" and "Mother of the Waters." An air energy name for creativity, fertility, power, and clarity of thought.

Ilmarinen (pronounced "ILL mar ee nayn"): The Weyland Smith of the Finnish sagas. A smith God. He forged a talisman from a swan's quill tip, the milk of a barren cow, a small grain of barley, and the dawn of a summer ewe. This name is good for those who wish to create something new within themselves, and for those who seek to forge ahead despite setbacks. This is a building, changing, growing, and transforming name.

Jumala (pronounced "YOO mah lah"): Supreme sky God. His symbol was the oak tree. An air elemental name bringing power, control, and creativity.

Nakki (pronounced "NAH key"): Shape-shifting water God. Bottomless lakes lead to the palace of Nakki. Swimmers must beware of him. He appears at the rising and setting of the sun. This is a water energy name, bringing immersion in one's inner emotions.

Paiva (pronounced "PIE vah"): God of the sun. A name to take to bring about the flames of passion, will, and determination. A fire elemental name.

Pellervoinen (pronounced "PAYL er voi nayn"): Vegetation God. Protector of trees and plants. This is an vibrant name to take to do environmental activism work (protesting clear-cut logging, for example), or just to help you get in touch with the energy of plants while gardening.

Rot (pronounced "roat"): God of the Underworld. Underworld Gods perform many functions. They are responsible for judgement, analysis, and understanding of one's inner self, synthesis, coming to terms with oneself, and rebirth or reward in a happier place. Thus, underworld names can help us do these things on our own. They can help us separate and identify aspects of our personality, analyze these aspects, synthesize this new awareness into our conscious mind, accept these aspects, and go through a rebirth of a new, improved person.

Surma (Pronounced "SOOR mah"): Guardian of the gates to the realm of Kalma, Goddess of graves. Surma is a frightening creature who represents fate and violent death. This name can acquaint us with death, the afterlife, and fate.

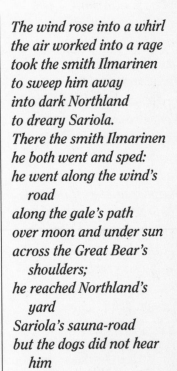

The wind rose into a whirl
the air worked into a rage
took the smith Ilmarinen
to sweep him away
into dark Northland
to dreary Sariola.
There the smith Ilmarinen
he both went and sped:
he went along the wind's
*   road*
along the gale's path
over moon and under sun
across the Great Bear's
*   shoulders;*
he reached Northland's
*   yard*
Sariola's sauna-road
but the dogs did not hear
*   him*
nor did the barkers notice.

—Elias Lonnrot
The Kalevala

Tapio (pronounced "TAHP pi oa"): God of the forest realm of Tapiola. Husband to Mielikki. He is pictured as dark-bearded, wearing a fir hat and a moss cloak. A God's name to invoke abundance, safety, protection, and oneness with forest energy.

Tuoni (pronounced "TUOAN ee"): God of the underworld. His daughters were the Goddesses of death, disease, and suffering. This is a good name to take to work through an illness or sorrow. Sometimes you are given an unpleasant thing in order to learn from it and the only way to do that is to immerse yourself in it, work through it, then move on.

Ukko (pronounced "OOK oh"): The supreme sky God (formerly Jumala). God of thunder and rain and he who supports the world. Husband to Akka, the Earth mother Goddess. A creation name bringing supreme power, fertility, and expression. Especially good for dealing with enormous responsibility.

Vainamoinen (pronounced "VINE am moi nayn"): The Finnish Adam. The son of the creator Goddess and the east wind. His name is probably derived from an archaic word meaning "slow-flowing river." He is also called the "calm waters man." He is a bard/shaman/creator God with a powerful water name for creativity, fertility, and insight.

Va-Kul (pronounced "VAHH kool"): An androgenous, malevolent water God. (See discussion of "evil" Gods under Hisi.)

Vu-Kutis (pronounced "VUAH coo tiss"): A healer water God. A good name for curing disease.

Vu-Murt (pronounced "VUAH moort"): Water God. A water elemental name.

Greek Gods

Achelous: A shape-shifting river God who during a wrestling match would change his form, but was eventually defeated and leapt into the river which then bore his name. At one point he became a bull; when his opponent tore off his horn, it became a cornucopia. This name suggests a wily nature, a shifting person who is hard to pin down, water energy, and a person who attracts abundance and plenty.

Achilles: Trying to make him invulnerable, his mother dipped him in the Styx when he was a baby. She held him by the heel and forgot to dip that as well, so it became his vulnerable spot. This name suggests a vulnerable person who is working on his weaknesses.

Adonis: A youth beloved by Aphrodite. When he was killed, Aphrodite begged Zeus to restore him to life, but Persephone had also become enamored of him and would not let him leave the underworld. Zeus decreed that he should spend half the year in the underworld and half in the upperworld. In the spring the festival of his rebirth was an occasion for wild celebrations, usually celebrated by women.

Aeacus: Son of Zeus. A god of such great integrity that after his death, Zeus made him a judge of the underworld. A name which brings honor, reward, integrity, and respect.

Aeolus: Father of the wind. An air name which brings to mind wisdom, flight, power, and freedom.

Ajax: A giant; the strongest of warriors. A name for those who wish to seem larger to others. A name which brings about increased body awareness and confidence about one's physique.

Anteros: Son of Aphrodite, brother of Eros; represents mutual love. A name for those who seek affection, friendship, and love to be reciprocated.

Antaeus: A God who could defeat any opponent as long as he remained in contact with the earth. He was defeated by being lifted into the air and strangled. A name which brings a strong connection to the earth, a bonding of the bearer with the energy flows of the earth, and a grounding effect.

Apollo: God of intellect, music, art, poetry, healing, and light. He was expanded with the advent of patriarchy to encompass the former domains of many goddesses. This is a name which brings strength, male beauty, compassion, sensitivity, lust, passion, and talent.

I shall sing of Zeus, the best and the greatest of Gods, far-seeing, mighty, fulfiller of designs who confides his tight-knit schemes to Themis as she sits leaning upon him. Have mercy, far-seeing Kronides, most glorious and great!

—Homer
The Homeric Hymns

Mighty Ares, golden-helmeted rider of chariots, stout-hearted, shield-carrying and bronze-geared savior of cities, strong-handed and unwearying lord of the spear, bulwark of Olympus, father of fair Victory, and succorer of Themis. You curb the unruly and lead truly just men, O paragon of manly excellence, wheeling your luminous orb through the seven-pathed constellations of the sky, where flaming steeds ever carry you above the third heavenly arch. Harken, helper of mortals and giver of flourishing youth, and from above shine a gentle light on my life and my martial prowess, that I may be able to ward off bitter cowardice from my head, to bend wisely my soul's beguiling impulse and to restrain the sharp fury of my heart, whenever it provokes me to enter chilling battle. But, O blessed one, give me courage to stay within the secure laws of peace and to escape the enemy's charge and a violent death.

—Homer
The Homeric Hymns

Ares: Also Aries. God of war. Lover of Aphrodite. Father to Gods of terror, tumult, fear, panic, and Goddesses of battle (Enos), discord (Eris), and fair victory. Sacred to him were the dog and the vulture. This is a warrior's name, bringing protection.

Cadmus: A builder God who gave the Greeks the alphabet. Husband to Zeus' daughter Harmonia. They became the rulers of Illyria and were associated with the snake God and Goddess of Illyrian myth. A name for any snake fanciers or for those who have great ambition.

Centaur: Means "those who round up bulls." Creatures with the body of a horse and the torso, arms, and head of a human. Originally Zeus thwarted a suitor of Hera by forming a cloud which resembled Hera. The suitor mated with the cloud, producing Centaurus. Centaurus mated with mares, creating the race of Centaurs. This name brings sexuality, fecundity, playfulness, swiftness, and power.

Dionysus (pronounced "dye oh NEE see us"): God of fertility, freer of emotions, remover of inhibitions. His rites were wild frenzies of female worshippers. This name is for overcoming shyness or inhibition.

Eros: Son of Aphrodite; God of love. A name to be chosen carefully in this day and age because it brings eroticism, sexual potency, attractiveness, fecundity, and stamina. This name is male sexuality personified. Be careful how you use it.

Glaucus: A sea God who had the gift of prophecy given to him by Apollo. He appeared to sailors in warning of danger. A good name for developing psychic abilities, getting in touch with water energy, finding your one true love (Glaucus was loved by none but his true love), or for those who like to sail.

Hades: God of the underworld. He abducted Persephone, daughter of Demeter (corn Goddess) and Zeus. Demeter was so distraught over losing her daughter that she refused to allow anything to grow upon the earth until her daughter was returned to her. In a compromise, Persephone was allowed to return to her mother for half the year but must return to Hades for the remainder of the year. This is symbolic of the cycle of growth of vegetation on the earth. Hades is a name for forceful energy, darkness, potency, faithfulness, wealth, and plenty.

Helios: Sun God. The name brings travel, passion, sexuality, glory, and determination.

Hermes: Messenger of the Gods. His symbols are a winged cap and sandals. As a name, it brings increased acuity for intellect, communication, commerce, and a sense of freedom.

Melanion: Husband to the nature and hunting Goddess Atalanta, who vowed she would only wed the man who could beat her in a foot race. A name of competition, victory, guile, fleetness, and union with nature.

Minos: Husband to Pasiphae and father to Ariadne. Poseidon caused his wife Pasiphae to fall in love with a white bull with whom she mated and gave birth to the Minotaur. After his death, Minos became a judge in the underworld. It is a name of sovereignty, honor, justice, and judgement.

Momus: God of mockery and spiteful criticism. This would be a good name for one who seeks to control his sarcasm, rudeness, cruelty, and overly critical nature.

Morpheus: God of dreams. Dweller in the underworld. Son of death and nephew of sleep. An excellent name for bringing prophetic dreams, awareness, release, rest, and goal-setting.

Orion: A hunter who loved the seven daughters of Atlas and pursued them. Zeus placed them in the sky to keep them from him. After death he was placed in the sky in endless pursuit of them. A name for bringing the essence of the hunt, pursuit, energy, determination, desire, and dealing with losing the object of your desire.

Pan: God of flocks. Body of a man but the horns, ears, and legs of a goat. He is playful, vigorous, lusty, and fertile. A powerful sexual name which brings lustiness, freedom, unabashed sexuality, eroticism, desire, longevity, and potency.

Paris: He was a prince of Troy who abducted Helen and began the Trojan war. This took place because he

Sing to me O Muse, of Hermes' dear child, the goat-footed, two-horned, din-loving one, who roams over wooded glades together with dance-loving nymphs....
Then only at evening he shouts as he returns from the hunt and on his pipes of reed he gently plays sweet music. In song he could even outdo that bird which sits among the leaves at flower-rich springtime and pouring forth its dirge, trills honey-voiced tunes... with him at that time are the clear-voiced mountain nymphs, dancing with swift feet and singing at some dark spring, as the echo moans about the mountain peak. The God glides now here, now there and then to the middle of the dance, setting the pace with quick feet. On his back her wears a bay lynx-skin as his heart delights in the shrill songs in a soft meadow where the crocus and the fragrant hyacinth blossom forth and entwine with the grass in fast embrace. They sing of the blessed Gods and of lofty Olympus...

*His was a festive wedding,
and inside the house she
bore to Hermes a dear son,
from birth monstrous to
behold, with goat's feet and
two horns, boisterous and
sweet-laughing. His mother
sprang up and fled; the
nurse in turn left the child
behind because she was
afraid when she saw his
wild and well-bearded
visage. Helpful Hermes
quickly received him into
his arms, and in his divine
heart the joy overflowed.
He wrapped the child in
snug skins of mountain
hares and swiftly went to
the abodes of the immor-
tals. He then set him down
beside Zeus and the other
Gods and showed them his
boy: all of them were
delighted in their hearts and
Bacchic Dionysos above all
others. They called him Pan
because he cheered the
hearts of all.*

—Homer
The Homeric Hymns

was challenged by the Gods to choose who was the fairest—Hera, Athena, or Aphrodite. Hera offered him wealth and power, Athena offered wisdom, and Aphrodite offered love of the most beautiful woman in the world. Aphrodite won, and Helen of Troy was his reward. Paris died during the Trojan War. This name is a good one for bringing about change, making decisions, choosing wisely, and developing diplomacy.

Satyr: Forest and mountain spirits who are crude, orgiastic, sexual, lusty, and wild. A good name for developing more potent sexuality.

Zeus: A supreme deity. A name for developing power, omnipotence, fecundity, creativity, and authority.

Gods of India

Adibuddha: Personification of masculinity. A good name for getting in touch with one's masculine side.

Ardhanarisvara: The androgenous aspect of Shiva. This is a good name for acknowledging and accepting the duality of the soul, the female within the male personality.

Bhrigus: Means "shining ones." Storm Gods. A name to choose when dealing with one's blustery temper or impatience.

Brahma: A creation God. Son of Kali. He divided himself into his male and female aspects. His wife was the Goddess of music, speech, and the arts. One of his wives gave birth to the Universe. A creative, vital, balanced name evoking a balance between male and female.

Budha: Beautiful and radiant God. Son of Tara the star Goddess and Soma the moon God. This is a powerful name with strong lunar influence.

Chandra: Means "moon." Pre-Vedic lunar God. Married to Rohini, the cow Goddess. A lunar influence name which brings about subtle change and gradual enlightenment.

Ganesha: God of good fortune, literature, and wisdom. He is a happy God. He has the head of an elephant and the body of a man. Husband to "intellect and intuition" and "achievement." He is worshipped before any new venture to ensure wealth and success. This is a success-oriented name which may bring wealth, wisdom, and respect.

Hanuman: Monkey God. He has incredible physical strength. He was virile, chaste, intelligent, and loyal. He was utterly devoted to Rama. This name suggests power through intellect and good intentions, a strong will, a strong body, a strong mind, and a strong set of ethics.

Indra: Warrior and storm God. A name which brings about rapid change.

Kama/Kamadeva: God of love. A winged child who has a bow and arrow, like Cupid. Husband to "pleasure." A name to choose to bring eroticism into one's life; also love, romance, and renewal of passion.

Krishna: An avatar of Vishnu. Charming, erotic, strong, and impudent. This is a name which brings popularity with women, strength, and daring.

Varuna: A sky and water God. Also God of the dead, justice and the moon. A good name for bringing justice, rewards, and fair compensation into one's life.

Irish/Celtic Gods

Aengus mac Og (pronounced "angis mack ock"): Irish. Also Angus or Oengus. Means young lad, son of a virgin. God of love. This name brings the brightness of youth, male beauty, wit, quickness, charm, and fated love. An excellent name for a young man.

Amergin (pronounced "a MORE gin;" g as in gone): Irish. The bard and spokesman of the Milesians. Author of the traditional poem which begins "I am a stag of seven tines." This is a good name for a poet, spokesperson, or a writer, for it brings poetry, inspiration, communication, and wisdom.

Balor: (pronounced "BAIL lore"): Irish. King of the Fomors. Husband to Danu. He possessed a magic eye which could kill just by looking at an opponent. His grandson Lugh killed him by throwing a rock into his magic eye. Balor is a good magical name for those who seek enlightenment, foresight, and the ability to see beyond the facades of others to their true motivations.

By the sensual pleasures he gives them, Krishna delights all women; at the touch of his limbs, as dark and gentle as a string of lotus-flowers, they know the delights of love, while the beauties in the heifer park kiss him to their hearts' content...May the learned souls, who seek ecstasy in Vishnu, learn from the song of Govinda awareness of what makes the essence of love!

—Gita-Govinda

Borvo: Celtic. European Celtic God of hot springs. This would be a good name for a hot tub. It is also a name which is beneficial for inducing healing, comfort, relaxation, and letting go.

Bres: Irish. Husband to Brighid. Was king of the Tuatha but lacked the generosity and compassion which are necessary to rule. He was satirized, ridiculed, and labelled unfit to rule. This is a name to take to learn from your mistakes; for developing generosity, compassion, leadership abilities, and, most importantly, to listen to and learn from those around you.

Cernunnos (pronounced "ker NU nos"): Celtic. Horned nature God. Portrayed with animals. The details of the mythology of Cernunnos are lost, but from our experiences during drawing down this God, it can be assumed that he was a God of the basic wild forest energies, the running of the deer, and the chattering of the tiny creatures. He is of moss and lichen, antler and wood. He is of wild mating and valiant dying. This, then, would be a name for one who seeks the hushed tranquillity of the forest, knowledge of the cycles of life, and the fertility, longevity, and strength represented by an old forest.

Creidhne (pronounced "KREEN nah"): Irish. Bronze worker who made the weapons with which the Tuatha de Danann defeated the Fomors. A name which works for any artesian, metal worker, sculptor, or smithy. It also speaks of skill, cunning, and victory.

Cu Chulainn (pronounced "koo HUH len"): Irish. The greatest warrior hero of the Irish myths. Setanta (his boyhood name) killed the hound of Culain and took up the dog's duties of guarding the dog's owner, earning the name Cu Chulainn ("hound of Culain"). He was a hero of many adventures from youth onward. His stamina was astounding. He died in a great single-handed defense of Ulster; when too tired to stand, he tied himself to a post and died still fighting. This is a powerful name which brings valor, honor, strength, dedication, strength of will, victory, dedication to the Goddess Morrigan, and all positive warrior traits. My husband carries this name to empower his work with Wiccan anti-defamation. His sword, too, is pledged to the Morrigan.

Daghda (pronounced "dagda"): Irish. The good God. Main God of the Tuatha de Danann. He was a warrior, magician, artisan, and sage. He was a mighty warrior who possessed the cauldron of plenty from which no one left unsatisfied. His name brings strength, wisdom, fertility, sexual potency, abundance, protection, valor, hospitality, and rebirth.

Diancecht (pronounced "DIANE kecked"): Irish. Healer God of the Tuatha de Danann. This name brings healing skill, artistry, compassion, and kindness.

Diarmuid (pronounced "dermud"): Irish. Hero of a love myth involving Grainne, who was betrothed to Fionn Mac Cumhail. She and Diarmuid fell in love and ran away. Diarmuid was eventually killed by a boar. The Celtic love God took pity on them and breathed life into Diarmuid's dead body. This is an excellent name to take when pursuing a love interest. The name brings romance, love, sexuality, passion, and desire.

Donn: Irish. Celtic God of the dead. A name for mourning the deceased and understanding death and rebirth.

Fergus: Irish. Lusty God of prodigious sexual appetites. A potent name for enhancing one's sexual capability.

Fergus Mac Roich (pronounced "fergus mack ROI"): Irish. King of Ulster who, for the love of Nessa, suffered exile. He became a tutor to Cuchulain. This name is one which brings the idea of a price tag attached to everything. One pays for things one wants. It is also about sacrifice, following your bliss regardless of the price, and moving on.

Fionn Mac Cumhail (pronounced "FINN mack COOL"): Irish. Also Fionn Maccumhaill. Son of the king of the Tuatha de Danann. All-knowing, long-lived (lived to be 200 years old) leader of the Fianna, a nomadic tribe of hunter warriors. This is a name which brings wisdom, longevity, and leadership.

Luchtaine (pronounced "luck TAINE"): Irish. The woodworker master who helped make the weapons with which the Tuatha de Danaan defeated the Fomors. This is a name that lends skill, craftsmanship, artistry, and creativity.

Lugh (pronounced "looh"): Irish. Also Lugh Samhioldanach ("of many arts") or Lugh Lamhfhada ("of the long hand"). Young God who supplanted the old God (Balor). This is a warrior name bringing power, youth, strength, and victory.

Mac Cecht (pronounced "mack KECKED"): Irish. Tuatha de Danann God who represents the Earth. Husband to Fodhla, the mother aspect of Ireland's trinity. This is an earth name bringing fertility, stability, and security.

Maccuill (pronounced "mack QUIHL"): Irish. Tuatha de Danann God symbolizing the primordial water element. Husband to Banbha, the crone aspect of the trinity which symbolized Ireland. This is a name for new beginnings, or for going back and exploring your own.

Macgreine (pronounced "mack GRAIN"): Irish. Tuatha de Danann God symbolizing the fire element. His wife, Eire, was the maiden aspect of Ireland's trinity. This name brings passion, youth, determination, and drive.

It happened long ago, and this is how we tell it to our children.

One day Earth went to her mate, Lugh sky God, and said "man, our youngest child, is forgetting me. He's prideful and won't even speak to his brother animals...Go and give him a swift kick since he's grown too full of himself to listen to me."

So Lugh called all of his children, the men, the fish, the birds and the animals, to stand before him, and he said to man: "now listen to your mother Earth."

They tried, but had truly forgotten the language. Then Lugh said "speak to your brother animals." But all had forgotten how except a few of the smallest men, who were among Earth's favorites because she made them first. Only these were able to speak to their mother and brothers.

The other man-children grew jealous. "What's so good about speaking to a wolf and cat and bird when we're bigger and better in

*every way? We don't even
call them brothers
anymore."*

*"Let it be so, then." Lugh
decided.*

*And Earth said "let it be
so. They're not your
brothers since you are no
longer my children. Go be
what you will, but only
these small ones who
remember me will be called
true men, my prydn, the
first ones, the only men
worthy of the name."*

*The other children have
been jealous ever since,
maybe because they wish
they'd kept the language of
Earth, but Earth meant
what she said.*

*...We never forget our
bond with Earth and Lugh.
Each year at Lughnassad,
the story is told to the
new children so that they
remember their real
parents and their true
name.*

—Parke Godwin
Firelord

Manannan Mac Lir (pronounced "manan ARN mack leer"): Irish. God of the sea. Husband to Fand, Goddess of healing. He possessed a magic cauldron which Cu Chulainn stole. This name brings water energy, swift movement, abundance, and power. It is also about the loss (and reclaiming) of valuable things.

Miach (pronounced "mee ACK"): Irish. A physician. When Nuada lost his hand, Miach made him a silver hand to replace it. Diancecht killed him for doing so. This is a name which brings healing powers, especially when suffering the loss of a limb.

Mider: Irish. Gaelic king of the underworld. Husband of the Goddess of reincarnation. This name lends the bearer an appreciation of the cycles of life, coping with death, renewed hope, and rejuvenation.

Nuada Argetlamh (pronounced "NU ada ahr GET lam"): Irish. King of the Tuatha de Danann who lost his hand in battle and because he was no longer physically perfect, gave up his throne. He obtained a silver hand and regained his throne, after which he was known as Argetlamh ("silver hand"). This is a good name for making the best out of a bad situation, for adaptation, creativity, and overcoming handicaps.

Oghma (pronounced "OG mah"): Irish. God of wisdom and writing. This name would be helpful to a writer, student, poet, philosopher, or someone who wished to become one of these.

Pooka: Irish. An ancient Pre-Celtic God who degenerated into a malicious spirit. This name is suggestive of a deterioration of fortune. It is for overcoming such downfalls and learning from them.

Shoney: Scottish and Irish Celtic. Sea God. A water energy name bringing with it the power of the sea, which can awaken psychic abilities and bring insight, prophetic dreams, and wisdom.

Norse/Teutonic Gods

Aegir: Scandinavian. Sea God. He lives with his wife and daughters in a palace under the sea lit by the gleam of sunken treasure. They work together to lure sailors to their doom. A water name. Also a name which brings a sense of working together as a team, an acceptance of death as part of the cycle, and working within that context.

Balder: Norse. Most beautiful of the Norse Gods; God of the sun. A name to use for improving self-esteem, confidence, wisdom, and pride.

Donar: Teutonic. Thunder God. Known as Thunar to the Anglo Saxons and Thor to Scandinavians. (See Thor.)

Farbauti: Scandinavian. Fire God. He gave birth to fire and his wife was a wooded isle who fed the fire. A fire name which brings the warmth of the home fire, domesticity, the magic of the flame, and rewards for labor.

Frey: Norse. God of weather and fruitfulness. Protector of marriage. A name which brings fertility, solidity, and the power to weather the storm.

Heimdahl: Norse. Guardian of the rainbow bridge, Bifrost, which leads from Earth to the home of the Gods. He is the son of many virgins and is tall, handsome, and fertile. This is a fertility name, a name for bringing safety on a trip, for travelling to extraordinary places, and for confidence in one's travels.

Hoder/Hodur: Norse. God of night. Blind son of Odin. A name for dealing with darkness and the unknown.

Hoeni/Hoenir: Norse. God who gave the first humans the ability to move and think. A name which suggests fleetness, intelligence, and the ability to bestow these traits in others. A good name for a physical therapist.

Loki: Scandinavian. Trickster God. A quick-witted, silver-tongued, cunning, crafty, and unpredictable God. A God who can be a great asset or painful liability, but always unique. A name to be used for breaking free of regimen, learning not to rely on routine, and accepting the crazy twists and turns in life and "lightening up." When you take on the name Loki, anything may happen. Just let it.

Mimir: Norse. God of prophecy. Guardian of the meadow of poets, and streams and lakes. A name for wisdom, prophecy, poetry, insight, inspiration, intuition, and water energy.

Njord: Norse. Also Niord or Njoerd. Husband to Skadi, who longed for her native mountains while she lived at Njord's seashore. She eventually left to return home. A name about allowing others the freedom to follow their bliss. A name for becoming less controlling, less commanding, and for no longer needing everything your way.

Odin: Norse. Supreme God. Warrior's God who also oversaw poetry, magic, and the underworld. A father name which brings fertility, creativity, power, strength, courage, and the poetic heart of the true warrior.

Sigmund: Norse. Warrior hero who pulled a sword from a tree, which Odin had placed there. He was thereafter a victorious warrior until Odin struck him down. Sigmund refused to be healed and chose to submit himself to Odin's will. This is a name for ridding oneself from being too controlling; for doing the best you can with the tools you have and leaving the rest to the Gods. This is a name for an overachiever, a workaholic, or a perfectionist who wants to be less controlling.

Thor: Norse. God of thunder and the sky. Peasant's God. A name which brings power, authority, support for the working class; useful for letting out pent-up anger and expressing one's feelings.

Ull: Norse. God of skiers. A good name to take when you hit the slopes.

Phoenician Gods

Adad: Also Addu or Hadad. Storm God who brings fertilizing rain. A fertility name. On a different level, a storm God name often brings rewards for dealing with one's stormy (or violent) emotions.

Adoni: Vegetation God. Mate of Astarte. He has his cycle of growth, death, and rebirth. This name is an excellent one for grasping the cycle of life and death, for rejuvenation, growth, and coping with growing old.

Aleyin: Also Aleion, Aleyn. God of springtime weather. Ruler of rainfall, clouds, and wind. A blustering, replenishing, fertility-causing name.

Baal: Vegetation and storm God. A fertility name that brings the winds of change.

Dagon: Sea God. A water elemental name.

Eliun: Primordial Father God. Husband to Beruth, the Mother Goddess. In terms of a magical name, Eliun is one to bring fertility, the components necessary for new beginnings, and rejuvenation.

Eshmun/Esmun: Healer God. Means "he whom we invoke." For use when healing is of paramount consideration.

Genos: Means "race." He was the first person. His children were "first-born" and "life." His grandchildren were "light," "fire," and "flame." This is a name which suggests beginnings; going back to one's origins to work on old baggage.

Hey-Tau: Ancient tree God. A forest God who brings stability, prosperity, and protection.

Kathar-Wa-Hasis: Craftsman God. A good name for a woodworker, sculptor, iron worker, or artist of any description.

Kolpia: Wind God. To invite the winds of change to sweep through your house.

Pontus: Means "sea." Sea God. Son of the Earth Mother. A water energy name involving creativity and new beginnings.

Salem: Also Shalem or Shelim. Means "evening star." A name which brings a faint glimmer of understanding, a subtle enlightenment, and the attainment of your wishes.

Roman Gods

Aeolus: Roman and Greek. God of wind. He keeps the wind chained in deep caverns on a distant island. This is a powerful air name bringing insight, intelligence, change, and power.

Bonus Eventus: Means "good outcome." God of good luck. Also a God of the harvest. A name to encourage prosperity, good fortune, and success.

Cupid: God of love. Son of Venus. He was the God of lovers. It was to him people came to ask for love and romance. This is a good name for a lonely man who seeks true love and romance to fill his empty life.

Faunus: God of forests and merrymaking. Means "the kindly one." He oversees the fruitfulness of the fields and of animals. He had psychic powers. This is a name of fertility, protection of the forests and the forest animals, and for learning to hear the whisper of the oracle in the depth of an old-growth forest.

Janus: God of beginnings. He watched over the doors and gates. He was seen as having two heads looking in opposite directions. Sacred to him were the first hour of the day, the first day of the week, and the first month of the year. This is an excellent name for new beginnings, new partnerships, business ventures, relationships, new jobs, or the beginning of anything to insure it goes smoothly.

Jupiter/Jove: Sky God. Supreme deity in Roman myth. Also known as Jupiter Lucetius (light-bringer). The full moon and the Ides were sacred to him. He is a God of thunder and lightning. His temples were erected upon places that had been struck by lightning. He acted as a conscience for his followers, being concerned with oaths, alliances, and treaties. He was also involved with protection and guardianship. This is a good name for a father to help guide, protect, guard, and teach the value of one's word.

Lares: Protector and God of crossroads. A good name to take to bring safe and uneventful travel.

Mars: War God. Father of Romulus. Also an agricultural God protecting the fields from disease in times of peace. He was summoned in the spring with a shaking of his sacred spears and the cry "Mars vigila!" ("Mars, wake up!") when war was at hand. Laurel is sacred to him. His name can be used as a protective, powerful, and awe-inspiring name. It can be used to increase your assertiveness, strength of will, conviction, and resolve.

Mercury: God of trade. He insures good harvests and abundant trading. This is a good name for those who seek success in business or who are looking for a job. It is especially good for sales work.

Neptune: Sea God. Husband to Salacia, Goddess of salt water. This is a powerful water name bringing the power of the sea, intuition, and a depth of emotion. This is a particularly good name for someone who is shut off from his emotions and unable to deal with his feelings.

Orcus: God of Death. An underworld God, and the name of the underworld itself. He stole the living from the earth by force and took them to the underworld. This is a name for dealing with the seemingly meaningless and cruel aspects of death.

Penates: Household Gods. The domain of these protective Gods is indoors, as opposed to the Gods of the outdoors (Lares). The Penates protected the hearth and home, pantry and larder. There was a shrine honoring the Penates just inside the front door of a house so one might honor them as they entered. This is a name to charge with protection of one's hearth and family.

Picunnus: God of newborn babies. He and his brother Pilumnus are protectors of babies. They were made welcome in the bedrooms of hopeful parents. This is a fertility name or one to bring protection to infants.

Saturn: God of agriculture. He is a God of sowing seed. He is seen holding a sickle or ear of corn which symbolizes abundance. This name brings with it abundance, fertility, plenty, success, and prosperity.

Silvanus: God of uncleared land. He oversees the clearing and ploughing of wild land. This is a good name to take when one begins a new garden or builds a house on uncleared land.

Summanus: God of nighttime thunder. Brings change, energy, courage, and power. In addition it also suggests mystery and dealing with that which is hidden (perhaps hidden fears?).

Vertumnus: Shape-shifting God of gardens and orchards. Consort of Pomona. This name brings fertility, abundance, protection, fruitfulness, and growth. Great name for a gardener.

Vulcan: God of Fire. Husband to Venus, Goddess of love. He was a feared God, bringing fire when it wasn't wanted. To placate him, shrines were set up outside the walls of the city to ask protection of things which might readily burn, such as storage houses full of dry grain. This is a name which brings fire energy, temper, rage, and destruction. Use it carefully; it can bring motivation, but it cuts both ways.

Welsh Gods

Amathaon (pronounced "am ah THAY on"): A magician, son of the Goddess Don. "Amaeth," the root word from which his name springs, means ploughman or farmer. In *The Mabinogi,* the book of Welsh folk tales, it says "The only husbandman who can farm land or prepare it is Amaethon son of Don, so wild is it." This suggests a name which is a combination of magician and farmer. Anyone who has gardened knows there is potent magic at work. This name would be taken to understand more about the magic that causes plants to grow. It would also be for helping to tame wildness, increasing fertility, and for planting the seeds of self-transformation.

Arawn (pronounced "ah ROAN"): King of the Otherworld, Annwn ("ah NOOIN"). He rides a white horse in pursuit of a stag and is followed by his red-eared, white hunting dogs. This is a name for understanding or accepting death, for recovering from grief at losing a loved one, or for dealing with troubling transitions in life.

Beli (pronounced "BAY ley"): Father God. Husband to Don, father to Arianrhod, grandfather to Lleu. Seen as a great progenitor. This is a name which brings fatherhood and being the head of a large extended family.

Belanus (pronounced "bell ANN ous"): Welsh/Roman. An underworld God. A name for a sage.

Bran: Welsh/Manx. Son of Llry and Iweridd, brother to Branwen. He was killed when avenging the death of his sister, but his head was brought back and it continued to speak, giving counsel for eighty years. Bran is a good name for one who likes to speak, or perhaps for endowing a shy person with the ability to speak comfortably (and at length). This is a name which brings strong communication skills.

Caswallawn (pronounced "cass WHAH hlaon"): A usurper of England. Uncle/cousin to Bran and Branwen. He has a cloak of invisibility which he used to cause calamity. This name suggests slyness, sneakiness, deviousness, and guile. If you have need of these things, then this is the name for you.

Dylan: Sea God. Son of Arianrhod and Gwydion. He married the Lady of the Lake, who bore him Vivienne (or Nimue), who became Merlin's lover. This is a name which brings magic, fertility, and magical children.

Gwydion (pronounced "gwid EE ohn"): Bard and magician. Son of Don and brother to Arianrhod; together they parented Lleu Llau Gyffes and Dylan. He was taught the secrets of magic by Math. Gwydion killed Pryderi. This is another of the many magical, mystical, and wizardly names in the Welsh pantheon.

Idris the Giant: He was an astrologer of such mastery that he could foretell the rest of history. A wonderful name for a student of astrology.

Llyr (pronounced "hleer"): Welsh, Manx, and Irish. Father to Branwen, Bran, Creiddylad, and Manannan mac Lir. His four eldest children were turned into swans by his second wife. Origin of Shakespeare's King Lear. A father name to bring responsibility, sound judgement, and fertility.

Mabon (pronounced "may BON"): Means "great son." Known as Maponus to the Romans. A hunter God, son of Modron (meaning "great mother"). He was kidnapped with he was an infant and rescued by Arthur. He is seen as a male version of Persephone. Gwair is another name of Mabon (the prisoner who must be released). This imprisonment aspect to the character is very strong. It can be used for those who find themselves trapped (in a dead-end job, bad marriage, debt, etc.) and seek ways to escape. Taking the name of one who was trapped and rescued would help release the bonds.

Manawyddan (pronounced "mana oo EETH ann"): Son of Llyr. Brother of Bran and Branwen. Husband to Rhiannon, Goddess of the Underworld. He was a tanner, but was a master of any task to which he set his hand. A good name for bringing skill, mastery, or a job in trade work.

Math ap Mathonwy (pronounced "math ap math OHN whee"): Father to Don. A magician. He has the ability to hear news on the wind. He is omniscient, well-rooted in the earth, stable, and severe. This is a name for a magician to bring out the stabilizing earth energy and further develop one's magical abilities.

Myrddin (pronounced "MIRTH in"): Welsh/British. Also Merlin, Emerys. The British Zeus. Early legendary wizard and bard. England once bore the name Clas Merdin

("Myrddin's enclosure"). He is a guardian of Britain, said to have been buried beneath Stonehenge (at sea, in a dense forest, and on Bardsey Island, say other myths), who will arise when he is needed. Has sky God attributes and his resting place is referred to as his airy tomb. A wise, magical, powerful, vulnerable, and protective name.

Nwyvre (pronounced "new EEE vear"): Means sky, space, or stars. Space God. Arianrhod's husband. He slipped into almost total obscurity. Since we know so little about his nature and his realm, we must assign our own meanings to him. He is a space God, dealing with that outside of the bonds of earth. Perhaps he has disappeared until we took up space travel and have need of him. It may be time to bring him back.

Pryderi (pronounced "PREED ahrie"): Son of Pwyll and Rhiannon. Rhiannon was thought to have killed him when he was an infant and was punished for it, but he returned and revealed that he had been abducted. His name means "free from anxiety." He suffered misunderstanding and enmity of the Gods. He was slain by the magician Gwydion. This is a name which describes a tolerance for abuse and an ability to wait out injustice and captivity to be free from anxiety. This is a good transitional name for someone who must suffer abuse while he plans the changes he must make to leave an abusive situation.

Taliesin (pronounced "tally EE sin"). Means "radiant brow." Son of Cerridwen. The supreme seer poet who lives in the region of the summer stars. He is a harper, sage, seer, poet, initiate, and wizard. The name suggests these talents.

Ysbadadden (pronounced "ees bah DATH ehn"): Father of Olwyn. He was to die if his daughter married, and he was not able to prevent her marriage. The father, daughter, and husband represent the sacrificial trinity as in Holly King/Oak King and May Queen archetypes. The maiden is fought over by an old love and a young love, with the youthful one always victorious. These three represent the spring maiden, her winter lover, and her summer lover. Ysbadadden is the older, winter figure, a father or older man who is bowing to the younger men and forgoing the young women. This is a good name to take at a saging ritual (a male equivalent of a croning).

NAMES FROM ENGLISH HISTORY

Since the departure of the Roman legions from Britain in the fifth century, England's government has been a monarchy. The names given to heirs to the throne were indicative of the trends in nomenclature of the day. I have listed those kings and queens before the Norman conquest. By seeing the changes in names of its rulers, you can see the passage of key events in Britain's history. Take note of the unusual (by today's standards) names of the rulers. These names soon became popular among the people. Some of the names listed here might make a good name for use as a public craft name, an SCA (Society for Creative Anachronism) name, pseudonym, literary character name, pet name, or coven or covenstead name.

The Rulers of Britain

SAXONS

Egbert (802–839), Queen Redburga

Aethelwulf ("ETHEL wolf") (839–858), Queens Osburga and Judith Aethelbald ("ETHEL bald") (855–860); Queen Judith (his stepmother)

Aethelberht ("ETHEL bert") (860–865)

Aethelred ("ETHEL red") (865–871)

Alfred (871–899), Queen Ealhswith ("ELS with")

Edward the Elder (899–924), Queens Ecgwynn ("eck WIN"), Aelfflaed, and Eadgifu ("ed GIFU")

Athelstan ("ETHEL stan") (924–939)

Edmond I (939–946), Queens Aethelflaed ("ETHEL layed") and Aelfgifu

Eadred ("EAD rid") (946–955)

Eadwig ("EAD wig") (955–959), Queen Aethelflaed

Edgar (959–975), Queens Aethelflaed and Aelfthryth ("ELF rith")

Edward the Martyr (975–978)

Aethelred II the Unready (979–1016), Queens Aelgifu and Emma

Edmund II Ironside (1016), Queen Ealdgyth ("EL gith")

DANISH KINGS

Canute (1016–1035), Queens Aelfgifu of Northhampton and Emma (widow of Aethelred II)

Harold I Harefoot (1035–1040)

Edward the Aetheling (1040), Queen Agatha (niece of Henry II, Emperor of Germany)

Harthacnut ("harth ACK nut") (1040–1042)

Edward the Confessor (1042–1066), Queen Edith

Harold II (1066), Queen Ealdgyth

9

Magical Names from Distant Circles

In this chapter, I have included some beautiful magical names from other languages; these are popular names in other lands. (Some of these names are also listed elsewhere in this book.) Many of these names are beautiful-sounding names whose magical meanings are hidden as the name is unfamiliar. This may be important to people who follow a Goddess religion but are not public about it. They may not want to name their daughter Moonlight, but the lovely name Chantrea appears as a beautiful, unusual name with no visible craft connection. You might like the lyrical sound of the name Mahina; you probably wouldn't call your daughter Moon, but that is what Mahina means in Polynesian. This is a great way to name your child a Pagan name without overtly labeling him or her a Pagan.

Many of the names attributed to one culture are based upon words from yet another culture, or from a smaller group within that culture. For example, the Native North American name Tuwa (Earth) is from the Hopi tribe.

Afghani

Badria: Moonlike.
Mallalai: Pashtu. Beautiful.
Palwasha: Spark of light.

Roxanna (pronounced "rokh SHA nuh"):
    Sparkling.
Shahla ("SHEH luh"): Beautiful eyes.

Arabian

Akilah ("ah KEE lah"): One who reasons; intelligent.
Anan ("a NAHN"): Clouds.
Falak ("fa LAHK"): Star.
Fatin ("FAH teen"): Captivating.
Hana ("hah NAH"): Happiness.
Hilel: The new moon.

Kadir ("HAH der"): Green.
Khoury: Priest.
Sabir: Patient.
Shadi: Singer.
Talib ("TAH lib"): North African. Seeker.
Umm ("OOM"): North African. Mother.

Armenian

Anahid: Goddess of the moon.
Astrid: Persian. Star.

Nairi: Land of canyons.
Siran: Lovely.

Basque

Izar ("ee SAHR"): Star.
Lur: Earth.

Nora: Greek. Light.
Pellkita: Latin. Happy.

Burmese

Mima: Woman.

Mya: Emerald.

Cambodian

Chan: Sweet-smelling tree.
Chantrea ("CHAN thee ay"): Moonshine.

Dara: Stars.

Danish

Asta: Greek. Star.

Ethiopian

Desta: Happiness.
Fannah: Fun.

Seble: Autumn.

Finnish

Ametisti ("AH may tis tea"): Amethyst.
Eeva ("EH vuh"): Life.
Haltijatar ("HAHL ti yah tahr"): Fairy.
Haukka ("HOUK kah"): Hawk.
Joki ("YOA key"): River.
Jumalatar ("YOU mah lah tar"): Goddess.
Kalevi ("KAHL ev ee"): Hero.

Kalwa ("KAHL wah"): Heroic.
Kesa ("KAY sah"): Summer.
Kevat ("KAY vaht"): Spring.
Kunta ("KOON tah"): Commune.
Kuu ("KOO"): The moon.
Lahde ("LAH day"): Spring.
Lilja ("LEEL yah"): Lily.

Linna ("LIN nah"): Castle.
Luuta ("LOO tah"): Broom.
Maaginen ("MAA gi nayn"): Magic.
Meri ("MAY ri"): Sea.
Metsa ("MAYT sa" [sa as in "sat"]): Forest.
Metsikko ("MAYT sik kur"): Grove.
Noita ("NOI tah"): Witch.
Moituus ("NOI tooss"): Witchcraft, magic.

Onnellinen ("OAN nayl li nayn"): Happy.
Onyksi ("OA newk si"): Onyx.
Satu ("SAH too"): Fairy tale.
Syksy ("SEWK sew"): Autumn.
Talvi ("TAHL vi"): Winter.
Timantti ("TI mahnt ti"): Diamond.
Vesiputous ("VAY si poo toa ooss"): Waterfall.

French

Artur: Celtic. Noble, bear man.
Blaise: Latin. Stammerer (also Blaize).
Candide: Pure white.
Demitri: Greek. From Demeter, Goddess of the harvest.
Denis: Greek. God of wine.
Fantine: Childlike.
Gustave: Teutonic. Staff of Gods.
Isidore: Greek. A gift of ideas.
Laure: Crowned with laurels (also Laurel, Laura, Laurelle).

Marlon: Little falcon (also Marlin, Merlin).
Morgance: Sea-dweller (Morgane).
Natacha: Born at Yule (also Nathalie, Natalie).
Prisca: The ancient.
Sylvie: From the forest (also Sylvianne, Sylvette, Silvia, Silvaine).
Tatiana: Russian. Fairy queen.
Vivien: Lively (also Vivienne, Viviane).

Greek

Aretha: Nymph.
Calandra: Lark.
Charis ("KAHR is"): Love.
Cloris: Goddess of flowers.
Damia: Goddess of the forces of nature.
Delia: Goddess of the moon.
Kalliope ("kahl ee O pee"): Beautiful voice.

Medea: Part Goddess, part sorceress.
Phaedra: Mythological figure.
Silas: Forest (also Silvanos).
Skatoulaki ("skah TOO lah key"): Little shithead.
Thea: Goddess.
Vanessa: Butterfly.

Hawaiian

Haimi: The seeker.
Kahoku ("kuh HOH koo"): The star.
Kaili ("kah EE lee"): Hawaiian deity.
Kaimi ("kah EE mee"): Polynesian. Seeker.
Kala ("kuh LAH"): Sun.
Kala: Princess.
Kalama: Polynesian. Flaming torch.

Kali ("KAH lee"): Spear carrier.
Kele: Seahorse.
Keoki ("keh OH kee"): Farmer.
Kika: From the forest.
Koka: A Scotsman.
Kolika: From the ocean.
Konane ("ko NAH neh"): Bright as moonlight.

Laka: Goddess of the hula.
Lani: Sky.
Leilani: Sky child.
Lono: God of peace and farming.
Luana: Enjoyment.
Lukela ("loo KEH luh"): Like a fox.
Mahina: Polynesian. Moon.
Makani: Wind.

Mana: Polynesian. Supernatural power.
Mapuana ("mah poo AH nuh"): Wind-blown fragrance.
Nahele ("nah HEH leh"): Forest, grove of trees.
Peni ("PEH nee"): Weaver.

Indian

Aditi: Hindu. Goddess.
Ambar: Hindu. Sky.
Ambika: Hindu. Goddess of power and destruction (also Sakti).
Amma: Mother Goddess (also Mata, Amba, Mahamba, Bimba).
Amritha: God.
Anala: Fire.
Anila: Hindu. Wine God.
Chandra: Hindu. Moon; moon God.
Daru: Hindu. Pine or cedar.
Devi ("DAY vee"): Hindu. Name of Goddess Sakti.
Ellama: Hindu. Mother Goddess.

Ganesha ("guh NAY shuh"): God of good luck and wisdom.
Guri: Hindu. Goddess of abundance.
Hema: Hindu. Daughter of the mountains.
Indra: Hindu. God of power.
Manda: Hindu. Saturn; God of the occult.
Matrika: Hindu. Mother.
Mitra: Hindu. God of daylight.
Sesha: Hindu. Symbol of time.
Shashi: Hindu. Moonbeam.
Sita: Hindu. Mother earth Goddess.
Soma: Hindu. Moon.

Italian

Argento: Silver.
Capra: Goat.
Cascata: Waterfall.
Chiaro di Luna: Moonlight.
Corrente: Stream, current.
Dea: Goddess.
Dio: God.
Incanto: Witchery.
Luce stellare: Starlight.
Luna: Moon.
Magico: Magician.
Mago: Mage.
Maliardo: Sorcerer.
Merlino: Merlin.
Mistico: Mystic.

Mita: Myth.
Pagano: Pagan.
Quercia: Oak.
Raggio lunare: Moonbeam.
Salice: Willow.
Scintillante: Twinkling.
Scintillare: Twinkle.
Sirena: Mermaid.
Stella: Star.
Stellato: Starlit.
Strega: Female Witch.
Stregone: Male Witch.
Stregoneria: Witchcraft.
Sucente: Starlike.
Torrente: Torrent.

Irish

GIRL'S NAMES

Affrica: Gaelic. Pleasant.

Arienh ("A reen"): Gaelic. Pledge.

Bebhinn ("BEH vin"): Melodious lady (also Bevin).

Briana: Celtic. Strong.

Bride: Celtic. Strength (also Briget, Bridget, Brighid, Brid, Breed).

Caitlin ("KAT leen" or "KATE lin"): Pure.

Erin: Gaelic. Peace.

Fiona ("FEE oh nah" or "FEE nah"): Celtic. White, fair.

Glynis: Gaelic. Valley.

Grainne ("GROH nyuh"): Grace.

Ide ("EED uh"): Old Irish. Thirst.

Kelly: Gaelic. Warrior.

Kennocha ("ken OH kuh"): Celtic. Beauty.

Kerry: Gaelic. Dark-haired (also Keriann).

Kinnat/Keenat: Traditional name.

Lasairiona ("las a REE nuh"): Flame wine.

Luighseach ("LOO seh"): Bringer of life (also Lucy).

Mave: Mirth.

Mavelle: Celtic. Songbird.

Morgan: Celtic. Sea dweller.

Moya: Celtic. Great.

Rowena: Celtic. White mane.

Sheena: God's gift.

Siobhan ("shuh VAHN"): Hebrew. Gracious.

Sorcha: Old Irish. Clear, bright.

Tara: Celtic. Tower.

Una ("OO nuh"): Unity.

BOY'S NAMES

Aidan: Celtic. Flame, fiery.

Aindreas ("AHN dree ahs"): Manly.

Artur: Celtic. Noble, bear man.

Baird: Ballad singer.

Bevan: Celtic. Youthful warrior.

Brenainn ("BREH neen"): Celtic. Sword.

Brendan: Gaelic. Raven.

Brett: Celtic. From Brittany.

Broin ("bree AHN"): Raven (also Brennan).

Carlin: Gaelic. Little champion.

Cian (keen): Ancient name (also Cein, Kian, Kean).

Cillian ("KEEL yan"): War (also Killian).

Colla: Ancient Irish name.

Conary ("KOH ner ee"): Ancient Irish name.

Conroy: Celtic. Wise man.

Conway: Gaelic. Hound of the plain.

Corey: From the hollow.

Cu Uladh ("koo ULL uh"): Hound of Ulster.

Cullan: Celtic. Handsome one (also Cullin, Cully, Collin).

Dagda: Good God.

Daibheid ("DEH vid"): Beloved (also David, Daibid).

Daire ("DEH ruh"): Old Irish. (also Dary, Darragh).

Dallas: Gaelic. Wise.

Daray: Gaelic. Dark.

Derry: Gaelic. Red-haired.

Devin: Celtic. A poet.

Donagh: Brown warrior, high king; son of Brian Boru.

Donahue: Gaelic. Dark warrior.

Donovan: Celtic. Dark warrior.

Dub h Dara: Black man of the oak.

Duncan: Celtic. Dark man.

Erin: Gaelic. Peace.

Evan: Young warrior.

Faolan ("FEH lahn"): Wolf (also Felan).

Farrell: Celtic. Courageous.

Farry: Manly.

Ferris: Greek. The rock (also Farris).

Fionan ("FIN ee ahn"): fair.
Gannon: Gaelic. Fair of face.
Giolla Bhrighde ("GIL a BREED"): Servant of bride.
Glen: Celtic. Valley.
Innis: Celtic. Island.
Kearney: Celtic. Warrior.
Keegan: Gaelic. Little and fiery one (also Kegan).
Keir (care): Celtic. Dark-skinned (also Kerr, Kern, Kearn, Kerry).
Labhras ("LAU rahsh"): Laurel.
Lochlain ("LOKH lan"): Home of Norsemen.
Logan: Gaelic. From the hollow.
Maghnus ("MAKH nus"): Great.
Mahon: Bear; brother of High King Brian Boru.

Mannix: Monk.
Morven: Celtic. Mariner.
Nealon: Celtic. Champion (also Neal).
Nolan: Gaelic. Famous.
Padraig ("PAH dreek"): Latin. Noble (also Patric, Padraic).
Roibin ("ROH bin"): Diminutive of Roibeard (Roh Bahrd).
Rory: Teutonic. Famous ruler.
Scully: Gaelic. Town crier.
Seamus ("SHEE a mus"): The supplanter (also Shemus).
Sean/Shawn: Hebrew. God's gift (also Seaghan, Shane, Shan).
Searlas ("SHAR las"): Full-grown; manly (also Charles).
Uaine ("OON yuh"): Old Irish.
Wynne: Celtic. White, fair.

Kenyan

Barika: Swahili. Bloom.
Dalila ("dah LEE lah"): Swahili. Gentle.
Machupa ("mah CHOO pah"): Likes to drink.
Makalani ("mah kah LAH nee"): One skilled in writing.
Mwasaa ("m wah SAH"): Swahili. Timely.

Paka: Swahili. Pussycat.
Pili ("PEE lee"): Swahili. Second-born.
Sadiki ("sah DEE kee"): Swahili. Faithful.
Sanura ("sah NOO rah"): Swahili. Kitten.
Shani ("SHAH nee"): Swahili. Marvellous.
Sikudhani ("see koo THAN nee"): A surprise; unusual.

Latin

Ardere: Fire.
Ars Magica: Arts magical.
Astrum: Star.
Cervus: Stag.
Deus: God.
Dia: Goddess.
Diva: Goddess.
Divus: God.
Fabula: Myth.
Lumen: Star.
Luna: Moon.

Lunae Lumen: Moonlight.
Magice: Magic.
Magus: Magician.
Paganus: Pagan.
Quercus: Oak.
Saga: Witch.
Sagus: Prophetic.
Siderbus Inlustris: Starlight.
Stella: Star.
Stellifer: Starlight.

Native North American

Aleshanee: Coos. She plays all the time.
Amitola: Rainbow.
Aponi: Butterfly.

Awenasa: Cherokee. My home.
Awenita: Fawn.
Ayita: Cherokee. First in the dance.

Elsu: Falcon flying.

Enola: Alone.

Gaho: Mother.

Hakan: Fiery.

Hinto: Dakota. Blue.

Hinun ("hee NOON"): God of clouds and rain.

Ilia: Meaning unknown.

Iye ("EE yeh"): smoke.

Jacy: Tupi-Guarani. Moon; creator of all plants.

Jolon: Valley of dead oaks.

Kachina: Sacred dancer.

Kai: Navaho. Willow tree.

Karmiti: Inuit. Trees.

Kaya: Hopi. My elder sister.

Kimama: Shoshone. Butterfly.

Leotie ("leh o TEE eh"): Prairie flower.

Litonya: Miwok. Hummingbird darting.

Lulu: Rabbit.

Luna: Zuni. Moon.

Macawi: Lakota. Motherly.

Macha: Lakota. Aurora.

Mahal: Woman.

Mahkah: Lakota. Earth.

Mamid: Chippewa. The star dancer.

Mascha: Navaho. Owl.

Masou ("mah SO OO"): Fire deity.

Meda: Prophet.

Miakoda: Power of the moon.

Migina: Omaha. Returning moon.

Mimiteh: Omaha. New moon.

Nahimana: Lakota. Mystic.

Nasnan: Carrier. Surrounded by a song.

Nata-Akon: Chippewa. Expert canoeist.

Niabi: Osage. Fawn.

Nidawi: Omaha. Fairy girl.

Nita: Choctaw. Bear.

Nokomis: Iroquois. White or fair woman.

Nova: Hopi. Chasing a butterfly.

Nuna: Land.

Omusa: Miwok. Missing things when shooting with arrows.

Onatah: Iroquois. Corn spirit, daughter of the earth.

Orenda: Iroquois. Magic power.

Pelipa: Zuni. Lover of horses.

Raini: Tupi-Guarani. Deity who created the world.

Satinka: Magic dancer.

Sedna: Inuit. Goddess of food.

Snana: Lakota. Jingles like little bells.

Tadewi: Omaha. Wind.

Taigi: Omaha. Returning new moon.

Taima: Crash of thunder.

Taini: Omaha. Coming new moon.

Tala: Wolf.

Tama: Thunderbolt.

Tateeyopa: Lakota. Happy hostess, her door.

Tuwa: Hopi. Earth.

Waitilanni: Laguna. Wonder water.

Wakanda: Lakota. Inner magical power.

Scandinavian

Davin ("DAH vin"): The brightness of the Finns.

Disa: Active spirit.

Freya ("FRAY yah"): After Goddess Freyja.

Kaia ("KAH ee ah"): From Gaia, earth Goddess.

Karen ("KAH rehn"): Pure (also Kari, Karine, Katinka, Trine).

Laila: Finnish. Unknown meaning.

Scottish

Aaid: Gaelic. Magpie.

Baird: Gaelic. Poet.

Blair: Gaelic. Child of the fields.

Cameron: Celtic. Crooked nose.

Campbell: Celtic. Crooked mouth.

Coleen: Gaelic. Girl.

Duncan: Dark-skinned warrior.

Gaisgeil: Gaelic. Heroic, brave.

Geas: Gaelic. Sorcery, religious vow, metamorphosis, charm.

Geasachd: Gaelic. Enchantment, astrology.

Geasadair: Gaelic. Wizard.

Geasadioma: Gaelic. Druidic wizardry.

Gointe: Gaelic. Bewitched, fay.

Grian: Gaelic. Sun.

Grianchrisos: Gaelic. Zodiac.

Grianghamhstad: Gaelic. Winter Solstice.

Grianghath: Gaelic. Sunbeam.

Muir: Gaelic. Sea.

Muireannach: Gaelic. Female champion.

Muirn: Gaelic. Joy.

Murdachan: Gaelic. Mermaid.

Nuin: Gaelic. Ash tree.

Orra: Gaelic. Incantation, charm, or amulet.

Orraidheachd: Gaelic. Enchantments.

Orrtha: Music or bewitchery.

Orrthannan: Gaelic. Enchantment.

Osran: Gaelic. Peace.

Pogadh: Gaelic. Kissing.

Ruis: Gaelic. Elder tree.

Sgaileach: Gaelic. Shadowy, ghost-like.

Suil: Gaelic. Willow tree.

Uilioc: Gaelic. Mistletoe.

Uchdbhan: Gaelic. Fair-breasted.

Ur: Gaelic. Yew tree.

NAMES OF MYTHICAL PLACES

Alfheim: The home of elves or dwarves in the Norse mythological home of the Gods. Mountainous, idyllic country. Nice name for a rural (or you wish it were rural) covenstead.

Asgard: City of the Gods in Norse myth; it included Valhalla, Odin's great hall. Another good coven name is "Children of Asgard."

Atlantis: Fabled island. A place of highly developed technology and spirituality. A good name for a covenstead of techno-Pagans.

Avalon: Fabled island where Arthur was taken to die. Brought to life as the teaching isle of priestesses and bards in *The Mists of Avalon* by Marion Zimmer Bradley. A good name for anything which suggests magic.

Beyond the Crest of the Ninth Wave: To the Celts, their domain went out to the crest of the ninth ocean wave, beyond which was sidhe ("she"), the land of enchantment.

Bifrost: Rainbow bridge in Norse myths which leads to Asgard, home of the Gods.

Camelot: Fabled castle and place of Arthur's court. Suggests peace, love, and romance.

Delphi: Site of the oracle of Apollo. Good name for a psychic.

Elysium: The home of the blessed in the afterlife. Nice name for a covenstead.

Gladsheim: The abode of the Gods in Norse myth. Another good house name.

Mount Olympus: Home of the Greek Gods. A good name for a covenstead in the mountains.

Sidhe ("she"): Irish land of enchantment. A lovely name for an individual, a coven, or covenstead. It suggests mystery.

Summerland: Mythical place the dead go while awaiting reincarnation. A happy place name.

The Happy Isles: The free, sunny section of Hades. Another good covenstead name.

Valhalla: The Great Hall in Asgard in Norse myth. The home of heroes who die bravely in battle. A good covenstead name.

Vingolf: The abode of the Goddesses in Norse myth. A name for a Dianic coven or covenstead.

GEOGRAPHIC PLACE NAMES

The names of distant places ring in our imaginations, conjuring up personal images of what we imagine that place is like. Everyone's image of a place name is unique. This is a name choice which can be exotic, unique, and inspire different images with everyone who hears it. These are good magical names for travellers, wandering spirits, adventurers, or those who long to be. They are unique names for unique people.

Not every place name mentioned here is a powerful place sitting squarely on a ley line radiating positive energy. Some I chose because of beautiful or exotic images which I associate with the places, or merely for the lyrical sound of the name itself. Because these places are not famous magical places doesn't mean that these names are without power. An important aspect to bearing a powerful name is to empower it yourself. I have a friend with whom I've circled many, many times. Each time I'm in circle with him he uses his magical name, a very short and simple one, to call the quarters and so forth, but as soon as the circle comes down, I cannot remember his magical name. He wanted it to be private. He wanted it used only in circle. "What's his name" empowered the name for that purpose. You, too, can empower your names with whatever power you want them to hold. A competent Witch can empower the name of "Cleveland" to possess all the power and mystery of "Stonehenge."

These names have a magic of their own and do not need to be defined by location. Perhaps it would

"Tonight I must go to Asgard," he said. "I must confront my father, Odin, in the great hall of Valhalla and bring him to account for what he has done."

"You mean, for making you count Welsh pebbles?"

"No!" said Thor. "For making the Welsh pebbles not worth counting!"

Kate shook her head in exasperation. "I simply don't know what to make of you at all," she said. "I think I'm just too tired. Come back tomorrow. Explain it all in the morning."

"No," said Thor. "You must see Asgard yourself, and then you will understand. You must see it tonight." He gripped her by the arm.

"I don't want to go to Asgard," she insisted. "I don't go to mythical places with strange men. You go. Call me up and tell me how it went in the morning. Give him hell about the pebbles."

—Douglas Adams
The Long, Dark, Tea-Time of the Soul

soil the image of a lovely, exotic-sounding name to know it was a polluted river near the Love Canal. Take the name and redefine it with your personality. Reclaim the name!

Islands

Avalon
Ceylon
Crete
Cyprus
Devon
Ellesmere

Java
Samar
Sicily
Sumatra
Summer

Mountains

Borah
Cameroon
Etna
Kilimanjaro
Logan

McKinley
Meru
Pelee
Shasta
Vesuvius

Rivers

Aldan
Amazon
Athabasca
Colorado
Congo
Euphrates

Japura
Nile
Tigris
Wisla
Yukon
Zambezi

More Exotic Places

Africa
Ajax
Alexandria
America
Andorra
Anjou
Ankara
Antigua
Asia
Athens
Atlanta
Azore
Baku
Bangkok

Bolivia
Bombay
Brea
Bristol
Burma
Calcutta
Cameroon
Canterbury
Casablanca
Chad
Cheyenne
China
Cody
Dacca

Darien
Delhi
Denver
Diva
Dixie
Djakarta
Dover
Dresden
Faeroe
Far Hills
Fiji
Gabon
Geneva
Genoa
Ghana
Ghea
Giza
Harmony
Havanna
India
Jandira
Jannali
Jasai
Kashmir
Kawara
Killarney
Kirby
Kismet
Lanae
Landon
Mali
Malone
Malta
Martinique
Mecca
Miki
Montana
Nauru
Nepal
Oceania
Olympia
Once
Palermo
Papua
Paris

"Where on earth did you get a name like that?"

Peru
Phoenix
Pomona
Ramos
Rye
Senegal
Sikkim
Singapore
Somalia
Sri Lanka
Stonehenge
Tama

Tamara
Tamath
Tamon
Tamura
Thana
Tigre
Tonga
Utah
Valencia
Valentine
Vienna

10

Names for Covensteads and the Things Which Lurk Inside Them

COVENSTEAD NAMES

In Victorian times it was customary to name one's home. It was a much more romantic and creative, albeit not as efficient, system than today's cold and dehumanizing addresses. Who wouldn't rather live at Oakendale Hall than at 124570–142nd Street East, #1704? Naming the house in which you dwell is still a practice so common in England as to be frowned upon as conformative. Here in North America, however, it is still rare enough to be a refreshing idea. My husband and I name every house we live in. We've made carved wooden signs with the house name on it for homes we've lived in. We were delighted to see that after we had gone the next tenant would not only keep the sign up, but refer to the house by those names (names like "Gull Cottage" or "Bay House").

House names are usually names which describe the house (House of Seven Gables, Cedar Gate House, White Cottage), its location (Seaside House, Bay View, Mountain Vista, Green Pastures, Springfield, Stonebank, Thistledum, Gothumview), distinctive vegetation growing on the property (Tall Trees, Holly House, Fir Cottage, Cedar Hall, Willowbrook, Pine Junction, Oak Hall, Rose Cottage, Mistletoe Manor, Forest Glen), the house's poetic aspects (Elfin's Whispers, Hobbit Hole, Avalon Hall, Merlin's Bryn), mythological aspects (Valhalla Hall, Thorhammer Hall, Diana's Den, Olympia Fields, Summerland Estate, Loki's Lookout, Athena Acres, Home of the Olde Gods, The Green Man, Morrigan Manor, Castle Eris, Odin Valley, Hecate Hill), its uses (Summerland House, Summerset Hall, Coven's Glen, Palamino Pastures, Slaphappy House, Winter Haven, Tarryton, Restful Meadows), or can be named for those who reside inside the house (Sutton's Corner, Moyer Manor, Caitlin's Castle, Feline Fields).

Pagans can use the name of the house or covenstead to help protect, bless, or in some way magically alter the energy surrounding the house. We can incorporate the naming of the house into our House Blessing Ritual (see Chapter 5). Also see Place Name Elements in Chapter 1, and Chapter 9 for more ideas for covenstead names.

ANIMAL NAMES

Cat Names from T.S. Eliot's "Old Possum's Book of Practical Cats"

Admetus
Alonzo
Asparagus (Gus)
Augustus
Bill Bailey
Bombalurina
Bustopher Jones
Coricopat
Demeter
Electra
Firefrorefiddle, The Fiend of the Fell
George
Griddlebone
Growltiger
Grumbuskin
Gumbie Cat

Jellicle
Jellylorum
Jennyanydots
Macavity
Morgan
Mr. Mistoffelees
Mungojerrie
Munkustrap
Old Deuteronomy
Plato
Quaxo
Rum Tum Tugger
Rumpelteazer
Skimbleshanks
Tumblebrutus

These names are so unusual it might by wise to use them as private names or coven names rather than children's names. They are nonetheless powerful names.

Insects

Ant: Social creatures who have a highly developed social order with a matriarchy, workers, soldiers, and a queen who reproduces. The queen possesses wings only for a brief mating flight when she flies to her own nest with her mates. Once there, the female bites off her wings, resigning herself to a lifetime of nestbound, egg-laying existence. The males die after copulating with the queen and their sperm is enough to last for a lifetime of reproduction. Ants are illustrative of the idea that together we can do things which we cannot do alone. They were once seen as a source of wisdom and used for divination purposes. It can be used as a name for invoking diligence, community, determination, fertility, drive, and hard work. A good name for one who is seeking employment.

Aphid: An insect which performs parthenogenesis (reproduction without sexual union) during part of the year and reproduces sexually during the winter. They give birth to fully formed young, with males appearing only at the end of the year when sexual mating takes place. A good name for one who desires fertility, ease of parenting burdens, or becoming a single parent.

Bedbug: A cozy-sounding name for one who enjoys bed sports. In actuality a parasite who lives off the lifeblood of people. A profound idea in this day and age.

Bee: A social insect with a matriarchal social order. The honey that bees make was very prized in ancient times. In *The Kalevala,* the Finnish epic poem, a mother used magic honey to bring her son back to life. Bees were associated with many Goddesses and their priestesses. In Greek culture, it was believed that the spirits of priestesses of Aphrodite resided in bees after their deaths. One of the titles of Demeter, the mother/vegetation/earth Goddess, translates to "the pure mother bee." It is a name for invoking energy, endurance, enthusiasm, determination, community involvement, sociality, and working toward a sweet reward. (Also Bumblebee, Honeybee, Queen bee, Yellowjacket, and Blessed Bee.)

Beetle: An insect group and a rock group who employ pheromones as sexual attractants. A beetle is a flying creature who, in the jungles of South America, sometimes grows to be as large as a house cat. Children leash the huge insects and treat them as pets. A good name which suggests durability, strength, adaptability, freedom, and the early sixties.

Butterfly: The lovely, colorful, graceful, and mystical insect which begins life as an ugly wormlike creature, hides within a cocoon, and emerges as the

Good night, sleep tight, don't let the bedbugs bite.

—Traditional

resplendent butterfly. In many cultures, the butterfly is believed to be the repository for the souls of departed ancestors. The Greeks, Celts, Chinese and many tropical cultures believed that butterflies were the souls of the dead searching for a new incarnation. This name and its transposed nickname (flutterby) are great magical names which speak of magical and spiritual transmutations. A name for rebirth, new beginnings, the turning of the wheel of life, change, growth, and evolution. You might also choose one of the thousands of butterfly species names, which are too numerous to mention here but can be found in any reference book on the subject.

Caterpillar: The pupal stage of the moth and butterfly before building its cocoon. A good name for a new Witch, just beginning to learn and grow. A name of beautiful potential.

Centipede: An insect with a hundred legs. This is a good name for invoking travel, progress, or movement. (Millepede means 1,000 legs.)

Cicada: An insect whose mating call is a loud, cricket-like chirp. For me, it brings to mind summertime in the forests of the American Midwest where, as a child, I would equate the coming of the fireflies at dusk to the thunderous hum of the cicadas. The cicada sings at dusk and dawn. There is a Greek myth of the lover of Eos, the dawn, who grows older and older, with his voice deteriorating until it is just a chirp of the cicada. The chirping of the cicadas in the morning is the lover of Eos saying "hello" to his love. The cicada takes a long time to mature (as long as seventeen years). This name would be a good growth-oriented name or one for dealing with growing older.

Cricket: In the Orient, it was believed that a cricket on the hearth would bring good luck, so cricket cages were built to house the cricket. The Orientals also found beauty in filling the house with the cricket's song. The idea of a homey cricket was carried forward by Disney's character Jimminy Cricket. In England, calling something "cricket" meant it was fair, honorable, and honest. This name, then, would manifest the comforts of hearth and home; also wisdom, kindness, fairness, and honesty.

Dragonfly: Dragonflies and the related damselflies are colorful, primeval-looking insects which come from the Carboniferous Era (up to 350 million years ago). They soared over Carboniferous swamps with twenty-four-inch wingspans. They existed long before even the flying pterodactyl evolved. Today's version of the dragonfly is smaller, but a powerful flier with a brilliantly-colored body. They are found all over the earth. These are marvellous names for longevity, durability, adaptability, power, and freedom. Dragonfly is also a good name for those who are friends of dragons. Dragons, as everyone knows, attract dragonflies.

Firefly: A member of the beetle family that uses light to attract a mate in the night. Many cultures, such as the ancient tribes on Leeward Island, Brazil, and the West Indies, used fireflies as a source of light by putting them in lanterns made of pierced gourds. The native tribes in the West Indies used a larger version of the luminescent firefly to light their huts and for use on nocturnal hunting expeditions. In the past, poor Eastern students used fireflies to read by. Today, Japanese people keep them in special lanterns and hold open-air viewing festivals for the appreciation of the beautiful greenish glow of the fireflies. A marvelous magical name for illumination and enlightenment. A mellow fire energy name. (Also Lightning Bug, Glowworm.)

Gnat: A tiny fly-like insect which often annoys humans. This is a good name to take to de-emphasize oneself when self-importance and egotism get the upper hand.

Grasshopper: A green, leaf-eating, jumping insect found all over the world. They often live in huge societies which have a tremendous impact on the crops they feed on. In Greek society, the landed nobility wore golden pins shaped like grasshoppers to signify their social rank. This name is good for movement, escape, travel, freedom, and humility. It is a name of much power and potential. This name might be useful when trying to buy a house or land, or when doing rituals to accomplish this. (Also Locust.)

Ladybug: A spotted beetle which eats huge amounts of other insects. Ladybugs are often sold in gardening stores as a natural pesticide. Ladybug is a good name for a mild-mannered person. It suggests maternal responsibility and mildness.

Mantis: A stick-like insect which is predatory in nature. It waits camouflaged against a tree and when an unsuspecting insect, such as an unlucky grasshopper, comes within range, it lunges at it, holds it with powerful forelegs, then delicately nibbles at the victim, often discarding a great deal of food as unpalatable. The females are larger and more powerful than the males and the females often eat their husbands. In Theban society, there was a priestess named Mante, from whom the insect got its name. Her name means "prophetess" or "one inspired by the moon." In Africa, the mantis is seen as the progenitor of the world in many creation myths. As a magical name, Mantis is aggressive, predatory, and well-protected. The female mantis is the one in power. This is a strong woman's name, a name for a victim who wishes to be more assertive. Taking a powerfully aggressive name is good for those who are usually the hapless grasshopper in life's scenarios.

Here in the highlands...we get the fireflies in the woods. On an evening you will see two or three of them, adventurous lonely stars floating in the clear air, rising and lowering, as if upon waves....To that rhythm of their flight they lighten and put out their... lamps. You may catch the insect and make it shine upon the palms of your hand, giving out a strange light, a mysterious message, it turns the flesh pale green in a small circle round it. The next night there are hundreds...in the woods. For some reason they keep within a certain height, four or five feet, above the ground. It is impossible then not to imagine that a whole crowd of children... are running through the dark forest carrying candles, little sticks dipped in magic fire, joyously jumping up and down...and swinging their small pale torches merrily. The woods are filled with a wild frolicsome life, and it is all perfectly silent.

—Isak Dinesen
Out of Africa

Mayfly: Together with dragonflies and cockroaches, the mayfly enjoys an ancient heritage beginning in the Carboniferous period of up to 350 million years ago. The longevity of the species is not carried forth to the individual mayfly, which is extremely short-lived. They live only a few hours as winged adults. The adult mayfly is incapable of eating. They are delicate creatures with tissue-like wings. Mayflies live for years under the water as larvae but leave the water to fly, mate, and die. As a magical name, mayfly is a bit reminiscent of Beltane (a May Day festival). It brings an appreciation of life, preparation for death, and a determination to live life to the fullest. Seize the day! Or in terms of mayflies, seize the afternoon!

Moth: Like a butterfly, a moth goes from a wormlike caterpillar stage into a cocoon from which the adult moth emerges. Many varieties are brilliantly colored, and some get to be huge in size; one African variety has a fourteen-inch wingspan. A transformational name, bringing change and growth.

Termite: A fully social creature that lives in large, rocklike nests (at least in Africa and Australia). They are socially less matriarchal than bees and ants, with the male consort to the queen holding a respected position within their society. There is more than just one female capable of reproduction within a nest, but only the queen reproduces. The other females are hormonally prohibited. The queen becomes huge and fertile until she is almost unable to move. If she dies, another female will be hormonally altered, become fertile, and take her place. This is a name which suggests the immense power of motherhood. It would be a good name for fertility workings.

Wasp: A stinging, social insect which kills a tremendous amount of other insects to feed the larvae in the nest. As a magical name, wasp is less preferable than hornet because of the social term W.A.S.P. (White Anglo-Saxon Protestant). Hornet is a name which brings power, freedom, fleetness, and protection.

Web-spinner: These are little known insects which resemble termites. The name web-spinner comes from the silky cocoon-like tunnels and webs which they construct. They live communally with the female tending the young, suggesting a rudimentary social organization. This is a superb name for a Pagan because this is what Pagans do—we help spin the web of life.

Reptiles and Amphibians

Alligator: These are remnants of the age of reptiles when gigantic ancestors of today's alligators and crocodiles roamed the earth in the Mesozoic Era (66 million years ago). They are carnivorous, sensitive to saline, and need to spend many hours in the sun to regulate their body temperature. They were worshipped in ancient Egyptian culture in the form of Sebek, the crocodile God, who represented rationality, clear vision, and was an agent of death. It is not surprising that the Egyptians worshipped crocodiles, as the Nile has an abundance of them, even today. I remember an unhappy tale of a ship which sank while on a moonlight cruise up the Nile, not very long ago. Many people died—some from the piranhas in the water and the rest from the crocodiles waiting along the shore. This kind of thing created a powerful impression on the ancients. This is a name which suggests a tough survivor. It is a name which brings about an awareness of antiquity, durability, longevity, death, and solidity. (Also Crocodile, Gharial.)

Frog: An amphibian which undergoes massive metamorphosis from egg to mature frog. It is like watching evolution in miniature as the egg develops a tail and comes to resemble a fish, then sprouts legs and eyes and reabsorbs its tail when it is ready to leave the water. Some frogs are horned or wildly colored or patterned as a camouflage device. One startling species has what looks like owl eyes on its rump to startle potential predators. Toads were traditionally associated with Witches, presumably as the Witch's familiar. They were seen as symbols of rebirth (probably because tadpoles resemble the human fetus). In South America, frogs are thought to be able to bring the rains. Folklore is full of frog and toad stories, such as the frog prince, toads giving people warts, and Witches turning people into frogs. Some ancient cultures used the frog in their regeneration rituals. As magical names, Frog, Toad, or Tadpole suggest rebirth, youth, enthusiasm, water energy, regenerative processes, untapped potential, and hidden strength. (Also Toad, Tadpole.)

Lizard: Families of lizards have interesting names, such as flying dragon, chameleon, iguana, gecko, skink, anguid, gila monster (pronounced "HEE la"), sungazer, xenosaur, and the giant komodo dragon. Lizards are widespread across the globe, including one species which is found above the Arctic circle. In folklore it is said that a lizard may bite the shadow of an unsuspecting person and that person is then doomed to die. In Asia it is believed that a happy life is guaranteed if a gecko lizard calls from the bedroom of newlyweds; consequently, well-wishers often endow the nuptial chamber with many lizards. The Salish of North America use the tail of lizards in a love potion. Live lizards are used in India in fertility rites known as serpent festivals. In terms of a name, this is a good name for suggesting quickness, agility, youth, and an appreciation of dragonlore.

Salamander: Salamanders resemble lizards, or more precisely, snakes with legs. They have moist, smooth skin. Being amphibians (meaning literally "a being with a double life," on land and in water), they swim like fish in water and waddle on land. This is a name for bringing earth and water energy. There is also a elemental connection to fire. Salamanders were long associated with fire as the sylphs were with air, undines with water, and gnomes with earth in ancient folklore. We still use these folk images when visualizing the elements. (Also Newt, Mudpuppy, Siren, Fire Salamander, and Axolotl.)

Snake: The fact that an old and wrinkled snake can shed its skin and appear young and beautiful again lends the snake a powerful symbolism to many cultures. In Egypt, the snake was a sign of imperial power. Cleopatra committed suicide by allowing an asp to bite her breast. The snake was seen as an Aztec God to the ancient Central Americans. Intertwining snakes in the caduceus are used as a symbol of healing in the medical profession. Pythons are sacred to the aboriginal people of Australia. The Goddess is represented often as a snake. The Goddess Gaia was also called "the female serpent." This is a good name for rejuvenation, sleekness, power, youth, regeneration, and agility. (Also Serpent.)

Tadpole: A baby frog. A good name for a child. It brings water energy and is a growth-oriented name, aiding transformation and metamorphosis.

Turtle: Long before there were mammals, birds, lizards, snakes, or crocodiles, there were turtles. Two hundred million years ago they thrived with an appearance very similar to today's turtle. Today they live in water and on land. They are extremely long-lived, living well over a century. There is evidence of pampered turtles living up to two centuries. The tortoise was sacred to Hermes. Turtles are a multicultural symbol of eternal life. Turtle is a good name for invoking longevity. (Also Tortoise, Chelonia.)

Mammals

Cat: The Egyptian cat Goddess Bast pounces to mind when one thinks of cats. The Goddesses Artemis and Diana were associated with Bast. In Norse mythology, cats pulled the chariot of the Goddess Freya. Sacrificial cats were used extensively by Finnish shamans to cure many illnesses. From the Middle Ages, the cat has been connected to Witches and many cats were burned with their owners during the Burning Times. This sad fact helped the bubonic plague take such a strong hold in Europe. The plague was carried by fleas on rats, which multiplied with ease without cats to hunt them and control their numbers. There seems to be a great affinity amongst Witches for cats above other pets. As magical names, cat names suggest varying degrees of fleetness, sleekness, mystery, grace, athletic prowess, and a person who follows their own bliss. This name brings a certain freedom from being controlled by other's expectations or demands. (Also Alley, Bobcat, Cheetah, Grimalkin, Leopard, Leonine, Lion/ess, Lynx, Manx, Mountain Lion, Panther, Snow Leopard, Tabby, Tiger/ess, Tomcat, Wildcat, or Siamese.)

Coyote: Sacred to many Native American tribes, the coyote is associated with the moon. The coyote was central to a creation myth in which he scratched the earth and the first people issued forth. This is a lunar name which suggests trickster energy.

There were always cats at Mark Twain's farm, and favorite cats had their own names—Blatherskite, Sour Mash, Stray Kit, Sin, Satan. His children inherited his love of them. His daughter Susy once said, "The difference between Papa and Mamma is, that Mamma loves morals and Papa loves cats."

—Albert Bigelow Paine
Mark Twain

Dog: The dog has an important place in mythology. Hecate was accompanied by a three-headed hound, the Irish hero Cu Chulainn became the "hound of Ulster" after slaying a watch dog, Artemis is accompanied by hunting dogs, the hounds of Annwn ("ann OON") were supernatural beasts with red ears, and Odin often hunted with supernatural dogs. The ancient fascination with canines is probably due to the great help a dog can offer when hunting. Dogs helped put food on the table and so were greatly revered. The name "dog," however, has come to be an insult, just as the expression "son of a bitch" was once a title of respect. As a magical name, it suggests a keen intellect, a sharp hunter, and a ferocious adversary. It is a name which could bring protection, courage, and strength. (Also Puppy, Cabal, Bran, Sirius, Sceolan, Cerberus, or you might find a name amongst the various dog breeds.)

Dolphin: The dolphin, sacred to Demeter, was seen by Greeks as symbolic of life passing into another dimension in death. This name brings water energy and suggests an easy flowing into the changes life brings. (Also Porpoise.)

Elephant: The Hindu elephant God Ganesha's name means "lord of hosts." Ganesha is the father of Buddha. Elephants are symbolic of great sexual energy. This name suggests potency, virility, and massive sexuality.

Ferret: A quick, playful, curious, and energetic trickster. This funny animal will, like a raccoon, get into anything, bringing endless entertainment. As a magical name, it is playful and carefree, bringing humor, a lack of inhibition, and spontaneity.

Fox: The fox is popularly seen as a wily, clever, and often dishonest character. In ancient times, the fox was sacred to the god Dionysus. It is suggested that the formal fox hunt is really a carryover of a Pagan sacrificial rite. The name Fox carries with it a degree of untrustworthiness, but also suggests fleetness, quick-thinking, cunning, and shrewdness. The expression "crazy like a fox" is suggestive of thinly disguised guile.

Then I went to get the other folks. Back with me came the dog, brave Horatius, and the crow, Lars Porsena, and the woodrat, Thomas Chatterton Jupiter Zeus, and the toad, Virgil, and the mouse, Felix Mendelssohn. When we were all come I did climb right into the pig pen and did tie on Aphrodite's new ribbon. I sang a little thank song and we had prayers and I gave Aphrodite little scratches on the back with a stick like she does like. That was to make up to her for not getting a walk.

—Opal Whiteley
adapted by Jane Boulton
Opal, the Journal of an Understanding Heart

Squirrel: There is an old legend that says that if you hunt and kill a squirrel, you will lose your hunting skill and have bad luck. This energetic, noisy, amusing, scolding creature is a good image for one who is shy and reticent, for it will lend the wearer more energy and fire.

Whale: In seagoing folklore, whales visiting areas they normally don't is a bad omen, although whales, in general, were seen to be symbols of good luck. Many cultures see being swallowed by a whale to be an initiatory rite. In Finland, for example, the God Ilmarinen was swallowed by the hag of Hiisi. In Babylonia, the sea Goddess Derceto swallowed and then gave birth to the god Oannes. The Christian myth of Jonah and the whale is also an example of this idea. The whale, then, is seen as a womb. As a name, it would bring fertility, rebirth, regeneration, and a fresh start.

Wolf: The wolf was an important figure in European mythology. Many of the names from the ancient Germanic tribes bore the name wolf. (Remember that these cultures made up their names with name words such as "wolf.") The Romans saw the Goddess as a she-wolf in the form of Lupa or Feronia. She nursed the infants Romulus and Remus. The ritual dressing up in wolf skins was common throughout Europe. In Egypt, there was a wolf god Up-Uat who was the son of Isis. In Ireland, people had festivals at Yule in which they dressed in wolf skins and masks and turned into wolves. As a magical name, Wolf brings with it a strong, aggressive, lunar-oriented energy which can help make you less afraid.

Hooved Creatures

Antelope: A hooved, horned, deer-like animal which roams the Western United States. I am particularly fond of the antelope because of an experience I once had while working outside Hanna, Wyoming, where the hills are dotted with herds of antelope. One morning at dawn I was driving down the road toward work when I heard an odd sound. I thought something was wrong with my car, so I stopped and listened. It was a roaring and it seemed to be getting louder, so I shut off the engine and rolled down the window. The sound was coming from all around me. I stepped out of my truck and gazed at a dark cloud forming along the horizon. I took a few steps away from the car and saw the leading edge of a huge herd of antelope stampeding across the land. The antelope herd thundered toward me and I did not move; I was too mesmerized by their beauty. I smelled them first as if I was struck by a wall of hot, musky, dusty odor, and then they came. They are quick animals and they were running at full speed. A break in the seemingly endless wave of animals opened around me and they dashed by me, brushing my arms with their heaving sides. I flinched at the racket as some of them galloped over the top of my car. I, for a few magic moments, knew what it was like to be a part of nature. I stood stock-still, laughing wildly as this river of antelope flooded around me. In a twinkle they were gone, leaving only dust, hoofprints, and dislodged sagebrush from the desert floor. I turned after them and raised my arm in salute as the thunder of their hooves receded in the distance. I associate this experience with earth energy; I call the thunder of the antelope when I call the north quarter.

Boar: The boar was sacred to the Celtic Goddess Arduinna (Goddess of forests). Boars were sacrificed in Indo-European, Celtic, and Greek societies. Oaths of a serious nature, such as the oath athletes took to play fairly in the Olympic games, were sworn over boar's meat. Many Gods held the boar sacred or were identified with them. The God Attis was killed by a boar in a ritual every spring, which was followed by an orgiastic ritual whereby his followers sought him in the wild. This tusked, fierce, and powerful beast was seen as divine because of its great strength and unbridled demeanor. The tamer, untusked domesticated pig was sacred to the Celts. In many myths, pigs were stolen from the Otherworld or given to the Celts by the Gods. The animals were highly prized and eaten by the spirits of the otherworld. Celts thought that in the Summerland, the Celtic afterlife, one ate pork. One of the heroes of Welsh mythology was born in a pigpen, a sacred place. His name, Culhwch ("KILL ooch"), means pigsty. As a magical name, Boar is a powerfully masculine, aggressive, and dominating name. It brings confidence, determination, grit, and courage.

Bull: The strong, virile, and well-endowed bull is admired in many cultures. Capturing a wild bull was the seventh labor of Heracles. The bull was the central figure in the cult of Mithras, a God of light who annually sacrificed a bull. The Romans adopted the Mithraic rituals. The sacrifice of bulls, especially white bulls, was widespread. Even today the Spanish bullfight is a continuation of this practice. The blood of a sacrificial bull was thought to create life, and it was used for initiations and in many other ritual contexts. I think that this was a patriarchal attempt to usurp the power of women (who are able to create life using blood) and shift the focus of the people to the masculine forces by dressing them up in female attributes. As a magical name, bull is strong, big, virile, and fertile. A very masculine name for bringing masculine attributes. Keep in mind, however, that like the notion of patriarchy usurping the regenerative power of the feminine, the current use of the name "bull" suggests a verbal challenge which, at best, means "nonsense," so public use of the name may detract from your intentions.

Deer: A graceful, fleet-footed, hooved, and antlered animal; the male (the stag) is often associated with the God. A human figure with antlers has been a powerful shamanic symbol since the time of the early cave dwellers. The deer remained important to people, as is evidenced by the antlered gods Cernunnos and Herne in Britain. Welsh mythology speaks of a supernatural white stag leading people into the Otherworld. As a name, it suggests fleetness, beauty, strength, and the mysteries which lie in ancient forests. (Also Fawn, Buck, and Roe.)

Goat: The goat is revered in many cultures. The Greek God Pan is known as the "goat-foot God." Amalthea, also in Greek myth, was a female goat and nurse to the god Zeus. The Norse had helpful goats as well. Odin's goat Heidrun was a female goat that gave mead from her teats in never-ending supply. As a name, Goat indicates fertility, sexual potency, and determination.

Horse: The horse plays a prominent part in many culture's mythologies. In the Celtic pantheon there was Epona, the horse Goddess. There is some record of leaders of Celtic tribes mating with a white mare who symbolized Epona. In doing so, the king would "marry the land" by mating with the Goddess. England has long been associated with the magical properties of the horse. For example, White Horse Hill in Berkshire is an ancient, huge chalk drawing of a horse on the side of a hill. The horse was sacred to the Goddess Rhiannon as well as Epona. Stories of flying horses are common in Greek mythology. Horses are also said to be omens of death, which is why a riderless horse appears at military funerals. In my family's Scottish traditions, a white horse is thought to bring good luck. Horses were also associated with fertility and strength. This was why the May queen would ride nude on horseback pursued by a young man, also on horseback, who would catch and mate with her, symbolizing the mating of the Goddess and the God. As magical names, horse names suggest fertility, change, freedom, and sexual prowess. (Also Mare, Stallion, Equine, Colt, Filly, Foal, Steed, Pony, Charger, Bronco, or Mustang.)

Moose: When discordians think of the moose, we think of Bullwinkle and Moosemas, not necessarily in that order. A wise and irreverent Pagan sometimes named Andulusa the Heretic wrote a slim volume of silliness called *Moosemas,* which outlines the rite of worshipping Bullwinkle the Moose to be performed whenever there is a lull in life. I, not knowing the identity of this inspired author, suggested to a friend that it was a book she should read. I told her that it would appeal to her as she is a particularly funny and quietly zany person. She said that she had liked the book, so much so that she had written it! (The only drawback to people having many magical names is that it's hard to keep track of who is who.) Moose, then, would make a good name for a discordian or someone who wants to loosen up a bit and let his or her sense of the ridiculous flourish. (Also Bull Moose, for bringing an exaggerated sense of masculine silliness.) May the moose be with you.

TOOL NAMES

Many Pagans name their magical tools as part of their consecration ritual. For more information on the naming of tools, see Chapter Five.

Anduril: "The flame of the west." Aragorn's sword in *The Lord of the Rings.*

Anglachel: The sword made from meteoric iron that Thingol received from Eol and which he gave to Beleg in *The Silmarillion.*

Angrist: "Iron cleaver," the knife made by Telchar of Nogrod in *The Silmarillion.*

Anguirel: Eol's sword, made of meteoric iron, found in *The Silmarillion.*

Balmung: Siegfried's sword in the *Nibelungenlied.*

Belthronding: The bow of Beleg Cuthalion in *The Silmarillion.*

Bright Rim: Shield of King Conchobar in Irish myth.

Caladcholg: Sword of Fergus mac Roich. A sword which was the length of the rainbow. Given to mac Roich by the sidhe.

Claidheamhmore: Gaelic for claymore (see below).

Claymore: A large, two-edged broadsword used by Scottish highlanders.

Cruaiden Cadatchenn: "Dear little hard one." Cu Chulainn's sword in Irish myth.

Crysknife: Sacred Fremen knife made from the teeth of a dead sandworm on the desert planet Arrakis in the novel *Dune* by Frank Herbert.

Culghlas: Blue-green spear carried by Conall the Victorious in Irish myth.

Durendal: Roland's sword in *The Song of Roland*.

Excalibur: Fabled sword of Arthur given to him by the Lady of the Lake (also Caliburn.)

Glamdring: Gandalf's sword in *The Lord of the Rings*.

Gram: Sigurd's sword in Norse mythology.

Grond: The mace of Morgoth in *The Silmarillion*.

Gurthang: "Iron of death." The name of Beleg's sword Anglachel after it was reforged for Turin in *The Silmarillion*.

Mjolnir/Miollnir: Thor's magic hammer in Norse mythology.

Narsil: Aragorn's broken sword in *The Lord of the Rings*.

Narya: "Ring of fire" or "red ring." One of the three rings of the elves in *The Lord of the Rings*.

Nauglamir: "The necklace of the dwarves" made for Finrod in *The Silmarillion*.

Nenya: One of the three rings of the elves, "the ring of water," from *The Lord of the Rings*.

Ringil: The sword of Fingolfin in *The Silmarillion*.

Retaliator: Name of a sword in the novel *The Wolves of Dawn* by William Sarabande.

Silmarils: The three jewels made by Feanor which contained the light of the trees of Valinor in *The Silmarillion*.

Vilya: One of the rings of the elves, "the ring of air," from *The Lord of the Rings*.

The sword of Elendil was forged anew by elvish smiths, and on its blade was traced a device of seven stars set between the crescent moon and the rayed sun, and about them was written many runes; for Aragorn son of Arathorn was going to war upon the Marches of Mordor. Very bright was that sword when it was made whole again; the light of the sun shone redly in it, and the light of the moon shone cold, and its edge was hard and keen. And Aragorn gave it a new name and called it Anduril, flame of the west.

—J.R.R. Tolkien
The Lord of the Rings

11

Which Witch Goes by Which Name?

The names in this chapter are public names used by Pagans. They are names of people I have met at festivals, seminars, lectures, read on book covers, or on bylines of articles. I have included a good selection of different styles of names to give you some idea of what others are doing in terms of their public magical names. Perhaps some of these will inspire, or at least amuse you.

DISCORDIAN AND/OR UNUSUAL MAGICAL NAMES

Andalusa the Heretic
Baldrick the Unfit
Bullwinkle
David the Forgetful
Erisian
Erisian Liberation Front
Fifi Trixibelle
"Hey Mike!" and His Brother "Hey Dave!"
Hey Zeus!
Johnny Quest
Kilgore Trout
Malaclypse the Younger

Marilyn Monroe, Hollywood Goddess
   of Sex
Myrth
Omar Ravenhurst
Nimrod, Lord of the Newts
Joshua, Self-Declared Emperor of the
   World
Random
Russell the Lug
Sugar Plum
The Joshua Norton Cabal
Thunder Bunny

COVEN NAMES

These are some interesting coven names which have already been published elsewhere or that I conjured out of the mists.

Abracadabra Coven
Ar nDraiocht Fein
Avalon
Blue Star Coven
Butterfly Garden Coven
Children of the Hundred Acre Wood
Children of the Tropical Moon
Church of the Crescent Moon
Circle of the Starry Starry Night
Circle of Stones
Clan of Cerridwyn
Clan of the Cauldron
Coven Lothlorien
Coven of the Sacred Stones
Coven of the Singing Tree
Coven of Danu
Coven Aurora
Coven of the Whispering Wind
Coven of the Dragon
Coven of the Dolphins
Covenant of the Goddess
Daughters of the Muse
Desert Henge Coven
Dragonfhain
Dreamdance Coven
Earth Song Circle
Earthaven
Earthcrafte
Elf
Elvenhome
Enterprise Coven
Every Witch Way
Gaia Group
Greenwood Grove
Grove of the Pegasus
Guardians of Avalon
House Atreides
Invisible Evening Twilight Tribe
Mississippi Moon

Moon Birch Grove
Moondance Coven
Moonfire
Moonweb Coven
Morning Star
Motherheart Coven
Mystery Cult of Bill the Cat
New Earth Coven
O.O.D.C. (Our Own Damn Coven)
O.O.P.S. (Our Own Pagan System—the
     "Tradition" of the O.O.D.C.)
Oak & Ash & Thorn
Oakrune Circle
Order of Osiris
Our Lady of Enchantment
Pale Horse
P.O.E.E. (Paratheoanametamystikhood
     Of Eris Esoteric)
Pendragon Coven
Rainbow Web Circle
Rowantree Circle
Silver Elves
Silver Acorn Coven
Silver Web
Silver Crystal Coven
Sisterhood (Brotherhood) of the
     Goddess
Sisters Circle
Spiritdancer Circle
Standing Stone Coven
Starmist Coven
Storm Circle
Sword and Stone
Temple of the Elder Gods
Temple Stardust
Temple of Danaan
Tuatha De Danaan
Wolfhaven Farms
Wychwood

FESTIVAL MONIKERS

These are some more of the interesting public names I've seen at festivals, gatherings, and workshops.

Aengus
Alia
Alva Uhl
Amber K
Antares
Archer Bowman
Aridawnia
Ariel
Ari Sekari Sepannen
Arynne
Aspen
Black Lion
Black Wolf
Bryony
Carnelian
Cattrin
Cerridwen Rose
Coyote Joe
Dragonfriend
Echo
Elazar
Epona
Fallingstar
Feather
Fox
Galadriel
Galain
Green Oak
Griffin
Jay Twelve Trees
Kelric
Kerr Cuhulain
Maia
Mysteries
Mystic
New Leaf

Nightwind
Nokomis
Ocean Breeze
Pagan
Penda
Phoenix
Questor
Rainbow
Red Hawk
Robin
Roe
Roy-Ke Khan
Sabrina
Sandara
Sarina
Scarab
Seamus
Sierra
Silverfoot
Skye
Soltahr
Spellbound
Starwalker
Starwyn
Sun Cat
Taliesin
Theora Ronin
Tobey
Udita
Venusia
Vixen
Weyland Smith
Wildfire Dragon
Windstalker
Wise

12

Names From
Whence We Came

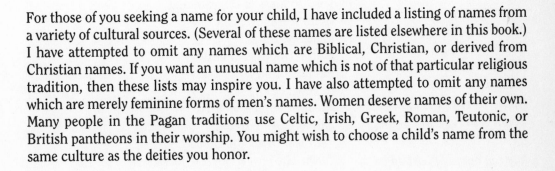

For those of you seeking a name for your child, I have included a listing of names from a variety of cultural sources. (Several of these names are listed elsewhere in this book.) I have attempted to omit any names which are Biblical, Christian, or derived from Christian names. If you want an unusual name which is not of that particular religious tradition, then these lists may inspire you. I have also attempted to omit any names which are merely feminine forms of men's names. Women deserve names of their own. Many people in the Pagan traditions use Celtic, Irish, Greek, Roman, Teutonic, or British pantheons in their worship. You might wish to choose a child's name from the same culture as the deities you honor.

GREEK NAMES

Greek Girls

Aileen: Light.
Aldora: Winged gift.
Aleris: Ancient name.
Alexandra: Helper of mankind.
Althea: Healing.
Amara: Unfading.
Amarantha: Immortal.

Ambrosia: Food of life.
Ambrosine: Immortal.
Anastasia: One who will rise again.
Aretha/Arethusa: Nymph.
Ariadne: Daughter of sun God; Goddess
   of spring.

Hither, huntress,
virgin, Goddess,
tracker, slayer,
to our truce!
Hold us ever
fast together;
bring our pledges
love and increase;
wean us from the
fox's wiles:
Hither, huntress!
Virgin, hither!

—Aristophanes
Lysistrata

Queen and Huntress, chaste
and fair,
Now the sun is laid to sleep,
Seated in thy silver chair
State in wonted manner
keep:
Hesperus entreats thy light,
Goddess excellently bright.

Lay thy bow of pearl apart
And thy crystal shining
quiver;
Give unto the flying hart
Space to breathe, how short
soever:
Thou that mak'st a day of
night,
Goddess excellently bright!

—Ben Jonson
"Hymn to Diana"

Aspasia: Woman famous for charm and intelligence.
Astra: Starlike.
Athena: Goddess of wisdom.
Calandra: The lark.
Calantha: Blossom.
Cassandra: Prophetess to whom no one listened.
Chloe: Flowering.
Clio: Celebrate.
Corinne: A maiden.
Crystal: Clear.
Cynara/Zinara: Ancient name.
Cynthia: Moon Goddess.
Damara: Gentle.
Delia: Goddess of the harvest.
Delphine: Derivation of Delphi, Oracle of Apollo.
Demeter/Demetra: Goddess of the harvest.
Despoina: Mistress.
Dorie/Dory/Dorissa: Sea.
Emma: Grandmother.
Hestia: Goddess of the hearth.
Ilona: Light.
Iona: Purple jewel.
Irene: Goddess of peace.
Iris: Goddess of the rainbow.
Isadora/Isadore: Gift of Isis.
Melaney: Dark.
Moira: Goddess of destiny.
Mona: Solitary.
Nerissa: Of the sea.
Nicole: People's victory.
Pandora: All gifted.
Panthea: Of all the Gods.
Pearl: The jewel.
Penelope: The weaver.
Phoebe: Brilliant; moon Goddess.
Rhea: Daughter of heaven and earth, mother of the Gods.
Rue: Plant used as an aspirilium in sacred ceremonies.
Selena/Selirra: Moon Goddess.
Terza/Tessa: The harvester.
Thaiassa: The sea.
Thalia: Joyful.
Theola: Divine.
Tressa: The harvester.
Trina: Pure.

Ursa: She-bear.
Vara: The stranger.
Vesta: Goddess of the hearth.
Xena: Distant place.
Zandra: Helper of humankind.
Zoe: Life-giving.

Greek Boys

Adonis: Beautiful youth.
Aeneas: Praiseworthy.
Ajax: Eagle.
Alexander: Great protector.
Ambrose: Immortal.
Anatole: The east.
Apollo: Manly.
Aristotle: The best.
Artemus: Safe and sound.
Cletus: Summoned.
Corydon: Lark.
Cosmo: The world.
Cyril: Lordly.
Damian/Damon/Daymond: Constant.
Darius: Wealthy.
Dorian: From the sea.
Erinys: Angry.
Fabian: Bean farmer.
Galen: Calm.
George/Goran/Jorgan: Farmer.
Homer: Promise.
Jason: The healer.
Leander: Lion-man.
Linus: Flax.
Nicholas: Victory of the people.
Orestes: Mountain.
Orion: Hunter.
Otis: Hears well.
Saunders: Son of Alexander.
Sebastian: Majestic.
Strephon: One who turns.
Ulysses: Wrathful.
Xanthus: Golden-haired.
Xenos/Zenos: Foreigner.
Yurik: Farmer.
Zeno: Shining.

Start the chorus dancing,
Summon all the Graces
Send a shout to Artemis in
*   invocation.*
Call upon her brother,
healer, chorus master,
Call the blazing Bacchus,
*   with his maddened*
*   muster.*
Call the flashing, fiery Zeus,
*   and*
call his mighty, blessed
*   spouse, and*
call the Gods, call all the
*   Gods,*
to witness now and not
*   forget*
our gentle, blissful Peace:
*   the gift,*
the deed of Aphrodite.

—Aristophanes
Lysistrata

LATIN NAMES

Latin Girls

Adora: Beloved.
Adrienne: Dark, rich.
Allegra: Lively.
Almeda: Pressing toward the goal.
Amabel: Loveable.
Amanda: Deserving of great love.
Andra/Andrea/Andreanna: Womanly (also Andriana, Aundrea).
April: Opening.
Arda/Ardelle: Warmth.
Ardis/Ardra: Enthusiasm.
Auerelie/Aurelia/Aurora: Golden.
Austin: Majestic.
Autumn: Fall.
Averyl/Avril: Opening.
Belinda: Beautiful serpent.
Bellona: Goddess of war.
Brina: From the boundary line.
Cerelia: Goddess of the harvest.
Chantal: Song.
Delcina/Dulce/Dulcinea: Sweetness.
Diana: Goddess of the hunt.
Emily/Emmaline: Hard-working.
Enid: Quiet.
Ermin: Regal.
Faline: Catlike.
Fawn/Fawna/Fawne: Young deer.
Felicity: Happiness.
Flora: Goddess of flowers.
Gelsey: Jasmine.
Gemma: Jewel.
Ginger: The spice.
Grace: Charm.
Hilary/Hillair: Full of cheer.
Imogene: Image.
Ivory: Made of ivory.
Julia/Juliet: Youthful.
Justine: Just.
Laura: Crown of laurel; honor.
Lauralee/Laureen/Laurel: Honor (also Laurette).
Lauren/Lauyrn/Lorrin: Laurel crown.

Verily, she is a magician, and of divine might, which hath power to bring down the sky, to bear up the earth, to turn the waters into hills and the hills into running waters, to call up the terrestrial spirits into the air, and to pull the Gods out of the heavens, to extinguish the planets, and to lighten the very darkness of Hell.

—Apuleius
The Golden Ass

Leandra: Lioness.
Lelia: Lily.
Lena: Temptress.
Leola/Leona/Leoni: Lion.
Lorelle: Little.
Lucina: Goddess of childbirth.
Lucretia: Riches.
Luna: Moon.
Maia: Goddess of springtime.
Maris/Marris/Meris: Of the sea.
Melena: Canary-yellow colored.
Merle/Merril/Merryl: Blackbird.
Miranda: Admirable.
Monica: Counselor.
Natalie: Born at Yule.
Nona: One of the three fates.
Nova/Novia: Newcomer.
Nydia: From the nest.
Ondrea: Womanly.
Oona: One.
Oriana/Riana: Golden.
Pomona: Goddess of fruit trees.
Portia: Offering.
Renata: Reborn.
Risa: Laughter.
Sabina: Sabine woman.
Sabrina: From the boundary line.
Season: Sowing, planting.
Selena: Salt.
Serena: Calm.
Sybil: Prophetess.
Terra: Goddess of the earth.
Tertia: The third.
Tessa: Essence.
Valene/Valery/Valora: Strong.
Valentine: Healthy.
Venus: Goddess of love.
Vesta: Goddess of the hearth.
Zia: Type of grain.

*O Blessed queen of heaven,
whether Thou be the Dame
Ceres which art the original
and motherly nurse of all
fruitful things in the
earth...or whether Thou be
the celestial Venus...or
whether Thou be the sister
of the god Pheobus...or
whether Thou be called
terrible Proserpine....Thou,
which dost luminate all the
cities of the earth by Thy
feminine light; Thou which
nourishest all the seeds of
the world by Thy damp
heat...by whatsoever name
or fashion or shape it is
lawful to call upon
Thee...Grant me peace
and rest.*

—Apuleius
The Golden Ass

Latin Boys

Adrian: Seacoast.
Alban: Pure heart.
Ardan/Arden/Ardin: Fiery.

tu Lucina dolentibus
Iuno dicta puerperis,
tu potens Triuia et notho es
deicta lumine Luna.

tu curseu, Dea, mensturo
metiens iter annuum,
rustica agricolae bonis
tecta frugibus exples.

sis quocumque tibi placet
sancta nomine, Romulique
antique up solita es bona
sospites ope gentem.

—Catullus
(87 BCE–54 BCE)

Austen/Austin: Great usefulness.
Bard: Bearded.
Basil: Magnificent.
Blase: Stammerer.
Branch: Claw.
Calvin: Bald.
Cash: Vain.
Clark: Scholarly.
Corbett/Corbin/Corvin: Raven.
Cornelius: Horn-colored.
Dex/Dexter: Dexterous.
Drake: Dragon.
Emlen/Emlyn: Charming.
Felix: Prosperous.
Forrest: Woodsman.
Foster: Keeper of the woods.
Griffin: Mythical beast.
Hadrian: Seacoast.
Jarl/Jarlath/Jarlen: Man of control.
Justin/Justinian: Just.
Linus: Flax-colored.
Lombard: Long-bearded.
Magnus: Great.
Max/Maxim/Maximillian: Most excellent.
Montgomery: Hill.
Myer: Great.
Myles: Soldier.
Oliver: Olive tree.
Orson: Bearlike.
Paine: Country peasant.
Patten/Paxton/Payton: Nobleman.
Quentin/Quincy/Quintin: Fifth.
Remus: Mythical founder of Rome.
Rex: King.
Romulus: Mythical founder of Rome.
Ross: Rose.
Rufus: Redhead.
Sebastian: Majestic.
Silvanus: The forest God.
Sumner: Summoner.
Sylvester: Woods.
Torin: Tender.
Trenton: Torrent.
Turner: One who works the lathe.
Ursa: Bear.
Vassily: Magnificent.

CELTIC/GAELIC NAMES

Celtic/Gaelic Girls

Abigail/Gobinet: Father rejoiced.
Aideen: Irish legendary lover of the fairy man.
Aine: Fairy queen at Knockany Hill.

Aislin: Dream.
Alina: Distant place.
Alyce: Noble.
Ashling ("ais LING"): Dream.
Asthore: Loved one.
Aurnia: Historic name.
Avril: April.
Banba: Irish Goddess.
Betha: Life.
Bonnie: Pretty.
Breeda: From Goddess Bried.
Brenna: Raven maid.
Briana: The strong; powerful.
Bride/Brigid/Bridget: Strong (from the Goddess).
Brona: Sorrow.
Caitlin: Kathleen.
Calum ("CAL um"): Dove.
Cara: Friend.
Catriona (pronounced "KAT ree own ah"): Catherine.
Daireen: Literary name.
Darcy: Dark one.
Deirdre (pronounced "DEE ur druh"): Sorrow.
Devin: (pronounced "dev IN"): Poet.
Doon: A landmark name.
Duvessa: Dark beauty.
Eavan: Fair form.
Edana: Little fire.
Edwina: Prosperous friend.
Enid: The spirit or soul.
Ennis/Erin/Erina: Island.
Fenella: Fair.
Finna: Medieval Icelandic name from Fionn (fair).
Finola/Fiona/Fionnagh: Fair or white.
Genevieve: Magic sighs.
Glenna: Valley.
Grainne: Grain Goddess.
Grania/Granna: Love.
Guinevere/Gweneth: White or fair lady.

*Thou art called Lucina
  Juno
By women in labor pains,
Called powerful Three:
  Ways and Moon
Of borrowed light.*

*Goddess, by Thy monthly
  course
Measuring the year's journey
Thou fillest up with good
  fruits
The farmer's barns.*

*Hallowed be Thou by the
  name
Of Thy pleasure, and
  protect
As in days of old from ill
Romulus' race.*

—Catullus
(87 BCE–54 BCE)

*I will pick the smooth
yarrow that my figure may
be more elegant, that my
lips may be warmer, that
my voice may be more
cheerful; may my voice be
like a sunbeam, may my
lips be like the juice of the
strawberries.*

*May I be an island in the
sea, may I be a hill on the
land, may I be a star when
the moon wanes, may I be a
staff to the weak one: I shall
wound every man, no man
shall wound me.*

—Traditional folk charm

Hazel: Tree.
Heather: Scottish. The flower.
Iseult: Lover of Tristram in Arthurian legend.
Ismenia: Irish name.
Isolda/Isolde/Isolt: The fair.
Izett: Irish name; a form of Iseult.
Janel/Jannel/Jannell: Darling.
Keelia/Keelin/Keely: Beauty.
Kelly: Female warrior.
Kerry: Dark-haired.
Kyla/Kylia: Lovely.
Mabbina/Maeve: Intoxicating one.
Mavelle: Celtic. Songbird.
Maili/Molly: Bitter.
Maiti (pronounced "MAT tee"): Irish name.
Margery: Form of Maeve.
Meara: Irish. Merry.
Morag (pronounced "MAW rack"): Princess.
Morrin: Longhaired.
Neala: Chieftainess.
Nessa: Form of Agnes.
Niamh: Irish mythical princess of the land of
     promise.
Nola: Noble.
Nora/Norah: Honor.
Nuala: Form of Fionnuala.
Onora/Ownah: Lamb.
Peigi (pronounced "PAEG ee"): Pearl.
Ranalt: Name dating from the twelfth century.
Rhona: Rough island.
Riona: Queenly.
Rona: Sea.
Ronat: Seal.
Rowena: Celtic. White mane.
Sabia/Sabina: Goodness.
Samhaoir: In Irish myth, Finn MacCool's daughter.
Saraid: Excellent.
Shannon: Little wise one.
Siobhan (pronounced "sha VAHN"): Ancient name.
Sorcha: Early Irish name.
Tara: Tower.
Ula: Jewel of the sea.
Vevina: Gaelic sweet lady.
Wynne: Fair; light-skinned.
Yseult: The fair.
Zaira: Irish name.

Celtic/Gaelic Boys

Ahern: Lord of horses.
Aidan: Hearth fire.
Angus: From the love God.
Arlen: Pledge.
Arthur: Noble.
Baird: Ballad singer.
Bevan: Warrior's son.
Bowen: Yellow-haired.
Brady: Spirited.
Bram: Raven.
Bren/Brendon/Brennon: Little Raven.
Brett: Briton.
Brian: Strength (from Brian Boru, famous Irish king).
Brock: Badger.
Broderick: Fertile flatland.
Brody: Ditch.
Calhoun: Warrior.
Callum: Messenger of peace.
Camden: From the winding valley.
Cameron: Crooked Nose.
Campbell: Crooked Mouth.
Carlin: Little champion.
Carson: Son of the family on the marsh.
Casey: Valourous, brave.
Cassidy: Clever.
Cathal: Great warrior; battle mighty.
Chalmers: Son of the lord.
Chay: Fairy place.
Cheney: From the oak forest.
Collin: Child.
Conlan: Hero.
Conway: Hound of the plain.
Cormac/Cormick: Charioteer.
Cory: Mountain glen.
Cowan: Hillside hollow.
Cullen: Handsome.
Curran: Hero.
Dacey: Southerner.
Dagda: The good God.
Daibhidh (pronounced "DA ee vee"): Beloved.
Dallan/Dallas: Wise.

Dane: After Goddess Danu.
Darby: Free man.
Darcy: Dark.
Daron: Great little one.
Darren/Darrin: Great.
Delaney: Descendant of the challenger.
Desmond: Man from Munster.
Devan: Poet.
Diancecht: Irish God.
Dillon: Faithful.
Donegal: Dark.
Donnelly: Brave dark man.
Donnovan: Dark warrior.
Doyle: Dark stranger.
Driscoll: Interpreter.
Druce: Wise man.
Duncan: Dark-skinned warrior.
Edan: Fiery.
Ennis: Island.
Evan/Ewan/Ewen: Young warrior.
Farrell: Valorous.
Fearghus (pronounced "FER ra ghuss"): Strong man.
Ferrell: Valorous.
Ferris: The rock; iron worker.
Finn: Fair-haired (from Irish mythical giant Finn MacCool).
Forbes: Prosperous.
Galen: Intelligent.
Gallagher: Eager helper.
Galvan/Galven: Sparrow.
Gavin/Gawen: White hawk.
Gilroy: Devoted to the king.
Glen/Glenn: Valley.
Glendon: From the glen castle.
Grady: Noble.
Hogan: Youth.
Inness: From the river island.
Innis: River island.
Kane/Kayne: Bright.
Kearney: Victorious.
Keefe: Cherished, handsome.
Keegan: Ardent little one.

Keenan/Kienan: Little and ancient.
Keene: Handsome.
Keir: Dark-skinned.
Kele/Kellen/Kelly: Warrior.
Kendrick: Son of Henry.
Kennedy: Helmeted chief.
Kennet/Kenneth: Handsome.
Kenyon: Fair-haired.
Kermit: Free man.
Kerr: Marshland.
Kerry: Dark-haired.
Kevan/Kevin: Loveable, gentle.
Kieran/Kiernan: Little and dark-skinned.
Killian: Little warrior.
Kyle: From the strait.
Laird: Landlord.
Laughlin: A land in Irish legend.
Liam: Gaelic.
Logan: From the hollow.
Mackenzie: Wise ruler's son.
Macnair: Son of the heir.
Maddock: Beneficent.
Mahon: Bear.
Miach: Son of Diancecht in Irish myth.
Morgan: Sea's edge.
Morolt: Brother of Iseult in Arthurian legend.
Muir: Of the moors.
Murdoch: Prosperous seaman.
Murray: Sailor.
Murrough: Sea warrior.
Neel/Nels/Niall: Champion.

Nolan: Famous.
Oren: Pale-skinned.
Owen: Young warrior.
Quinlan: Very strong.
Quinn: Wise.
Renan/Ronan: Little sea.
Revelin: Irish name.
Rierdan/Riordan: King's poet.
Rory: Red king.
Ross: Promontory, headland.
Rowan: Little red one.
Ryan: Little king.
Shamus: Supplanter.
Shay/Shea: Fairy place.
Sheridan: Wild man.
Skelly: Storyteller.
Sloan: Warrior.
Somerled: Scottish. Viking.
Somhairle: Irish. Viking.
Synan: Old.
Tadleigh: Poet.
Teague: Poet, bard.
Thorfinn: Norse chief.
Tiernan: Lord.
Torc: Irish. Boar.
Torin: Chief.
Trahern: Strong as iron.
Trevor: Prudent.
Turlough: Shaped like Thor.
Uileos: Ulysses.
Ultan: Town of Ulster.

TEUTONIC NAMES

Teutonic Girls

Ailsa/Alyssa: Of good cheer.
Alda: Rich.
Amelia: Industrious.
Ara: Eagle maid.
Ardith: Rich gift.
Audris: Wealthy.
Bianca: White.

Blenda: Dazzling.
Dagna: Fair as the day.
Dena: Valley.
Emera: Industrious.
Ethelind: Nobly wise.
Farica: Peaceful ruler.
Felda: A field.

Garda: Protected.
Gisela: Pledge.
Griselda: Grey heroine.
Gudrun: Daughter of the king of the Nibelungs.
Haldis: Stone spirit.
Hazel: Commander.
Hertha: Mother Earth (after the Goddess of fertility).
Ida: Happy.
Ilsa: Gaiety.
Lorelei: Destruction.
Marelda: Famous battle maid.
Melisande: Industrious, strong.
Minetta/Minna: Loving memory.
Raina: Mighty.
Ramona: Wise protectoress.
Vedis: Sacred spirit of the forest.
Velda: Of great wisdom.
Wanda: The wanderer.
Wandis: Lithe and slender.

Teutonic Boys

Abelard: Resolute.
Adalard: Brave and noble.
Alaric/Alarick: Ruler of all.
Aldrich: Wise ruler.
Allard: Resolute.
Archaimbaud/Archambault: Bold.
Archibald: Truly bold.
Arvin: Friend of the people.
Aubrey: Elf king.
Axel: Father of peace.
Baldwin: Bold friend.
Ballard: Bold.
Baron: Noble warrior.
Barret: Mighty as a bear.
Bevis: Archer.
Bond: Farmer.
Chalmers: Lord of the manor.
Charles: Manly.
Conrad: Honest councellor.
Crosby: Dweller near the crossroad.
Derek/Derrick/Dirk: Great ruler.
Derwin: Friend to the animals.
Dustin: Brave fighter.

*Now went she forth, the
   loveliest, as forth the
   morning goes
From the misty clouds
   outbeaming; then all his
   weary woes
Left him, in the heart who
   bore her, and so long
   time had done.
He saw there stately
   standing the fair, the
   peerless one.*

*Many a stone full precious
   flashed from her vesture
   bright;
Her rosy blushes darted a
   softer, milder light
Whate'er might be his
   wishes, each could not
   but confess
He ne'er on earth had wit-
   nessed such perfect
   loveliness.*

*As the moon arising
   outglitters every star
That through the clouds so
   purely glimmers from
   afar,
E'en so love: breathing
   Kriemhild dimmed every
   beauty nigh.
Well might at such a vision
   many a bold heart beat
   high.*

—The Nibelungenlied

He bowed with soft
emotion, and thanked the
blushing fair;
Love's strong constraint
together impelled
th'enamored pair;
Their longing eyes
encountered, their
glances every one
Bound knight and maid for
ever; yet all by stealth
was done.
That in the warmth of
passion he pressed her
lily hand,
I do not know for certain,
but well understand
'Twere surely past believing
they ventured not on this:
Two loving hearts, so
meeting, else had
done amiss.
No more in pride of
summer nor in bloom
of May.
Knew he such heartfelt
pleasure as on this happy
day,
When she, than May more
blooming, more bright
than summer's pride,
His own, a dream no
longer, was standing by
his side.

—The Nibelungenlied

Dwight: Fair one.
Garner: Guardian warrior.
Goddard: Divinely firm.
Graham: From the grey house.
Haines: Vined cottage.
Hardy: Bold, daring.
Humphrey: Man of peace.
Ingram: Angel raven.
Kirby: Norse. From church town.
Lombard: Long beard.
Loring: Famous in war.
Merrill: Famous.
Meyer: Farmer.
Paxton: Pack man.
Roscoe: Deer forest.
Sprague: Lively.
Talbot: Valley bright.
Tate: Cheerful.
Thayer: Of the nation's army.
Thorp: Hamlet.
Tyson: Son of the German.
Ulrich: Wolf ruler.
Waldron: Mighty raven.
Warner: Armed defender.
Warren: Defender.
Warrick: Defending ruler.
Wayne: Wagon.
Wolfe: Wolf.

ENGLISH, WELSH, AND ANGLO-SAXON NAMES

English, Welsh, and Anglo-Saxon Girls

Afton: One from Afton.
Alodie: Wealthy.
Arden: Eagle valley.
Ashleigh/Ashley: From the ash tree farm.
Audrey: Strength to overcome.
Avis: Refuge in battle.
Billie: Strong-willed.
Blake: One with a swarthy complexion.
Bliss: Joy.

Blythe: Joyful.
Brook: Near the stream.
Chelsea: A port of ships.
Clover: Clover blossom.
Cody: A cushion.
Dawn: Break of day.
Dove: The bird.
Eadwine: Valuable friend.
Eartha: The earth.
Edlyn: Noble one.
Edmee: Prosperous protector.
Edris: Prosperous ruler.
Edwina: Valuable friend.
Edyth/Edythe: Rich gift.
Elfin: Elf-like.
Ella: Elf; beautiful fairy woman.
Ellette: Little elf.
Elvina: Befriended by elves.
Erlina: The elfin.
Esme: Gracious protector.
Fancie: Imagination.
Farra/Farrah: Beautiful, pleasant.
Fleta: Swift.
Genna/Gennifer/Guenna: White; fair.
Guinevere/Gwen/Gwendolen: White.
Gwenora/Gwyneth: Fair.
Harley: From the long field.
Harper: Harp player.
Hazel: Commanding authority.
Holly: Tree.
Isolde/Isolt: Fair lady.
Jolene: She will increase.
Kendra: Knowing woman.
Kimberlyn/Kimbra: From the royal fortress meadow.
Lane: From the narrow road.
Lark: Skylark.
Leigh: From the meadow.
Lindsay/Lindsey: From the linden tree island.
Lynn: A cascade.
Maida/Mayda: A maiden.
Megan: Strong or able.
Merry: Happy.
Olwen: White track.
Ora: Money.
Piper: Pipe player.

And she came, wearing a flame-red silken tunic, and a massive collar of red gold round the girl's neck, with precious pearls and rubies in it. Her head was yellower than the flowers of the broom; her flesh was whiter than the foam of a wave; her palms and fingers were whiter than the flowers of the melilot among the small pebbles of a gushing spring. No eye was fairer than hers, not even the eye of the mewed hawk nor the eye of the thrice-mewed falcon. Whiter than the breast of the white swan were her two breasts; redder than the foxglove were her cheeks. All who saw her became filled with love for her. Four white clover flowers would grow up in her footprints wherever she went; and hence she was called Olwen.

—*White Footprint*
(Tenth-century Welsh)

Pixie: Sprite.
Rae: Doe.
Raven: Like the bird.
Rhiamon: Mythological; a Witch.
Rhiannon: Mythical name.
Robin: Like the bird.
Rowena: Famous friend.
Ruadh ("RUE ahd"): Red.
Shandeigh/Shandy: Rambunctious.
Shelby: From the ledge estate.
Skye: Sky.
Skylar: Sheltering.
Sorcha (pronounced "SOR kah"): Bright.
Storm: Stormy.

Summer: Summertime.
Velvet: Velvety.
Vivien: Full of life.
Wallis: From Wales.
Wesley: From the western meadow.
Whitney: From the white island.
Wilda: Willow forest dweller.
Willa: The desired.
Wilona: Wished for.
Winnie: Short form of Gwyneth.
Winter: Wintertime.
Wynne: Fair.
Yetta: To give.

English, Welsh, and Anglo-Saxon Boys

Aelfric: Elf ruler.
Aethelweard: Noble protector.
Aethelwine: Noble friend.
Aethelwulf: Noble wolf.
Aiken: Oaken.
Ainsley: From the near meadow.
Alcott: From the old cottage.
Alden/Aldin/Aldis: Old friend.
Aldrich: Old wise ruler.
Aldwyn: Protector.
Alfred: Elf counselor.
Allard: Noble and brave.
Archer: Bowman.
Averell/Averill: Born in April.
Aylwyn: Old friend.
Bancroft: Of the bean field.
Barclay: From the birch meadow.
Baron: Nobleman.
Barton: From the barley farm.
Baxter: Baker.
Bayard: Having auburn hair.
Benton: Of the moors.
Berwyn: Bright friend.
Birch: Of the birch tree forest.
Blake: Fair-haired.
Bond: Tiller of the soil.
Booth: From the hut.
Borden: From the valley of the boar.

Brad: Broad.
Braden: Of the wide valley.
Bradley: From the broad meadow.
Bradshaw: From the broad grove.
Bramwell: Fierce-willed.
Bran: Raven.
Brand: Fiery.
Brandon: From beacon hill.
Brenton: From the steep hill.
Broderick: From the broad ridge.
Bronson: Son of a dark man.
Buachaill: Sheep herder.
Burgess: Castle dweller.
Burleigh: A field with knotted tree
    trunks.
Burne: From the brook.
Burris: Of the town.
Burton: From the castle.
Calder: Stream.
Caldwell: Dweller by the cold spring.
Calon: Ancient name.
Calvert: Herdsman.
Carleton: Farmer's town.
Carlisle: From the castle.
Carter: Cart driver.
Chad: Warlike.
Chadwick: From the warrior's town.
Chapman: Merchant.

Cliff: Steep rocks.
Clifton: From the town by the cliff.
Cody: A cushion.
Colby: From the black farm.
Collier: Miner.
Cutler: Knifemaker.
Darnell: From the hidden place.
Denver: Green valley.
Draigh: Dragon.
Dudley: From the people's meadow.
Dunstan: From the brown stone castle.
Eadgar: Fortunate spearman.
Eadmund: Rich protector.
Elden: Protector.
Elton: From the town.
Elwin: Friend of the elves.
Elwood: From the old wood.
Emlyn: Winning.
Fairfax: Fair-haired.
Falkner: Falcon master.
Fenton: From the marshland estate.
Fleming: Flemish.
Garland: From the battlefield.
Garrett: With a mighty spear.
Garrick: Oak spear.
Garrnet: Armed with a spear.
Garwin: Comrade in battle.
Gladwin: Cheerful.
Graham: The grey home.
Grayson: Judge's son.
Harley: From the hare's meadow.
Hereward: Army guard.
Hereweard: Soldier protecting.
Hollis: From the holly grove.
Houston: From the hill town.
Kendall: From the bright valley.
Kenway: Bold in battle.
Kingsley: From the king's meadow.
Landon: From the open grassy meadow.
Lane: From the narrow road.

Langdon: From the long hill.
Langley: From the long meadow.
Leland: Meadowland.
Lowell: Beloved.
Mabon: Son.
Maddison: Son of the powerful soldier.
Marlow: From the hill by the lake.
Merlin: Falcon.
Merlin Emrys: Wonderous youth.
Merrick: Ruler of the sea.
Newbold: From the new building.
Oakes: From the oak trees.
Perry: Rock.
Ramsay: Raven's island.
Rand: Shield warrior.
Regenbeald: Rainbow.
Sawyer: Woodsman.
Sheldon: From the hut on the hill.
Shepard: Sheep watcher.
Sherwood: Of the bright forest.
Stanton: From the stony farm.
Taliesin: Radiant Brow.
Thackeray/Thatcher/Thaxer: Roofer.
Thorley: Thor's meadow.
Tilden: From the liberal one's estate.
Tyler: Tile maker.
Wade: From the river crossing.
Waite: Guard.
Walden: From the woods.
Ward: Guardian.
Waverly: From the meadow of aspens.
Wayland: From the land by the road.
Weston: From the western estate.
Weylon: From the land by the road.
Wildon: From the wooded hills.
Winslow: From the friend's hill.
Winston: From the friendly town.
Yale: From the corner of the land.
Yates: Dweller at the gates.
Yul/Yule: Born at Yuletide.

13

Names From Literature

I have consulted a wide variety of texts to create the following listing, which includes names from science fiction, fantasy, ancient texts, poetry, novels, children's books, and modern Pagan-oriented historical novels. I have included several Arthurian works to illustrate some of the differences in characters names involved for any Arthurian buffs who may be interested. Just for fun, I included a Puritan work whose character names struck me as funny and which illustrated the nomenclature of the day. I have included the works of the science fiction and fantasy genres because of the remarkably creative names in such works. I have attempted to include names from many different eras, excluding works whose characters bore strictly Christian names (with the exception being the Puritan work mentioned above). I have also included names from the cult phenomenon of *Star Trek: The Next Generation*. I've included these in this chapter on literature because these stories appear in book form as well as on the television show. The names, as well as the stories and characters, are seductively interesting and warrant a listing. For those Trekkers who would admonish me for omitting a name or two, this isn't intended as a comprehensive chronicle of Trek names, merely a listing of some of my favorites. It is important to give serious attention to cultural phenomena such as this, for it is the stuff of our own mythology.

When choosing a name from something which already exists, one must be sensitive to what in pop psychology is called the universal or collective unconscious. This is a stock of symbols universally understood by almost everyone. An example would be a baby representing beginning and an old man representing ending. To become part of

217

the collective unconscious, a symbol must be understood by a large part of the world to mean a certain thing. To choose such a symbol and try to redefine it as something else is very difficult. It is nearly impossible to swim against the tide of collective understanding. Ask Richard Nixon's former public relations people. The media has a lot to do with putting ideas into the collective unconscious, regardless of whether the ideas are based in reality or not. Many people connect into this when they say "I don't know why I think such as thing is true, but it's everywhere, on television, in the papers; it must be true." A small-scale example is the Pagan use of the pentagram, which is understood by many Westerners to be a symbol of Satanism (thanks to the exploitative and sensationalistic media). You can tell people that you define the pentagram differently, that it doesn't mean Satanism to you, but the stigma is persistent. Many Pagans have come to realize they can't overcome their own aversion to the symbol, despite their understanding of what Pagans mean it to be. Another example would be to say that the very ancient and holy symbol of a swastika is an appropriate Pagan symbol based solely on its antiquity. Much of the world knows that to be a symbol of the Nazis, and it is so engrained with this meaning in the collective unconscious that it would be impossible to use the symbol without the emotional baggage associated with it.

The same idea works in the choosing of names. Most literary names, geographic names, and magical place names would work well when taken as a magical name, because there isn't a universally understood definition involving such names. If one has read the particular book, he or she has an idea about what one author meant the name to be, but one name can be used by many authors for many different characters, thereby muddying the collective understanding of the name. The same holds true for geographic place names; there are many rivers that share the same name. These sorts of names are easily chosen, cleansed, and consecrated to you.

However, the collective understanding of what Biblical names are and what they symbolize is far from reclaimable. If you compare a name from the Bible and a name from a science fiction novel, the Biblical name has a great deal of energy attached to it from thousands of years of use by millions of people. It was often used in times of trauma or upset. The Bible, don't forget, was often read aloud over the crackle of the fires of the Burning Times. The science fiction name, on the other hand, has very little "feeling" or "energy" attached to it. What little there is comes from relaxed reading for pleasure and a fleeting association with a particular character, if you happen to have read the novel. Of course, the better known the book, the more ingrained it is in the collective consciousness. Scarlett O'Hara, for example, could never be used to indicate shyness and modesty; it is too well understood as selfish, beautiful, greedy, and bold.

You do not have to have read the particular books listed in this chapter to get a feeling for the name listed. Remember that when the author named the character (often by invention) the chosen name had no meaning attached to it, but the author breathed life into it by attaching it to the character. Breathe life into these names and redefine them as they are attached to you as one of your magical names. If you like a particular name, take it off the shelf, check it out, and wear it home.

The Acts of King Arthur and His Noble Knights
By John Steinbeck

Accolon
Alardine
Alyne
Anguyshaunce
Arthur
Balan
Balin
Bawdewyn
Bors
Brastias
Carados
Clarivaus
Claudas
Colombe
Cradilment
Ector
Elaine
Ettarde
Ewaine
Fergus
Galahad
Garlon
Gawaine
Gilmere
Grastian
Gryfflet
Guinevere
Hugh
Igraine
Kay

Ladynas
Lamorake
Lancelot
Launcelor
Lodegrance
Lyle
Lyonel
Lyonse
Margawse
Marhalt
Merlin
Mordred
Morgan Le Fay
Naram
Nentres
Nyneve
Outlake
Pelham
Pellinore
Percival
Phariance
Placidas
Raynold
Royns
Sanam
Tarquin
Torre
Ulfius
Uryens
Uther Pendragon

Aeneid
By Publius Vergilius Maro (17 BCE)
(By Order of Augustus Caesar)

Acestes
Aeneas
Amata
Anchises
Anius
Anna
Aruns

Ascanius
Camilla
Celaeno
Creusa
Dido
Evander
Latinus

*Their swords and shining
    armor I descry
Some hostile God, for some
    unknown offense,
Had sure bereft my mind of
    better sense;
For, while thro' winding
    ways I took my flight,
And sought the shelter of
    the gloomy night.*

—Publius Vergilius Maro
Aeneid

Lavinia
Nautes
Nisus
Opis
Palinurus
Pallus
Turnus

Bartholemew Fair
By Ben Jonson (1614)

This is the work which has nomenclature representative of the Puritan era. It is also representative of descriptive names which became surnames.

Alice the Harlot
Bristle
Rabbi Busy
Zeal of the Land Busy
Ezekiel Edgeworth
Bartholemew Fair
Filcher
Haggis
Langthorn Leatherhead
John Littlewit
Win the Fight Littlewit
Mooncalf
Nightingale
Adam Overdo
Dame Overdo
Pocher
Dame Purecraft
Tom Quarlous
Sharkwell
Joan Trash
Troubleall
Ursula
Humphrey Waspe (Numps)
Grace Wellborn
Ned Winwife

Beowulf
(725–750 CE)

Aeschere
Beowulf
Brosing
Ecglaf
Ecgtheow
Ecgwela
Eormenric
Finn
Fitela
Folcwalda
Freawaru
Frisian
Gotar
Grendel
Halga the Good
Hama
Healfdene
Heorogar
Heorot
Hnaef
Hrothgar
Hunlaf
Hygelac
Naegling
Offa
Oslaf
Scyld of the Sheaf
Sigemund
Unferth
Waels
Waelsing
Wealtheow
Weder
Weohstan
Wulfgar

They praised his great deeds and his acts of courage, judged well of his prowess. So it is fitting that man honor his liege lord with words, love him in heart when he must be led forth from his body. Thus the people of the Geats, his hearth-companions, lamented the death of their lord. They said that he was of world-kings the mildest of men and the gentlest, kindest to his people, and most eager for fame.

—Beowulf

Bevis of Hampton
(1200–1250? CE)

Ascapard: Giant.
Bevis: Hero and knight.
Bradmond: King.
King Edgar

Ermyn: Saracen king.
Guy: Prince.
Inor: King.
Josyan: Heroine; lady fair.

Miles: Prince.
Sir Murdour: Murderer.
Saber: Knight.

Castle of Wizardry
By David Eddings

Adara
Aldur
Aloria
Ariana
Barak
Belar
Beldaran
Belgarath
Belgariad
Brand
Ce'nedra
Cherek
Ctuchik
Durnik
Garion
Gorek the Wise
Gorim
Issa
Kharel
Lelldorin

Mandorallen
Nedra
Olban
Polgara
Poppi
Relg
Rhodar
Riva Iron-Grip
Salmissra
Silk
Torak
Tupik
Ulgo
Valgon
Vordai
Xantha
Zakath
Zedar
Zelik

A Celtic Miscellany
By Kenneth Hurlstone Jackson

Aeron: Place name.
Ainnle: Brother of Noise.
Arianrhod: Lugh's mother.
Arran: Place name.
Arthur: Mythical king.
Athairne: Poet.
Balar: Legendary Fomorian chieftain.
Bassa: Place name.
Bedwyr: Sir Bedivere of Arthurian legend.
Beli: Legendary British king.
Berwyn: Place name.
Boadhagh: Mythical king of the happy otherworld.
Boann: Nymph of the River Boyne.

Bron: Ancient name.
Cadwalader
Cailidin: A wizard killed by Cu Chulainn.
Cailte: One of Finn's chief heroes.
Camlan: King Arthur's last battle.
Caradawg
Cashel: Chief place of the early kings.
Celyddon: Forest in Scotland.
Conall: One of the early Ulster heroes.
Conn: Legendary ancient king of Tara.
Connaught: Place name.
Cork: Place name.
Cu Chulainn: The hound of Culann.
Drem

Edain: Fairy woman.
Elfan (Elvan): Brother of Cynddylan.
Emhain (Evin): Place name.
Emlyn: Place name.
Ethal Anbhuail: One of the kings of the
    Fairies.
Finn: Legendary Irish hero.
Galway: Place name.
Gwaddn: Sole.
Gwenddydd: Merlin's sister, a poetess.

Llanddwyn: Place name.
Llew: Sun God, Welsh equivalent of
    Lugh.
Morann: A mythical wise judge.
Moy: River.
Muirinn: Imaginary midwife.
Olwen: Daughter of the ogre Ysbad-
    daden.
Sedanta: Cu Chulainn's real name.
Tara: Place name.

Crusade
By James Lowder

Alusair
Azoun
Balin
Brunthar
Brunthar Elventree
Chanar
Cyric
Dargor
Dimswart
Farl
Filfaeril
Fonjara
Jad
Kiri
Koja
Lugh

Lythrana
Mourngrym
Myrmeen
Rhigaerd
Salember
Susail
Tanalasta
Torg
Torm
Tuigan
Tymora
Tyrluk
Vanderdahast
Vrakk
Winefiddle

The Crystal Shard
By R. A. Salvatore

Agorwal
Akar
Beorg
Beornegar
Biggrin
Bruenor
Cassius
Catti-Brie
Crenshinibon
Dendybar
Dineval

Dorim
Drizzt
Dualdon
Dumathoin
Eldeluc
Errtu
Glensather
Grock the Goblin
Guenhwyvar
Heafstaag
Jensin

Kemp
Kessell
Konig
Luskan
Mithril
Moradin
Morkai
Pasha Pook
Regis

Rumblebelly
Shander
Targos
Telshazz
Termalaine
Tirith
Torga the Orc
Wulfgar

Crystal Singer
By Anne McCaffrey

Andurs
Borella
Borton
Carigana
Carrick
Enthor
Falanog

Gorren
Jezerey
Killashandra
Rimbol
Shillawn
Tukolom
Valdi

The Darkling Hills
By Lori Martin

Adrell
Armas
Ayenna
Baili
Bainne
Boessus
Carden
Dalleena
Desja
Ditta
Envy
Ferra
Forlas
Gharei
Heila
Inama
Kellstae
Kentas
Lilli
Lindis
Lissor

Nesmin
Nialia
Nichos
Nilsor
Phenna
Pillyn
Proseras
Raynii
Rena
Rendell
Sanlin
Seani
Shandel
Sillus
Simsas
Teleus
Telph
Temhas
Traehi
Valtah

The Darkover Novels*
By Marion Zimmer Bradley

Alanna
Aldaran
Aleki
Alexis (Lexie)
Alida
Allart
Allira
Anjali
Ann'dra
Annelys
Aquilara
Ardrin
Arielle
Arilinn
Auster
Avarra
Aven
Barak
Bard
Barron
Bethany
Brynat
Byrna
Calinda
Callista
Carlina
Carolin
Caryl
Cathal
Chandria
Chieri
Cholayna
Clariza
Cleindori
Colin
Colryn
Coryn
Cressa
Cyrillon

Dalereuth
Damon
Danilo
Danvan
Darill
Darissa
Darnack
Deonara
Desideria
Devra
Dezi
Dika
Donal
Donell
Dorilys
Dyan
Edric
Eduin
Elhalyn
Ellemir
Ellers
Elorie
Felix
Ferrika
Fianna
Fiona
Garin
Garris
Gwynn
Hali
Hilary
Idriel: A moon.
Irmelin
Jaelle
Jandria
Janetta
Janine
Javanne
Jerana

* Including *The Bloody Sun, City of Sorcery, The Forbidden Tower, Hawkmistress, The Heritage of Hastur, Sharra's Exile, The Shattered Chain, Star of Danger, Stormqueen!, Thendara House, Two to Conquer,* and *The Winds of Darkover.*

"Yes, you will all learn to protect yourselves, by force if you cannot do so by reason or persuasion; but this in itself will not make you the equals of men. Even now, a day is coming here in Thendara when every little matter need not be put to the sword, but will be decided more rationally. For now, we accept the world as men have made it because there is no other world available, but our goal is not to make women as aggressive as men, but to survive— merely to survive—until a saner day comes. Yes, you will all learn a way to earn a living, but being independent of a husband is not enough to free you of dependence; even a rich woman who marries a poor man, so that they live upon her bounty, considers herself, by custom, bound to serve and obey her husband. Yes, you will learn to wear women's clothes by choice and not from necessity, and to speak as you wish, not to keep your words and your

Kadarin

Karinn

Keitha

Kennard

Ker

Kermiac

Kerstal

Kerwin

Kieran

Kilghard

Kindra

Kyntha

Kyril

Kyrrids: A moon.

Laurens

Lauria N'ha Andrea

Laurinda

Lella

Leominda

Leonie

Lerrys

Li

Linnea

Linnell

Liriel: A moon.

Lisarda

Loran

Lorenz

Lorill

Luciella

Lyondri

Magda

Magdalen (Magda, Margali) N'ha Ysabet

Mallina

Mallinson

Margwenn

Mariel

Marius

Marsiela

Marya

Maura

Mayra

Melisendra

Melora

Melora

Merelie
Merryl
Mhari
Mikhail
Millea
Mirella
Montray
Mormallor: A moon.
Neskaya
Neyrissa
Nira
Orain
Rafaella
Rafe
Ragan
Rakhaila
Rannath
Rannirl
Rannvil
Rayna
Reade
Renata
Rezi
Ria
Rima
Rohana
Romilly
Rory
Rumal
Sharra
Shaya
Sherna
Stefan
Sunstar
Taniquel
Tella
Thyra
Valdir
Varzil
Wolf
Yllana
Zandru

minds in bonds for fear of being thought unmannerly or unwomanly. But none of these is the most important thing. Mother Lauria, will you tell them the most important thing they will learn?"

Mother Lauria leaned forward a little, to emphasize what she was saying.

"Nothing you will learn is of the slightest importance, save for this: you will learn to change the way you think about yourselves, and about other women."

—Marion Zimmer Bradley
Thendara House

Darkover Novels with the Friends of Darkover*
By Marion Zimmer Bradley and the Friends of Darkover

Alais	Cyril
Alar	Cyrilla
Alaric	Damrys
Alessandro	Danilys
Allira	Danla
Amara	Danlyn
Amaury	Darla
Amrek	Darriel
Anya	Dawyd
Ariane	Denita
Arielle	Deonara
Artros	Derik
Asharra	Dione
Auster	Donal
Avarra	Dorata
Belloma	Dorian
Beltran	Eadar
Bredan	Edric
Brigid	Elena
Bronwyn	Elholyn
Bruna	Elinda
Buartha	Elorie
Caelly	Elys
Caillean	Enid
Caitlin	Erharth
Caitrin	Farren
Caltus	Finn
Cara	Gabriela
Carolin	Gaelan
Casilda	Garrik
Cassalina	Garris
Catlyn	Harkspell
Catriona	Jamilla
Cerdic	Janella
Chimene	Janetta
Clea	Janna
Colryn	Jaqual
Coryn	Jemel
Corys	Jharek
Crystal	Julana
Cullen	Kadi

* Including *The Four Moons of Darkover*, *Sword of Chaos*, and *Free Amazons of Darkover*.

Katria
Kayeta
Keithyl
Kell
Kennard
Kennet
Kiera
Kyla
Kyria
Larissa
Lauria
Liane
Linnet
Lionora
Lira
Liriel
Lisandra
Lora
Loran
Lori
Macrae
Maellen
Maol
Mara
Margali
Margalys
Margatta
Margolys
Mari
Marissa
Marji
Marna
Merryl
Mhari
Mikhael
Millim
Mirrei
Morag
Naella

Nemma
New Skye
Nyal
Peidro
Rabharty
Rael
Raghall
Raimon
Ramhara
Rannan
Ranwyn
Ranyl
Reva
Rima
Robard
Roualeyn
Ruyven
Sabrynne
Sarena
Seanon
Shandra
Shilla
Stelle
Tani
Tarisa
Temora
Terel
Torayza
Torcall
Toria
Valaena
Valentine
Vardis
Verdis
Veynal
Wellana
Xiella
Ysabet
Zhalara

The Deryni Novels*
By Katherine Kurtz

Alain
Alaric

Alroy
Alyce

* Including *Deryni Checkmate, Deryni Rising,* and *High Deryni.*

Arilan	Graham
Barrett	Gryphon
Bennett	Gwydion
Bethane	Gwyllim
Bradene	Gwynedd
Bran	Hamilton
Brendan	Hillary
Brion	Hort
Bronwyn	Hugh
Burchard	Ian
Camber	Istelyn
Cara	Jared
Cardiel	Jatham
Carsten	Jehana
Charissa	Kelson
Conall	Kevin
Conlan	Kirby
Coram	Kyri
Cordan	Laran
Coroth	Lewys
Corrigan	Liam
Corwyn	Loris
Creoda	Mal
Culdi	Malcolm
Danoc	Marluk
Davency	Mclain
Davis	Medras
Dawkin	Merritt
Deegan	Moira
Deforest	Morag
Derryd	Morgan
Derry	Nigel
Dobbs	Payne
Donal	Ralf
Duncan	Ralson
Elas	Rhafallia
Elsworth	Rhemuth
Elvira	Rhodri
Eric	Rhydon
Ewan	Rhys
Fathane	Richenda
Fianna	Rimmell
Garon	Rogier
Giles	Rolf
Godwin	Ronal

Rory
Royston
Selden
Shannis
Thorne
Tolliver

Torin
Torval
Vera
Vivienne
Wencit

The Dragonriders of Pern
By Anne McCaffrey

B'dor
B'rant
Brand
Brekke
Celina
Dunca
Elgion
F'lar
F'lon
F'nor
Fandarel
Fanna
Fax
Felena
Gemma
Groghe
Jaxom
Jora
Kern

Kylara
Lessa
Lidith
Lytol
Manora
Menolly
Merika
Moreta
Nadira
Piemur
Rannelly
Sanra
Sharra
Talina
Toric
Wansor
Yanis
Zurg

Dune
By Frank Herbert

Alia: Psychic sister to hero.
Arrakis: Planet name.
Atreides: Clan name.
Bene Gesserit: Priesshood of psychics.
Caladan: Planet name.
Chani: Hero's wife, desert warrior.
Fedaykin: Fremen warriors.
Fremen: Desert warrior tribe.
Giedi Prime: Evil planet name.
Gom Jabbar: Poison pin.
Great Mother: Space Goddess name.
Gurney Halleck: Troubador warrior.
Harkonnen: Evil clan.

Jessica: Priestess.
Kwisatz Haderach: Male seer.
Leto: Hero's father.
Maud'dib: Hero's magical name (means mouse).
Melange: Spice drug.
Mentat: Human computer.
Sandrider: Fremen who ride giant sandworms.
Shai-hulud: Giant sandworm.
Shari
Stilgar: Fremen leader.
Thufir Hawat: Warrior.

Usul: Nickname of hero.

Vladimir Harkonnen: Evil leader.

Weirding: Witchcraft.

Elven Star
By Margaret Weis and Tracy Hickman

Aleatha
Arianus
Bane
Calandra
Daidlus
Drakar
Drugar
Durndrun
Elixnoir
Gregor
Griffith
Haplo
Kevanish

Lenthan
Lucillia
Paithan
Patryn
Peytin
Pundar
Rega
Roland Redleaf
Sigla
Thillia
Ulaka
Zifnab

The Epic of Gilgamesh
(Third Millenium BCE)

Adad: Storm, rain, weather God.

Anunuki: Gods of the Underworld.

Anshan: A bow-making location in Persia.

Antum: Wife of Anu.

Anu: Father of the Gods.

Apsu: Primeval waters under the earth.

Aruru: Goddess of creation.

Aya: The dawn; wife of the sun God.

Belit-Sheri: Scribe to the Gods.

Dilmun: Sumerian paradise.

Dumuzi: God of vegetation and fertility, husband to Inanna.

Ea: God of the sweet waters and wisdom; patron of the arts.

Egalmah: Home of the Goddess Ninsun; a great palace.

Enlil: God of earth, wind, and space.

Ereshkigal: Goddess of the underworld; once a sky Goddess.

Gilgamesh: Son of Goddess Ninsun and a priest.

Gizzida: See Ningizzida.

Hanish: One who forewarns of storms.

Humbaba: Guardian of the cedar forests.

Igigi: Collective name for the Gods.

Ishtar: Goddess of love and fertility; also of war. Patroness of Uruk.

Ki: Earth.

Lugulbanda: A shepherd God, protector of Gilgamesh.

Magan: Land of the dead.

Mammentum: Goddess of fate or destiny.

Mashu: The mountain where the sun goes at night.

Nergal: Underworld God. Was once an air God who "fell" to being an underworld plague God, much as the Christian Satan.

Neti: Underworld gatekeeper.

Ningal: Wife of the moon and mother of the sun.

Ningizzida: Fertility God called "lord of the tree of life." Later a healer God of magic.

Ninhursag: Mother Goddess; also called Nintu (meaning lady of birth).

Ninki: Mother of Enlil, God of earth.

Ninsun: Mother of Gilgamesh. Goddess of wisdom.
Ninurta: Warrior and wind God.
Nisaba: Goddess of grain.
Samuquan: God of cattle.
Shulpae: God of feasting.
Siduri: Goddess of winemaking and brewing. She lives in the garden of the sun.
Silili: Horse Goddess.
Sin: The moon God, father of the sun and of Ishtar.
Tammuz: Dying God of vegetation.
Uruk: Town in Southern Babylonia between Fara and Ur (Gilgamesh was king of Uruk).

The Faerie Queene
By Edmund Spenser (1590)

Acrasia: Circe-like temptress in her bower of bliss.
Adonis
Amoret: Scudamour's bride.
Archimago: Evil wizard.
Arthur: Prince.
Atin: Servant.
Belphoebe: Virgin huntress reared by Goddess Diana.
Diana
Duessa: Diana's seductive assistant.
Error: Monster in the wandering wood.
Faunus: Satyr.
Florimell: Lovliest and gentlest lady in Faerieland.
Gloriana: Faerie Queene.
Ireana: Victim.
Kirkrapine: Church robber.
Mammon: God of riches.
Marinell: Son of a sea nymph.
Merlin: Wizard.
Mollana: Nymph.
Neptune: Sea God.
Panope: An old nymph.
Phaedria: Coquette.
Scudamour: Knight skilled in lovemaking.
Snowy Florimell: Made a Witch.
Timias: Price Arthur's squire.
Una: Daughter of the King and Queene.
Venus: Goddess of love.

*There, whence that Musick
   seemed heard to bee,
Was the faire Witch her
   selfe now solacing,
With a new Lover, whom
   through sorceree
And Witchcraft, she from
   farre did thither bring:
There she had him now
   layd a slombering,
In secret shade, after long
   wanton joyes:
Whilst round about them
   pleasauntly did sing
Many faire Ladies, and
   lascivious boyes,
That ever mixt their song
   with light licentious
   toyes.*

—Edmund Spenser
The Faerie Queene (1590)

The Fall of Atlantis
By Marion Zimmer Bradley

Arkati
Arvath of Alkonath
Cadamiri
Chedan
Demira
Deoris
Domaris
Elara
Elis
Isarma
Karahama
Lissi
Lydara

Maleina
Micail
Micon of Ahtarrath
Mother Ysouda
Nadastor
Ragamon
Rajasta
Rathor
Riveda
Simila
Talkannon
Tiriki
Woman Clothed With the Sun

Firelord
By Parke Godwin

Agrivaine
Ambrosius
Arthur
Avalon
Bedivere
Bedwyr
Belrix
Bors
Bredei
Cador
Caius
Carline
Cerdic
Coel
Cradda
Cunedag
Dafydd
Dorelei
Drost
Druith
Eleyne
Fhain
Flavia

Gareth
Gawain
Geraint
Gryffyn
Guenevere
Imogen
Kay
Lancelot
Maelgwyn
Melga
Merlin
Modred
Morgana
Nectan
Nectin
Peredur
Prydn
Rhian
Trystan
Uredd
Urgus
Uther
Ygerna

Grettir the Strong
(Thirteenth Century)

Aesa: Wife of Onund.
Asmund Longhair: Father of Grettir.
Atli: Grettir's brother.
Bjorn: Jealous man.
Einar: Farmer.
Glam: Shepherd.
Grettir the Strong: Icelandic hero.
Grim: Outlaw.
Illugi: Grettir's brother.
Karr the Old: Father of Thorfinn.
Ofeig: Father of Aesa.

Ogmund: Raider.
Onund: Viking ancestor of Grettir.
Redbeard: Outlaw.
Skeggi: Killed by Grettir.
Thorbjorn Slowcoach: Enemy.
Thorbjorn Oxmain: Kin of Slowcoach.
Thorfinn: Norwegian landlord.
Thorir of Gard: Father.
Thorir: Raider.
Thorodd: Kinsman of Oxmain.
Thrand: Hero.

Gulliver's Travels
By Jonathan Swift (1726)

Calin
Clumglum
Clustril
Drunlo
Flimnap
Galbet
Golbasto Momaren Evlame Gurdilo
      Shefin Mully Ully Gue
Grildrig
Gulliver
Hurgo
Island of Blefuscu

Lalcon
Laputa
Lilliput
Limtoc
Lustrog
Mildendo
Nardac
Reldresal
Skyresh Bolgolam
Slamecksan
Tramecksan

Guy of Warwick
(Thirteenth Century)

Anlaf: King of Denmark.
Athelstan: King of England.
Colbrand: Giant.
Ernis: Emperor of Greece.
Felice La Belle: Heroine.
Guy: Knight.
Loret: Ernis' daughter.

Morgadour: Knight.
Otous: Duke of Pavia.
Reignier: Emperor of Germany.
Rohaud: Earl.
Segyn: Duke of Louvain.
Segyn: Prisoner.
Tirri: Knight.

The Heart of the Fire
By Cerridwen Fallingstar

Amergin
Annie

Anu
Ashtara: Sexual Goddess of passion.

Avalon
Bearhearth
Bess
Blouwedd: Goddess of beauty and
    flowers.
Briget
Cailitie: The cat.
Cailleach: A dark aspect of the Goddess.
Cernonus
Cerridwen
Chanda
Colin
Copper
Crosby
Druaderia: Gypsy Tantra (sex magick).
Elana
Eostre
Ewan
Fiona Mcnair
Galen
Grizelda Greediguts the Cat
Ian
Jesses
Jonet
Kelpie: Sea or lake monster.
Kyairthwen
Leman: Lover.
Lindsay
Litha
Lizbet
Lochlan

Magpie Maiden
Mairead
Malcolm
Mannanon MacLir
Mari
Marianna: Goddess of the sea.
McTavish
Mina
Minstrel
Mist the Cat
Moonsock the Cat
Morrigan
Myrrhiana
Nimue
Oberon the Cat (Obie)
Orrin Argyle
Peat Moss the Cat
Queen of the Night
Ragni: Spider Goddess.
Robin the Good
Roxanne
Sari Snowflower
Scotia Cailleach
Sean
Sooktart Machlana
Staghorn
Taliesin
Verado
Violet
Wind Mare
Winter

The Heimskringla
By Snorri Sturluson (Thirteenth Century)

Aethelred: King of England.

Aethelstan: King of England.

Crippled Inge: Harald Gille's most
    popular son.

Ellisiv: Daughter of the Tussian king,
    wife of Harald the Stern.

Eric Blood-Ax: Hakon's brother.

Hakon Magnusson: Nephew to Olaf the
    Quiet.

Hakon the Good: Harald's son. He is a
    Christian, but does not force it
    upon his subjects.

Halfdan the Black: King of Norway. A
    good king. He died young and his
    body was quartered and sent to
    separate provinces to spread his
    goodness.

Harald Gille: From Ireland. Claiming to
    be Sigurd's brother, he proves his
    paternity in an ordeal by hot iron.
    He is a cruel sovereign.

Harald Godwinsson: Successor to
    Edward the Good of England.

Harald Sigurdsson the Stern: Brother of Olaf the
Saint. He won great wealth in plundering and
gave half to his nephew in return for rule of
half of Norway.

Harald the Fairhaired: Halfdan's brother. A girl
refused him because he had little territory, so
he conquered all of Norway for her. He eventually married her.

Hardacnute: King of Denmark and King of England.

Magnus Barefoot: Son of Olaf the Quiet.

Magnus the Blind: Son of Sigurd. A foolish king. He
retired to a monastery.

Magnus the Good: Stepson of Olaf Haraldsson.

Mime: Odin's friend who was beheaded. Odin caused
the preserved head to speak and tell him
secrets.

Odin: Conqueror who settled in the Scadinavian
peninsula.

Olaf Haraldsson the Saint: Descendant of Harald the
Fairhaired.

Olaf the Quiet: Son of Harald the Stern.

Olaf Tryggvesson: Son of Tryggve. Became a Viking
chieftain at the age of twelve. He converted all
of Norway to Christianity.

On Jorundsson: King of Sweden; he extended his life
by sacrificing a son to Odin every ten years.

Sigurd the Crusader: Son of Magnus Barefoot.

Sigurd Slembedegn: Pretender to the throne.

Olaf the Stoat:
Vermin, Martyr, Saint

—A T-shirt seen
at a Pagan festival

The Horse Goddess
By Morgan Llywelyn

Basl
Brydda
Dasadas
Drui
Epona
Esus
Goibban
Kazhak
Kelti
Kernunnos Shapechanger
Kolaxis
Kwelon
Mahka

Nematona
Okelos
Poel
Rigatona
Ro-An
Suleva
Talia

Taranis
Tena: She who summons fire.
Toutorix
Tsaygas
Uiska
Vilma

Ivanhoe
By Sir Walter Scott (1820)

Athelstane of Coningsburgh: A descendant of ancient Saxon kings.
Aymer: Lazy prior captured by Robin Hood.
Cedric the Saxon: Master of Rotherwood.
Friar Tuck: Robin Hood's follower.
Gurth: Cedric's jester.
Issac of York: Kindly jew.
Lady Rowena: Beautiful, young ward of Cedric.
Lucas De Beaumanoir: Head of Templars who presides over Rebecca's trial on charges of Witchcraft.
Albert Malvoisin: Templar executed by Richard for treason.
Philip Malvoisin: Templar executed by Richard for treason.

Maurice De Bracy: Norman who captures Rowena.
Prince John: Richard's unscrupulous brother.
Rebecca: Lovely Jewess.
Reginald Front De Boeuf: Savage Norman.
Richard the Lion-Hearted: King.
Robin Hood (Robin of Locksley): Outlaw.
Sir Brian De Bois-Guilbert: Templar who kidnaps Rebecca.
Ulrica: Saxon hag.
Waldemar Fitzurse: Prince John's wily follower, banished by Richard.
Wilfred Of Ivanhoe: Chivalrous hero, son of Cedric, Rowena's husband.

The Jungle Book
By Rudyard Kipling

Akela: a wolf.
Bagheera: The black panther.
Baloo: Brown bear.
Chuchundra: The muskrat.
Darzee: The tailorbird.
Hathi: The white elephant.
Ikki: The porcupine.
Kaa: The rock snake.
Kala Nag: The elephant.
Lungri: The lame one.
Mang: The bat.

Mao: The peacock.
Mowgli: The frog.
Mysa: buffalo.
Nagaina: The cobra.
Raksha: The demon.
Rann: The kite.
Rikki-Tikki-Tavi: The mongoose.
Shere Khan: The tiger.
Tabaqui: The jackal.
Toomai: The boy.

The Kalevala
By Elias Lonnrot (Oral, originating prior to 1000 CE)

Ahti: Matchless boy.
Aino: Joukahainen's sister, wife to Vainenoinen.
Air Daughter: Elemental Goddess.
Annikki: She of good name, girl of the night, maid of dusk.
Antero Vipunen: Full of tales.
Birdberry Daughter
Fir Daughter
Great Bear's Daughter
Ilmarinen: The smith.
Joukahainen: The young bard.
Jack Frost: The evil one, a trickster.
Juniper Daughter
Kaleva Daughter: Fair maid.
Karelia: Ox.
Kullervo: Kalervo's son.
Kylli: An island maid; island flower.
Kyllikki: An island maid; island flower.
Lemminkainen: Wanton, luckless one.
Louhi: Mistress of the northland.
Marjatta: Nice young maid.
Mieliki: Forest Daughter.
Mist Girl: Maid of the fog.
Moon Daughter
Nyyrikki: Tapio's son.
Osmo: The brewer woman.
Pellervionen: The field's son.
Piltti: Tiny wench.
Rowan Daughter
Sampsa: Tiny boy.
South Daughter
Star Daughter
Summer Daughter
Sun Daughter
Tellervo: Tapio's maid.
Tiera
Tuoni: River.
Tuulikki: Forest girl.
Utamo: Fisherman.
Vainamoinen: The timeless old bard.
Water Mother: Gaia figure.

Vainamoinen grew angry at that, angry and ashamed. He himself started singing himself began reciting: the songs are not children's songs children's songs, women's songs but for a bearded fellow which not all the children sing nor do half the boys nor a third of the suitors of this evil age with time running out. Then old Vainamoinen sang: the lakes rippled, the earth shook the copper mountains trembled the sturdy boulders rumbled the cliffs flew in two the rocks cracked upon the shores.

—Elias Lonnrot
The Kalevala
(The battle between the Old Bard and the Young Bard)

Le Morte d'Arthur
By Sir Thomas Malory (1469)

Agravaine: Gawain's brother.
Arthur: King of Britain.
Balan: Brother of Balin.
Balin Le Sauvage: Knight.
Brangwaine: Isoud's maid.
Breunor Le Noire: Knight.
Dodinas Le Sauvage: Knight.
Ector De Maris: Knight.
Elaine Le Blanc: The fair maid of Astolat.
Elaine: Pelle's daughter, Galahad's
    mother.
Gaheris: Gawain's brother.
Galahad: Launcelot's son.
Gareth: Brother of Gawain.
Gawain: Arthur's nephew.
Gouvernail: Tristram's tutor.
Isoud: Irish princess, lover of Tristram.
Isoud La Blanche Mains: Tristram's wife,
    in name only.
King Pelles: The Fisher King.
King Evelake: Ancient ruler.

Launcelot du Lake: Knight, lover of the
    queen.
Linet: Damsel.
Lionel: Knight.
Liones: Linet's sister, Gareth's wife.
Mark: Isoud's husband.
Meliogrance: Kidnapper of Guenevere.
Merlin: Wizard.
Mordred: Arthur's son.
Morgan Le Fay: Arthur's half-sister.
Numue: Lady of the Lake, Merlin's
    mistress.
Palamides: Valiant Pagan knight.
Pellinore: Knight who continuously pur-
    sues the Questing Beast.
Percival: Knight.
Queen Guenevere: Queen of Britain.
Sagramore: Knight.
Sir Kay: Arthur's foster brother.
Tristram: Knight.

Lion of Ireland
By Morgan Llywelyn

Ailill
Amlaff
Anluan
Aoife
Ardan
Bebinn
Benin
Brian Boru
Brigid
Brodir
Cahal
Callachan
Camin
Carroll
Cashel
Cennedi
Cet
Conall Cernach

Conn
Connlaoch
Conor
Corc
Cuchullain
Cullen
Damon
Deirdre
Dermott
Donncuan
Donogh
Echtigern
Emer
Ferdiad
Fiacaid
Fiona
Fithir
Flann

Gilli
Gormlaith
Guaire
Ilacquin
Ivar
Kernac
Kian
Kincora
Lachtna
Leti
Liam Mac Aengus
Macliag
Maelmordha
Mahon
Malachi Mor

Mangus
Marcan
Molloy
Muiredach
Murrough Mac Brian
Nessa
Niall
Olaf Cuaran
Ospak
Padraic
Sabia
Sigurd
Sitric
Svein
Teigue

The Lord of the Rings and *The Silmarillion*
By J. R. R. Tolkien

Aerin
Aglon
Ainur
Aldaron
Aldor
Almaren
Aman
Amandil
Amlach
Amon Obel: Place name.
Amon Amarth: Place name.
Amon Gwareth: Place name.
Amon Ethir: Place name.
Amon Sul: Place name.
Amon Uilos: Place name.
Amon Rudh: Place name.
Amon Ereb: Place name.
Amras
Amrie
Amroth
Anach
Anarion
Aragorn (Arathorn, Elessar, Elfstone, Strider): King of Gondor.
Arien
Arthad

Arwen Evenstar (Undomiel): Elvish princess.
Atani
Avallone
Avari
Azaghal
Bain: Dwarf lord.
Balin: Dwarf lord.
Balar
Baldor
Balin: Dwarf lord.
Balrog: Creature that nearly killed Gandalf.
Barahir: Warrior of Gondor.
Bard the Bowman
Barliman Butterbur: Innkeeper in Bree.
Beechbone: An Ent (tree creature).
Beleg
Belfalas: Place name.
Beorn: A Warrior of the Mark.
Bereg
Beregond: A Warrior of Gondor.
Beren
Bergil
Beruthiel
Bifur: A Hobbit.

Bilbo Baggins: The finder of the Ruling
    Ring; a Hobbit.
Blue Mountains
Bombadil, Tom: The oldest creature in
    Middle Earth.
Borlach
Borlad
Boromir: A warrior prince of Gondor.
Brand: A legendary warrior.
Brandir
Bregalad: An Ent.
Brego
Brodda
Cardolan
Carnil
Celeborn
Celebrimbor
Celon
Ceorl
Cirdan: The ancient shipwright.
Ciryon
Daeron
Dagnir
Dagorlad: A battle plain.
Dain: A Dwarf lord.
Dairuin
Deagol: An ancient Hobbit, brother of
    Smeagol.
Denethor: Steward of Gondor.
Deor
Dernhelm: A warrior of the Mark.
Dimbar
Dior
Dolmed
Dori: A Dwarf lord.
Doriath
Dorlas
Draugluin
Drengist
Dunadan: Man of the west.
Durin: A Dwarf lord.
Dwalin: A Dwarf lord.
Dwarrowdelf: Place name.
Ea
Earendil
Earnur

Ecthelion
Edain
Elbereth Gilthoniel (Varda): An Elvish
    princess.
Eldar
Elendil: A king of Westernesse.
Elenna
Elerrina
Elfhelm: A warrior of the Mark.
Elladan: An Elvish warrior.
Elrohir: An Elvish warrior.
Elrond Halfelven (Elrond): An Elvish
    king.
Elwe
Elwing
Emeldir
Eomer: Heir to the throne of the Mark.
Eomun
Eorl: Legendary warrior king of the
    Mark.
Eothain
Eowyn: Warrior princess of the Mark.
Erkenbrand: A warrior of the Mark.
Fangorn (Treebeard): Leader of the Ents.
Faramir: A Captain of Gondor.
Feanor
Fimbrethil: An Ent.
Finglas (Leaflock): An Ent.
Fingon
Finrod
Floi: A Dwarf lord.
Forlong: A lesser king of Gondor.
Fredegar Bolger: A Hobbit.
Frodo: The hero of the story; a Hobbit.
Fundin
Galadriel: Elvish queen of lorien.
Galdor
Gamling
Gandalf the Grey (Mithrandir): A wizard.
Garulf
Gildor: An Elvish warrior.
Gimli: A Dwarf, Frodo's companion.
Gladden Fields
Gloin: A Dwarf lord.
Glorfindel: An Elvish warrior.
Goldberry: Tom Bombadil's wife.

Goldwine
Gorlim
Gram
Grimbeorn
Grimbold
Guilin
Guthlaf
Gwindor
Hador
Haladin
Halbarad
Haldir
Halflings: Hobbits.
Hama
Harding
Helm: A legendary warrior of the Mark,
     founder of "Helm's Deep."
Herefara
Hirgon
Hirluin
Horn
Hurin
Iarwain Ben Adar
Idril
Imrahil
Ingold
Ioreth
Iorlas
Isengrim
Isildur: Legendary warrior king of
     Westernesse.
Legolas Greenleaf: An Elf, Frodo's
     companion.
Lindon
Lorien: An Elvish land.
Luthien Tinuviel: An Elvish princess.
Magor
Mahal
Malbeth the Seer
Mauhur
Melian
Meneldil
Meneldor
Meriadoc Brandybuck (Merry): Frodo's
     companion.
Mim

Miriel
Mirkwood: Place name.
Misty Mountains
Mordor: Sauron's realm.
Nandor
Narvi: An Elvish smith.
Narya: An Elvish ring.
Nenya: An Elvish ring.
Nimrodel: A river.
Noldor
Nori
Ohtar
Oin: A Dwarf lord.
Olorin
Ori: A Dwarf.
Orome
Orophin
Peredhil
Peregrin Took (Pippin): A Hobbit,
     Frodo's companion.
Quenya
Quickbeam: An Ent.
Radagast The Brown: A wizard.
Ragnor
Rian
Rumil
Salmar
Seeing Stones (Palantir): Crystal balls
     used to see afar.
Slimbirch: An Ent.
Taras
Targon
Tauron
Telchar
Thengel: A legendary king of the Mark.
Theoden: King of the Mark.
Theodred
Thingol
Thistlewood: An Ent.
Thorin Oakenshield: A legendary warrior
     Dwarf.
Thrain: A Dwarf lord.
Thranduil
Thror
Turgon
Turin

Ulfang
Valandil
Vana
Vanyar

Vorondil
Wandlimb: An Ent.
Widfara
Yavanna

The Mabinogi
(Tenth Century)

Annwen
Aranrhod
Arawn
Arberth
Arthur
Bendigeidfran
Branwen
Bres
Bwlch
Cei
Ceridwen
Cigfa
Coraniaid
Cyfwlch
Diaspad: Cry.
Drwg: Bad.
Dyfed
Dylan
Efnisien
Elphin
Fir Bolg
Formorian
Garm: Shout.
Gawain
Gilfaethwy
Glewlwyd
Glyn Cuch
Goewin
Gwaeth: Worse.
Gwaethaf Oll: Worst of all.
Gwales
Gwion Bach

Gwydion
Gwynedd
Hafgan
Harlech
Lleuelys
Llew Llaw Gyffes
Llew
Lludd
Llwyd
Llyr
Lugh
Maelgwn
Manawydan
Math
Matholwch
Nisien
Nuadha
Och: Alas.
Olwen
Owaen
Pen Annwfn: Lord of the otherworld.
Pendaran Dyfed
Pryderi
Pwyll
Rhiannon
Sefwlch
Silver-Hand
Taliesin
Teyrnon
Tuatha de Danaan
Twrch Trwyth
Ywain

Macbeth
By William Shakespeare

Angus
Banquo

Caithness
Donalbain

Duncan
Fleance
Hecate
Lennox
Macbeth
MacDuff
Malcolm
Menteith
Ross
Seyton
Siward
Weird Sisters

The Masters of Solitude
By Marvin Kaye and Parke Godwin

Arin
Bern
Bowdeen
Callan
Callee
Cat
Charzen
Deak
Echo
Elin
Gannell
Garrick
Hoban
Holder
Janny
Jay
Jenna
Karli
Kon
Korbin
Lams
Loomin
Lorl
Magill
Maysa
Moss
Mrikan
Myudah
Samman

The characters presented as "the three witches" in Macbeth *were never referred to as Witches by Shakespeare, or by any characters in the play. They are identified as Witches in the director's notes of the original (and undoubtedly pressured by the attitudes of King James I, during whose reign it was written). These three sisters appear on the battlefield, which suggests that they may have been intended to represent the three Goddesses of battle that attended the Morrigan. Shakespeare called them "weird sisters" and cast them as oracles, identifying them with the Norse Wyrds or the Greek Moirae.*

Sand
Shalane
Shando
Sidele
Singer
Suffec
Thammay
Tilda
Uhian
Wengen

I swear to thee by Cupid's
strongest bow,
By his best arrow with the
golden head,
By the simplicity of Venus'
doves,
By that which knitteth souls
and prospers loves,
And by that fire which
burn'd the Carthage
queen,
When the false Troyan
under sail was seen,
By all the vows that ever
men have broke,
In number more than ever
women spoke,
In that same place thou
hast appointed me,
To-morrow truly will I meet
with thee.

—William Shakespeare
A Midsummer
Night's Dream

The Merlin Novels*
By Mary Stewart

Branwen
Cadal
Camlach
Cei
Cerdic
Dyved
Galapas
Keridwen
Merlin
Merlinus
Moravik
Myrddin Emrys
Niniane
Ulfin
Uther
Vortigern
Ygraine

A Midsummer Night's Dream
By William Shakespeare

Cobweb: Fairy.
Egeus: Hermia's father.
Francis Flute: A bellows master.
Helena: In love with Demetrius.
Hermia: Egeus's daughter.
Hippolyta: Queen of the Amazons.
Lion: Snug in the interlude.
Lysander: Loved by Hermia.
Moonshine: Robin Starveling in the interlude.

---

* Including *The Crystal Cave, The Hollow Hills,* and *The Last Enchantment.*

Moth: Fairy.
Mustardseed: Fairy.
Nick Bottom: A weaver.
Oberon: King of the Fairies.
Peaseblossom: Fairy.
Peter Quince: A carpenter.
Philostrate: Theseus's master of the revels.
Prologue: Peter Quince in the interlude.
Puck: Or Robin Goodfellow.
Pyramus: Nick Bottom in the interlude.
Robin Starveling: A tailor.
Snug: A joiner.
Theseus: Duke of Athens.
Thisbe: Francis Flute in the interlude.
Titania: Queen of the Fairies.
Tom Snout: A tinker.
Wall: Tom Snout in the interlude.

The Mists of Avalon
By Marion Zimmer Bradley

Ambrosius
Arthur
Avalon
Balan
Balin
Caerleon
Cai
Galahad
Gawaine
Gorlois
Gwenhwyfar
Gwydion
Igraine
Kevin
Lancelet
Lot
Merlin
Morgaine of the Fairies
Morgause
Niniane
Pellinore
Taliesin
Uriens
Uther Pendragon
Viviane

The sun was rising as they led her outdoors, robed in a cloak like the old woman's, with the magical signs painted on it—the moon, the antlers of the deer... They were leading forth a young man. She could not see him clearly; the rising sun was in her eyes, and she could see only that he was tall, with a shock of fair hair, and strongly built... The men of the tribe were painting the youth's body from head to foot with the blue woad, covering him with a cloak of untanned raw skins, smearing his body with the deer fat. On his head they fixed antlers... he swung his head to make certain they could not be dislodged...Morgaine looked up to see the proud swing of that young head, and suddenly she felt a ripple of awareness run down her body, cramping her calves, running into the secret parts of her body. This is the Horned One, this the God, this the consort of the Virgin Huntress...

—Marion Zimmer Bradley
The Mists of Avalon

*'Tis more than I can tell
    you what afterwards
    befell,
Save that there was
    weeping for friends
    beloved so well;
Knights and squires, dames
    and damsels were seen
    lamenting all.
So here I end my story. This
    THE NIBELLUNGENS'
    FALL.*

—*The Nibelungenlied*

The Nibelungenlied
Author Unknown (1203)

Alberich: A Dwarf, warden of the treasure.

Aldrian: Father of Hagen and Dankwart.

Alzei: A town northwest of Worms.

Amelrich: Brother of the ferryman on the Danube.

Amelungland: Country in northern Italy.

Arras: A city in France famous for its tapestries.

Astolt: Lord of the castle in Medelick.

Azagouc: A mythical land somewhere in the Orient.

Balmung: Seigfried's sword.

Bechelaren: Town in Austria.

Bern: Verona, Dietrich's home. Capital of
        Amelungland.

Bloedel: Etzel's brother.

Botelung: Etzel's father.

Brunhild: Queen of Isenland, Gunther's wife.

Dankrat: Ute's husband.

Dankwart: Hagen's brother.

Dietrich: King of Amelungland.

Eckewart: Margrave of the Burgundian kings.

Else: Ruler of the border province.

Gelfrat: Else's brother.

Gere: Margrave in Burgandy.

Gernot: Son of Ute and Dankrat.

Gibeche: A king.

Giselher: A king.

Gotelind: Wife of Margrave Rudeger of Bechelaren.

Gran: City in Hungary.

Gunther: A king.

Hadeburg: Mermaid.

Hagen of Troneg: Son of Aldrian.

Hawart: Danish prince.

Helca: Etzel's first wife.

Helfrich: One of Dietrich's vassals.

Helmnot: One of Dietrich's vassals.

Hildebrand: Dietrich's teacher and armor bearer.

Hildegund: Fiancee of Walther of Spain.

Hornboge: One of Etzel's vassals.

Hunolt: Chamberlain of the Burgundian kings.

Irnfried: Landgrave of Thuringia.

Isenstien: Brunhild's castle in Isenland.

Kriemhild: Daughter of Ute and Dankrat, wife of
        Siegfried and Etzel.

Liudegast: King of Denmark.

Liudeger: King of the Saxons.
Natwin: Father of Herrat.
Nibelungs: Possessor of the Nibelung tresure.
Nudung: Kinsman of Gotelind.
Ortlieb: Son of Etzel and Kriemhild.
Ortwin: Son of Hagen's sister.
Ramung: Duke from the land of the Walachs.
Rudegar of Belchelaren: Margrave of Bechelaren,
      Gotelind's husband.
Rumolt: Master cook.
Schrutan: Participant in tournament.
Siegmund: King of the Netherlands.
Sindolt: Cupbearer.
Spessart: Hilly forestland northeast of Worms.
Swemmel: Minstrel.
Troneg: Troja.
Ute: Dankrat's widow.
Vergen: Town on the Danube.
Volker: A minstrel.
Walther: Hero from Spain.
Waske: Iring's sword.
Werbel: Minstrel.
Witege: Warrior.
Witchart: One of Dietrich's vassals.
Wolfhart: one of Dietrich's vassals.
Xanten Castle: Capital of the Netherlands.
Zazamanc: Mythical land in the Orient.

Opal, the Journal of an Understanding Heart
By Opal Whiteley, Adapted by Jane Boulton

Aidan of Iona come from Lindisfarne: A shepherd.
Alfric of Canterbury: A sheep.
Aphrodite: A mother pig.
Aristotle: A bat.
Bede of Jarrow: A sheep.
Ben Johnson: A chicken.
Brave Horatius: A dog.
Dallan Forgaill: A sheep.
Edmund Spenser: A chicken.
Elizabeth Barrett Browning: A calf with musical
      mooings.
Euripides: A lamb.
Felix Mendelssohn: A mouse.
Good King Edward I: A fir tree.
Homer: A lamb.

When I feel sad inside I talk things over with my tree. I call him Michael Raphael. It is a long jump from the barn roof into his arms. I might get my leg or my neck broken and I'd have to keep still a long time. So I always say a little prayer and do jump in a careful way. It is such a comfort to nestle up to Michael Raphael. He is a grand tree. He has an understanding soul.

—Opal Whiteley,
adapted by Jane Boulton
*Opal, the Journal of an
Understanding Heart*

John Fletcher: A chicken.
Lars Porsena: A wise black crow.
Madame Lapine: A gentle rabbit.
Marcus Aurelius: A lamb.
Michael Raphael: A tree.
Minerva: A chicken.
Mozart: A wood mouse.
Oliver Goldsmith: A chicken.
Peter Paul Rubens: A pig.
Plutarch: A lamb.

Savonarola: A sorrel horse.
Sir Frances Bacon: A chicken.
Solomon Grundy: A pig.
Thomas Chatterton Jupiter Zeus: A
    lovely woodrat.
Virgil: A toad.
William Makepeace Thackeray: A hurt
    bird.
William Shakespeare: A horse.

The Song of Hiawatha
By Henry Wadsworth Longfellow (1855)

Bemahgut: Grape vine.
Bena: Pheasant.
Ishkoodah: The comet.
Kahgahgee: Raven.
Keewaydin: Northwest wind.
Kwo-Ne-She: Dragonfly.
Maskenozha: Pike.
Meenahga: Blueberry.
Minnehaha: Laughing water.
Mudgekeewis: West wind.
Nahma: Sturgeon.
Nepahwin: Spirit of sleep.
Nokomis: Moon/Mother Goddess.

Odahmin: Strawberry.
Okahahwis: Herring.
Opechee: Robin.
Owaissa: Bluebird.
Pah-Puk-Keena: Grasshopper.
Sebowisha: Brook.
Shahbomin: Gooseberry.
Shawgashee: Crawfish.
Shuh-Shuh-Gah: Heron.
Subbekashe: Spider.
Wash-Wah-Taysee: Firefly.
Wawonaissa: Whippoorwill.
Wenonah: First-born daughter.

The Song of Roland
(1050-1096?)

Acelin
Aelroth
Apollin
Aude: Damsel engaged to Roland.
Balagant: Emir of Babylon, leader of the
    Saracens.
Basan
Basilie
Blancandrin: The wisest of the Pagans,
    he plots with Ganelon.
Bramimond: Widow of King Marsilion.
    Chalemagne takes her to France
    where she is baptised and named
    Juliana.
Canabeus

Capuel
Charlemagne: 200-year-old Emperor
    (King Charles or Carlon);
    Possessed a militant zeal for
    Christianizing Pagans.
Clarin
Climborin
Durendal
Esprieris
Estamarin
Eudropin
Ganelon: Traitor knight who conspires
    with Pagans.
Gefrey
Gerer

Gerin
Grandonies
Guarlan the Bearded
Jouner
Jozeran
Jurfaret the Blond
Maheu
Malbien
Malduit
Malprimis
Marsilium: Saracen king.
Milun
Oger
Oliver: Roland's friend.
Priamun
Rabel
Roland: Favorite nephew of Charlemagne; a hater of Pagans. He doesn't use his weapons when the Saracens attack, trusting in his Christ's supremacy over the Pagans. He was killed.
Saracen
Tedbalt
Timozel
Turpin: Archbishop.
Valdabrun

Star Trek: The Next Generation
Created By Gene Roddenberry

Aldea (a legendary planet)
Armus
Bachra
Barclay
Benzar
Brahms, Dr. Leah
Crusher, Beverly
Crusher, Wesley
Data
Duras
Elbrun, Tam
Endar
Fajo, Kivas
Gowron
Guinan
Haftel, Admiral

All through that host the drums sound, and their horns and their clear trumpets, and the Pagans dismount to put on their armor. The Emir bestirs himself, not to be the last...He hangs from his neck his great broad shield with its golden boss and crystal border; it is swung on a thick strap of silk embroidered with circles. He grasps his spear named "Maltet," with its shaft as thick as a club. Its iron head alone would make a full load for a pack mule. Then...Baligant mounts his war horse. He has a good broad stride in the saddle, this brave knight. He is narrow in the hips, but big ribbed, and his chest is deep and beautifully molded, his shoulders are massive, his color fair and his face proud. His curling hair is as white as a summer flower. His courage has been proved many times. God, what a Baron, if only he were a Christian!

—The Song of Roland

Helmsley, Admiral
Jarada
Jono
K'hleyr
K'mpec
Kahlest
Keiko
Kiko
Kurn
LaForge, Geordi
Lal
Lore
O'Brian, Miles
Okona
Picard, Jean Luc
Polaski, Doctor
Q
Ral, Devinoni
Riker, Will Commander

Riva
Salia
Sarjenka
Sarek
Shelby, Lt. Cmdr.
Soong, Dr.
Stubbs, Dr. Paul
T'pei
Tamarac, Admiral
"The Picard"
Troi, Ian
Troi, Lwaxana
Troi, Deanna
Uthat, Tox
Varria
Worf
Yanar
Yar, Tasha
Yar, Ishara

RACES

Antedian
Betazoid
Borg
Bynar
Calamarian
Edos

Ferengi
Mariposan
Pakled
Romulan
Talarian
Vorgon

The Story of Burnt Njal
Author Unknown (Thirteenth Century)

Aumund
Bergthora
Bork the Waxy-Toothed Blade
Fiddle Mord
Flosi
Geir the Priest
Glum
Grim
Gunnar
Hallgerda
Hauskuld
Helge
Helgi
Hildigunna
Hogni

Hrvt
Kari
Kettle of the Mark
Kolskegg
Lything
Mord
Njal
Olaf
Otkell
Rodny
Skapti
Skarphedinn
Starkad
Thangbrand
Thiostolf

Thord
Thorgeir of Lightwater
Thorgerda
Thorwald
Thrain
Unna

The Tempest
By William Shakespeare (1611)

Alanso: King and father of Ferdinand.
Antonio: Prospero's brother who plots against him.
Ariel: Spirit released by Prospero.
Caliban: Monstrous servant of Prospero. Represents
    brute force with no intelligence and is con-
    trolled only by Prospero's magic.
Ferdinand: Lover of Miranda.
Gonzalo: Faithful courtier.
Miranda: Prospero's daughter who was brought
    up on an island on which her father is the
    only man.
Prospero: Hero; interested more in philosophy and
    books on magic than in affairs of state.

*We are such stuff as dreams
are made on...*

—William Shakespeare
The Tempest

Tristan and Isolde
By Gottfried Von Strassburg (1210)

Blanchefleur: Wife to Rivalin, Tristan's mother.
Brangene: Companion to Isolde.
Duke Morolt: Brother of Isolde.
Duke Morgan: Enemy of Rivalin.
Isolde of the White Hands: Wife of Tristan in name
    only.
Isolde the Fair: Lover of Tristan.
Mark: King of Cornwall.
Queen Isolde of Ireland: Mother of Isolde the Fair.
Rivalin: Tristan's father.
Rual the Faithful: Tristan's foster father.
Tristan: Hero.

Wizards' Worlds
By Andre Norton

Alizon
Craike
Dagmar

The storm came out of the north. It came from across the Sea of Mists, from beyond the moors and highlands, and now, at last, it struck full force at Albion, that fabled isle that men of later days would name and know as England. Merciless, devastating, the storm was a great, black beast running wild across the fens, consuming the dawn, making a mockery of spring. Lightening snagged the sky and ripped open the belly of the clouds as sleet-stung, wind-driven rain poured down into the vulnerable earth that could hold no more.

—William Sarabande
Wolves of the Dawn

Dairine
Elfanor
Elfreda
Elyn
Elys
Erlia
Fallon
Farne
Fritigen
Gunnora
Herdrek
Hertha
High Hallack
Horla
Inghela
Jabis
Jervon
Jonkara
Jorik
Kara
Kas
Koris
Kuno
Mafra
Malka
Nadi
Ortis
Porpae
Rinard
Rivery
Roth
Rothar
Salzarat
Sibbald
Simond
Starrex
Sulcar
Sylt
Takya
Tamisan
Tanree
Thasus
Thra
Trystan
Tursla
Uletka Rory

Unnanna
Urre
Vidruth
Volt

Wowern
Xactol
Zackuth

Wolves of the Dawn
By William Sarabande

Albion
Balor
Bracken Fen
Cethlinn
Dana
Dianket
Donar
Dragda
Eala
Elathan
Falcon
Fomor Maclir

Huldre
Keptah
Manannan
Mealla
Morrigan
Munremar
Nemed
Nia
Star Gazer
The Sword "Retaliator"
Uaine

Yvain
Chretien De Troyes (Transcribed after 1164)

Calogrenant: Yvain's cousin.
Harpin of the Mountain: Giant slain by
     Yvain.
King Arthur
Lady Noroison: Championed by Yvain.
Laudine De Landuc ("LOW deen"):
     Yvain's wife.
Lunete: Damsel serving Laudine.

Queen Guinevere
Sir Kay: Cynical Seneschal humbled by
     Yvain.
Sir Gawain: Yvain's friend, Arthur's
     nephew.
Yvain ("eee-VAN"): Knight of the Round
     Table.

Appendix 1

Index of Names by Characteristic

Abundance/Wealth

Achelous, 154
Adoni, 164
Aestas, 144
Annona, 144
Audris, 210
August, 96, 184
Autumn, 96, 172-173, 204
Celynnen, 119
Cerelia, 145, 204
Ceres, 145, 205
Clove, 123
Comfrey, 123
Dagda, 116, 141-142, 160, 175, 209
Damona, 141
Darius, 203
Delia, 138, 173, 202
Demeter, 49, 53, 138-139, 156, 173, 184-185, 191, 202
Fall, 96

Forbes, 209
Gaia, 35, 53, 75, 78, 133, 139, 144, 189, 198, 239
Grainne, 77, 160, 175, 207
Guri, 174
Hey-Tau, 164
Holly, 113, 119-120, 213, 215
Honeysuckle, 124
Lucretia, 205
Lughnasadh, 96
Mabon, 36, 71, 96-97, 146, 167, 215
Mercury, 130-131, 165
Nutmeg, 125
Ora, 178, 213
Osiris, 117, 135, 150-152, 198
Pomona, 166, 182, 205
Ric, 5-7, 13-14, 21, 40, 81-82, 90-91, 94, 107, 124-125, 138, 140, 204-205, 210, 213, 215, 218, 226, 230, 233, 238

Rick, 5, 7
Rich, 5-7, 218, 230, 238
Riches, 14, 125, 205, 233
Saturn, 128, 131, 166, 174
Tapio, 79, 154, 239
Tinne, 113, 119
Terza, 202

Tessa, 202, 205
Tressa, 202
Tuulikki, 79, 136, 239
Vertumnus, 166
Wealth, 14-15, 221
Wealthy, 14-15, 81, 203, 210, 212
Yalluc, 123

Air Names

Adad, 164, 232
Aeolus, 76, 127, 155, 165
Aleyn, 76, 164
Ambar, 174
Anan, 140, 172
Aria, 76, 137, 146, 201, 222, 228, 232
Ariel, 35, 76, 199, 225, 228, 253
Aurora, 76, 128, 131, 177, 198, 204
Baal, 144, 164
Bhrigus, 158
Boreas, 76
Breeze, 76, 199
Celestial, 76
Cirrus, 76
Cloudy, 76
Cumulus, 76
Cyclone, 76
Doldrum, 76
Donar, 163, 255
Dustdevil, 76
Eos, 76, 96, 186, 236
Ethereal, 76, 129
Eurus, 76
Frey, 143, 163, 177, 190
Gale, 76, 86-87, 93, 153, 203, 209, 236
Gannet, 100
Gusty, 76
Hathor, 76, 135
Hinun, 177
Hurricane, 76
Ilma, 49, 53, 135, 152-153, 192, 239
Indra, 159, 174
Jumala, 76, 153-154, 172
Jupiter, 99, 116, 130-131, 165, 250

Kolpia, 164
Lani, 23, 174
Leilani, 29, 174
Maelstrom, 76
Makani, 174
Mapuana, 174
March, 7, 14, 61, 69, 97, 195
Nebula, 130
Nimbus, 76
Notus, 76
Nwyure
Puff, 76
Skye, 76, 199, 214, 229
Storm, 75-76, 198, 214
Stratus, 76
Tadewi, 177
Taima, 177
Thor, 5, 8-9, 35, 66-67, 76, 112, 116-117, 143, 149, 163-164, 179, 184, 195, 198, 210, 212, 215, 231, 235, 243, 253
Thunar, 163
Thunder, 76, 79, 87, 116, 139, 150, 154, 163-166, 177, 186, 192, 197
Tornado, 77
Tradewind, 77
Tsunami, 77
Turquoise, 94-95
Typhoon, 77
Ukko, 77, 154
Whirlwind, 77, 79
Wind, 76-77, 198-199, 236, 250
Zephyrus, 77

Balance

Aeacus, 155
Amber, 80-81, 199
Anubis, 150
Arkose, 82
Astra, 128, 137, 202
Athena, 35, 101, 137, 145, 158, 184, 202
Beryl, 82-83, 85
Bittersweet, 122
Blueberry, 107, 250
Bryony, 108, 199
Dandelion, 109-110
Dove, 99, 213
Eostar, 96
Equinox, 96-97, 116, 119, 130
Fall, 96

Hisi, 152, 154
Lempo, 152
Libra, 130
Maat, 135
Mabon, 36, 71, 96-97, 146, 167, 215
Onyx, 91, 173
Osiris, 117, 135, 150-152, 198
Paha, 152
Polaris, 131
Robin, 7-9, 17-18, 71, 98, 100-102, 199, 214, 236, 238
Solstice, 119, 178
Turquoise, 94-95, 98
Varuna, 159
Yule, 97-98, 215

Beauty

Adonis, 155, 203, 233
Agate, 80, 89, 91
Aphrodite, 49, 52, 99, 103, 132, 137-138, 146, 155-156, 158, 185, 191, 203, 249
Apollo, 138, 155-156, 178, 202-203
Balder, 35, 115, 143, 163
Barika, 176
Belinda, 204
Bonnie, 207
Cliona of the Fair Hair, 141
Cullan, 175
Cullin, 175
Cytherea, 138
Ella, 17, 174, 213, 242
Farra, 34, 147, 213
Farrah, 213
Fionan, 176
Freya, 143, 177, 190
Gannon, 176
Gold, 87-88, 111, 242-243

Hathor, 76, 135
Holly, 113, 119-120, 213, 215
Iris, 113-114, 139-142, 201-202
Jasper, 89-90
Keelia, 208
Keelin, 208
Keely, 208
Kennet, 210, 222, 229
Kenneth, 210, 222
Kennocha, 29-31, 175
Mafdet, 135
Mallalai, 171
Nix, 143, 149, 218
Opal, 18, 80, 91-92, 95, 191, 249
Orchid, 18, 116, 126
Shahla, 171
Siran, 172
Swan, 103, 129, 153, 167, 213
Tamarisk, 117

Change

Akhnaton, 150
Aspen, 105, 116, 199, 215
Baal, 144, 164
Candleberry, 108

Chameleon, 189
Dolphin, 48, 191, 198
Indra, 159, 174
Mira, 123, 130, 205, 253

Moon, 118, 128-132, 134, 142-146, 153, 158-159, 165, 171-174, 176-177, 187-188, 190, 195, 198, 202, 205, 207-208, 211, 220, 225-228, 232-233, 246-247, 250
Moth, 35, 89, 103, 110, 119, 123, 141-142, 146-147, 161, 164, 167, 177, 188, 202, 211, 239-240, 249-250, 253

Osiris, 117, 135, 150-152, 198
Paris, 88, 157-158, 181
Quicksilver, 35, 92-93
Spin, 20, 59, 75, 111-112, 120, 188
Web-Spinner, 188

Clarity/Communication

Aldebaran, 127
Amergin, 34, 159, 235
Balor, 159, 161, 255
Bran, 60, 62-63, 65, 79, 99, 104, 110, 114-116, 118, 146, 167, 191, 206, 214, 222, 230-231, 240, 242-244, 246, 253
Bres, 160, 244
Crystal
Diamond, 84-85, 95, 173
Eidana
Gort, 114, 119
Hermes, 130, 157-158, 190

Iris, 3, 10, 49, 61-62, 77-78, 100, 102, 113-114, 124, 139-142, 146, 149, 159-162, 167, 175-176, 178, 191, 194-195, 201-202, 207-210, 223, 240
Ivy, 18, 114, 119-120
Jade, 89
Math ap Mathonwy, 167
Mercury, 93, 130-131, 165
Mert, 135, 149
Mica, 88, 90, 234
Obsidian, 90
Quartz, 81-84, 86, 88-89, 92-93
Sorcha, 175, 208, 214

Crone

See Sage

Earth Names

Acres, 78, 184
Adoni, 155, 164, 203, 233
Aker, 78, 150
Amber, 80-81, 199
Antaeus, 155
Antelope, 192
Axolotl, 189
Ay, 5, 9, 17, 136, 172, 176, 214, 224, 232, 238
Bonton
Brandon, 214
Brenton, 214
Broderick, 209, 214
Burleigh, 214
Burne, 108, 115, 121, 190, 214
Cernunnos, 160, 193
Chalk, 78, 194
Chestnut, 78, 108
Clay, 83, 94, 195
Cliff, 35, 79, 99, 214-215, 239

Coast, 5, 74, 78, 100
Cybele, 138
Demeter, 49, 53, 97, 138-139, 156, 173, 184-185, 191, 202
Den, 5, 9, 12, 52, 66, 71, 75, 80, 87, 145, 149-150, 181, 184, 215, 228, 235, 237, 248
Desert, 78, 85, 100, 151, 192, 195, 198, 231
Don, 2-3, 9, 16, 18, 22, 24, 31, 36, 44, 49, 61, 63-65, 83, 101, 134, 146-147, 151, 160, 162-163, 166-167, 179, 185, 192, 209, 211-212, 218, 225, 228, 240, 244, 255
Dun, 9, 35, 76, 175, 178, 195, 209, 215, 230-231, 242, 245
Earth, 13, 15, 35, 40, 44, 46-48, 54, 60, 62-63, 67, 70, 72-75, 77-83, 85, 87-91, 93-97, 99, 101-105, 107, 111, 117-119, 121, 127-132, 134-136, 138-140, 143-146, 150, 152, 154-157, 161-165, 171-172, 174, 177, 181, 185-186, 188-190, 198, 202, 204-205, 211, 232, 239, 242, 254

Eartha, 78, 198, 213

Ennis, 207, 209

Ey, 6, 9, 23, 26, 31, 41, 46-47, 56, 58-59, 64, 76, 79, 85, 87, 89-90, 95, 99, 101, 105, 109, 115, 117, 122, 127, 139, 149, 152, 159, 171, 189, 212-213, 247

Faunus, 78, 145, 165, 233

Fir Daughter, 135, 239

Fire Salamander, 189

Flidais, 78, 142

Flora, 78, 145, 204

Forest, 9, 26, 43, 48, 54, 78-81, 103-104, 135-136, 143, 149, 154, 158, 160, 164-165, 168, 173-174, 186-187, 193, 206, 209, 211-212, 214-215, 222, 232, 239, 249

Gaia, 35, 53, 75, 78, 83, 110, 133, 139, 144, 177, 189, 198, 239

Ghe, 144, 181

Glade, 78, 157

Glen(n), 9, 78, 176, 183-184, 207, 209, 223

Glenna, 207

Gondwanaland, 78

Granite, 82, 88, 90, 94

Grove, 78, 103-104, 120, 142, 198, 214-215

Hema, 91, 174

Hey-Tau, 164

Holm, 9, 113

Inland, 78, 100

Island, 9, 74, 78, 94, 121, 136, 138, 149, 165, 168, 176, 178, 180, 186, 207-209, 213-215, 235, 239, 253

Keoki, 173

Kika, 173

Kimberlyn, 213

Kimbra, 213

Lane, 213, 215

Langdon, 215

Langley, 215

Laurasia, 74, 78

Law, 9-10, 20, 29-30, 71, 103, 120, 140, 205

Lay, 9, 80, 89, 93, 95, 117, 142, 169, 202, 233

Lee, 9, 100, 162, 172-173, 175-176, 186

Leigh, 213

Leland, 215

Ley, 9, 166, 179

Lindsay, 213, 236

Lono, 174

Low, 9, 16-17, 99, 110, 149, 187, 223, 255

Luonnotar, 136

Lur, 24, 42, 85, 104, 133, 143, 162, 172, 183, 185, 187, 189, 191, 193, 195

Mac Cecht, 161

Magma, 74, 78, 82

Mahkah, 177

Math ap Mathonwy, 167

Meadow, 9, 79, 157, 163, 184, 213-215

Mesa, 79

Metsa, 173

Mielikki, 79, 136, 154

Montgomery, 206

Mo(o)r(e), 9, 19, 154, 210, 214, 254

Moraine, 79

Moss, 79, 154, 160, 236, 245

Mud Puppy

Nahele, 174

Nairi, 172

Nerthus, 143

Nuna, 177

Ocre

Onatah, 177

Pangaea, 74, 79

Pellervoinen, 153

Planet, 73-75, 77, 79, 81-83, 85, 87, 89, 91, 93, 95, 97, 99, 101, 103, 105, 107, 109, 111, 113, 115, 117, 119, 121, 123, 125, 127-132, 134, 138, 195, 204, 231, 251

Raini, 177

Rhea, 79, 139, 202

Rock, 2, 18-19, 30-31, 35, 67, 70-72, 74-75, 78-80, 82-83, 86-90, 92, 95, 138, 159, 175, 185, 188, 209, 214-215, 238-239

Salamander, 77, 189

Salt, 26, 44-47, 56, 79, 83, 88, 100, 165, 205

Sandy, 79, 94

Savanna(h), 79

Shaw, 9, 176, 250

Shore, 2, 53, 79, 102, 188, 239

Silvanus, 166, 206

Siren, 143, 174, 189

Sita, 174

Slate, 94

Stan, 9, 14, 16, 18, 45, 52, 56-58, 61-62, 64-66, 76, 127, 142, 148, 160-161, 168-169, 198, 211-212, 215

Staun, 9
Steppe, 79, 192
Stone, 1, 9, 27, 45, 50, 65-66, 71, 79-81, 84-
    95, 142, 149, 168, 179, 182-183, 198,
    211, 215, 243
Sycamore, 117
Sylvester, 206
Talus, 79
Tapio, 79, 154, 239
Tellus, 146
Terra, 35, 72, 77, 79, 132, 146, 205
Terrain, 77, 79
Terrestrial, 79, 99, 101, 204
Tundra, 79
Turquoise, 94-95, 98

Tuulikki, 79, 136, 239
Tuwa, 171, 177
Vedis, 211
Wald, 5, 9, 212, 215, 238
Walden, 215
Waverly, 215
Weald, 5, 9
Wildon, 215
Winslow, 215
Winston, 215
World, 3-4, 11-12, 14, 18, 21, 29, 31, 42, 50-
    51, 56-57, 67, 69, 80, 84, 88-89, 93-94,
    98, 101-102, 105, 118, 124, 132, 134,
    146-147, 149, 151-152, 154, 158, 177,
    187, 197, 203, 205, 218, 221, 226, 253

Fertility

Achelous, 154
Adad, 164, 232
Aleion, 164
Aleyin, 164
Amathaon, 166
Amba, 174
Amma, 174
Anguid, 189
Apple, 48, 103-105, 115, 120, 143
Baal, 144, 164
Beli, 2, 21-23, 25-27, 31, 34, 40, 57, 73, 81,
    84-85, 88, 90, 92-93, 95, 99, 101, 106,
    108-111, 114-116, 122, 125-126, 134,
    138, 146, 150, 166, 185-186, 189, 204,
    212, 222, 232
Bes, 11, 31, 36, 52-55, 62, 80, 82, 103, 107-
    108, 113, 118, 129, 147, 151, 154-155,
    158, 162-163, 193, 203, 236, 246, 251
Bimba, 174
Boann, 141, 222
Bona Dea, 144-145
Brid, 11, 104, 112, 123, 137, 141, 148, 163,
    175-176, 178, 207, 233
Bride, 11, 123, 137, 141, 148, 175-176, 233
Brighid, 77, 141, 160, 175
Brigid, 141, 207, 228, 240
Brigit, 117, 141
Brimo, 138
Bronco, 194

Broom, 44, 107-108, 112, 120, 173, 213
Cerelia, 145, 204
Ceres, 145, 205
Cernunnos, 160, 193
Cerrdiwen
Chameleon, 189
Charger, 194
Checkerberry, 108
Colt, 194
Damona, 141
Dana, 141, 160-162, 198, 244, 255
Danu, 141, 146, 159, 198, 209, 248-249
Don, 2-3, 9, 16, 18, 22, 24, 31, 36, 44, 49, 61,
    63-65, 83, 101, 134, 146-147, 151, 160,
    162-163, 166-167, 179, 185, 192, 209,
    211-212, 218, 225, 228, 240, 244, 255
Earth, 13, 15, 35, 40, 44, 46-48, 54, 60, 62-63,
    67, 70, 72-75, 77-83, 85, 87-91, 93-97,
    99, 101-105, 107, 111, 117-119, 121,
    127-132, 134-136, 138-140, 143-146,
    150, 152, 154-157, 161-165, 171-172,
    174, 177, 181, 185-186, 188-190, 198,
    202, 204-205, 211, 232, 239, 242, 254
Eliun, 164
Ellama, 174
Epona, 141, 193-194, 199, 237
Equine, 194
Ernmas, 141
Esbat, 96, 129
Fabiana, 111

Faunus, 78, 145, 165, 233
Flying Dragon, 189
Foal, 194
Fodhla, 49, 53, 141-142, 161
Freya, 143, 177, 190
Full Moon, 10, 96, 128-129, 139-140, 165
Gaia, 35, 53, 75, 78, 83, 110, 133, 139, 144,
    177, 189, 198, 239
Gecko, 189
Gila Monster, 189
Goat, 124, 128, 157-158, 174, 193
Godiva, 134
Goleuddydd, 147
Herne, 149, 193
Horse, 71, 128, 134, 138, 141, 156, 166, 177,
    193-194, 198, 209, 233, 237, 250-251
Iguana, 189
Ilmatar, 49, 53, 135
Jumala, 76, 153-154, 172
Juno, 49, 53, 113, 145, 207
Kadir, 172
Komodo Dragon, 189
Lammas, 96
Linden, 115, 213
Lizard, 189-190
Llyr, 116, 167, 244
Lucina, 142, 145, 205-207
Lucina, 142, 145, 205-207
Luighsearch
Macawi, 177
Mahamba, 174
Maia, 112, 144-145, 199, 205
Mare, 156, 193-194, 211, 236
Mata, 174
Matrika, 174

May, 112, 144-145, 199, 205
Mielikki, 79, 136, 154
Mustang, 194
Mya, 172
Nerthus, 143
Oak, 9, 35, 43, 104, 115-116, 119-120, 149-
    150, 153, 168, 174-177, 183, 198-199,
    209, 214-215, 243
Ochre, 91
Omicle, 144
Osiris, 117, 135, 150-152, 198
Pan, 25, 49, 62, 74, 79, 90, 110, 133, 139-140,
    149, 151, 156-158, 166-167, 190, 193,
    201-202, 233, 238
Picunnus, 166
Pony, 194
Raina, 211
Raka, 140
Saturn, 128, 131, 166, 174
Sebele
Selene, 103, 139-140
Skink, 189
Stallion, 194
Steed, 140, 148, 156, 194
Stork, 103
Summer, 19, 24, 36, 96-97, 109, 116, 127,
    136, 143-144, 153, 168, 172, 179-180,
    184, 186, 193, 212, 214, 239, 251
Sungazer, 189
Termite, 188
Ukko, 77, 154
Vainamoinen, 154, 239
Whale, 192
Xenosaur, 189

Fire Names

Aestas, 144
Agate, 80, 89, 91
Agni, 77
Aidan, 17, 175, 209, 249
Akhnaton, 150
Amun, 150, 152
Anala, 174
Arani, 77, 140
Ardan, 205, 240

Arden, 205, 209, 212
Ardere, 176
Ardor, 77
Asta, 144, 164, 172
Astrid, 172
Aton, 77, 143
Balder, 35, 115, 143, 163
Basalt, 82
Bask, 36, 47, 77, 84, 107

Beorht, 4
Bert, 4, 19, 169
Blaise, 173
Blast, 62, 77
Blaze, 77
Bowl, 45, 61, 115
Brand, 62-63, 214, 222, 231, 242-243
Brighid, 77, 141, 160, 175
Calamine, 36
Cayenne, 121-122
Cinnamon, 121, 123
Comet, 129, 152, 250
Copper, 83-84, 132, 140, 236, 239
Crackle, 77, 218
Curry, 123
Dara, 172, 175
Dazzle, 77, 149
Didin, 115
Didthin, 115
Dirocco
Draco, 128-129
Drake, 110, 206
Edan, 207, 209
Electric, 77, 83
Ember, 35
Falak, 172
Farbauti, 163
Fearn, 104, 119
Fever, 77, 105
Fire, 11, 35-36, 40, 43-47, 52, 70, 72-75, 77,
    79-80, 82-83, 87, 90-94, 96, 110, 116,
    119, 123, 125, 128-130, 140-141, 144,
    150, 161-164, 166, 174, 184, 186-187,
    189, 195, 207, 209, 234-235, 238, 250
Firecracker, 77
Firefly, 72, 77, 186, 250
Flame, 77, 129, 135, 153, 163-164, 175, 194-
    195, 213
Flash, 63-65, 77, 82, 203, 211
Galaxy, 129-130
Garnet, 87
Glow, 35, 62, 77, 81-82, 86, 93, 140, 187
Gold, 2, 35, 47, 58, 81-82, 84, 87-88, 92-93,
    105, 111, 134, 138-140, 154, 156, 187,
    203-205, 213, 242-243, 246, 250-251
Grainne, 77, 160, 175, 207
Gwernen, 119
Hakan, 177
Helios, 157

Izar, 172
Kala, 23, 173, 238
Kalama, 173
Karan, 115
Keegan, 176, 209
Khepera, 151
Li, 77
Lightning Bolt, 77
Lightning Bug, 77, 187
Lumina, 130, 205
MacGreine, 77, 161
Masou, 177
Merr, 48, 140, 151, 165, 187, 205, 208, 212-
    213, 215, 227, 229-230, 243
Meteor, 129-130, 132, 194
Midsummer, 97, 110, 119, 246
Mira, 123, 130, 205, 253
Mirra, 115
Mopper
Myrrh, 115-116, 122, 236
Nora, 172, 208
Paiva, 77, 153
Palwasha, 171
Paprika, 121, 125
Phoenix, 19, 35-36, 44, 147, 182, 199
Ptah, 152
Pyre, 77, 99, 143
Ra, 152
Roxanna, 171
Ruby, 18, 87, 91, 93, 95
Salamander, 77, 189
Salem, 15, 164, 223
Sapas, 144
Scorpio, 127, 130, 132
Seb, 77, 172, 188, 203, 206, 250
Seker, 77
Set, 152
Shamish, 77
Solar, 77, 129-132, 152
Spark, 35, 46, 77, 84-85, 87-88, 90, 92-93,
    129-130, 132, 171
Sparkle, 77, 84, 87, 90, 92, 132
Star, 13, 19, 22, 40, 49, 63-64, 66-67, 102,
    107, 121, 125, 127-132, 135-137, 140,
    151-152, 164, 168, 172-174, 176-177,
    187, 192, 195, 198-199, 208, 211, 217,
    225, 239, 246-247, 251-252, 254-255
Sultry, 77, 97

Summer, 19, 24, 36, 96-97, 109, 116, 127, 136, 143-144, 153, 168, 172, 179-180, 184, 186, 193, 212, 214, 239, 251
Summerwind, 36
Sundance, 35, 77
Sunny, 36, 77, 103, 109, 179
Sunshine, 18, 77, 79

Surya, 77, 140
Tannus, 150
Tara, 140, 158, 175, 208, 222-223, 238, 243
Tina, 150
Tunnus
Vulcan, 34, 166
Wildfire, 35, 77, 199

Growth

Acorn, 43, 104, 198
Cicada, 186
Crescent, 129, 131, 195, 198
Cynthia, 145, 202
Eithin, 119
Furze, 112, 119-120
Half Moon, 129

Imbolc, 96
New Moon, 129, 131-132, 136, 145, 172, 177
Nova, 131, 177, 205
Onn, 119, 173
Spin, 20, 59, 75, 111-112, 120, 188
Starling, 102
Waxing Moon, 132

Happiness

Ailsa, 210
Aleshance
Alyssa, 210
Apple, 48, 103-105, 115, 120, 143
Bast, 133, 135, 190
Bliss, 144, 147, 150, 163, 190, 203, 212, 233
Bluebird, 98, 250
Blythe, 213
Bull Moose, 194
Bullwinkle, 194, 197
Clover, 109, 117, 213
Cumin, 123
Delight, 13, 138-139, 151-152, 157-159, 183
Desta, 172
E(a)d, 4, 116, 119, 169, 213, 215, 228
Elf Leaf, 125
Fannah, 172
Faunus, 78, 145, 165, 233
Felicity, 204
Ferret, 191
Gladwyn
Guardrobe, 125
Hana, 172
Hillair, 204
Hillary, 230
Ida, 211
Ilsa, 211
Iris, 3, 10, 49, 61-62, 77-78, 100, 102, 113-114, 124, 139-142, 146, 175-176, 178, 191, 201-202, 207-210, 223, 240

Joy, 13, 19, 24, 53, 84, 101, 109, 114, 124, 126, 134-135, 138, 140, 152, 158, 178, 187, 202, 212-213, 233
Joy of the Mountain, 124
Lark, 8, 101, 173, 202-203, 213
Luana, 174
Marjoram, 124
Mave, 175, 208
Meara, 208
Merry, 48, 151, 205, 208, 213, 227, 229, 243
Millair
Mint, 124, 126
Moose, 97, 194
Mountain Mint, 124
Muin, 117, 119
Onnellinen, 173
Pellkita, 172
Peppermint, 124
Risa, 205
Rosemary, 125-126
Sea Dew, 125
Shamrock, 117
Tamra, 140
Tate, 177, 212
Tateeyopa, 177
Thalia, 202
Vine, 108, 114, 117, 119, 138, 154, 212, 250
Volupia, 146
Weyland, 150, 153, 199
Wintersweet, 124

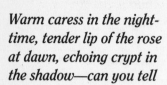

Warm caress in the night-time, tender lip of the rose at dawn, echoing crypt in the shadow—can you tell me where she's gone?

Do you remember when God was a Woman? She had many names. We called Her Isis, Astarte, Diana, Hecate, Demeter, Kali, and Inanna.

She was the Mother, the Earth, and all Her children from the sky, the land, and the sea. She was the Green One, growing, ripening, sustaining, giving life abundantly.

She was the sunlight, starlight, waxing moon and waning, and the Queen of Heaven, too. She was the deep space and the galaxies of planets that we ride twirling through.

We heard Her voice in the force of the whirlwind. We felt Her pulse in the tide and the driving rain, we saw Her blood at the birth of our children, we'd taste Her flesh in the growing grain.

She was the Young One, the holy maiden huntress, new life that blooms in the

Healing

Allspice, 121
Althea, 201
Angelica, 121
Apollo, 138, 155-156, 178, 202-203
Ariadne, 114, 137, 157, 201
Bettersweet
Borvo, 160
Chamomile, 122
Checkerberry, 108
Cloacina, 145
Comfrey, 123
Coriander, 123
Diancecht, 160, 162, 209-210
Dew of the Sea, 125
Elf Leaf, 125
Emery, 86, 149, 167
Eshmun, 164
Esmun, 164
Goldenrod, 111
Gooseberry, 111, 120, 250
Guardrobe, 125
Induna, 143
Jasper, 89-90
Kipu-Tytto, 136
Kivutar, 136
Lucina, 142, 145, 205-207
Maythen, 122
Miach, 162, 210
Mint, 124, 126
Ocre
Our Lady's Mint, 124
Pine, 48, 79, 116, 120, 174, 183
Rhiannon, 54, 102-104, 147-148, 167-168, 194, 214, 244
Rosemary, 125-126
Salus, 146
Spearmint, 124, 126
Sulla, 143
Thyme, 126
Valentine, 11, 95-97, 116, 182, 205, 229
Vammatar, 136
Velvet, 95, 214
Vu-Kufis

Hearth and Home

Awenasa, 176
Broom, 44, 107-108, 112, 120, 173, 213

Burgess, 214
Cardea, 144
Chestnut, 78, 108
Clover, 109, 117, 213
Cricket, 186
Fern, 18, 104, 107, 111, 120
Fraech, 113, 120
Grasshopper, 187, 250
Heath(er), 106-107, 113, 119-120, 208
Hestia, 139, 202
Linna, 173
November, 97, 131, 141
Penates, 166
Raith, 111, 120
Ratis, 134
Surya, 77, 140
Vanilla, 121, 126
Vesta, 146, 203, 205

Love

Aengus Mac Og, 141, 159
Amabel, 204
Amanda, 204
Anteros, 155
Aphrodite, 49, 52, 99, 103, 132, 137-138, 146, 155-156, 158, 185, 191, 203, 249
Astarte, 144, 164
Bilberry, 106-107
Charis, 173, 230
Chocolate, 35, 109
Coriander, 123
Cupid, 96-97, 139, 159, 165, 246
Cytherea, 138
Diarmuid, 160
Dove, 99, 139, 181, 207, 213, 246
Eros, 35, 74-75, 81, 83, 86, 92, 96-97, 138-139, 155-156
Freya, 143, 177, 190
Gorse, 107, 112
Grania, 207
Heath, 106-107, 113, 119-120, 208
Kama, 159
Kamadeva, 159
Lavender, 114, 121
Mistletoe, 115-116, 178, 183
Sjofna, 144
Thyme, 126
Vanilla, 121, 126
Venus, 35, 49, 113, 131-132, 146, 165-166, 205, 233, 246

spring. She was the seed, the key, the power of beginning, the door that's opening.

She was the Old One, the hag, the crone of wisdom, The deep grave under the earth. She was the Queen of Night, the face of death and darkness, the cauldron of rebirth.

Is She forgotten? Can we find her resting place? When is the hour of Her return? We are without Her and the pain is all around, the forest dies, the Witches burn.

Can we remember? Dreams will take us in our hearts to the place where she has gone. She's still among us. We sing Her name, She answers...and she still lives on and on.

And She is the world outside us and the world inside, she is birth, life, love, and death. Well, She's both near and far, the boundary and the center, she is north, south, east, and west.

—Lyrics by Sparky T. Rabbit
and Greg Johnson
God Was a Woman

*Of august gold-wreathed
and beautiful Aphrodite I
shall sing, to whose domain
belong the battlements of all
sea-laved Cyprus where...she
was carried over the waves
of the resounding sea in soft
foam. The gold-filleted
Horae welcomed her and
clothed her with heavenly
raiment. Then on her divine
head they placed a well-
wrought crown...Round her
tender neck and silver-white
breasts they decked her with
golden necklaces such as the
Horae themselves are
adorned with whenever they
go to lovely dances of the
Gods and to their father's
house. And after they decked
her body with every sort of
jewel, they brought her to
the immortals, who saw and
welcomed her, giving her
their hands, and each one
wished that he might take
her home as his wedded
wife; for they marvelled at
the looks of violet-crowned
Kythereia. Hail, honey-
sweet goddess with the
fluttering eyelids!*

—Homer
The Homeric Hymns

Luck

Bonus Eventus, 165
Draenen Wen
Emerald, 82, 84-85, 91, 95, 172
Elder, 35, 47, 57, 81, 84-85, 87-89, 91, 106, 110-111, 119-
120, 169, 177-178, 198
Falling Star, 129-130, 132
Ganesha, 158, 174, 191
Honeysuckle, 124
Nutmeg, 125
Shamrock, 117
Star Anise, 121, 125
Stork, 103
Uath, 112, 119

Magician/Wizard/Bard Names

Baird, 175, 177, 209
Devin, 175, 207, 252
Dylan, 78, 167, 244
Elfin, 184, 213
Ellette, 213
Elvina, 213
Erlina, 213
Geas, 178
Geasachd, 178
Geasadair, 178
Geasadioma, 178
Genevieve, 207
Gointe, 178
Gwydion, 146, 167-168, 230, 244, 247
Khoury, 172
Magice, 176
Magico, 174
Mago, 174, 243
Magus, 176
Maliardo, 174
Math ap Mathonwy, 167
Meda, 177
Merlin, 71, 101, 147-149, 167, 173-174, 184, 215, 219, 223,
233-234, 240, 246-247
Merlin Emrys, 215
Merlino, 174
Mistico, 174
Myrddin, 19, 149, 167-168, 246
Nahimana, 177
Odin, 105, 163, 178-179, 184, 191, 193, 237
Orenda, 177

Orra, 178
Orraidheachd, 178
Orrtha, 178
Orrthannan, 178
Owl, 45, 94, 101, 177, 189
Pagano, 174
Paganus, 176
Rierdan, 210
Riordan, 210
Saga, 143, 153, 176
Sagus, 176

Satinka, 177
Sgaileach, 178
Strega, 174
Stregone, 174
Stregoneria, 174
Tadleigh, 210
Taliesin, 146, 168, 199, 215, 236, 244, 247
Teague, 210
Wakanda, 177
Web-Spinner, 188
Wren, 36, 103

Maiden Names

April, 7, 95-96, 107, 132, 204, 207, 214
Artemis, 49, 111, 114, 137-138, 190-191, 203
Bona Dea, 144-145
Chloris, 138
Corinne, 202
Daisy, 18, 109
Diana, 35, 49, 139, 144-145, 190, 204, 233
Eire, 49, 141-142, 161
Erin, 141, 175, 203, 207
Flora, 78, 145, 204

Kyllikki, 49, 136, 239
Maia, 112, 144-145, 199, 205
Maida, 213
March, 7, 14, 61, 69, 97, 195
Mayda, 213
Ruis, 110, 119, 178
Trina, 202
Virgo, 130, 132, 137
Ysgawen, 119

Moon/Stars

Aldebaran, 127
Algol, 127
Alioth, 127
Altair, 127
Anahid, 172
Antares, 127, 199
Argento, 174
As(t)ra(l), 128, 137, 144, 164, 172, 202
Astrid, 172
Astrum, 176
Badria, 171
Bendis, 137
Beorht, 4
Budha, 158
Chandra, 158, 174
Chantrea, 171-172
Chiaro di luna, 174
Coyote, 190, 199
Cynthia, 145, 202
Delia, 138, 173, 202
Diana, 35, 49, 139, 144-145, 190, 204, 233
Falak, 172

Galaxy, 129-130
Half Moon, 129
Hilel, 172
Izar, 172
Jacy, 177
Kahoku, 173
Konane, 173
Koo, 42, 154, 160, 172-173, 175-176
Luce Stellare, 174
Lumen, 176
Luna, 93-94, 96, 106, 118-119, 129-130, 145,
    158, 174, 176-177, 190, 192, 205-206
Lunae, 176
Lunar, 93-94, 96, 129-130, 158, 174, 190, 192
Mahina, 171, 174
Mamid, 177
Miakoda, 177
Migina, 177
Mimiteh, 177
Nebula, 130
New Moon, 129, 131-132, 136, 145, 172, 177
Nova, 131, 177, 205

Phoebe, 202
Polaris, 131
Raggio Lunare, 174
Rigel, 131
Salem, 15, 164, 223
Scintillare, 174
Selena, 202, 205
Selirra, 202
Shashi, 174
Siderbus Inlustris, 176
Silver, 41-42, 60, 87, 93-94, 111, 119, 130,
    138-139, 146, 149-150, 162-163, 174,
    198-199, 202, 244
Sirius, 132, 191
Soma, 158, 174, 182

Star, 13, 19, 22, 40, 49, 63-64, 66-67, 107,
    121, 125, 127-132, 140, 151-152, 158,
    168, 172-174, 176-177, 187, 189, 192,
    195, 198-199, 202-203, 211, 217, 225,
    232, 239, 246-247, 251-252, 254-255
Stella(to), 132, 174, 176
Stellifer, 176
Sucente, 174
Taigi, 177
Taini, 177
Tanit, 144
Tara, 140, 158, 175, 208, 222-223, 238, 243
Vega, 132, 150
Waning Moon, 132, 140
Waxing Moon, 132

New Beginnings

Acorn, 43, 104, 198
Aker, 78, 150
Anumati, 140
April, 7, 95-96, 107, 132, 204, 207, 214
Ariadne, 114, 137, 157, 201
Bri(e)d(e), 11, 104, 112, 123, 137, 141, 148,
    163, 175-176, 178, 207, 233
Brig(h)id, 77, 141, 160, 175, 207, 228, 240
Brigit, 117, 141
Butterfly, 173, 176-177, 185-186, 188, 198
Cerridwen, 61, 146, 168, 199, 235-236
Cynthia, 145, 202
Eliun, 164
Emery, 86, 149, 167
Etain, 141
Genos, 164
Ilmarinen, 153, 192, 239
Ilmatar, 49, 53, 135
Imbolc, 96

January, 96
Janus, 116, 145, 165
Khepera, 151
Kyllikki, 49, 136, 239
Mimiteh, 177
Nu, 158, 160
Omicle, 144
Oriole, 101
Pyrite, 87, 92
Spring, 2, 35-36, 59-60, 66, 74, 78, 95-97, 99,
    102-104, 112, 119, 134, 138, 143, 145,
    155, 157, 160, 164-166, 168, 172, 183,
    193, 201, 205, 213-214, 254
Taigi, 177
Taini, 177
Wayland, 150, 215
Weyland, 150, 153, 199
Whale, 192

Passion/Sexuality

Adonis, 155, 203, 233
Anann, 140
Anu, 140-142, 150, 232, 235
Aphrodite, 49, 52, 99, 103, 132, 137-138, 146,
    155-156, 158, 185, 191, 203, 249
Apollo, 138, 155-156, 178, 202-203
Arani, 77, 140
Babhbh
Babi, 1, 11, 48, 52, 60, 103, 145, 151, 166

Barberry, 106
Bedbug, 185
Beltane, 43, 96-97, 188
Bendis, 137
Cayenne, 121-122
Cernunnos, 160, 193
Cinnamon, 121, 123
Comet, 129, 152, 250
Copper, 83-84, 132, 140, 236, 239

Coriander, 123
Cumin, 123
Cytherea, 138
Dagda, 116, 141-142, 160, 175, 209
Damara, 134, 202
Dionysus, 114, 117, 137, 156, 191
Eagle, 79, 99-100, 142, 203, 210, 212
Elephant, 26, 40, 158, 191, 238
Eros, 35, 74-75, 81, 83, 86, 92, 96-97, 138-139, 155-156
Fabiana, 111
Fergus, 161, 194, 219
Flidais, 78, 142
Freya, 143, 177, 190
Goat, 124, 128, 157-158, 174, 193
Hawthorn, 112-113, 119-120
Herne, 149, 193
July, 96, 107
June, 71, 96, 112, 145
Juniper, 114, 136, 239
Krishna, 159
Kundalini, 140

Lena, 205
Mandrake, 108, 115
May, 112, 144-145, 199, 205
Midsummer, 97, 110, 119, 246
Morrigan, 49, 62, 66, 102, 140-142, 160, 184, 236, 245, 255
Orchid, 18, 116, 126
Pan, 25, 49, 62, 74, 79, 90, 110, 133, 139-140, 149, 151, 156-158, 166-167, 190, 193, 201-202, 233, 238
Paris, 88, 157-158, 181
Parsley, 125
Pichi, 111
Ruby, 18, 87, 91, 93, 95
Satyr, 116, 158, 233
Stallion, 194
Suratamangari, 140
Ura, 25, 119, 128, 131
Valentine, 11, 95-97, 116, 182, 205, 229
Vanilla, 121, 126
Venus, 35, 49, 113, 116, 131-132, 146, 165-166, 199, 205, 233, 246

Power

Ambika, 174
Anu, 140-142, 150, 232, 235
Badhbh, 140-142
Bride, 11, 123, 137, 141, 148, 175-176, 233
Briana, 175, 207
Briget, 175, 236
Brighid, 77, 141, 160, 175
Chanda, 140, 236
Condor, 99
Damselfly
Dragonfly, 186, 250
Dwarf, 110, 119, 241-243, 248
Eagle, 79, 99-100, 142, 203, 210, 212
Garbh Ogh, 142
Ginger, 124, 204
Hornet, 188
Indra, 159, 174
Jumala, 76, 153-154, 172
Jupiter, 99, 116, 128, 130-131, 165, 191, 250
Leo, 42, 109, 130, 132, 177, 190, 205, 226
Lugh, 96, 159, 161-162, 222-223, 244
Macha, 140-142, 177
Mantis, 187

Mars, 9, 78, 98-100, 102-103, 128, 130-131, 165, 209-210, 215, 226, 250-251
Medbh, 142
Morgause, 134, 149, 247
Morrigan, 49, 62, 66, 102, 140-142, 160, 184, 236, 245, 255
Myrtle, 116, 120
Odin, 105, 163, 178-179, 184, 191, 193, 237
Olwyn, 147-148, 168
Peith, 119
Snake, 25, 99, 101, 151, 156, 189-190, 238
Star Anise, 121, 125
Tamarisk, 117
Taurus, 127-128, 131-132
Thor, 5, 8-9, 35, 66-67, 76, 112, 116-117, 143, 149, 163-164, 179, 184, 195, 198, 210, 212, 215, 231, 235, 243, 253
Wald, 5, 9, 212, 215, 238
Wasp, 81, 188, 220
Weald, 5, 9
Weard, 5, 41
Zeus, 35, 99, 103, 116-117, 128, 130-131, 138-140, 149, 155-158, 167, 191, 193, 197, 203, 250

Protection

Achilles, 155

Aethelweard, 1, 9, 19, 214

Aldwn

Alexander, 22, 203

Andromedia

Angelica, 121

Area, 22, 44, 59-60, 69, 75, 95, 105, 192

Aries, 128, 156

Artemis, 49, 111, 114, 137-138, 190-191, 203

Asmindr, 5

Bay, 78, 108, 121-122, 124, 157, 166, 183, 214

Bes, 11, 31, 36, 52-55, 62, 80, 82, 103, 107-
108, 113, 116, 129, 147, 151, 154-155,
158, 162-163, 193, 203, 236, 246, 251

Bittersweet, 122

Blackthorn, 106, 120

Branwen, 146, 167, 244, 246

Broom, 44, 107-108, 112, 120, 173, 213

Caraway, 122

Cardea, 144

Clove, 109, 117, 123, 213

Cumin, 123

Curry, 123

Dew of the Sea, 125

Dike, 138

Dog, 11, 84, 117, 128, 132, 149, 153, 156,
160, 166, 191, 249

Edmee, 213

Elden, 215

Elf Leaf, 125

Esme, 213

Fern, 18, 104, 107, 111, 120

Garda, 211

Garner, 212

Guardrobe, 125

Helm, 4, 210, 243, 248, 252

Hornet, 188

Jupiter, 99, 116, 128, 130-131, 165, 191, 250

Lares, 165-166

Mars, 9, 78, 98-100, 102-103, 128, 130-131,
165, 209-210, 215, 226, 250-251

Mistletoe, 115-116, 178, 183

Parsley, 125

Pepper, 26, 121-122, 124-125

Picunnus, 166

Raith, 111, 120

Ratis, 134

Rosemary, 125-126

Rowan, 117, 119-120, 198, 210, 239

Tapio, 79, 154, 239

Tuulikki, 79, 136, 239

Velvet, 95, 214

Vesta, 146, 203, 205

Ward, 5, 10, 110, 156, 215, 238, 248

Warner, 212

Warren, 8, 212

Warrick, 212

Yew, 118-120, 178

Psychic Ability

Alder, 104, 119-120

Allum, 121

Amethyst, 81, 84, 91-92, 172

Anise, 121-122, 125

Aquamarine, 82

Bay, 78, 108, 121-122, 124, 157, 166, 183, 214

Cassandra, 202

Cicely, 122

Copper, 83-84, 132, 140, 236, 239

Delphine, 202

Egeria, 78, 145

Faunus, 78, 145, 165, 233

Glaucus, 156

Gwendydd, 147

Gypsum, 88-89

Laurel, 31, 71, 121-122, 165, 173, 176, 204

Man(d)a, 19, 78, 162, 167, 174, 244, 255

Mandrake, 108, 115

Meda, 177

Mica, 88, 90, 234

Mimir, 163

Morgan, 18, 34, 82-83, 117, 147, 173, 175,
184, 210, 219, 230, 234, 237, 240, 253

Myrrh, 115-116, 122, 236

Quartz, 81-84, 86, 88-89, 92-93

Saga, 143, 153, 176

Shoney, 78, 162

Silver, 41-42, 60, 87, 93-94, 111, 119, 130,
138-139, 146, 149-150, 162-163, 174,
198-199, 202, 244

Sybil, 205

Thyme, 126

Purification

Basil, 122, 126, 206, 250
Bedwen, 119
Beth, 106, 119, 207, 225, 230
Birch, 106, 118-120, 198, 214
Broom, 44, 107-108, 112, 120, 173, 213
Candleberry, 108

Clove, 109, 117, 123, 213
Holle, 143
Sage, 59, 96, 125, 149, 160, 167-168, 192
Tamarisk, 117
Thyme, 126

Rebirth/Transformation

Adoni, 155, 164, 203, 233
Adonis, 155, 203, 233
Ambrose, 203
Anastasia, 201
Aquamarine, 82
Arianrhod, 146, 166-168, 222
Butterfly, 173, 176-177, 185-186, 188, 198
Caterpillar, 186, 188
Cerridwen, 61, 146, 168, 199, 235-236
Dolphin, 48, 191, 198
Donn, 160, 209, 240
Eiddew, 119
Emery, 86, 149, 167
Etain, 141
Frog, 189-190, 238
Gort, 114, 119
Ilmarinen, 153, 192, 239
Induna, 143
Ivy, 18, 114, 119-120
Khepera, 151

Mider, 162
Migina, 177
Nion, 105, 119
Omicle, 144
Osiris, 117, 135, 150-152, 198
Phoenix, 19, 35-36, 44, 147, 182, 199
Renata, 205, 227
Rot, 69, 153, 238, 254
Serpent, 134, 139-140, 189, 204
Snake, 25, 99, 101, 151, 156, 189-190, 238
Spin, 20, 59, 75, 111-112, 120, 188
Spring, 2, 35-36, 59-60, 66, 74, 78, 95-97, 99,
    102-104, 112, 119, 134, 138, 143, 145,
    155, 157, 160, 164-166, 168, 172, 183,
    193, 201, 205, 213-214, 254
Tadpole, 189-190
Toad, 189, 191, 250
Udun, 143
Vine, 108, 114, 117, 119, 138, 154, 212, 250
Whale, 192

Romance

Basil, 122, 126, 206, 250
Caraway, 122
Clove, 109, 117, 123, 213
Coriander, 123
Ginger, 124, 204
Joy of the Mountain, 124
Lavender, 114, 121

Marjoram, 124
Mint, 124, 126
Mistletoe, 115-116, 178, 183
Mountain Mint, 124
Our Lady's Mint, 124
Spearmint, 124, 126
Wintersweet, 124

Sage and Crone Names

Adoni, 155, 164, 203, 233
Aeld, 110
Ailm, 111, 119
Aspen, 105, 116, 199, 215
August, 17, 96, 112, 132, 184, 219
Autumn, 35-36, 96-97, 105-106, 108, 116,
    119, 130, 172-173, 204

Banbha, 49, 54, 141-142, 161
Banshee, 141
Belanus, 167
Briar, 107, 120
Broom, 44, 107-108, 112, 120, 173, 213
Burtree, 110
Cerridwen, 61, 146, 168, 199, 235-236

Cicada, 186

Crow, 91, 93-94, 98-100, 102, 114, 126, 134, 140, 145, 173, 187, 191, 204, 250

December, 96, 128

Eadha, 116, 119

Elder, 35, 47, 57, 81, 84-85, 87-89, 91, 106, 110-111, 119-120, 169, 177-178, 198

Eldrum, 110

Elm, 111, 120

Emerys, 149, 167

Emma, 6, 17, 169, 202, 204

Falcon, 100-101, 173, 177, 213, 215, 255

Falling Star, 129-130, 132

February, 96, 131

Fincoll, 113, 120

Fir, 110-112, 114-116, 141, 144-145, 149-151

Gold, 2, 35, 47, 58, 81-82, 84, 87-88, 92-93, 105, 111, 134, 138-140, 154, 156, 187, 203-205, 213, 242-243, 246, 250-251

Hecate, 49, 54, 118, 139, 184, 191, 245

Hylantree, 110

Hyldor, 110

Ivy, 18, 114, 119-120

Jana, 145

Merlin, 71, 101, 147-149, 167, 173-174, 184, 215, 219, 223, 233-234, 240, 246-247

Meteor, 129-130, 132, 194

Myrddin, 19, 149, 167-168, 246

Myrtle, 116, 120

Oak, 9, 35, 43, 104, 115-116, 119-120, 149-150, 153, 168, 174-177, 183, 198-199, 209, 214-215, 243

Pethboc, 110

Poplar, 116, 119-120

Prisca, 173

Raven, 3, 99-100, 102, 142, 175, 197, 206-207, 209, 212, 214-215, 250

Ruis, 110, 119, 178

Sage, 59, 96, 125, 149, 160, 167-168, 192

Samdhya, 140

Samhain, 43, 97, 141

September, 97, 130

Shooting Star, 129, 132

Talvi, 173

Trom, 110, 120

Waning Moon, 132, 140

White Poplar, 116, 120

Winter, 24, 60, 89, 97-98, 108, 111, 124, 128, 134, 143, 168, 173, 184-185, 214, 236

Ysbadadden, 148, 168

Yule, 97-98, 111, 113, 119, 128, 173, 192, 205, 215

Self-Esteem

Aphrodite, 49, 52, 99, 103, 132, 137-138, 146, 155-156, 158, 185, 191, 203, 249

Aquamarine, 82

Aspasia, 137, 202

Balder, 35, 115, 143, 163

Barberry, 106

Diamond, 84-85, 95, 173

Holly, 113, 119-120, 168, 183, 197, 213, 215

Venus, 35, 49, 113, 116, 131-132, 146, 165-166, 199, 205, 233, 246

Shadow Side/Underworld/Death

Aegir, 162

Aker, 78, 150

Alligator, 188

Ambika, 174

Anubis, 150

Arawn, 166, 244

Athtor, 135

Banshee, 141

Belanus, 167

Bellona, 144, 204

Crocodile, 26, 188-190

Crow, 91, 93-94, 98-100, 102, 114, 126, 134, 140, 145, 173, 187, 191, 204, 250

Cyhiraeth, 146

Dolphin, 48, 191, 198

Donn, 160, 209, 240

Gemini, 129

Hades, 156-157, 179

Hecate, 49, 54, 118, 139, 184, 191, 245

Helygen

Hisi, 152, 154

Hoder, 163

Idho, 118-119

Kalma, 49, 136, 153

Mayfly, 188

Melanie, 139

Melusine, 142
Mider, 162
Minos, 157
Modur
Morpheus, 157
Nox, 49, 54, 145
Obsidian, 90
Odin, 105, 163, 178-179, 184, 191, 193, 237
Orcus, 165
Rot, 69, 153, 238, 254
Saille, 118-119
Samdhya, 140

Samhain, 43, 97, 141
Set, 3, 5-6, 9, 11, 29-31, 33, 37, 43, 45, 47, 50,
    54-55, 57, 62, 65, 70, 88, 95, 114, 143,
    151-153, 157-160, 166-167, 195, 237
Sgaileach, 178
Summanus, 166
Surma, 153
Tuonetar, 136
Tuoni, 154, 239
Varuna, 159
Yew, 118-120, 178
Ywen, 119

Sobriety

Abstinence, 12
Abuse Not, 12
Amethyst, 81, 84, 91-92, 172
Ametisti, 172
Braken
Cokil, 110
Darnel, 110, 215

Drake, 110, 206
Ivy, 18, 114, 119-120
Machupa, 35, 176
Refrain, 14
Temperance, 14, 147
Zirwan, 110

Strength

Adecock, 8
Alioth, 127
Antares, 127, 199
Apis, 150
Arcturus, 127-128
Aries, 128, 156
Brant, 99
Breed, 141, 175-176, 191, 207
Brian(a), 175-176, 207, 209, 238, 240-241, 252
Brid(e), 11, 104, 112, 123, 137, 141, 148, 163,
    175-176, 178, 207, 233
Bri(d)get, 175, 207, 236
Centaurus, 128, 156
Cuchulain, 61-64, 142, 148, 161
Fearghus, 209
Flint, 81, 86, 90, 92
Galena, 86-87, 93

Granite, 82, 88, 90, 94
Hanuman, 159
He(a)rd, 5, 24, 31, 54, 93, 111, 138, 141, 192,
    214, 233, 254
Jarnsaxa, 143
Lugh, 96, 159, 161-162, 222-223, 244
Mahogany, 115
Mars, 9, 78, 98-100, 102-103, 128, 130-131,
    165, 209-210, 215, 226, 250-251
Medbh, 142
Megan, 213
Oak, 9, 35, 43, 104, 115-116, 119-120, 149-
    150, 153, 168, 174-177, 183, 198-199,
    209, 214-215, 243
Valene, 205
Valery, 205
Valora, 205

Success

Annona, 144
Basalt, 82
Capricorn, 128
Chamomile, 122
Durwen

Duir, 116, 119-120
Elden, 215
Emerald, 82, 84-85, 91, 95, 172
Ganesha, 158, 174, 191
Ginger, 124, 204

Honeysuckle, 124
Mercury, 93, 130-131, 165
Minerva, 101, 145, 250
Nike, 139
Nova, 131, 177, 205

Oak, 9, 35, 43, 104, 115-116, 119-120, 149-
    150, 153, 168, 174-177, 183, 198-199,
    209, 214-215, 243
Vine, 108, 114, 117, 119, 138, 154, 212, 250
Ward, 5, 10, 110, 156, 215, 238, 248

Trickster Names

Brendan, 102, 175, 230
Coyote, 190, 199
Ferret, 191
Hisi, 152, 154
Jay, 100-102, 199, 245
Loki, 143, 163, 184

Magpie, 101, 177, 236
Moosemas, 97, 194
Pyrite, 87, 92
Raven, 3, 99-100, 102, 142, 175, 197, 206-
    207, 209, 212, 214-215, 250

Warrior Names

Ajax, 155, 180, 203
Amethyst, 81, 84, 91-92, 172
Anu, 140-142, 150, 232, 235
Ares, 130, 137, 156
Aries, 128, 156
Ash, 12, 16, 52, 105, 112, 117-120, 178, 198,
    207, 212, 228, 235, 239
Audrey, 212
Avis, 212
Babu
Badhbh, 140-142
Baron, 211, 214, 251
Barret, 211, 230, 249
Beald, 4
Bellona, 144, 204
Beorn, 4, 223, 241
Beorn, 4, 223, 241
Bevan, 175, 209
Bevis, 211, 221
Born, 4, 7, 13, 16, 22-23, 31, 34, 91, 96, 128,
    134, 137-139, 173, 193, 205, 214-215
Brenainn, 175
Calhoun, 209
Casey, 209
Cathal, 209, 225
Cillian, 175
Cuchulain, 61-64, 142, 148, 161
Dagda, 116, 141-142, 160, 175, 209
Donagh, 175
Donahue, 175
Duncan, 175, 178, 209, 230, 245
Dustin, 211
Eagle, 79, 99-100, 142, 203, 210, 212

Evan, 175, 209, 219
Ewan, 209, 230, 236
Farrell, 175, 209
Farry, 175
Fionn Mac Cumhail
Gaisgeil, 178
Garner, 212
Hardy, 212
Hazel, 112-113, 119-120, 208, 211, 213
Her(e), 183, 248
Kalevi, 172
Kalwa, 172
Kearney, 176, 209
Kele, 173, 210
Kellen, 210
Kelly, 175, 208, 210
Killian, 175, 210
Kyllikki, 49, 136, 239
Loring, 212
Lugh, 96, 159, 161-162, 222-223, 244
Macha, 140-142, 177
Marelda, 211
Mars, 9, 78, 98-100, 102-103, 128, 130-131,
    165, 209-210, 215, 226, 250-251
Medbh, 142
Minerva, 101, 145, 250
Morrigan, 49, 62, 66, 102, 140-142, 160, 184,
    236, 245, 255
Muireannach, 178
Murrough, 210, 241
Nealon, 176
Nels, 210
Nemontana, 142

Niall, 210, 241
Nuada, 149, 162
Odin, 105, 163, 178-179, 184, 191, 193, 237
Owen, 210
Poplar, 116, 119-120
Raina, 211

Rand, 89, 197, 215
Scathach, 61-62, 64-65, 142, 148
Sigmund, 163
Sloan, 210
Thayer, 212
Yarrow, 118, 208

Water Names

Adrian, 205
Aegir, 162
Aleyin, 164
Aquamarine, 82
Aquarius, 127
A(r)chelous, 78, 154
Atlantic, 74, 78
Axolotl, 189
Bay, 78, 108, 121-122, 124, 157, 166, 183, 214
Belisma, 134
Blackbird, 98, 205
Boann, 141, 222
Brook, 78, 213-214, 250
Cascade, 35, 72, 78-79, 213
Cascata, 174
Corrente, 174
Cove, 24, 36, 39-42, 46, 56, 60, 73, 83, 105-
    106, 119, 131, 135, 150, 168, 178-179,
    183-185, 187, 189, 193, 197-198, 247
Creek, 78
Dagon, 164
Deep, 11, 22, 43-46, 49, 53, 81-82, 85, 87, 90,
    92-93, 118, 122-124, 131, 165, 243, 251
Dolphin, 48, 191, 198
Dorian, 203, 228
Dorie, 202
Dorissa, 202
Dory, 202
Drizzle, 78
Dwyvach, 147
Dylan, 78, 167, 244
Ebb, 78
Egeria, 78, 145
Flow, 7, 13, 18, 51, 59-60, 72, 78, 80, 82, 97,
    103-104, 106-112, 121, 126-127, 130,
    134, 136, 138-139, 145, 151, 157, 173,
    177, 191, 202, 204, 208, 213, 239, 251
Gannet, 100
Geyser, 78
Glacier, 78

Glaucus, 156
Gull, 71, 100, 183, 235
Gypsum, 88-89
Hadrian, 206
Hail, 46-48, 78, 137, 140, 152
Harbor, 78
Ilmatar, 49, 53, 135
Jade, 89
Jet, 78, 81
Joki, 107, 172
Kele, 173, 210
Kolika, 173
Lagoon, 36, 78, 90
Lake, 77-78, 88, 134, 153, 163, 167, 195, 215,
    236, 239-240
Lapis, 90
Llud, 149, 244
Lynn, 213
Mac Cuill
Manannan Mac Lir, 78, 162, 167
Mar(r)is, 205, 229, 240
Marsh, 9, 78, 98-100, 102-103, 209-210, 215
Meri(s), 35, 173, 205, 231, 243
Monsoon, 78
Morgan(ce), 18, 34, 82-83, 117, 147, 173, 175,
    184, 210, 219, 230, 234, 237, 240, 253
Mudpuppy, 189
Muir, 178, 210, 223, 241
Murdachen
Nakki, 153
Neptune, 131, 165, 233
Nerissa, 202
Nick, 7-9, 19, 33, 36, 71, 149, 186, 232, 247
Nion, 105, 119
Nu, 2-3, 6, 11, 18-19, 23, 26, 34, 40, 53, 56-
    57, 64, 78, 90, 103-104, 106, 113, 125,
    129, 133, 144, 149, 151, 158, 162, 171,
    189-190, 205, 208, 240, 244, 249
Ocean, 45, 52, 71, 74, 78, 82, 88-89, 100, 140,
    173, 178, 181, 199

Onnen, 119

Opal, 18, 80, 91-92, 95, 191, 249

Pacific, 74, 78, 102, 106

Pisces, 128, 131

Pond, 55, 60, 78, 102

Pontous

Quicksilver, 35, 92-93

Rain, 5, 19, 36, 75, 78-79, 85, 87, 89, 92, 95,
    113, 134, 139, 154, 163-164, 176-178,
    189, 194, 198-199, 202, 211, 215, 232,
    254

Raindrop, 78

Rainforest, 78

Rana, 78, 143, 208

Rapid, 36, 78, 100, 159

River, 19, 23, 74, 78-80, 134, 141, 143, 149,
    154, 172, 180, 192, 209, 215, 218, 222-
    223, 239, 243, 254

Rona, 208, 210, 230

Ronan, 210

Saegrmr, 5

Salamander, 77, 189

Sandpiper, 102

Sea, 2, 14, 23-24, 26, 42-43, 52, 67, 71, 74-75,
    77-79, 85, 91-92, 97, 100, 104-105, 107-
    108, 114, 125, 127, 131, 143-144, 156,
    162-165, 167-168, 173, 178, 183, 199,
    202-203, 208, 210, 224, 229, 236

Sea Priestess, 78

Shoney, 78, 162

Siren, 143, 174, 189

Sirena, 174

Snowflake, 54, 78

Splash, 78, 98

Spring, 2, 35-36, 59-60, 66, 74, 78, 95-97, 99,
    102-104, 112, 119, 134, 138, 143, 145,
    155, 157, 160, 164-166, 168, 172, 183,
    193, 201, 205, 213-214, 254

Stream, 9, 64, 74-75, 78-79, 90, 100, 102,
    143, 163, 174, 213-214

Sulla, 143

Tamesis, 78, 134

Tefnut, 78, 135

Thaiassa, 202

Torrente, 174

Trenton, 206

Tuonetar, 136

Twilight, 36, 46, 77, 103, 140, 198

Ula, 175, 208, 232

Va-Kul, 154

Vainamoinen, 154, 239

Varuna, 159

Vellamo

Vu-Kufis

Vu-Murt, 154

Waitilanni, 177

Waterfall, 48, 78, 173-174

Wave, 20, 45, 48, 53, 57, 64-65, 78, 136, 178,
    187, 192, 213, 215

Whirlpool, 78

Whitewater, 78

Willow, 118-120, 174, 177-178, 183, 214

Wheel of the Year/Time Names

April, 7, 95-96, 107, 132, 204, 207, 214

August, 17, 96, 112, 132, 184, 219

Autumn, 35-36, 96-97, 105-106, 172-173, 204

Beltane, 43, 96-97, 188

Blizzard, 36

Brisk, 36

Dawn, 1, 45, 76, 103, 128, 153, 186, 192, 195,
    213, 232, 254-255

December, 96, 128

Eostar, 96

Equinox, 96-97, 116, 119, 130

Esbat, 96, 129

February, 96, 131

Fall, 96

Grianghamhstad, 178

Imbolc, 96

Jack Frost, 36, 239

Jana, 145

January, 96

June, 71, 96, 112, 145

Lammas, 96

Litha, 36, 236

Lughnasadh, 96

Mabon, 36, 71, 96-97, 146, 167, 215

March, 7, 14, 61, 69, 97, 195

May, 112, 144-145, 199, 205

Midsummer, 97, 110, 119, 246

Moira, 202, 230, 245

Moosemas, 97, 194

Mwasaa, 176

Natalie, 173, 205

Nova, 131, 177, 205

November, 97, 131, 141

Novia, 205

October, 97, 114, 132

Robin, 7-9, 17-18, 36, 71, 98, 100-102, 199, 214, 236, 238, 246-247, 250

Samhain, 43, 97, 141

Season, 24, 36, 43, 52, 71, 95, 97, 107, 111-112, 114, 118, 144, 205

Sebele

September, 97, 130

Sesha, 174

Silver, 41-42, 60, 87, 93-94, 111, 119, 130, 138-139, 146, 149-150, 162-163, 174, 198-199, 202, 244

Solstice, 36, 97, 119, 128, 178

Spring, 2, 35-36, 59-60, 66, 74, 78, 95-97, 99, 102-104, 112, 119, 134, 138, 143, 145, 155, 157, 160, 164-166, 168, 172, 183, 193, 201, 205, 213-214, 254

Summer, 19, 24, 36, 96-97, 109, 116, 127, 136, 143-144, 153, 168, 172, 179-180, 184, 186, 193, 212, 214, 239, 251

Time, 1-4, 6, 8, 10-11, 16-17, 23, 26, 45-46, 49-53, 55-56, 58-59, 61-62, 69-71, 108, 110, 112-113, 115, 119, 129, 133, 142, 147, 157, 165, 168, 174, 176, 179, 183, 185-186, 190-191, 193, 211, 218, 239, 249, 251

Tulip, 36

Twilight, 36, 46, 77, 103, 140, 198

Valentine, 11, 95-97, 116, 182, 205, 229

Winter, 24, 60, 89, 97-98, 108, 111, 124, 128, 134, 143, 173, 178, 184-185, 214, 236

Yul, 97-98, 111, 113, 119, 128, 173, 192, 205, 215

Yule, 97-98, 111, 113, 119, 128, 173, 192, 205, 215

Wisdom

Acorn, 43, 104, 198

Akilah, 172

Amethyst, 81, 84, 91-92, 172

Apollo, 138, 155-156, 178, 202-203

Aspasia, 137, 202

Ate, 42, 137, 142, 193

Athena, 35, 101, 137, 145, 158, 184, 202

Beech, 106, 241

Branwen, 146, 167, 244, 246

Bres, 160, 244

Cassidy, 209

Cerdinen, 119

Coll, 19, 33-34, 70, 74, 82, 89, 113, 119-120, 129, 140-142, 147, 175, 209, 213, 215, 217-218, 232

Collen, 119

Conroy, 175

Crescent, 129, 131, 195, 198

Crystal, 42, 44, 50, 79-86, 88-89, 91-95, 149, 198, 202, 223-224, 228, 243, 246, 251

Dagda, 116, 141-142, 160, 175, 209

Dallan, 209, 249

Dallas, 175, 209

Diamond, 84-85, 95, 173

Experience, 13, 29, 34, 41-42, 53, 60, 71, 81-82, 88, 97, 104, 113-114, 133, 148, 160, 192

Falcon, 100-101, 173, 177, 213, 215, 255

Fennel, 124

Fincoll, 113, 120

Fox, 4, 174, 191, 199, 202, 213

Galen, 86-87, 93, 203, 209, 236

Galena, 86-87, 93

Hanuman, 159

Hazel, 112-113, 119-120, 208, 211, 213

Hazelnut, 113

Induna, 143

Jade, 89

Launfal, 149

Luis, 117, 119

Mert, 135, 149

Nanna, 143

New Moon, 129, 131-132, 136, 145, 172, 177

Oghma, 162

Oriole, 101

Our Lady's Mint, 124

Owl, 45, 94, 101, 177, 189

Peppermint, 124

Raed, 4-5
Red, 5, 7, 26, 31, 36, 43, 51, 70-71, 83, 87, 91-
    93, 96, 102, 104, 109, 113, 121-123,
    125, 130, 142, 166, 169, 175, 191, 195,
    199, 206, 210, 213-214, 218, 232, 235
Rede, 5, 7, 70, 180, 218

Writing Ability

Amergin, 34, 159, 235
Beech, 106, 241
Calliope, 138
Ibis, 100
Makalani, 176

Sage, 59, 96, 125, 149, 160, 167-168, 192
Slate, 94
Spearmint, 124, 126
Vanilla, 121, 126
Velda, 211

Mimir, 163
Odin, 105, 163, 178-179, 184, 191, 193, 237
Oghma, 162
Slate, 94
Thoth, 34, 100, 152

Appendix 2

Pronounciation Guide for Difficult Names

Many of the hard to pronounce names in this book include a pronouciation explanation next to the name. To help you understand the reasoning behind the often odd way a name is pronounced in some languages, I have included this section. These rules to pronounciation will help you pronounce other difficult foreign words or phrases which you may come into contact with in the course of your studies of ancient cultures.

WELSH PRONOUNCIATION RULES

The second to last syllable in a multisyllabic word is accented.

Consonants

Consonants are pronounced in normal English fashion, except for the following:

- *c* as in caer is pronounced as a *k,* thus *kyer.*
- *ch* as in Gwalchmai is pronounced as in Scottish *loch.*
- *dd* as in Gwenydd is pronounced as a *th* sound, thus *Gweneth.*
- *f* is soft and sounds like a *v.*
- *ff* is hard and sounds like an *f* in English.

- *ll* is pronounced in an alien sound to the English-attuned ear. You know you are saying it fairly closely if your tongue is on the roof of your mouth when you say Llew Llaw Gyffes, thus *Hlew Hlou Guffes.*
- *rh* is pronounced as *hr;* Rhiannon is *Hriannon.*
- *r* is rolled.

Vowels

- *y* is pronounced as an *i* in *pin.* Glyn, for example, is pronounced *Glin.* Y can also be pronounced as *u* in *us.* Thus Yspaddaden is pronounced *Uspathaden.*
- *w* is pronounced as *oo* in *look.* Thus Arawn is *ara OON,* or Annwn is *an NOON.*
- *u* is pronounced as *i* in *sill.* Cu'lhwch is *kill OOCH.*

Diphthongs

- *wy* is pronounced as *ooh-i* (as in *ill*). Pwyll is *pooh ILL.*
- *aw* is pronounced as *ou* (as in *ouch*); Llaw is *HLOU.*
- *oe* is pronounced as *oy* (as in *boy*); Goe'win is then *goy WIN.*

FINNISH PRONOUNCIATION RULES

The first syllable in a multisylabic word is accented.

Consonants

- *g* is always hard, as in *go.*
- *h* is always pronounced, even after vowels.
- *ng* is pronounced with the g silent.
- *r* is rolled.
- *s* is always hard, as in *so.*

Vowels

- *aa* is pronounced as the *a* in *car.*
- *ah* has no English equivalent sound. It falls between *a* in *cat* and *u* in *cut.*
- *ae* is pronounced like *a* in *cat.*
- *aeae* is a long *ae* sound.
- *ew:* The only way to explain this diphthong is to say that it is the sound a Valley Girl makes when disgusted. As you are saying *ee* (as in *see*), round your lips as if saying *ooh,* but keep your tongue in the *ee* position.
- *igh* is pronounced as *igh* in *sigh.*
- *ur* is pronounced as in *fur,* but with rounded lips.

Bibliography

Abrams, M. H. *The Norton Anthology of English Literature*. New York: W. W. Norton & Co., n.d.

Adams, Douglas. *The Hitchhiker's Guide to the Galaxy*. London: Pan Books Ltd., 1981.

_____. *The Long, Dark Tea-Time of the Soul*. New York: Simon and Schuster, 1988.

Adler, Margot. *Drawing Down the Moon*. Boston: Beacon Press, 1986.

Alfred, William, trans. *Beowulf*. New York: Dutton, 1962.

Ames, Winthrop. *What Shall We Name the Baby?* New York: Pocket Books/Vistacam, 1974.

Andalusia the Heretic. *The Complete Discordian Moosemas Celebration Handbook*. Blue Mound, WI: Moonstone Press. n.d.

Anderson, William. *The Green Man: The Archetype of our Oneness with the Earth*. San Francisco: HarperCollins, 1990.

Apuleius, Lucius. *The Golden Ass*. New York: Collier Books, 1962.

Aristophanes. *Lysistrata*. New York: New American Library, 1964.

_____. *The Wasps, The Poet and the Women, and The Frogs*. New York: Penguin, 1964.

Athanassakis, Apostolos N., ed. *The Homeric Hymns*. Baltimore, MD: John's Hopkins Press, 1976.

Avto, John. *Dictionary of Word Origins*. New York: Arcade, 1990.

Bain, Robert. *The Clans and Tartans of Scotland*. Glasgow: Collins Publishing, 1968.

Bardsley, Charles Wareing. *Curiosities of Puritan Nomenclature*. London: 1880. (Gale Research Co., facsimile reprint 1970.)

Bartlett, John. *Familiar Quotations*. New York: Little, Brown & Co., 1919.

Benjamin, Alan. *A Treasury of Baby Names*. New York: New American Library, 1991.

Boulton, Jane, ed. *Opal: The Journal of an Understanding Heart*. By Opal Whitely. Palo Alto, CA: Tioga Publishing Co., 1984.

Bradley, Marion Zimmer. *The Bloody Sun*. New York: Ace Science Fiction Books, 1979.

_____. *City of Sorcery*. New York: Daw Books, 1984.

_____. *The Fall of Atlantis*. New York: Baen Publishing, 1983.

_____. *The Forbidden Tower*. New York: Daw Books, 1977.

_____. *Hawkmistress*. New York: Daw Books, 1982.

_____. *The Heritage of Hastur*. New York: Daw Books, 1975.

_____. *The Mists of Avalon*. New York: Ballentine/Del Rey, 1982.

_____. *Sharra's Exile*. New York: Daw Books, 1981.

_____. *The Shattered Chain*. New York: Daw Books, 1976.

_____. *Star of Danger*. New York: Ace, 1983.

_____. *Stormqueen!* New York: Daw Books, 1978.

_____. *Thendara House*. New York: Ace, 1983.

_____. *Two to Conquer*. New York: Daw Books, 1980.

_____. *The Winds of Darkover*. New York: Ace, 1982.

_____. *The World Wreckers*. Ace Science Fiction Books, 1971.

Bradley, Marion Zimmer and the Friends of Darkover. *Free Amazons of Darkover*. New York: Daw Books, 1985.

_____. *Sword of Chaos*. New York: Daw Books, 1982.

Bradley, Marion Zimmer with the Friends of Darkover. *Four Moons of Darkover*. New York: Daw Books, 1988.

Buckland, Raymond. *Scottish Witchcraft*. St. Paul, MN: Llewellyn Publications, 1992.

Budge, E.A. Wallis. *The Egyptian Book of the Dead: The Papyrus of Ani*. Egyptian text transliteration and translation. New York: Dover Books, 1985.

Cannon, John and Ralph Griffiths. *The Oxford Illustrated History of the British Monarchy*. New York: Oxford University Press, 1988.

Cassell's Italian Dictionary. London: Cassell & Co., 1958.

Chadwick, Nora. *The Celts*. New York: Penguin, 1991.

Chaucer. *The Canterbury Tales*. New York: Bantam, 1964.

Coghlan, Ronan, Ida Grehan and P. W. Joyce. *Book of Irish Names: First, Family & Place Names*. New York: Sterling Publishers, 1989.

Cottle, Basil. *Names*. London: Thames and Hudson, 1983.

Cruden, Alexander. *Cruden's Complete Concordance to the Old and New Testaments*. Grand Rapids, MI: Zondervan Publishing House, 1968.

Cunningham, Scott. *Magical Herbalism*. St. Paul, MN: Llewellyn Publications, 1982.

_____. *Cunningham's Encyclopedia of Magical Herbs*. St. Paul, MN: Llewellyn Publications, 1988.

Delaney, Frank. *Legends of the Celts*. London: Grafton/HarperCollins, 1991.

Delderfield, Eric R. *Kings and Queens of England and Great Britain*. New York: Facts on File, 1990.

Dickens, Charles. *Great Expectations*. New York: Scholastic Book Services, 1968.

Dinesen, Isak. *Out of Africa*. New York: Vintage Books/Random House, 1985.

Dolan, J.R. and Clarkson Potter. *English Ancestral Names*. New York: Crown Publishing, 1972.

Dunkling, Leslie. *English Country House Names.* 1971.

Eddings, David. *Castle of Wizardry.* New York: Del Rey/Ballantine, 1984.

_____. *Enchanters' End Game.* New York: Del Rey/Ballantine, 1984.

_____. *Magician's Gambit.* New York: Del Rey/Ballantine, 1983.

_____. *Pawn of Prophecy.* New York: Del Rey/Ballantine, 1982.

_____. *Queen of Sorcery.* New York: Del Rey/Ballantine, 1982.

Eliot, T. S. *Old Possum's Book of Practical Cats.* London: Faber & Faber, 1988.

Ellefson, Connie Lockhart. *The Melting Pot Book of Baby Names.* White Hall, VA: Betterway
    Publishing, 1987.

Ellis, Peter Berresford. *Dictionary of Celtic Mythology.* London: Constable & Co., 1992.

Evslin, Bernard, Dorothy Evslin and Ned Hoopes. *The Greek Gods.* New York: Scholastic Book
    Services, 1969.

Fallingstar, Cerridwen. *The Heart of the Fire.* San Geronimo, CA: Cauldron Publications, 1990.

Farrar, Janet and Stewart. *A Witches' Bible.* New York: Magickal Childe, 1984.

_____. *The Witches' God.* Custer, WA: Phoenix Publishing, 1989.

_____. *The Witches' Goddess.* Custer, WA: Phoenix Publishing, 1987.

Ford, Patrick K. *The Mabinogi and Other Medieval Welsh Tales.* London: University of Califor-
    nia Press, 1977.

Gimbus, Marija. *The Goddesses and Gods of Old Europe.* Berkeley, CA: University of California
    Press, 1990.

Godwin, Parke. *Firelord.* New York: Bantam Books, 1982.

Graves, Robert. *The White Goddess.* New York: Farrar, Straus & Giroux, 1974.

Grieve, Mrs. M. *A Modern Herbal.* New York: Dover, 1971.

Grimal, Pierre. *Larousse World Mythology.* New York: Excalibur Books, 1984.

Haley, Alex. *Roots.* New York: Bantam/Viking, 1977.

Halliday, Tim and Dr. Kraig Adler. *The Encyclopedia of Reptiles and Amphibians.* New York:
    Facts on File, 1986.

Hamilton, Edith. *Mythology: Timeless Tales of Gods and Heroes.* New York: New American
    Library, 1969.

Hanks, Patrick and Flavia Hodges. *A Dictionary of First Names.* New York: Oxford University
    Press, 1990.

_____. *A Dictionary of Surnames.* New York: Oxford University Press, 1989.

Hart, Mickey. *Drumming at the Edge of Magic.* San Francisco: Harper San Francisco, 1990.

Heinlein, Robert. *Stranger in a Strange Land.* New York: Ace Books, 1987.

Herbert, Frank. *Dune.* Philadelphia: Chosen Books, 1965.

Hope, Murry. *Practical Celtic Magic: A Working Guide to the Magical Heritage of the Celtic
    Races.* Wellingborough, Northamptonshire, UK: Aquarian Press, 1987.

_____. *The Psychology of Ritual.* Longmead Shaftesbury UK: Element Books, 1988.

Houston, Dr. Percy Hazen and Dr. Robert Metcalf Smith. *Types of World Literature.* New York:
    Doubleday, Doran, & Co., 1930.

Jackson, Kenneth Hurlstone. *A Celtic Miscellany.* New York: Viking/Penguin, 1971.

Jonson, Ben. *Bartholemew Fair*. From Magill, Frank. *Cyclopedia of Literary Characters*. New York: Harper and Row, 1963.

_____. *Hymn to Diana*. From Abrams, M. H. *The Norton Anthology of English Literature*. New York: W. W. Norton & Co., n.d.

K, Amber. *True Magick: A Beginner's Guide*. St. Paul, MN: Llewellyn Publications, 1990.

Kaye, Marvin and Parke Godwin. *The Masters of Solitude*. New York: Avon, 1979.

Keats, John. "Ode to Psyche." in Abrams, M. H. *The Norton Anthology of English Literature*. New York: W. W. Norton & Co., n.d.

Kolatch, Alfred J. *The Jonathan David Dictionary of First Names*. New York: J. David Publishing, 1980.

Kurtz, Katherine. *Deryni Checkmate*. New York: Ballantine/Del Rey, 1991.

_____. *Deryni Rising*. New York: Del Rey, 1982.

_____. *High Deryni*. New York: Del Rey, 1983.

Lansky, Bruce. *The Best Baby Name Book in the Whole Wide World*. New York: Meadowbrook, 1991.

Leach, Maria, ed. *Funk & Wagnall's Standard Dictionary of Folklore, Mythology and Legend*. New York: Funk & Wagnall's, 1972.

Lee, Guy, ed. *The Poems of Catullus*. New York: Oxford University Press, 1991.

LeGuin, Ursula. *A Wizard of Earthsea*. New York: Puffin Books of Viking/Penguin, 1986.

Lonnrot, Elias. *The Kalevala: An Epic Poem after Oral Tradition*. Keith Bosley, trans. New York: Oxford University Press, 1989.

Longfellow, Henry Wadsworth. *The Song of Hiawatha*. Edmonton: C. E. Tuttle Co., 1975.

Loomis, Roger Sherman and Laura Hibbard Loomis. *Medieval Romances*. New York: New Modern Library, 1957.

Lowder, James. *Crusade*. New York: Random House, 1991.

Llywelyn, Morgan. *Lion of Ireland*. New York: Playboy Paperbacks, reprinted Houghton Mifflin Co., 1981.

_____. *The Horse Goddess*. Boston: Simon and Schuster, 1982.

Lucas, Randolph, ed. *The Illustrated Encyclopedia of Minerals and Rocks*. London: Octopus Press, 1977.

MacCana, Proinsias. *Celtic Mythology*. New York: Peter Bedrick Books, 1983.

Magill, Frank. *Cyclopedia of Literary Characters*. New York: Harper and Row, 1963.

Maro, Publius Virgilous. *The Aeneid*. New York: Library of Liberal Arts, 1965.

Martin, Lori. *The Darkling Hills*. New York: New American Library, 1986.

Matthews, Caitlin. *Elements of the Celtic Tradition*. Rockport, MA: Elements, 1991.

_____. *Mabon and the Mysteries of Britain: An Exploration of the Mabinogion*. London: Arkana, 1987.

McCaffrey, Anne. *Crystal Singer*. New York: Del Rey, 1982.

_____. *Dragonflight*. New York: Del Rey, 1978.

Mehrabian, Dr. Albert. *Name Game: The Decision that Lasts a Lifetime*. Bethesda, MD: National Press Books, 1990.

Merwin, W. S., ed. *The Song of Roland.* New York: Vintage Books, 1963.

Miles, Joyce C. *House Names Around the World.* Newton Abbot, UK: David & Charles, 1972.

Moore, Robert and Douglas Gillette. *King, Warrior, Magician, Lover: Rediscovering the Archtypes of the Mature Masculine.* San Francisco: HarperCollins, 1991.

Mustard, Helen, ed. *Nibelungenlied.* From Houston, Dr. Percy Hazen and Dr. Robert Metcalf Smith. *Types of World Literature.* New York: Doubleday, Doran, & Co., 1930.

National Geographic Society. *Mysteries of the Ancient World.* Washington, D.C.: National Geographic Society, 1979.

Norton, Andre. *Wizards' Worlds.* New York: Tor Books, 1989.

Nurnberg, Maxwell and Morris Rosenblum. *What to Name Your Baby, From Adam to Zoe.* San Francisco: HarperCollins, 1962.

O Corrain, Donnachadh and Fidelma Maguire. *Gaelic Personal Names.* Dublin: 1981.

Paine, Albert Bigelow. *Mark Twain: A Biography.* New York: Harper & Bros., 1912.

Peterson, Roger Tory. *A Field Guide to Western Birds.* Boston: Houghton Mifflin Company, 1961.

Reaney, P. H. *The Origin of English Place Names.* London: Routledge & Kegan Paul, 1969.

Rolleston, T. W. *Celtic Myth and Legends.* New York: Dover, 1990.

Sarabande, William. *Wolves of the Dawn.* New York: Bantam, 1986.

Saunders, N. K., trans. *Epic of Gilgamesh.* London: Penguin Books, 1971.

Shakespeare, William. *A Midsummer Night's Dream.* New York: Penguin, 1967.

_____. *Macbeth.* New York: Signet, 1987.

_____. *The Tempest.* New York: Signet, 1987.

Spenser, Edmund. *The Faerie Queene.* From Abrams, M. H. *The Norton Anthology of English Literature.* New York: W. W. Norton & Co., n.d.

Squire, Charles. *Celtic Myth and Legend.* Van Nuys, CA: Newcastle Publishing, 1975.

Stein, Lou. *Clues to Family Names: What Do they Mean? How Did they Begin?* Bowie, Bowie, MD: Heritage Books, 1986.

Steinbeck, John. *The Acts of King Arthur and His Noble Knights.* New York: Ballantine, 1976.

Stewart, George R. *American Given Names.* New York: Oxford University Press, 1979.

Stewart, Mary. *The Crystal Cave.* New York: Faucett Crest Books, 1970.

_____. *The Hollow Hills.* Ballantine/Faucett Crest Books, New York: 1973.

_____. *The Last Enchantment.* New York: Ballantine/Faucett Crest Books, 1979.

Stewart, R. J. *Celtic Gods and Celtic Goddesses.* London: Blandford Press, 1990.

Stone, Merlin. *When God Was a Woman.* New York: Harvest/Harcourt, Brace & Jovanovich, 1976.

Strieber, Whitley. *Cat Magic.* New York: Tom Doherty Associates, 1987.

Sujata. *Beginning to See.* San Francisco: Apple Pie Books, 1985.

Swift, Jonathan. *Gulliver's Travels.* New York: Oxford University Press, 1977.

Tennyson, Lord Alfred. *Selected Poems.* New York: Dover, 1992.

Tolkien, J. R. R. *The Lord of the Rings.* Boston: Houghton Mifflin, 1983.

_____. *The Silmarillion.* London: George Allen Pub., 1977.

Turner, Nancy J. *Food Plants of British Columbia Indians.* Victoria, BC: British Columbia Provincial Museum. 1982.

Walker, Barbara G. *The Women's Dictionary of Symbols and Sacred Objects.* San Francisco: HarperCollins, 1988.

_____. *The Women's Encyclopedia of Myths and Secrets.* San Francisco: HarperCollins, 1983.

Waring, Philippa. *A Dictionary of Omens and Superstitions.* Seacaucus, NY: Chartwell Books, 1987.

Weis, Margaret and Tracy Hickman. *Elven Star.* New York: Bantam, 1990.

Withycombe, E. G. *The Oxford Dictionary of English Christian Names.* New York: Oxford University Press, 1971.

Whitney, A. H. *Finnish.* New York: David McKay Co., 1970.

Wooton, Anthony. *Insects of the World.* New York: Facts on File Publications, 1984.

Zappa, Frank with Peter Occhiogrosso. *The Real Frank Zappa Book.* New York: Poseidon Press, 1989.

Television and Films

Dances With Wolves. Orion Home Pictures, 1990. Directed by Kevin Costner. Produced by Kevin Costner and Jim Wilson. Screenplay by Michael Blake.

Mickie and Maude. Columbia Tri-Star Pictures, 1984. Directed by Blake Edwards. Produced by Tony Adams. Screenplay by Jonathan Reynolds.

The Wicker Man. British Lion Film Productions, 1971. Directed by Robin Hardy. Screenplay by Anthony Shaffer.

Star Trek: The Next Generation. Paramount, 1987 (pilot). Directed by Cory Alan. Produced by Gene Roddenberry.

Songs

"The Morrigan." Earth Tone Studios, 1995. From the album *The Seeker.* Written and performed by Teara Jo Staples.

"God Was a Woman." 1990. From the album *Hand of Desire.* Written by Sparky T. Rabbit and Greg Johnson. Performed by Lunacy. Refrain adapted from "The Goddess Chant" by Deena Metzger and Caitlin Mullin.

Index

Abundance/Wealth, names to invoke, 257

Afghanistan, 90

Air names, 76, 129

Anglo-Saxon names, 5, 212

Animal names, 98, 184

Arabia, 117

Baby names, 1, 33

Balance, names to invoke, 259

Basque, 172

Beauty, names to invoke, 259

Biblical names, 6, 8, 11, 69-70, 218

Bibliomancy, 42

Birds, names from, 18, 86, 97-104, 127, 140, 148, 157, 161, 190, 213-214, 239, 250

British goddesses, 134

British gods, 148-150

Burma, 23, 180

Burning times, 2, 11, 23, 190, 218

Celestial objects, names from 127, 132

Celtic/Gaelic names, 140-143, 159-162, 175-176

Celtic tree alphabet, 104, 119

Change, names to invoke, 260

Changing names, 24

Christian names, 69-71, 201, 217

Clarity, names to invoke, 260

Coven names, 184, 198

Covenstead names, 183-184

Croning ritual, 59-61

Denmark, 5, 71, 110, 235, 237, 248

Discordian names, 197

Earth names, 73-75, 78-79

Egyptian goddesses, 135

Egyptian gods, 150

Elemental names, 40, 72-73, 75

Eleusian mysteries, 26

English history, names from, 169

Exotic places, 180

Fertility, names to invoke, 262

Finland, 26, 192

Finnish goddesses, 135

Finnish gods, 152

Fire names, 35, 77, 83, 123, 129

First moon ritual, 48

Folklore, 21-23, 25, 27, 91, 121, 144, 189, 192

Gaelic names, 207

Geological names, 73

Greek goddesses, 137-140

Greek gods, 154-158, 178

Growth, names to invoke, 265

Handfasting, 44-45

Happiness, names to invoke, 265

Healing, names to invoke, 266
House blessing ritual, 44, 184
House names, 183
India, god names from, 158-159
India, goddess names from, 140
Initiation, 33-34, 61-62, 145
Ireland, god names from, 78, 160-162, 209
Ireland, goddess names from, 62, 78, 117-118, 139-142, 146, 202, 207
Islands, 121, 180
Italy, 248
Latinized names, 17
Literature, names from, 217-256
Love, names to invoke, 267
Luck, names to invoke, 268
Luther, Martin, 10-11, 16
Magical tools, 27, 35, 96, 194
Magician/wizard/bard names, 268
Maiden names, 269
Meditations, 39, 41, 43, 45, 47, 49, 51, 53, 55, 57, 59, 61, 63, 65, 67
Middle ages, 2, 7-8, 81, 84, 89, 92, 190
Moon/stars, names from, 269
Mountains, 72, 79, 88, 99, 105, 144, 163, 174, 178, 180, 239, 242-243
Mythological names, 133
Mythology, 17, 49, 100, 110, 115, 127-128, 130-132, 160, 190-195, 217
Name chant, 39, 43, 46
Name making, 11, 71
Name quest, 41
Naming ritual, 26, 40, 45
New beginnings, names to invoke, 270
Nicknames, 7-9, 33, 36, 71
Norman names, 6, 12
Norse goddesses, 143-144
Norse gods, 162-164
North American Indian, 23
Norway, 5, 236-237
Old English names, 4, 6, 17
Passion/sexuality, names to invoke, 270-271
Patronymic system, 9
Pet names, 33, 45
Phoenician goddesses, 144
Phoenician gods, 164
Place names, 8, 12, 179, 218
Plants, names from, 104-118

Popular culture, 18
Power, names to invoke, 271
Pronounciation guide, 281
Protection, names to invoke, 272
Psychic ability, names to invoke, 272
Purification, names to invoke, 273
Puritan names, 12, 14
Quickie name exercise, 41
Rebirth, names to invoke, 273
Reformation, 11, 14, 16, 69, 151
Rocks, names from, 79-95
Roman goddesses, 144
Roman gods, 165
Romantic movement, 17
Rulers of Britain, 169
Sage (and crone) names, 273-274
Science fiction, 19, 34, 127, 217-218
Scotland, 5, 8, 12, 82, 109-110, 222
Seasonal name, 36, 144
Self-esteem, names to invoke, 274
Sexual orientation, 23, 30, 42
Shadow side, names for your, 274-275
Sobriety, names to invoke, 275
Spells, 39-45
Spices, 45, 72, 104, 121-127
Strength, names to invoke, 275
Subjugation of women, 9
Success, names to invoke, 275-276
Surnames, 8, 10, 16, 71, 220
Teutonic names, 210
Tool names, 40, 194
Totem animal, 25, 42, 72, 128
Tractarian movement, 17
Trickster names, 276
Victorian era, 18, 81, 92
Warrior names, 3
Water names, 77
Welsh goddesses, 146
Welsh gods, 166
Wheel of the year, names from the, 278-279
Wiccaning ritual, 47
Wisdom, names to invoke, 279-280
Women's rite of passage, 48-59
Writing ability, names to invoke, 280
Zappa, Frank, 18-19

STAY IN TOUCH

On the following page you will find listed, with their current prices, some of the books now available on related subjects. Your book dealer stocks most of these and will stock new titles in the Llewellyn series as they become available. We urge your patronage.

TO GET A FREE CATALOG

You are invited to write for our catalog, *Llewellyn's New Worlds of Mind and Spirit*. A sample copy is free. Or you may subscribe for just $10 in the United States and Canada ($20 overseas, first class mail). Many bookstores also have *New Worlds* available to their customers. Ask for it.

In *New Worlds* you will find news and features about new books, tapes and services; announcements of meetings and seminars; helpful articles; author interviews and much more. Write to:

Llewellyn's New Worlds of Mind and Spirit
P.O. Box 64383, Dept. K251-8, St. Paul, MN 55164-0383, U.S.A.

TO ORDER BOOKS AND TAPES

If your book store does not carry the titles described on the following pages, you may order them directly from Llewellyn by sending the full price in U.S. funds, plus postage and handling (see below).

Credit Card Orders: VISA, Master Card, American Express are accepted. Call us toll-free within the United States and Canada at 1-800-THE-MOON.

Special Group Discount: Because there is a great deal of interest in group discussion and study of the subject matter of this book, we offer a 20% quantity discount to group leaders or agents. Our Special Quantity Price for a minimum order of five copies of *The Complete Book of Magical Names* is $79.80 cash-with-order. Include postage and handling charges noted below.

Postage and Handling: Include $4 postage and handling for orders $15 and under; $5 for orders over $15. There are no postage and handling charges for orders over $100. Postage and handling rates are subject to change. We ship UPS whenever possible within the continental United States; delivery is guaranteed. Please provide your street address as UPS does not deliver to P.O. boxes. Orders shipped to Alaska, Hawaii, Canada, Mexico and Puerto Rico will be sent via first class mail. Allow 4-6 weeks for delivery.

International Orders: Airmail—add retail price of each book and $5 for each non-book item (audiotapes, etc.); Surface mail—add $1 per item.

Minnesota residents add 7% sales tax.

Mail orders to:
Llewellyn Worldwide
P.O. Box 64383, Dept. K251-8
St. Paul, MN 55164-0383, U.S.A.

For customer service, call 1-800-THE-MOON (In Minnesota, (612) 291-1970).

THE FAMILY WICCA BOOK
The Craft for Parents & Children
Ashleen O'Gaea

Enjoy the first book written for Pagan parents! The number of Witches raising children to the Craft is growing. The need for mutual support is rising—yet until now, there have been no books that speak to a Wiccan family's needs and experience. Finally, here is *The Family Wicca Book,* full to the brim with rituals, projects, encouragement and practical discussion of real-life challenges. You'll find lots of ideas to use right away. When you want to ground your family in Wicca without ugly "bashing;" explain life, sex, and death without embarrassment; and add to your Sabbats without much trouble or expense, *The Family Wicca Book* is required reading. You'll refer to it again and again as your traditions grow with your family.

0-87542-591-7, 240 pp., 5¼ x 8, illus., softcover   **$9.95**

ANIMAL-SPEAK
The Spiritual & Magical Powers of Creatures Great & Small
Ted Andrews

The animal world has much to teach us. Some are experts at survival and adaptation, some never get cancer, some embody strength and courage while others exude playfulness. Animals remind us of the potential we can unfold, but before we can learn from them, we must first be able to speak with them.

In this book, myth and fact are combined in a manner that will teach you how to speak and understand the language of the animals in your life. *Animal-Speak* helps you meet and work with animals as totems and spirits—by learning the language of their behaviors within the physical world. It provides techniques for reading signs and omens in nature so you can open to higher perceptions and even prophecy. It reveals the hidden, mythical and realistic roles of 45 animals, 60 birds, 8 insects, and 6 reptiles.

0–87542–028–1, 400 pp., 7 x 10, illus., photos, softcover   **$17.95**

CUNNINGHAM'S ENCYCLOPEDIA OF MAGICAL HERBS
Scott Cunningham

This is the most comprehensive source of herbal data for magical uses ever printed! Almost every one of the over 400 herbs are illustrated, making this a great source for herb identification. For each herb you will also find: magical properties, planetary rulerships, genders, associated deities, folk and Latin names and much more. To make this book even easier to use, it contains a folk name cross reference, and all of the herbs are fully indexed. There is also a large annotated bibliography, and a list of mail order suppliers so you can find the books and herbs you need. You will be able to discover which herbs, by their very nature, can be used for luck, love, success, money, divination, astral projection, safety, psychic self-defense and much more. Besides being interesting and educational it is also fun, and fully illustrated with woodcuts from old herbals. This book has rapidly become the classic in its field. It enhances books such as *777* and is a must for all Wiccans.

0-87542-122-9, 336 pp., 6 x 9, illus., softcover   **$12.95**